THE CLASSICAL GREEKS

Michael Grant is a highly successful and renowned historian of the ancient world. He has held many academic posts including those of Fellow of Trinity College, Cambridge; Professor of Humanity at Edinburgh University; Vice Chancellor of The Queen's University, Belfast and Vice Chancellor of the University of Khartoum. He is a Doctor of Letters at Dublin and a Doctor of Laws at Belfast. He has also been President of the Classical Association of England, the Virgil Society and the Royal Numismatic Society, and is a Medallist of the American Numismatic Society. He lives and writes in Italy.

A SELECTION OF WORKS BY MICHAEL GRANT
AVAILABLE IN PHOENIX PRESS

The Twelve Caesars
The Classical Greeks
The Climax of Rome
The Fall of the Roman Empire
The Roman Emperors
The Rise of the Greeks
The Myths of the Greeks and Romans
The History of Ancient Israel
The Jews in the Roman World
The Roman World
Cleopatra
Cities of Vesuvius

THE CLASSICAL GREEKS

Michael Grant

PHOENIX
PRESS

5 UPPER SAINT MARTIN'S LANE
LONDON
WC2H 9EA

A PHOENIX PRESS PAPERBACK

First published in Great Britain
by Weidenfeld & Nicolson in 1989
This paperback edition published in 2001
by Phoenix Press,
a division of The Orion Publishing Group Ltd,
Orion House, 5 Upper St Martin's Lane,
London WC2H 9EA

A CIP catalogue record for this book
is available from the British Library.

Printed and bound in Italy by
Grafica Veneta S.p.A.

ISBN 1 84212 447 1

CONTENTS

Lists of events are inserted at the beginnings of Chapters 1, 5, 11, 16, 25, 29 and 35.

ILLUSTRATIONS

MAPS

INTRODUCTION

This book deals with the period of Greek history and civilization extending between the external wars of the early fifth century BC, against Persia and Carthage, and the accession of Alexander the Great in 336.

Never in the history of the world has there been such a multiplication of varied talents and achievements within so limited a period. Much of what happened, however, is not easy to assess. The surviving ancient literary sources, although they add up to an impressive quantity, are often incomplete or even fragmentary, and can be prejudiced to an extent which other evidence, notably from inscriptions and coins, archaeological finds and works of art, proves not wholly able to correct. Modern interpretations have been innumerable and frequently excellent, and it may seem presumptuous to add yet another. But at this juncture in our own affairs, when the world's instabilities make it so important to examine our origins – and when current educational systems are not making it very easy to do so – there seems to be room for one more endeavour.

The old mistake of concentrating too much on political and military affairs must be avoided (although it would be equally mistaken to neglect them). There remains, then, the problem of how a book of this kind ought to be organized and arranged. It would be possible to aim at a straightforward chronological survey, or, alternatively, to tackle one topic or theme after another. Neither of those courses, however, suits the peculiar character of the epoch. Another possible arrangement would have been geographical – to consider each of the principal areas and city-states of the Greek world in turn, as I tried to do in *The Rise of the Greeks*.* That seemed appropriate in dealing with a period during which the Greek world was assuming its regional configuration. But now that we have reached the next period, when that configuration has been established, it appears best to interpret this new age by accepting that its outstanding deeds and thoughts were produced not by communities but by individuals.

*Weidenfeld & Nicolson (1987).

Of course, it was within the framework of their communities that they worked, and, indeed, it was the existence and circumambience and tradition of those communities that made their work practicable. But it was they, as individual persons, who did what was done and wrote what was written. I have listed nearly forty of these men, and grouped my narrative round them.

The list could have been extended to an almost indefinite length, but I have tried to single out those whose contribution seems enormous. This is, perhaps, a somewhat unfashionable way of proceeding, in an age which believes that the ancient writers concentrated too much, not only on politics and military affairs as was suggested above, but also on individual personages at the expense of general, underlying impersonal movements. And indeed it may well be true that the Greek and Roman authors went too far in that direction, out of their desire to point a moral or tell a picturesque story. They were right, however, in principle, and the proof is that if you subtracted the achievements of these almost forty persons there would not be a great deal of the classical world left. More on this subject will be said in the Epilogue.

I shall also try, from time to time, to correct a few impressions that I believe to be misleading. I mentioned the blatant biases which are detectable in the ancient literary sources. In particular, these sources are overwhelmingly Athenian and concerned with Athens, to such a degree that they often hardly mention people belonging to other city-states except when their lives and doings happen to impinge on Athenian affairs. This may seem justified, to some extent, in that a remarkably large number of the greatest personages of the time were Athenian or worked in Athens. But it is misleading because men who came from other parts of the Greek world deserve and demand a larger proportion of our attention than they habitually receive. This applies especially to citizens of, and from, city-states outside, and often far outside, the Greek mainland. That mainland, it is true, was the origin and originator of classical Greece. Yet it comprised only a small part of that Greek world, despite much propaganda, antique and modern, to the contrary. For patriotic reasons, too, conscious or unconscious, the ancient authorities obscured the recurrent domination of Persia over Greek affairs.

Our roots, it has been constantly and correctly declared, are to be found, to a large degree, among these classical Greeks – and the discovery of earlier, near-eastern strands in our heritage, during the course of the past century, has not caused this indebtedness to look any less significant. To a marked extent, what we are doing and thinking today was anticipated by those Greeks. But the story of fifth- and fourth-century Greece has to be heard in its own right as a phenomenon of its own time, infinitely worthwhile as such, without any updating.

INTRODUCTION

The present book forms the middle part of a three-volume attempt to summarize the history of Greece, taking its place, chronologically, between *The Rise of the Greeks* and *From Alexander to Cleopatra*, which discussed the archaic and Hellenistic periods respectively: the periods preceding and following the 'classical' epoch (in so far as one may use these vague but convenient labels) which is my subject here. If I have succeeded in conveying even one hint of what was the most wonderful civilization in the world's history, I shall be content.

As to the inadequacy of such an attempt, nobody is better able to appreciate this than myself. It is indeed a reason for humility that every generalization I have ventured to offer has been the subject of five hundred books. My debts to modern authorities are so extensive that I cannot enumerate them here, although some slight impression of their dimensions can be obtained from the bibliography at the end of the book. I am also grateful to Miss Candida Brazil and Miss Alison Kemp, of Messrs Weidenfeld and Nicolson, for their extremely effective editorial assistance, and to Miss Maria Ellis, Dr Martin Henig and Mr Peter James. The staff of the Joint Library of the Hellenic and Roman Societies have also provided very useful assistance. And my wife has, as always, helped me greatly.

Michael Grant
1988

PART I
Wars Against External Enemies

LIST OF EVENTS

499–494	Ionian Revolt against the Persians; 495 battle of Lade
c.494	Spartans defeat Argives at Sepeia
493	Miltiades returns to Athens from Thracian Chersonese
493/492	Themistocles archon at Athens
490	Battle of Marathon won by Miltiades
500–480	Temple of Aphaea at Aegina
490/488	Suicide of King Cleomenes I of Sparta
489	Miltiades' expedition to Paros and death
488	Theron becomes dictator of Acragas (d.472)
487	Reform at Athens gives greater power to generals (*strategoi*)
486	Xerxes I becomes King of Persia (d.465/4)
485	Gelon becomes dictator of Syracuse (d.478)
c.483/482	Themistocles uses Laurium silver to build up Athenian navy
481	'Panhellenic' Congresses at Corinth
480s	Archaeanactid rulers in Cimmerian Bosphorus (Panticapaeum; Chapter 27)
480	Invasion of Greece by Xerxes I. Battles of Thermopylae (Leonidas I), Artemisium and Salamis (Themistocles)
480	Invasion of Sicily by the Carthaginians. Battle of Himera (Gelon and Theron)
479	Battles of Plataea (Pausanias) and Mycale
479–478	Persians lose Sestus, Byzantium and the Thracian Bosphorus
c.477 (or 472/470)	Pausanias expelled from Byzantium by Cimon

c.474	Hiero I of Syracuse defeats the Etruscans off Cumae
c.472 (?)	Themistocles ostracized
c.469/466	Pausanias starved to death
c.469/468 (?)	Battle of River Eurymedon against the Persians (Chapter 5)
c.462	Death of Themistocles

CHAPTER 1

MILTIADES: VICTOR AT MARATHON

The Persian empire – the greatest empire the world had ever known – was founded by King Cyrus II the Great (559–529 BC). It extended as far as Pakistan to the east and as far, in the other direction, as westernmost Asia. The empire came close to Greece when its founder overwhelmed Croesus, King of Lydia in western Asia Minor, and annexed his state (546), thus assuming suzerainty over the Greek cities on the western seaboard of the mainland and adjoining islands, in regions which had hitherto been dependent on the Lydian rulers.

One of the two Persian dominions, or satrapies, which henceforward influenced the Greeks was based on Sardis, the former Lydian capital. The other was ruled from Dascylium in Lesser Phrygia, beside the Propontis.* It was Darius I (521–486) who, after suppressing revolts in his eastern territories, reorganized the empire into a series of these satrapies, each of which, under a prince or great noble, enjoyed a substantial degree of internal autonomy, while remaining more or less obedient to the central authority. Darius developed trade, consolidated the imperial frontiers and sought to enlarge them by crossing over to Europe (*c*.513–512). His expedition did not make effective progress against the Scythians of the east European hinterland, north of the Danube, but the annexation of Thrace was a major success.

It was also an event which brought the Persians into close contact with Athens. The Athenians had for some time been intent on dominating the strategic waters leading into the Black Sea, because they needed the grain that came from that region. This meant that the passages of the Hellespont, Propontis and Thracian Bosphorus had to be under Athenian control. With these aims in mind Miltiades the elder, a member of the noble Athenian family of the Philaids, had set up an Athenian colony in the Thracian Chersonese which adjoined the northern (European) shore of the Hellespont (*c*.547). Although his father was a political opponent of the Athenian dictator Pisistratus, it

*For the modern equivalents of ancient place-names see the index.

was probably with Pisistratus' support that he established himself in the Chersonese, where he fortified his position by building a wall across the isthmus.

He was succeeded by his nephew Stesagoras, after whose death his brother Miltiades the younger was sent out from Athens to succeed him – by Pisistratus' son and successor Hippias (? *c.*524 or 518/516) – in the hope that, on arrival, he would shore up the position of Hippias' half-brother Hegesistratus, who ruled over neighbouring Sigeum. Encouraging Athenians to come and settle in the area, this younger Miltiades put down Thracian unrest in the Chersonese by imprisoning the local chiefs, but married Hegesipyle, daughter of the Thracian (Sapaean) king Olorus.

When Darius arrived in Europe on his expedition of *c.*513–512, Miltiades commanded a contingent in his army. As the King, however, was preparing to return from Scythia across the Danube, Miltiades (so he later claimed) advised his fellow Greeks to destroy the river bridge, so as to cut off the Persian army's withdrawal.[1] Since, however, Darius left him undisturbed, Miltiades' story may have been a subsequent invention, found convenient at a time when the Persians had become the enemies of Athens and he needed to explain away his earlier allegiance to their rule.

Moreover, it could be said in Miltiades' favour that, after Darius' departure, he detached the islands of Lemnos and Imbros from Persian rule and handed them over to Athens (*c.*500, or a little later). And then again, when in 499 the Greek cities of Ionia (western Asia Minor) revolted from the Persians, he supported their cause, surviving a brief exile caused by a Scythian invasion (496/495) and reinstating himself with Thracian help. Not long after the Ionian revolt collapsed (494), however, he fled to Athens, where he was impeached for 'tyranny' (dictatorship) – a charge brought forward by his political enemies, now that the Pisistratid 'tyrant' house, which had established the two Miltiadeses in the Chersonese, had been replaced at Athens by a government of more democratic inclinations (guided by Cleisthenes). In spite of opposition, Miltiades became a powerful politician at Athens – taking the lead in anti-Persian initiatives.

For Persia now presented an immediate threat to Greece. When Darius had first invaded Europe in *c.*513–512 it is uncertain whether, and to what degree, he wanted to extend his hold over the Greek city-states. Those on the Asian side of the Aegean were already under his control, and so, to a large extent, were the cities on the Thracian and Macedonian coasts, and he and his advisers must have considered whether it would not be logical to occupy mainland Greece as well.

At all events, the question arose in a more acute form when the

Greek cities of Ionia revolted against him, since Athens and Eretria (in Euboea) came to their assistance – and helped to sack the capital of Persia's satrapy in western Asia Minor, Sardis (498). Their contingents withdrew soon afterwards, but from that time onwards Darius decided to take vengeance on Athens and Eretria. Once again, we cannot tell whether at this stage his plans were limited to those cities only, or possessed a wider scope. But if they both succumbed, it was inevitable that he would seek to extend his conquests to other parts of Greece as well.

In *c*.492 Darius' able young nephew and son-in-law Mardonius calmed down the defeated Ionian cities on the Asian mainland by dismissing some of their puppet dictators – previously set up by the Persians – and allowing democratic forms of government. Then, in spite of a shipwreck and a wound, he completed the reduction of Thrace; and the kingdom of Macedonia, too, became Persia's subject ally. This achieved, the Persian generals Datis (a Mede) and Artaphernes (son of the satrap of Sardis) launched, by sea, their punitive expedition against Athens and Eretria, accompanied by the fugitive Athenian ex-dictator Hippias, who expected that a Persian victory would restore him to power.

After the surrender of the Cycladic islands, Eretria fell to the Persians by treachery, following a six-day siege. A few days later the Persians sailed on, and landed their force of heavy-armed infantry, cavalry and archers, amounting to 15,000–20,000 men, in the Bay of Marathon, forty-one miles north of Athens. The Bay possessed a sheltered beach, and was one of the few places in the region which provided good watering facilities, as well as autumn pasture for horses; and Hippias hoped to find supporters in this part of Attica.

Technically speaking, the Athenian commander-in-chief was a civil official, the polemarch Callimachus – the war archon, one of the nine elected archons who were the titular heads of the Athenian state. But in practice the command was jointly vested in the ten generals (*strategoi*), each elected from his tribe. One of them was Miltiades the younger, familiar with the Persian army after Darius' Thraco-Scythian campaign, and credited (as he had made sure) with an anti-Persian record; tradition was right in allotting him the leading role in what followed.

He and his colleagues decided not to await a Persian attack upon Athens, but to march north to Marathon instead. This was a crucial decision and a perilous one, since the Persians might try to hold the Athenian army at Marathon and meanwhile sail round and assault Athens itself – which the departure of its army would leave dangerously unprotected. But what weighed with the Athenians was the need to prevent the enemy from securing a base in eastern Attica to which traitors might be attracted.

So they sent out a force of about 10,000 hoplites (heavy-armed infantry). A party of about 600 men from Plataea, on the borders of Attica and Boeotia, joined them, but no one came from the principal land state of Sparta, which could not – the Athenian runner Pheidippides reported – dispatch troops for several days, until a religious festival was over. The pretext was perhaps authentic, but the delay may also have reflected sharp Spartan differences of opinion about Persia.

The Greek force occupied foothills facing the Persian position and blocking the routes to Athens. The deliberations of its generals are clouded by anecdote. At all events, however, despite the strength of their position, and despite arguments in favour of waiting for the Spartan army, the Athenians finally decided to take the offensive; either because the Persian cavalry were away (we know that they were away, but we do not know why), or because they feared that the Persians would re-embark and make for Athens, or – once again – for fear of treachery within their own ranks if they delayed any longer. Miltiades, proposing to attack, believed that the superiority of his weapons, and his greater familiarity with local conditions, would counterbalance his numerical inferiority.

Planning for the battle that lay ahead, he thinned his centre so as to make his line equal in length to the enemy's and reinforced both his wings. Then, at dawn on 9 September (?), his men charged for a mile across the plain, 'at the double', Herodotus says,[2] but presumably only breaking into a run when in range of the enemy arrows. The Persian centre penetrated its Greek counterpart, but the Greek wings threw back their opponents and wheeled inwards onto the Persian centre, putting it to flight. The defeated Persian soldiers streamed towards the sea, and their fleet moved inshore and took them aboard. They had lost 6,400 dead, as against 192 Athenian casualties, including the polemarch Callimachus on the right wing. The Spartans arrived after the battle, and gazed upon the scene.

After re-embarking, the Persians sailed round Sunium and made for Phaleron Bay, in the hope of assaulting Athens before its army came back. Herodotus reports a story that, soon after they had started their voyage, a fifth column in the city flashed them a signal with a shield telling them to come on. This is possible, although if so it remains uncertain who the traitorous signallers were (the great but often uncooperative family of the Alcmaeonids was blamed, perhaps unfairly). In any case, however, the victorious Athenian force, marching rapidly homewards – it must have taken them about eight hours – got there first. So the Persians sailed back to Asia, and for the time being the peril was over.

Miltiades and his Athenian force had won one of the most famous victories of all time. They had demonstrated to the world that the great state of Persia was not invincible, that the Greek heavy-armed infantryman was more than a match for any soldier in the Persian empire – and that Athens, whose middle-class citizenry provided these hoplites, was the heroic victor, and a power for the future. True, the Persians had not been repelled for ever. But they had been shown that Greece could not be invaded by sea, when no secure base for disembarkation was available; and other Greek cities had been encouraged to resist them. A painting of the battle, probably by Micon, was set up in the Painted Portico (Stoa Poikile) of Athens.

Miltiades was a man of courage and determination. But he came to the usual unhappy end which awaited successful Greek individuals. Commissioned by his city to regain control over the Aegean, he sailed off in early spring of 489 (or possibly in the previous autumn) to capture the island of Paros, a task which he failed to achieve, damaging himself severely as he tried to jump over a fence. On his return, the Alcmaeonids arranged his impeachment 'for having deceived the people', and after being brought to court on a stretcher he was fined a large sum. Before he could hand it over, however, he died of his injury. The fine was then paid by his son Cimon (Chapter 5) – who later rehabilitated his memory; and he was included in the group of heroes sculpted by Phidias for the Athenian Treasury at Delphi (*c.*465).

CHAPTER 2

THEMISTOCLES: VICTOR AT SALAMIS

Themistocles (*c*.528–*c*.459 (?)) was, on his father Neocles' side, a member of an old, respectable and fairly prosperous but unpolitical Athenian family, the Lycamidae – who still lived outside Athens, near Sunium. His mother, however, was said to have been of humble and non-Greek origin, probably Carian (Chapter 28). In a period when family statuses and alliances were potent political factors, this dubious pedigree deprived him of support among the governing class. Indeed he would not even have been an Athenian citizen at all had it not been for the constitutional and social reforms of Cleisthenes at the end of the sixth century.

Making a determined move away from old-fashioned oligarchical institutions, Cleisthenes had supplemented, and in effect replaced, the antique tribal system founded on brotherhoods and clans by ten national tribes that were no longer based on family and property. He had also created a Council (Boule) of Five Hundred which, largely superseding the political authority of the conservative, aristocratic Areopagus, formed the nucleus, together with the Assembly (Ecclesia), of the democracy which was gradually emerging. Cleisthenes also carried out a franchise reform encouraging resident aliens or metics (an important commercial class, Appendix III) to become citizens, and cancelling an earlier removal from the citizen roll of those 'not of pure descent'. It was this measure that enabled Themistocles to fulfil his role in political life.

He made his way quickly. The most important of the nine annually elected archons who presided over the Athenian state was the *archon eponymos*, and (despite modern doubts) Themistocles was elected to this office as early as 493/492, at the age of thirty-five or less. During his archonship he may well have begun the development of the Piraeus – the safest and largest harbour on the Greek mainland – in place of the inadequate roadstead of Phaleron. His intention was partly, it would seem, to safeguard Athens against the neighbouring island city-state of Aegina, which was hostile. But he also intended, farsightedly, to create

a means of resisting the Persians, whom Aegina might help (though Herodotus' informants, hostile to Themistocles, preferred to discount this patriotic anti-Persian motive).[3] However this may be, Themistocles precociously understood the potential importance of Athens' navy and sea-power, markedly breaking with the old principle of just defending one's own territory. But the return of the younger Miltiades from exile, and the subsequent battle of Marathon (Chapter 1), distracted attention from this aspect, and postponed all Themistocles' naval plans, since the victory was won on land by the hoplite infantry.

Themistocles served at Marathon, as one of the generals for the year. Nevertheless, the trophy of Miltiades, who had such different ideas from his own, 'kept him awake at night'.[4] But in 489 came Miltiades' downfall and death. The sequel was savage rivalry among Athenian politicians. In particular, there was frequent resort to ostracism. This practice seems to have been another of the innovations of Cleisthenes, although it was not utilized until the 480s – after Marathon had taught the danger of treachery from within, and the need for good leadership. Ostracism was a method of getting rid of a politician who had become unpopular, by sending him into exile. Every citizen could inscribe the name of the Athenian whose banishment he favoured on a piece of pottery (potsherd, *ostrakon*), and then, provided that the number of *ostraka* totalled 6,000, the man whose name figured most frequently in this ballot was sent away. He had to leave within ten days, and stay in exile for ten years.

Nearly 1,500 *ostraka* have been found. Most are of the 480s BC; and no less than 542 of them carry the name of Themistocles. This indicates that he was at risk every year: there was a concerted attempt to get rid of him. But it failed, for it was others who were ostracized instead. They included, in successive years from 487 onwards, a member of the deposed family of the former dictators Pisistratus and Hippias, an Alcmaeonid, another Pisistratid, and an Alcmaeonid supporter: all were believed, no doubt, to be potential supporters of Persian invasion and favourable to the restoration of the dictator Hippias. The further decision, probably in 483/482, to ostracize another statesman, Aristides, is significant; because he had supported Miltiades' plans at Marathon, whereas Themistocles favoured a naval policy instead – and was therefore in a position, now that times and attitudes had changed, to secure his opponent's elimination.

Themistocles was able to achieve this success owing to a great stroke of luck. For just at this time rich new veins of silver ore were found on Attic territory, at Laurium, where the mines of that metal were Athens' largest industrial asset. As was customary in Greek city-states – to which prescient economic planning was alien – a proposal was made that this

surplus revenue should be distributed among the citizen body. But Themistocles, remarkably enough, persuaded the Assembly to use the money to multiply the size of the navy instead, despite the loss of profits to individuals which this would entail, not to speak of the heavy strain on skilled Athenian personnel needed to man the ships. Aristides, who still thought of Marathon and would have preferred to build up the land forces instead, sought to censure the policy – and that is why he was ostracized. And so the navy, which had consisted of 70 triremes before, possessed the unprecedented number of 200 ships by 480 BC.

The transformation came just in time. For the Persians had no intention of letting Marathon go unavenged. Their counterstroke was delayed by the death of Darius I and by rebellions in Egypt (486) and Babylonia (482), but Darius' son Xerxes I (486–465) moved into action as soon as he could, planning a co-ordinated invasion by land and sea – possibly with as many as 1,000 ships and 100,000 soldiers, or even more. Thus the most formidable force yet seen in Mediterranean waters crossed the Hellespont, bridged for the purpose, in late spring 480.

The idea that 'Medism', support for Persia (or failure to fight against it), was a disgrace had hardly taken root among the Greek city-states – many of which saw the Persian empire as unoppressive and open to intercourse. Or, at any rate, the imperatives of fear or necessity prevailed in their minds: so that Xerxes was able to win the favour or neutrality of Thessaly and most of central Greece (including the Delphic oracle), as well as Argos, which hated the Spartans.

Sparta and Athens, on the other hand, took a decisive step in 481 by murdering Persian envoys who had arrived in their cities. And it was the Spartans, by far the greatest land-power in Greece, who on this occasion led the common defence against Persia, by summoning the earliest of what were later called 'Panhellenic' congresses at the Isthmus of Corinth (autumn 481). The Congress was attended by representatives of thirty-one city-states which had the will to resist.

Although thirteen of these states were in the Peloponnese, so that the new union was something like an enlargement of the existing Peloponnesian (Spartan) League, they also included Athens; and it was Themistocles (occupying one of the city's generalships, an office recently strengthened still further at the expense of the archonship) who designed the plan of campaign. Indeed he seems to have been granted supreme command over the Athenian forces, something very rare at Athens, although the overall inter-allied command, both on land and sea, remained in Spartan hands, a decision which encouraged a unitary, coherent strategy. Nevertheless, the inter-city preparations, which

included such decisions, displayed the usual Greek mixture of clever suggestions and opportunistic squabbles.

The initial Greek intention was to hold the narrow valley of Tempe between Macedonia and Thessaly, and a force of 10,000 men, commanded by the Spartan Euaenetus (with Themistocles under him) was sent north for this purpose. But the project was rapidly abandoned, when it became clear that the Persians could force their way through the mountains elsewhere – and, besides, as we saw, the Thessalians (especially the Aleuad rulers of Larissa) could not be trusted, and must therefore be left to their own devices, though it was a pity to lose their horses and grain.

The Greeks now had to form another plan instead; and they decided to concentrate their forces on the east coast, stationing their army and fleet (which the Persians would not dare to bypass) at the interdependent positions of Thermopylae and Artemisium (northern Euboea) respectively. At Thermopylae – a narrow pass which extended for five miles between the cliffs of Callidromus (Mount Oeta) and the sea – 6,000 hoplites were posted under the Spartan King Leonidas I; and off Artemisium in northern Euboea, 271 triremes were commanded by his compatriot Eurybiades, advised and guided by Themistocles, whose Athenian contingent was far the largest.

The Persian fleet, advancing down the perilous Thessalian coast, suffered heavy damage from gales. But after three days of fighting, costly to both sides, it became clear to the Greeks that, although they had inflicted serious losses, they would soon have to withdraw into narrower waters. Meanwhile Leonidas I at Thermopylae, after repelling attacks for two days, had his mountain flank (unsuccessfully protected by 1,000 not very courageous Phocians) turned by a Persian force guided by a Greek collaborator, Ephialtes of Anticyra in Malis. And so Leonidas, after dismissing most of his force, fought with his own men to the death, falling in defeat but creating a saga of Spartan heroism; and he had at least delayed the Persians for a week, thus saving the Greek fleet at Artemisium. But when the final disastrous news of Thermopylae came to that fleet, it retired southwards, hastily and after dark, through the Euripus strait between Boeotia and Euboea.

Bowing to the agonizing necessity, most of the Athenians evacuated their city, which Xerxes took and burned. The fugitive wives and children left for Troezen, Aegina and Salamis, and the Athenian government transferred itself to Salamis. It did not matter, declared Themistocles, because they had their ships, and Athena was showing them their way to the sea.[5]

The Spartans now wanted to fall back to the Gulf of Argos and fortify the Isthmus of Corinth. But Themistocles – reportedly by threatening to sail off to south Italy if he was not listened to – advised the allies strongly against this. As long as the Persian fleet remained undefeated, he pointed out, any Greek land fortification could be turned, and the allied navy should instead put into the narrow strait of Salamis. Legend encrusts what happened next. But it was said (perhaps accurately, though not everyone agrees) that Xerxes, knowing that the end of the campaigning season was at hand without any conclusive success having been gained, and that provisioning would thereafter present him with a problem, was persuaded by a deceitful message from Themistocles that the disunited Greeks were about to get away. To forestall such a move, Themistocles urged him, the Persians must attack immediately.

And this they did, in a congested area which suited their vessels worse than those of the Greeks, which although slower – and that did not matter in those narrow waters – were heavier and more stoutly constructed for ramming than their own; and the result was a total Persian defeat, under the eye of King Xerxes himself. The Greeks were said to have destroyed or captured two hundred enemy ships, for the loss of forty on their own side. As for what remained of Persia's fleet, it was still superior in numbers, but its morale had been heavily dented and it had lost command of the sea, so that it could no longer supply food to Xerxes' large army. He therefore returned with most of his troops to Sardis, capital of his satrapy of western Asia Minor – where a renewed Ionian insurrection was now feared.

Salamis had been the turning point of the war, and one of the most famous victories of all time; as Thucydides declared, it 'most obviously saved our cause'.[6] Athens, with 180 or 200 out of the total of 334 allied ships, had done more than all the rest of Greece together to win the battle; and as Themistocles himself was not slow to point out (with support from the poet Simonides),[7] the victory was unmistakably his. After it had been won, he received honours, even at Sparta, that had never been seen before.

But then things began to go wrong for him, as they had also gone wrong for Miltiades, the acclaimed victor at Marathon ten years earlier. Some of Themistocles' principal rivals had been recalled from exile during a general amnesty before this second Persian invasion, and in 479, under their guidance, popular feeling swung against him: because he wanted to carry the naval war to the Hellespont. This appeared too rash to the Athenians – who in any case did not like overweeningly successful citizens. And so, possessing too few clients to provide a firm basis of support, Themistocles lost his generalship to his political opponents.

Nevertheless, he still remained powerful enough, during the ensuing winter, to assert a novel view that he had formed, to the effect that the real enemy was now not Persia but Sparta – which seemed to him too conservative and jealous to be compatible with the Athenian expansion he wanted. In pursuance of this new conviction, he deliberately outwitted the Spartans when they tried to prevent his rebuilding of the walls of Athens and the Piraeus (479/478) – which they suspected was directed against themselves.

However, prevailing opinion at Athens was pro-Spartan – or at least did not want war, or the threat of war, against Persia and Sparta at one and the same time. In *c.*472/471 (?), therefore, Themistocles was ostracized. He went to live at Argos. Resenting this recourse to their enemy, and reciprocating his hostility, the Spartans charged him with involvement in the alleged treason of their own King Pausanias (Chapter 3). Under their influence, Themistocles' enemies at Athens secured his conviction for pro-Persian activity, or 'Medism' (*c.*468): though whether he was guilty of secret communication with Persia, then or earlier, remains impenetrably obscure.

After an adventurous, circuitous flight, he escaped into Asia Minor (467/466?). Athens condemned him to death in his absence. But he approached the new Persian King Artaxerxes I (465–424), who welcomed him and gave him the princedom of Magnesia on the Maeander and other towns, which he held until he died (*c.*462?). He had taken traitorous refuge with their old enemy, Athenians said. Yet his own country, rightly or wrongly, had rejected him.

The handicap of his suspect origins meant that Herodotus' informants magnified his faults. Yet the stories telling of his sharp practice, vanity and crafty acquisitiveness are probably not without substance; great war-leaders are rarely very pleasant. However, his oratory, a talent which appealed to the Greeks, could be superbly persuasive, and Thucydides, who does not usually indulge in character sketches, emphasized his powers of intelligent analysis and anticipatory foresight.[8] And indeed these qualities emerge from the course of events: the Salamis campaign, in particular, displayed his decisiveness and genius for rapid improvization. Here was a man whose outstanding qualities foreshadowed future Greek trends towards individualism.

Salamis also secured the political future of the unpropertied Athenian oarsmen who had so largely contributed to the victory, in contrast to the middle-class hoplites who had won at Marathon. Yet it would not be right to credit or debit Themistocles with any conscious urge towards democracy, because what he was concerned with was winning the Persian war.

After the war, however, he had performed a political somersault, becoming one of the first Athenians to turn against Sparta instead of against Persia. Hereby he anticipated Athenian policies of the future. But whether they were wise policies is a different matter. For they ensured the disunity and eventual disintegration of Greece. It could be argued, however, on his side, that Persia was so powerful that to adopt a permanent anti-Persian policy was equally or even more self-destructive.

However, these were questions for the future. For even after Salamis there were still Persian invaders in Greece. When Xerxes retreated after the battle, and took most of his army back to Asia, he did not take it all. That would have meant too severe a loss of face; and in any case his hopes of success in Greece were not extinguished. So he left a picked force in friendly Thessaly under Mardonius – to try again in the following year.

CHAPTER 3

PAUSANIAS: VICTOR AT PLATAEA

During the period preceding the Persian Wars Sparta had been incomparably the most important land power in Greece, incorporating numerous cities in what has been known in modern times as the 'Peloponnesian League' but was usually described by ancient Greeks as 'the Lacedaemonians (Spartans) and their allies'.

In this permanent alliance, the Spartans held the military command during wartime, and convened and presided over the inter-city Assembly comprising representatives of the allied states. It was only after the majority of this Assembly had ratified a proposal to go to war that the Spartans could demand the support of its entire membership. Nevertheless, they were predominant in the League, which remained unparalleled elsewhere on the Greek mainland.

The unique Spartan constitution, with its stability protected by a favourable agricultural economy, attracted interest, often combined with fascination, among Greeks from other regions. It included a rigorous system of checks and balances between two jointly ruling kings (of the Agiad and Eurypontid houses); five powerful administrative, annually elected, officials named ephors; a Council of Elders (*gerousia*) consisting of twenty-eight members over sixty years of age drawn from a limited range of noble families; and an Assembly (*apella*) to which all the citizens (known as Spartiates) belonged.

Through their membership of the Assembly every Spartiate participated in the government. But other large groups of the population, although not slaves, were excluded from the central government altogether. These included *perioikoi*, 'dwellers around', particularly in Laconia, who served in the Spartan army and paid taxes; and many helots, in Laconia and conquered Messenia, who stood 'between the free men and the slaves' and were 'owned by the state'.[9] They have been loosely described as serfs, bound to the soil, which they cultivated for their Spartan masters (Appendix IV).

The history of Sparta centred round the perpetual need to repress these helots and keep them in order, a need recalled by recurrent rebellions and threats of rebellion. As a result, Spartan society gradually lost its more liberal archaic character, in which literary and artistic interests had been prominent, and transformed itself into a ruthlessly austere regime (*agoge*) of military training and obedience clamped upon every Spartan from the age of seven onwards: a regime which produced an army not only capable of repressing the helots but recognized by other Greek city-states as unequalled anywhere else throughout the Aegean world.

The rigorous equality among Spartan citizens, however, upon which this system depended, was not enough to prevent the emergence of a few remarkable individuals. True, Lycurgus, the traditional founder of the Spartan system, may have been a fictitious product of legend, standing for a conglomeration of primitive tribal customs surviving from early times. But the ephor Chilon can be recognized as a historical figure (556/555), 'the first to yoke the ephors alongside the kings',[10] and probably the prime mover in the development of the Peloponnesian League. And then the Agiad King Cleomenes I (*c*.519–490) played a large, if controversial, part in Greek affairs, expelling the dictator Hippias from Athens in 510 (Sparta was proud of its actions against 'tyrants') but failing to establish a pro-Spartan regime there (owing to obsruction from his fellow monarch Demaratus). However, Cleomenes and his army crushed Sparta's age-long rival Argos at Sepeia (*c*.494).

Cleomenes also, rather belatedly, showed his appreciation of the Persian danger by attempting to penalize Aegina for 'Medism' (*c*.491?); but this intention, too, was frustrated by Demaratus. Various other internal disputes followed, involving Cleomenes' temporary flight from Sparta, and when he returned he stabbed himself to death (490/488), in circumstances that pointed to his virtual murder by the Spartan government. He had been resented by his half-brothers as an intruder, and his fellow Spartans could no tolerate his personal power. It was even harder for a Spartan than for an Athenian to be allowed to excel.

In 490 the Spartan army, for whatever reason, had arrived too late for the battle of Marathon. But in the next Persian invasion of 480 (after announcing a firm stand by joining the Athenians in slaying Persian envoys) their organization of the Hellenic League, and their military predominance, had earned them the command over all participating Greek states by land and sea; and Cleomenes' brother and successor Leonidas I gained everlasting fame by his self-immolation at Thermopylae (Chapter 2). Thermopylae was followed by the sea battle of Salamis, and when after his defeat there Xerxes returned to Asia Minor, he left some 30,000 to 40,000 men in Thessaly under his son-in-law Mardonius, son of his principal helper Gobryas.

During the months that followed Mardonius, employing King Alexander I of Macedonia as his intermediary, made determined attempts to win the Athenians away from the Spartan alliance – because he needed their fleet. But the endeavour, although accompanied by a mixture of theats and alluring inducements, did not prove successful, and a renewal of the war in spring 479 became inevitable.

Mardonius marched south, ravaged Attica and, finding Athens abandoned, inaugurated its second Persian occupation in ten months, accompanied by thorough devastation. However, the Athenians, although their city was now held as Mardonius' hostage, persisted in their rejection of his advances. This showed determination, since they were disconcerted because no Spartan force had responded to their appeals and moved north. But finally (after secret preparations) a Spartan army started out, and proceeded as far as the Isthmus of Corinth. Its commander was Pausanias, son of Cleombrotus of the Agiad royal house, a man in his early or mid thirties who was regent for his uncle Leonidas' young son, Pleistarchus (480–459). Pausanias' army consisted of 5,000 Spartiates, 5,000 *perioikoi* and (according to Herodotus) 35,000 helots – the largest Spartan force ever to be sent outside the Peloponnese.

Learning of this move, and realizing that he would not convince the Athenians, Mardonius retired from Attica into Boeotia. Since the best force in his army was his cavalry, perhaps 10,000 strong and superior to anything that his enemies could put into the field, he hoped to persuade the Greek army – which had moved forward from the isthmus – to give battle in the plain between the River Asopus and Plataea which favoured cavalry movement. The Greeks, to avoid this, encamped on low hills three miles east of Plataea. Their force had now been strengthened by 8,000 Athenians and 5,000 Corinthians, and raised to a total of 110,000 men from twenty-four cities.

The course of the subsequent campaign, culminating in August, contains many obscurities, further clouded by Herodotus. At first, however, the two armies apparently remained facing each other on either side of the Asopus, for between twelve and twenty-one days. Then, however, after the Persian cavalry had ridden round and blocked springs needed by the Greek troops for their drinking water, Pausanias decided to move to still higher ground during the night. This perilous withdrawal (resisted for too long, it was said, by one pig-headed Spartan commander) caused disarray, and at dawn the Greek army was still widely spread out.

So Mardonius changed his plan. Hitherto he had deliberately delayed, in the hope of exploiting Greek dissensions – and of fighting an eventual battle in the plain. But now, instead, he immediately passed to the attack, with his main force, focusing his assault on 11,500 Spartan and Tegean hoplites who constituted the Greek right wing. Pausanias' army, however, counterattacked by charging downhill at the double. The charge was a complete success; and Mardonius himself, riding his white horse, was killed. The Athenians, on the left wing, extricated themselves from an enemy force of Boeotian collaborators, and joined up with Pausanias, who pursued the Persians to a stockade they had built, north of the Asopus, in case just such an emergency should arise. But this fort fell, and the Persian army was annihilated, except for a contingent under Mardonius' second-in-command Artabazus, which (perhaps through disloyalty, because the two generals were rivals) had never been engaged in the battle. Artabazus succeeded in leading these survivors back home, through Thessaly and Thrace.

Pausanias' success, in this greatest land battle the Greeks had ever fought, was described by Herodotus as 'the finest victory in all history known to me'.[11] The tribute is all the more notable in the light of the abundant anti-Spartan propaganda the historian must have heard at Athens (Chapter 13). Pausanias' troops at Plataea, in which Spartans predominated, had saved Greece as surely as the Athenians had saved it at Marathon and Salamis: and, indeed, even more conclusively, since henceforward the Persians never invaded mainland Greece again.

Pausanias' personal contribution, too, was inestimable. Young though he was, he had held squabbling and insubordinate contingents from many cities together for weeks; he had warded off continual cavalry menaces, lethally threatening his food and water supplies; and his counter-charge, although undertaken in untidy and chaotic conditions, had justified his confidence in the training and fighting capacity of the rock-like Spartan infantry. After the battle, he put Thebes' Medizing leaders to death; whether he had consulted his own government before doing so is uncertain. But otherwise the Hellenic League, under Sparta's guidance, showed little enthusiasm for seeking out Persian collaborators in northern Greece – and Artabazus was not pursued.

While the Greek army had been at Plataea preparing for the battle, the Greek fleet, under the command of the Eurypontid Spartan King Leotychidas II, was urged by Samian envoys to move from Delos, where it was now stationed, in order to liberate Ionia, which was ready to revolt. So Leotychidas, with 250 triremes, sailed to Samos, only to find that the Persians, suspicious of Ionian intentions and lacking confidence in their own fighting fitness after Salamis, had retired to the promontory of Mycale on the mainland opposite, enclosing their beached ships, and the troops that had joined them, within a palisade. Leotychidas, however, launched an assault on this stronghold, which succumbed to him after many of the Ionians in the Persian army, notably the Milesians, had changed sides.

Their defection foreshadowed a general uprising of the Asian and island Greeks against Persia. Greek tradition, which enjoyed synchronizations, liked to suppose that Plataea and Mycale had been fought on the same day. In fact, Mycale was slightly the later of the two; yet the engagements deserved to be bracketed, since, between them, they ended the Persian Wars of 480–479. What Mycale had done was to show the Greeks passing, for the first time, from the defensive to the offensive – and the new potentialities of sea power were made clear.

As for Pausanias, his exceptional success, like those of his earlier Spartan compatriot Cleomenes I and of the Athenians Miltiades and Themistocles, brought him to a sticky end, accelerated, in his case, by the swollen-headedness to which successful Spartans abroad, rendered naive by their blinkered training, were particularly liable.

At first, all went well: in 478, as commander-in-chief of an allied Greek fleet, he captured Byzantium, in order to command the crossing between Europe and Asia. But his dictatorial arrogance – reflected in a grandiose thank-offering dedication at Delphi (later erased by the Spartans), and displayed by the adoption of Persian clothes and the employment of an Asian bodyguard from Thrace – provoked his Greek allies and fomented suspicions of treachery. Recalled to Sparta for trial, he avoided conviction on this major charge (though not on minor ones), and returned to Byzantium (*c.*477), on his own initiative, it was said, though Spartan official connivance (to be disowned in the event of failure) can be supposed.

This was the time when Sparta's Aegean allies were going over to Athens, and Pausanias was dislodged from Byzantium by the Athenian Cimon (*c.*477/475 or 472/470, Chapter 5). Moving to Colonae in the Troad (north-west Asia Minor), where the Spartans suspected him of renewing negotiations with Persia, he was again recalled home for trial (*c.*470?). Once more he was acquitted. However, the discovery or fabrication of a letter written by him to Artabazus, now the Persian satrap of Dascylium, together with an alleged overheard conversation between Pausanias and a messenger – accorded credence, and every possible emphasis, by his Athenian enemies – led to his fatal incrimination. To avoid arrest by the ephors, he sought sanctuary in Sparta's temple of Athena of the Brazen House, but was walled in and left to starve, though removed in time to die on unconsecrated ground (*c.*469/466).

Spartans at the time must have been divided about the rights and wrongs of the matter. He had his supporters. Disgraceful though his autocratic behaviour no doubt seemed, it is impossible to tell whether the charges of Medism – in which he allegedly shared complicity with Themistocles – were justified or merely a pretext. In any case, Pausanias' fellow Spartans were sore because they had lost the leadership of Hellas to Athens – and they derived satisfaction from making him a scapegoat.

The ephors, when they set out to ruin Pausanias, were not merely acting out of traditional hostility to the royal houses, but believed that he was planning a coup against them, and in the end, if not earlier, they may have been right. Above all, his political enemies became sure that he was inciting the helots to revolt, promising them freedom and citizenship. Indeed, some believed that he had already made such assurances to the helot contingents under his command before the battle of Plataea, but had been, at the time, unable to honour his promises.

About these accusations it is impossible to be certain, although they cannot be rejected out of hand, since, to protect himself, and to realize his dreams of an imperial Sparta, he had to find a weapon against his own compatriots – and needed the help of the helots. Be that as it may, in Sparta, at any time, conspiracy with the helots was the most alarming and lethal suspicion that could possibly arise (Appendix IV), and once it became directed against Pausanias there was no saving him. It was of no avail that, along with Themistocles, named as his co-plotter, he was 'the most famous man of his time in Hellas'[12] – and the architect of an outstandingly glorious victory over a foreign foe: as subsequent honours to his tomb tardily recognized.

But all the victories over the Persians had been glorious. They had filled the Greeks with immeasurable confidence about their own potentialities and their future. They had also confirmed, in Greek minds, a powerful conviction of the difference and distinction between Greeks and 'barbarians' (foreigners) – and an assurance that the former, free men and members of free communities, were superior to the latter – slaves of despots – and constituted their national enemies, and could defeat them. The Greeks had been given an identity, or the means of recognizing what it was.

Yet these new invigorating conceptions, often hailed as the beginning of European history, did not result, as might have seemed logical, in any strengthening of the Panhellenic political union which had been, partially, realized during the emergency. On the contrary, so strong were the centrifugal tendencies that many independent Greek city-states, and especially Athens and Sparta, preferred to derive their own, parochial propaganda messages from the Persian Wars – each allocating all the credit to itself – and continued to do everything possible to flourish and expand at the expense of other *poleis*. This was to give the

Persians the opportunity to intervene once more, decisively, before the end of the century, and again in the century that followed – without the need for any further military invasions (Chapters 24, 29).

CHAPTER 4

GELON AND HIERO I: VICTORS AT HIMERA AND CUMAE

Modern Greece is only one of the heirs of ancient Greece. There was also not only a Greece of the near east and a Greece in southern Russia, but a Greece of the west – southern Italy and Sicily. This, like those two others, tends to be underestimated, partly because the works of its own historians, unlike those of the great historians working on the mainland, did not survive.

The expansion of the Greeks into Italy and Sicily, undertaken from the early eighth century onwards, had been their most adventurous and far-reaching series of enterprises. Within a brief space of time there were colonies in Campania and beside the Gulf of Taras, and in eastern Sicily too.

The Phoenicians as well as the Greeks colonized Sicily, but a suggestion that the Phoenicians arrived first cannot be confirmed. At all events their settlements, eventually, were concentrated in the western part of the island, while the Greeks came in relatively large numbers to its eastern areas. For those territories resemble the coastal regions of the Aegean, while offering, however, more abundant and cultivable lowlands – which were, above all, what the Greek colonists wanted, although the ratio between agricultural and commercial desiderata varied from place to place. At first, relations between the two immigrant peoples, Greeks and Phoenicians, were not necessarily unfriendly, though they deteriorated in the course of the sixth century.

Seven hundred and thirty-three BC was the traditional date of the foundation of Syracuse on the eastern Sicilian coast (one year later, it was said, than the earliest Greek colony on the island, at Naxos, farther to the north). The colonists at Syracuse were Corinthians, though Corinth's desire to retain control over the new city was resisted. The initial site of the settlement was on the offshore island of Ortygia, joined to the mainland by a causeway; the protection provided by the island created two excellent ports, one of which, the Great Harbour, was the most spacious in all eastern Sicily. But already before 700, with the assistance of unlimited building stone from a nearby limestone plateau, the habitation centre had spread to new quarters on the Sicilian mainland itself. Two miles to the south-west stood a temple of Olympian Zeus, just beyond the River Anapus, of which the plain produced an abundant cereal crop. This enriched the aristocratic ruling class of the city, who were known as the *gamoroi*, 'those who divide the land', and formed an Assembly six hundred strong.

This oligarchic government gained control of a broad surrounding territory, expelling or subjugating its native Sicel population. Yet at Syracuse itself the *gamoroi* were continually involved in tensions with later waves of Greek settlers and others of under-privileged status – notably the *kyllyrioi*, serf-like helots – who lived discontentedly in the hills, so that already, by the beginning of the fifth century, the city's achievements had to be measured against a background of savage and almost perpetual internal strife.

Moreover, for a time Syracuse was eclipsed by Gela on the south coast, where Hippocrates (*c*.498) became the richest and most powerful among a crop of island dictators. In *c*.492 he heavily defeated the Syracusans and, although prevented by Corinthian mediators from occupying the city itself, superseded Syracuse as suzerain of the region's Sicel inhabitants.

But in *c*.491/490 the Sicels killed him in a battle, whereupon his cavalry commander Gelon, disregarding his role as guardian of the dead man's sons, seized the dictatorship for himself, becoming the founder of the Deinomenid dynasty, named after his father Deinomenes, member of a family of hereditary priests.

In 485 Gelon fulfilled Hippocrates' aims by seizing control of Syracuse – in response to an appeal from the *gamoroi* (threatened by internal discontents), who did not, however, find their own authority restored after all, since Gelon himself moved into Syracuse (leaving his brother Hiero to take charge of Gela). Under Gelon Syracuse became the biggest, richest, most formidable and most cultured Greek centre of the age. The Sicilian towns of Megara Hyblaea and Camarina suffered destruction at his hands, and many of their citizens, together with a large part of Gela's own population, were transferred to Syracuse. Complex marriage links were formed with Theron, dictator of the city of Acragas on the south coast, and powerful Syracusan armed forces were built up by the recruitment of mercenaries and the construction of an imposing fleet in the city's fine harbours.

Early in his reign Gelon had become involved in warfare with Carthage, the Phoenician colony in northern Africa which was now a major mercantile power and had taken over the control, or leadership, of Phoenicia's settlements in western Sicily. His position strengthened by what he was able to present as this foreign threat, Gelon had intended to invade north Africa, but the assistance from the Spartans which he hoped for failed to arrive, and the plan had to be abandoned.

When, however, Greece, in its turn, was threatened by Persian invasion under Xerxes I, the Hellenic alliance appealed to him for help (481). But it refused to pay the prices he demanded, which were, first, the supreme command, and then, when that was not granted, the inter-allied command at sea. But by this time, in any case, it had become clear to Gelon that Sicily itself was menaced by a major Carthaginian invasion. Why the Carthaginians chose this particular time to embark on such a large-scale aggressive policy has been debated. But they had probably come to feel that their essential metal supplies from Spain were threatened by the Greek cities on the island. And a measure of collusion between the more or less simultaneous invasions launched by Carthage (a Phoenician foundation) and the Persians (whose fleet so largely consisted of Phoenician ships and men), seems likely enough.

At all events, when the Carthaginians received appeals from one of the island's dictators, Terillus, who had been expelled from the north-coast city of Himera by Theron of Acragas, and from Terillus' son-in-law Anaxilas of Rhegium, with whom he had taken refuge, they responded by sending a fleet of 200 warships and numerous transports under Hamilcar (I). The 30,000 (?) soldiers these vessels carried, including mercenaries from Phoenician and Carthaginian settlements throughout the central and western Mediterranean, formed the strongest expedition that had ever invaded Sicily; and Gelon and Theron united to repel its assault. Hamilcar marched from his base at Panormus in order to besiege Himera. He hoped to join forces with Anaxilas, but, before he could achieve this, Gelon attacked him with 50,000 infantry and 5,000 cavalry. This cavalry squadron, a speciality of Syracuse's horse-breeding aristocracy and much superior to its enemy counterpart (diminished by shipwreck during the crossing from Africa), penetrated Hamilcar's stockade by masquerading as a force from one of his local allies (Selinus), and set fire to his ships. Hamilcar was killed, and Gelon's infantry forced the Carthaginian troops back into a strongpoint, where lack of water compelled them to surrender. Their entire army was captured or killed, and Carthage, in addition to losing a vast booty, bought an end to hostilities by paying a substantial indemnity; they presented Gelon's wife Demarate with a golden crown for her good offices in arranging the peace.

Although the Phoenician–Carthaginian settlements in western Sicily survived (and trading between them and the Greeks was resumed), seven decades were to pass before the Carthaginians ventured to invade Sicily again. The decisive battle of Himera won Gelon enormous fame, and he dedicated a golden tripod and statue of Victory to Apollo at Delphi. A statue of Zeus was also set up at Olympia, and temples were built at Syracuse, Acragas and Himera to celebrate the triumph. The rescued city of Himera was placed under Theron's son Thrasydaeus; Selinus and Rhegium made peace with the victorious leaders; and Hiero, pursuing the Sicilian dictators' propensity for political weddings, married the daughter of Anaxilas.

Gelon had now become the most powerful man in the Greek world and, indeed, in Europe. But in 478 he died: despite all the anti-tyrant propaganda of later epochs, his reign was looked back upon as a period of prosperity and happiness.

After his death Hiero I moved from Gela to become dictator of Syracuse in his place, overcoming the counterclaims of his brother Polyzalus – who possessed close links with Theron, so that relations between Hiero and Theron were now damaged, at least for a time. Hiero concerned himself with Greek interests on the Italian mainland. There, after various interventions, he came into open conflict with the Etruscans. These constituted the other rival power, or powers, which, along with the Carthaginians, threatened the Greeks of the west. Our lack of information compels us, very often, to speak of the 'Etruscans', although in fact they comprised a number of independent and rarely collaborating Etruscan city-states, not only in their homeland in west-central Italy, north of the Tiber, but also south of that river, in Latium and Campania, where many archaeological sites display occupation by one Etruscan state or another, or varying degrees of their political, commercial and cultural influence.

Campania was the inevitable site of a clash between the Greeks – one of whose principal centres was the seaport of Cumae – and the Etruscans, who possessed important bases at Capua and Cales, which were uncomfortably close to Cumae. Hostilities developed in the later sixth century BC, when Aristodemus the Effeminate, ruler of Cumae, repelled an invasion by northern and local Etruscan forces (*c.*525/524), and then won a further victory at Aricia (506/504). These setbacks deprived the Etruscans of their land-route, and stressed the need for them to secure a sea passage along the Italian coast instead, so as not to lose access to the commercially vital Sicilian Strait.

Co-operation between some of the Etruscan city-states and Carthage against the Greeks was nothing new, and when in *c.*474 an Etruscan navy sailed against Cumae it had Carthaginian support. Hiero I of Syracuse, in the light of his interest in the Italian mainland, realized that the defeat of the Greek cause would be a disaster for himself, and sent a fleet, which defeated the Etruscans in the Gulf of Cumae. The power of the Etruscan city-states, by this time, was already on the wane, and Hiero had ensured that it would not revive. By his success, he secured western Greece against one of its two principal menaces, just as Gelon had driven off the other. A bronze helmet was dedicated at Olympia; and the Boeotian poet Pindar celebrated the triumph.[13]

Although their constitutional position remained ambiguous – they identified themselves with their states, yet did not call themselves kings – the dictators of the Sicilian city-states created alliances and coalitions which could never have been brought about by any oligarchic or democratic city-state. Moreover, amid a brilliant upsurge of cultural life, the poets Pindar, Bacchylides and Simonides were successfully mobilized to praise the glamour and splendour of these rulers' victories and courts, and the court of wealthy Syracuse in particular – thus fulfilling the dictators' desire that their eulogies should resound on the Greek mainland, where they were assiduous to Delphi and Olympia.

They had repelled the two great national enemies in the west, and now they took the lead in fostering local peace and wealth. Yet their methods were tough, and to some extent counter-productive. Gelon remarked that 'the common people is a most thankless house-mate',[14] and he and Hiero were aristocratic by birth and inclination, relying upon the wealthy horse-breeding classes rather than upon the *demos*. Nevertheless, by a paradox, the two dictators' policies encouraged democracy, because their massive transplantations of men and women, and their enfranchisements of the foreign mercenary soldiers on whom they depended, chipped away the local, conservative traditions that bound the people to the aristocrats. Yet the dictators were able to trust no one; Hiero organized an elaborate system of spies to watch his own citizens. In his last years, he forcibly induced Acragas (after Theron's death) to join his alliance.

But when he himself, suffering painfully from gallstones, died in 467/6 having earned a less favourable reputation than Gelon, though both men were honoured as heroes after their deaths – the Syracusans rose against his brother Thrasybulus, and the local dictatorship came to an end. The 'democracy' that succeeded it, however – as in other Sicilian city-states – remained all too true to the chronic instability that plagued democratic governments on the island. For the new 'democratic' government of Syracuse very soon became involved in ferocious strife between its old and new citizens, who were trying and failing to live together in this first great cosmopolitan centre in the Greek world.

PART II

Between the Wars: First Phase

LIST OF EVENTS

478	Athenians form Delian League
477	Bronze statue of tyrant-slayers by Critius and Nesiotes (see Chapter 14)
477–*c*.463	Campaigns of Cimon transform Delian League into Athenian empire
476 or 474	Bronze statue of charioteer at Delphi
476–474	Pindar guest of Hiero I at Syracuse (Chapter 4): also Aeschylus (between 478 and 472).
475/473	Taras (with Rhegium) defeated by Iapygians, democracy established (Chapter 26)
472	Aeschylus' *Persians*
470s(?)	Beginnings of Polygnotus' career as a painter
470s(?)	Philosophical poem of Parmenides
470s or 460s	Spartan victories over Tegea and Argos at Tegea and over the Arcadians at Dipaea
470–457	Temple of Zeus at Olympia
c.469/468(?)	Cimon defeats the Persians at the River Eurymedon
468	Death of Simonides
466	Democracy replaces dictatorship at Syracuse (Chapter 4)
460s(?)	Philosophical poems of Empedocles
465	Artaxerxes I becomes King of Persia (d.424)
c.465	Earthquake at Sparta
c.465/464–461/460 or mid-450s	Revolt of helots in Messenia
462	Anaxagoras comes to Athens
462	Cimon sent to Messenia by the Athenians but dismissed by the Spartans
462/461	Ephialtes' reform of the Areopagus

461 Cimon ostracized (d.*c*.451) and Ephialtes assassinated

458 The *Oresteia* of Aeschylus(d.456)

CHAPTER 5
CIMON: CREATOR OF EMPIRE

When Pausanias, the Spartan victor of Plataea, captured Byzantium which dominated the crossing from Europe to Asia and access to the Black Sea – at the head of a fleet made up from the Greek city-states that had taken part in the war and now rebelled against Persia – his overbearing behaviour, combined with the suspicion of treasonable negotiations with Persia, brought about his recall to Sparta (Chapter 3).

At this juncture the allies who had complained about him, led by Chios, Samos and the cities of Lesbos, appealed to Aristides, the honest and methodical Athenian commander, to take over their leadership. And so, by his initiative, the confederacy of the 'Greeks' or the 'Athenians and their allies', later known as the Delian League, came into existence.

This was a decisive *volte face*. Hitherto, and notably against the Persians, every endeavour to achieve Hellenic and Panhellenic collaboration had been guided by the Spartans, and was modelled on their Peloponnesian League. Now, however, Athens, a seapower and therefore more suited to the role, had replaced them. The Spartans accepted the new situation – how reluctantly we cannot tell, but they always included a party which was unwilling for their city, with its primary Peloponnesian preoccupations, to commit its forces too extensively overseas. Moreover, recurrent strife between kings and ephors – and between local commanders in the field and the government at home – exercised a paralysing effect upon Spartan claims to Panhellenic leadership.

The purpose of the new Athenian confederacy was mutual protection against Persia, as well as retaliation, whenever possible, for the damage caused by the Persian invasions. The Athenians, whose port the Piraeus was being developed by Themistocles (Chapter 2), were to provide the federal commanders-in-chief and decide which city-states would supply ships and which would contribute money; these funds were to be controlled by ten Athenian 'treasurers of the Greeks' (*hellenotamiai*).

Representatives of the allied city-states were enjoined to meet together once a year, each with an equal vote. Their meeting-place and treasury was on the sacred island of Delos, an ancient Ionian religious and festival centre.

It was understood, though perhaps only implicitly, that the autonomy of all member states would be respected; and their representatives took an oath of loyalty to the League – an oath which was permanently binding. The initial size of the confederacy has been much disputed. It included a good many eastern Greek states. Chios, Samos, Lesbos, Thasos and other maritime centres provided ships. The money supplied by the rest was spent by the Athenians, at their sole discretion.

Their statesman Aristides, after organizing the initial assessment, vanished from political view, and the leading figure of the new League was his fellow-Athenian Cimon. Cimon was the son of the younger Miltiades, victor at Marathon, and of Hegesipyle, daughter of the Thracian (Sapaean) monarch Olorus. When his father died in 489 he paid the large fine which Miltiades had incurred after his failure at Paros (Chapter 1). Cimon served, with distinction, at Salamis and on a mission to Sparta (479), and then in the following year was on the staff of Aristides at Byzantium, where he subsequently assumed the command himself as one of the Athenian generals (an office he continued to hold frequently year after year). After Pausanias had returned to Byzantium, he was driven out again by Cimon.

The dating of events in the period that followed is hard to establish, since the historian Thucydides is selective and impossible to check (Chapter 23). But it was apparently in 476 that Cimon's confederate army expelled the Persian garrison from Eion at the mouth of the River Strymon in Thrace, establishing Athenian settlers to prevent its return. In *c.*475 he occupied the island of Scyros – strategically located for the control of the northern Aegean – clearing it of non-Greek (Dolopian) pirates and once again replacing them by colonists from Athens. This was also the occasion of a major propaganda coup, since Cimon found on the island the supposed bones of the Athenians' founder hero Theseus, and took them to Athens.

Probably, too, he presided over two subsequent happenings, in the late 470s and early 460s, which made it clear that the Delian League was becoming an Athenian empire. First Carystus, at the southern tip of Euboea, was compelled to become a member of the confederacy, since its location was deemed too vital (and too close to Athens) for neutrality to be tolerable. Then the island city of Naxos in the Cyclades, which tried to secede because it felt that the League had lost its purpose, was brought to heel by the Athenians. This was the first occasion, says Thucydides, when an ally was treated in such a coercive fashion, although the Naxians were reminded that, legally speaking, their oath of loyalty had not included a time limit.

Cimon was able to distract attention from these ominous events by leading an allied fleet to Lycia in southern Asia Minor, where he drove out Persian garrisons and enrolled new members of the League. And then came the greatest military achievement of his life, his victory over the Persians at the River Eurymedon in Pamphylia (?469/468). The Persians, in a last attempt to restore their fortunes in the Aegean, had concentrated an army and naval force at the mouth of the river, and were expecting reinforcements from Cyprus. Cimon, confident of friends in the cities of the region, struck at them on sea and land, annihilating their fleet in the cramped river basin – with a loss of 200 Persian ships – and then inflicting a heavy reverse on their land troops. The Persians' camp was sacked; and then their flotilla from Cyprus likewise met with disaster. 'No one', said Plutarch, 'did more to humble the Great King and deflate his ambitions than Cimon.'[1] Eurymedon was a culmination and completion of the Greek victories in the earlier Persian Wars (490–479), and meant that the Persians had decisively lost their coastal and island bases in the eastern Aegean and Mediterranean regions, so that the members of the Delian League could feel safe, and their old Levant trade-routes could be reopened.

Enriched by enormous plunder – part of which he passed on to his fellow citizens – and satisfied that Athens under his leadership had become a great power, Cimon next attacked the Thracian Chersonese, forcing the Persians (who had hitherto remained there) to depart.

But he was prevented from further exploitation of his victory at Eurymedon by a revolt on the large northern island of Thasos, rich in wine and timber and metals (465/464). The Athenians' infiltrations into this region, aimed at expanding their own commercial interests on the adjacent Thracian mainland, had come into conflict with the Thasians' mining interests, and Thasos seceded from the Delian League. After a two years' siege, however, the island city succumbed to Cimon, and lost its mainland possessions (and its walls). The issue, however, had been an Athenian one, scarcely justifiable from the League's Panhellenic point of view; and there was grumbling, which his political enemies at Athens exploited.

When Cimon returned there, they showed their hand. The Thasians had received private encouragement from Alexander I, king of Macedonia (Chapter 35), and Cimon was put on trial on the charge of taking bribes from Alexander and thus refraining from the annexation of mainland territory which he might otherwise have seized on behalf of Athens. He was acquitted; but it now became clear what was at stake.

His prosecutors had included the young Pericles, making his political début and speaking for older men such as Ephialtes who were opposed to Cimon's principal political aim: which was friendship and partnership and shared leadership with the other leading Greek power Sparta, in the interests of a common anti-Persian policy. This pro-Spartan attitude seemed wrong to Ephialtes and Pericles, who, like Themistocles earlier (Chapter 2), were convinced that Athenian and Spartan power, in the long run, must prove incompatible.

By the same token, Cimon's opponents at Athens were far more closely wedded to democracy than he was. He himself, married to an Alcmaeonid noblewoman Isodice, was an attractive, well-born, conservative land-owner, notable for his ostentatious wealth – of which land-owning was the best source and index at Athens – and for his genial, open-handed generosity (including lavish building), which helped to strengthen his political base. At the same time, however, this semi-feudal princely style, redolent of the old aristocratic slogan of *eunomia*, good (hierarchical) order, left him out of touch with the democratic elements in Athenian politics. These he found less understandable, and less sympathetic, than the Spartan way of life. And indeed the Delian League, which Cimon virtually converted into an Athenian empire, had won a free hand only because the Spartans did not impede the process – putting their trust in Cimon.

This relationship, however, was put to the test in *c.*465 when Sparta, disabled through an earthquake, became threatened by a large-scale revolt of its subject helots in Messenia (?*c.*465/464–461/460 or mid-450s), the most serious helot rebellion in living memory (see Appendix IV). The Spartans succeeded in penning the rebels in and besieging them upon Mount Ithome, but nevertheless felt obliged to appeal to Athens for assistance.

Cimon, despite opposition from Ephialtes, obtained leave from his Athenian compatriots to proceed to Ithome to help them, with 4,000 hoplites (*c.*462). But when the Athenian troops arrived, an extraordinary thing happened. For the Spartan government proceeded to send them home again – because they seemed politically unreliable, and were even believed capable of intriguing with the helots: since this was the very time when the Athenian Assembly, guided by Ephialtes with the assistance of Pericles, was launching major and almost revolutionary reforms, stripping the venerable Areopagus of most of its powers in the interests of democracy (Chapter 11).

The Spartans cannot have suspected their friend Cimon of disloyalty to themselves (and indeed they tried to smooth over the rejection of his force in order to protect him). Yet it was he, as the contingent's commander, who became the principal sufferer. The pro-Spartan policy, which he had so successfully directed at Athens, was discredited and abandoned – with the immediate result of an inter-city war (460–445), involving hostilities which affected the rest of the century. Moreover, he himself, after failing to secure the repeal of Ephialtes' constitutional measures, was ostracized (461): not the first, or last, Greek or Athenian war-winner to suffer rejection from his countrymen.

For the next ten years Cimon is not heard of; though during the 450s he was recalled, on the proposal of Pericles himself – during a period when Athens, after setbacks on the mainland and in Egypt, feared invasion from the Spartans and wanted peace with them after all. So Cimon negotiated a Five Year Truce with Sparta (*c.*451), and was permitted by his fellow citizens to revert to his familiar anti-Persian preoccupation by leading a League expedition to Cyprus.

But there, at the siege of Citium, he was killed. The forces he left behind him, after naval victories off Cypriot Salamis, returned home, bringing his bones. His fight against Persia was at an end – there was no politician left who wanted to keep it going – and his death, followed by those convenient successes at sea, gave Athens a badly needed opportunity for peace on favourable terms.

CHAPTER 6

PINDAR: THE OLD VALUES

Non-epic, non-dramatic Greek verse, a combination of words and music and dancing, is grouped together as 'lyrical'. Greek lyric poetry displays more analytical and introspective aims than epic: its approach (like its metres) is different. But a 'lyric age', succeeding an 'epic age', is a fallacious conception. There had been non-epic, 'lyrical' songs long before Homer; they are mentioned in the *Iliad* and the *Odyssey*.

First-class lyric poetry, however, did not continue for ever. It reached its natural termination in the fifth century BC, when Simonides of Ceos (*c*.556–468), bridging the archaic and classical epochs, wrote many kinds of verse, but was especially famous for his epigrams and epitaphs. And Pindar of Cynoscephalae in Boeotia (*c*.518–*c*.438) gained unprecedented renown.

Although anecdotes and surmises relating to Pindar's family and teachers remain conjectural, it is clear that he had already acquired a reputation in early youth. During the Persian Wars of 480–479 he was as neutral as any other Theban. His career recalls that not every distinguished Greek fought, or sided, against the Persians. Afterwards, however, this pacifist attitude must have caused him some embarrassment, since he duly praised the Greek victories at Salamis and Plataea.

In 476 Pindar went to Sicily at the invitation of Hiero I, dictator of Syracuse (Chapter 4), and stayed there for about two years. Thereafter, he was commissioned by rich patrons in many parts of the Greek world, on a scale that had not been seen before, and for fees about which he was not reticent. We have reached a period when far more writers and artists travelled widely throughout Hellenic lands than had ever been the case before. Aegina and Athens (where he had studied) were centres to which he showed particular devotion. He died at Argos.

Within a few centuries after his death his works were collected into seventeen books of poetry. These included poems of many descriptions, mostly choral, but covering a wide range of subjects. From these various types of poetry only fragments – though in some cases fragments of considerable size – have survived: with one exception. That is to say, his only works to have come down to us more or less intact are four books containing forty-five Epinician (Victory) Odes – choral songs written in honour of athletic and musical victories in the competitions at Greek Games. Inheriting all the Greek competitive spirit that had already made itself manifest in Homer, this peculiar Epinician literary form had already been shaped by Simonides, but Pindar developed the genre much more elaborately.

Each of the four books of his Epinicians is concerned with one of the four principal festivals, the Olympian, Pythian, Isthmian and Nemean Games. These festivals – blends of public feast and competition, religious experience, and great art, extensions of the heroic, Homeric ethos – had developed round sanctuaries of ancient origin, though the precise degree of their prehistoric antiquity is disputed. At Olympia the worship of Zeus of Mount Olympus within his Altis precinct had been introduced by Dorian immigrants or invaders at about the turn of the millennium, perhaps in more or less direct continuity with an earlier, pre-Greek cult. A local athletic competition was being held at the place by *c.*900, and the Games, in their developed form, seem to go back to the eighth century, though the criteria for the date 776, to which the Greeks ascribed their inauguration, are unstable.

In this Olympic festival, subsequently held in every fourth year, the foot-race always remained the principal event, but jumping and wrestling and boxing also came to be included, and when chariot-races were added they gained enormous prestige. The Olympic Games, although they provided no facilities for music and poetry, were seen as the greatest of the four, and won their Panhellenic status and renown – displayed by the presence of forty or fifty thousand visitors – two centuries before the others.

Delphi derived its reverential fame from Apollo, a god of Anatolian antecedents who, after absorbing the features of northern divinities, was once again brought there by the Dorians. He pronounced his oracles through a priestess, the Pythia. From an early date the cult included a festival held every eighth year, and the four-yearly Pythian Games were inaugurated in 582/581 (or 586/585). Musical competitions – singing and reciting, and instrumental contests – remained pre-eminent, but athletic and equestrian contests modelled on those of Olympia were added.

It was probably likewise in *c.*581 that the Isthmian Games, held every second year, were established by the leading families of Corinth, to celebrate the replacement of its dictatorship by republican, oligarchic government. Then, in 573, the Nemean Games, of legendary origin associated with Heracles' slaying of the Nemean Lion, were elevated by the Argives (who controlled Nemea and its festival through their dependency Cleonae) to Panhellenic status, thus becoming the fourth and last of the great Games, once again celebrated in alternate years.

These various Games were contested by individuals, and not by their cities, although the cities took intense pride in their citizens' victories. The prizes were only wreaths: of wild olive at Olympia, bay leaves at Delphi, pine branches at Isthmia, wild celery at Nemea. But the victors won undying local and also Panhellenic fame, which celebration by the great lyric poets supremely enhanced.

In particular, such festivals formed the background of the Epinician (Victory) Odes of Pindar.

These Odes are anything between twenty-five and two hundred lines long. Their structure is variable – and there has been much debate about their internal unity, or lack of it. Yet at all events they are disciplined compositions, and reveal certain more or less constant elements. An allusion to the victor is indispensable, and the location and nature of his success are also to be found, together, in some cases, with references to earlier athletic achievements by his relatives, or praises of his trainer.

As for the specific victory that is the subject of each poem, it is never described in a straightforward fashion. For example, a mythical narrative is often inserted, possessing some relevance to the occasion but designed to set it against a causative yet timeless background, related to the great sagas of Greek religion. Highlights in the traditional myths are selected, or their character, even, may be partially recast, to point a moral, or to suggest to Pindar's hearers how extraordinary competitive success should be experienced (and he gloats brutally over the crushing dishonour of failure).[2]

Oracles and proverbs too, wise maxims and moral sayings, are included, with oblique, enigmatic effects – some derived from ancient origins and others coined by the poet himself. Progress is rarely unambiguous, or denoted in neat chronological sequence; the Odes trace involuted circles round their themes, developing a series of dazzling, shimmering, lightning images, amid which changes of topic and mood are sharp and disjointed and abrupt.

Pindar exploited the poetic conventions that he inherited with masterly skill, loosening them so as to incorporate vast new reaches of wider experience. His concern with his athletic victors is not to delineate their feats or deeds but to celebrate the whole way of life lying around and behind the moment of their triumph, and to see them as mortals elevated or illuminated by a divinely inspired force, in the climactic manifestation of their excellence represented by this victory. For Pindar is one of the most deeply religious of all Greek poets. When this metaphysical transfiguration comes upon a victor in the Games he is seen to achieve, in a flash – despite the gulf that normally separates gods and men – a well-being comparable to that of the gods themselves. The happy attainment of this life-enhancing effulgence is the ultimate justification of existence upon this earth.

Moreover, Pindar believes himself uniquely empowered to fasten upon these awesome moments that illuminate the holiness of beauty, self-consciously employing his poetic gifts to capture them for ever. His soaring imaginative vigour ranges freely and excitedly, and with deep, impetuous, sensuous or even sensual emotion, from acrobatic, light-footed, deft delicacy to the sublime grandeur for which he is most famous (and which seems, to us, so curiously discordant with the sporting occasions).

To achieve these imposing contrasts he made flexible use of a wide variety of lyric metres, and employed an intricately patterned diction which, although founded on the Doric dialect, moved beyond this when necessary, building up mighty, cumulative, rhythmical masses of poetic language which captured audiences throughout the Greek world. We can only guess at the music (of flute and lyre) and the singing – needing weeks of rehearsal – which formed integral elements of his complex art.

However, Pindar was a nostalgic figure, out of sympathy with many aspects of his age. Thus, for all the admiration of Athens which he eventually developed, his social and moral convictions remained alien from the democratic effervescence that increasingly motivated so many Athenians of his time (Chapter 11). Pindar's values, on the contrary, were those of an old-fashioned, hierarchical oligarchy which esteemed hereditary nobility and family tradition, and admired the display and self-expression made possible by inherited wealth. It is these characteristics, he pronounced, that exemplify god-given *areta*, an excellence which is not only physical but also moral, intellectual and practical. Yet the achievement of this lofty standard, and of the virtues that it embodied – friendship, courage, hospitality, moderation, civic peace – was impossible without laborious endeavour and brave enterprise and fine character. In this regulated world of archaic *eunomia*, good order (the ideal of Cimon, Chapter 5), the powerful man must make use of his authority with generosity and courtesy, worthy of the universal order of Zeus himself.

Even in his own time Pindar encountered opposition. Simonides and Bacchylides were his rivals in Sicily; and he incurred criticism for his admiration of Sicilian dictators. Thebans, too, felt that he paid too little attention to themselves, and that he had become too fond of Athens – although a careful reading of his Odes (even if he is never altogether explicit in his topical references) shows that Athenian imperialism in the 450s was now causing him disquiet.

After his death, he rapidly came to look obsolete and outdated, since few of his cherished values survived him. But from Alexandrian times onwards he reassumed his position, as a poet's poet or scholar's poet, it is true, but also as the greatest lyric poet whom Greece, and perhaps the world, had ever produced, earning a host of admirers in many centuries: though there have always been some who hated his unabashed conservatism.

CHAPTER 7

AESCHYLUS: GODS AND HUMAN BEINGS

Athenian tragedy, when it had first emerged, was a gradually dramatized improvement upon various kinds of more or less poetical entertainment already existing in different parts of Greece.

In Athens, it was under the dictator Pisistratus (546–527) that the presentation of tragic drama became established as a regular feature of the annual festival of the City Dionysia, staged beneath the Acropolis. Athenian festivals were tragedy's motivating force. According to tradition what passed as the first tragic play was presented in *c.*534 by Thespis, who seems to have supplemented earlier choral performances (mime, impersonation and so on) by a prologue and set speech or speeches, spoken or declaimed to the music of a double flute. Thespis won a prize, and so, in 511/508, did Phrynichus, remembered for the beauty of his lyrics, the variety of his dances and the introduction of female characters (though still acted by men). In due course, it became the custom for playwrights to produce four plays (a tetralogy) at each competition, comprising three tragedies and a satyric drama.

This tragic poetry, even though the music and dancing which were essential to its performance are lost, remains one of the decisive theatrical and literary innovations and achievements of all time. It was designed to express the deepest thoughts of which men and women are capable, and in particular, to examine and assess their relationships with the divine powers.

Spoken, recited passages – long speeches or dialogues – alternate with lyrics sung and danced by choruses (granted to competitors by the authorities); and these choral contributions, although alien to modern dramatic conceptions, effectively set the action against a more generalized and contemplative background. The structure of a tragic play is tight-packed and concise: and it says a great deal for the intelligence and stamina of Athenian audiences that they could understand what was going on, seated in the open air watching actors wearing standardized masks (and unable to secure texts of the plays to be read before, during, or after the performances).

Characterization, though often broadly vivid, is restricted to the requirements of the play itself. Neither the sayings of the characters nor the words of the choruses should necessarily be seen as reflecting the views of the authors themselves – that is to say, Aeschylus, Sophocles and Euripides, the only tragic dramatists whose works have, in part, come down to us. Their own opinions can only be reconstructed from their surviving plays at a distance, obliquely and uncertainly. Moreover, these plays themselves are not only few in comparison with the number they had composed, but different from one another, even within the corpus of each single dramatist, to an extent which illustrates their phenomenal versatility – and makes it all the harder to pin down what the three playwrights themselves thought.

The plays of Thespis and Phrynichus have vanished, and the real foundation of Greek tragedy is generally ascribed to Aeschylus (525/524–456). It was he, it seems, who introduced a second actor – thus making dialogue possible. He also formalized the role of the choruses alternating with these spoken passages, and organized the stage presentation of his plays on the lines that subsequently became habitual.

The son of Euphorion, an aristocratic land-owner, Aeschylus was born at Eleusis in Attica, and may have been initiated into the Eleusinian Mysteries of Demeter that lay at the heart of Greek piety. Patriotic as well as religious, he fought in the battle of Marathon (490), and probably at Salamis too (480). He visited the court of Syracuse in Sicily three times, residing there for a considerable period, and died on the same island at Gela. But his principal dramatic successes had been achieved at his native city of Athens, where he won thirteen festival victories from 484 onwards. Seventy-two titles of his tragedies are recorded in a catalogue, and ten more probable titles are known. Seven plays have survived.

The earliest, the *Persians* (472), handles a recent historical event, a very rare occurrence in tragic drama. For the play tells of Xerxes I's invasion of Greece eight years earlier. In his absence, Persian elders, who form the play's chorus, conjecture what may have happened, expressing anxiety about the lack of news. They are joined by the king's mother Atossa, who seeks their interpretation of an ominous dream. Then, in haste, arrives a messenger, who announces the destruction of the Persian fleet at the battle of Salamis; and he goes on to recount the sufferings of the Persian army on its homeward journey. On learning what has happened, Atossa sacrifices at the tomb of her husband Darius I, whose spirit then appears, warning against any further plans to invade

Greece and ascribing Xerxes' downfall to his insanely presumptuous obsession with revenge.

The Seven Against Thebes (467) turns to Greece's incomparably rich mythology, the source of nearly all the themes of Athenian tragedy. The play describes the Theban Polynices, son of the blinded and exiled Oedipus, and the six companions from Argos whom he enlisted to help him win the throne of Thebes from Eteocles, his brother. Eteocles calms the wailing of the Theban women (the chorus), and hears from a scout how each of the Seven is standing ready for battle at the seven gates of the city.

One of them is Polynices himself, and Eteocles strides out to confront him, brushing aside the plea of the chorus (mindful of the longstanding, inexorable curse that has deluged his family in blood) that he should not slay his brother. Their father Oedipus had prophesied that his two sons would perish at one another's hands, and so, as a messenger now comes to report, it turns out. While their sisters Antigone and Ismene mourn for the two brothers, a herald comes to announce that, whereas Eteocles is to be given honourable burial, Polynices, seeing that he had attacked his own city, must lie unburied, food for the dogs. Antigone insists that she will ignore the order, at whatever price; and half the chorus agree with her, while the rest depart to join Eteocles' funeral procession.

The Suppliant Women – now known to date from 462/461, and not from the earlier date to which its archaic form had seemed more appropriate – tells of the fifty Danaids (the chorus of the play), daughters of the mythological Danaus whom the fifty sons of Danaus' brother Aegyptus have endeavoured to compel to marry them. The women seek to avoid this fate by taking refuge with their father at Argos, the home of Zeus' mistress Io, from whom they were descended. Pelasgus, king of Argos, is unwilling to grant them sanctuary, but the contrary vote of the Argive people prevails, and although the frustrated suitors arrive to seize their brides, the women are not given up.

The story, which stresses the theme of the protection of the weak, and contrasts the laws of the Greek city of Argos, with oriental arbitrariness, was continued in two other tragedies, of which only fragments have survived, so that the entirety of the picture delineated by Aeschylus escapes us. Together with the *Suppliant Women* these two lost plays constituted a trilogy, a form which Aeschylus favoured, or even perhaps created, as a vehicle for his extended plots.

The only completely surviving example of such a trilogy is the *Oresteia* (458), which was described by Algernon Swinburne as 'the greatest achievement of the human mind'. It tells of the mythical Argive house of Atreus, in which one crime led to another, over many generations. The end of the Trojan War is close at hand – and in the royal palace awaiting Agamemnon's return there are elusive, disquietingly mingled hopes and fears, redolent of the growing suspense which the dramatist was adept at building up to breaking-point.

For at the Boeotian port of Aulis, before sailing to Troy, Agamemnon had sacrificed his own daughter Iphigenia as the only means of obtaining a favourable wind from the gods. Throughout the ten years of his absence at the war, his alienated and remorseless wife Clytemnestra, sending their son Orestes away and ruling over the kingdom with her lover Aegisthus, had planned revenge. Now Agamemnon reappears, accompanied by his captive Trojan mistress Cassandra. After a tense exchange of speeches between the royal pair, exemplifying the interaction of personalities at which Aeschylus excelled, Clytemnestra lures him into the palace. There she savagely puts him to death; and Cassandra, after evoking the past and present crimes of the house of Atreus, dies as well. The chorus of elders declares its horror, but Clytemnestra reminds them that the sacrifice of Iphigenia had to be answered for, and Aegisthus tries to overawe them with threats. The elders, however, hope that, one day, Agamemnon's son Orestes will avenge his father's death.

In the *Libation-Bearers* (*Choephori*) Orestes returns with this very purpose, enjoined upon him by Apollo. He watches his sister Electra, accompanied by slave-women (the chorus), preparing to pour libations at Agamemnon's tomb. Brother and sister recognize one another, and swear to destroy the slayers of their father. Orestes kills Aegisthus and then, his determination strengthened by his friend Pylades, he murders Clytemnestra as well. But avenging Furies (Erinyes) come to haunt him, and he takes flight, insane, to Apollo's temple at Delphi, in the hope of purging what he has done, and of somehow making the crime of matricide endurable.

The third play of the trilogy, the *Eumenides*, opens at Delphi. The Furies – who are the chorus – representing a powerful, primitive world-order, lie asleep around the suppliant Orestes. But Apollo orders him to depart and proceed to Athens for judgment; while the Furies, aroused by the ghost of Clytemnestra, set off in pursuit. The next scene is at Athens, where Orestes and his pursuers assert their conflicting arguments, in front of Athena's temple on the Acropolis – and indeed before the goddess herself, who creates the homicide court of the Areopagus to hear the case. Apollo is Orestes' advocate, and when the judges are equally divided, Athena awards the youth her casting vote. She persuades the angry Furies to calm down, and they are led to their new shrine beneath the Areopagus, where henceforward they will be known as the Kindly Ones (Eumenides).

The *Prometheus Bound* has been the subject of massive controversy, since its Aeschylean authorship has been seriously contested, on grounds of computer analysis and tricks of style and metre; but the objections are not wholly convincing. The theme of this tragedy is the attempt of the hero Prometheus to resist Zeus (his cousin), and the result of that endeavour. Zeus, when he supplanted his father Cronus as the supreme deity, had decided to annihilate the human race, because of its inadequate respect for the gods. But Prometheus, the universal culture-hero, who had stolen Hope and Fire – the source of all progress – from heaven and given them to mortals, opposed Zeus' decision to exterminate the human race. In consequence, Zeus commands that he should be chained to a rock upon the Caucasus for evermore: and it is now that the play begins.

Zeus' subordinates, Might and Violence, bring Prometheus to the rock, where Hephaestus, god of fire, nails him down. He is visited by the Daughters of Oceanus, the chorus, who lament his fate. His next visitor is their father, who advises submission. Then comes the woman Io, who had been seduced by Zeus, transformed into a heifer by his jealous wife Hera, and maddened by a gadfly which pursued her over vast regions of the earth. Prometheus prophesies to Io that in the distant future a descendant of hers will liberate him. He also foretells that a son of Zeus will overthrow his own father, but does not reveal the name of the mother from whom the boy will be born. Zeus' messenger Hermes orders him to disclose what he knows: but Prometheus refuses. The crag is then shattered by lightning, and Oceanus' daughters, who insist on staying with him, are engulfed in an earthquake.

The *Prometheus Bound* seems to have been part of a trilogy, first performed on one (the last?) of Aeschylus' visits to Sicily; but the remaining plays of the trilogy are fragmentary and conjectural, in subject and order. It appears, however, that after 30,000 years Zeus became reconciled with Prometheus, who then saved him by revealing his secret. This fuller picture would, no doubt, eliminate some of the shock caused by the *Prometheus Bound* because of its depiction of Zeus as a tyrant.

As Aeschylus' plots move remorselessly forward, most of his characters embody an austere overriding passion or principle, illustrating some religious and moral problem or law. As the *Oresteia* and Prometheus plays emphasized, the dramatist insists on the fulfilment of providential evolution, in which divine and human aims are ultimately reconciled, and cosmic justice, however long delayed and hard to understand, is satisfied in the end, so that even the most catastrophic pattern of evil and suffering may eventually be seen as part of an exalted, beneficial design.

Aeschylus is concerned with traditional concepts: inherited taints, the dreadful challenges of punitive, family-destroying curses – and the perils of overmuch prosperity. Yet one of the keys to his thought is a heart-racking ambiguity. For destiny does not wholly eclipse human free will (this is the first time that this ethical, social and personal problem had ever been so clearly stated), since all these perils will not strike a victim down unless he is already afflicted with *hubris*, arrogant self-confidence. Much in Aeschylus is Homeric, as he himself declared[3] – too modestly, since he infused the old material with new form and thought and feeling.

Abundant care, lately, has been devoted to the possible identification of topical political issues in Aeschylus' words. Indeed, although it was not a tragedian's function to comment directly on contemporary events, such issues cannot have been entirely absent from his plays, since what he wrote, however universalized, must have had some contemporary relevance to his public. He lived and worked at a time when the contrast between tyranny and freedom was in every Athenian mind. *The Persians* displayed Xerxes' downfall through *hubris*, and reflections of Aeschylus' experiences of Sicilian autocracies have also been detected. The *Eumenides* praises Athens as the home of reconciliation under divine auspices, and (although this is disputed) the poet seems to acquiesce in the contemporary restriction of the Areopagus, formerly the chief council of state, to a (revered) tribunal of homicide cases (462/461; Chapter 11). Efforts to decipher his political attitudes, for example with reference to democracy, in further detail have not proved successful – for he does not wish or intend us to do so; he seems both to endorse the values of the developing democracy and to hesitate about their implementation at one and the same time.

Although effective translations exist, an exceptionally large amount of Aeschylus becomes irrecoverably lost once his own language is left behind. Reinforced, as we must imagine, by impressive staging, his poetry is intricately loaded with a lavish, gorgeous grandeur, manifested in oracular pronouncements displaying an almost infinite wealth of vocabulary and ever-returning, convoluted imagery. By means of this accumulation of word-magic the poet infused tragedy with lofty imaginative power, capable of employing the traditional mythology in order to convey almost incommunicably profound and complex verities relating to the role of human beings in the world and the universe.

When Aeschylus had died, the Assembly decreed that any citizen desirous of reviving one of his plays should be granted a chorus in order to do so; and such revivals, it is recorded, gained him numerous posthumous victories in dramatic competitions. He was the creator of the tradition followed by Sophocles and Euripides (Chapters 17, 18), and later by the entire tragic drama of western Europe.

CHAPTER 8
PARMENIDES: AND THREE REACTIONS

The sixth century had produced the first, rich crop of 'pre-Socratic philosophers', as they are known today – misleadingly enough, because they knew of no boundaries between philosophy and other fields of human knowledge, and asked the questions out of which science as well as philosophy was to develop.

These men were so versatile that the full extent of their range of enquiries defies any brief definition. But the questions which, above all others, interested them were: What is everything made of? How do things come into existence, undergo change and cease to exist? And what permanent substance or substances exist behind appearances? Such questions had been asked before, notably by the Mesopotamians and Egyptians, but without the emancipation from irrationality and magic which the Greeks, gradually and painstakingly, achieved; and without the new Greek assumption that the subject of their investigations was a *cosmos* governed by logical laws which could be defined.

The conclusions, however, about the basic material constituting reality and the universe to which these sixth-century enquiries had led proved extremely varied. Thales, of Ionian Miletus, said it was water. Anaximenes declared it to be air or vapour – for which Heraclitus of Ephesus (*c.*500) substituted fire. However, Heraclitus also sought to explain the problem of evolution, by pronouncing that the universe is in a state of continual change and decay, which he was believed to have summed up by the saying *panta rhei* – everything is in a state of flux.[4]

But all such speculations, and the whole process of the earlier sort of pre-Socratic 'philosophy' were brought to an abrupt end by Parmenides of Elea (Velia) in southern Italy, who was born in *c.*515 and died at an unknown date in the following century. This epoch-making development is revealed in his short poem *On Nature*, of which about 160 incisive, though unpoetical, lines have survived.

After an allegorical introduction, in which the poet claims to have received a solemn revelation from 'the goddess',[5] she declares to him in the second part of the poem – *The Way of Truth* – how he ought to direct his enquiry. In this passage, constituting the first sustained discussion of philosophical method in European thought, she defines three philosophical approaches. It is possible to hold either (1) that the reality which is under investigation necessarily is and exists, or (2) that it necessarily does not exist, or (3) that it both exists and does not exist (i.e. comes into existence and changes and ceases to exist). But (2) and (3), the goddess points out, have to be rejected, because nothing except what exists can be known. (1) therefore is the only valid choice; the way of truth starts from the proposition '*it is*, and not being is impossible'. *What is* is uncreated and ungenerated, since it cannot be derived from not-being; it will never perish, since it cannot pass into non-being; it is indivisible, continuous and unchangeable, since nothing else can come into existence and impinge on it or make a breach in its continuity; it is homogeneous and motionless and balanced in perfect equilibrium like a solid sphere, but occupying the whole of space, because there can be no void.

Earlier thinkers had framed their questions and answers about the nature of reality and the universe in physical terms. But Parmenides felt convinced that this was a total delusion. When our senses demonstrate to us the plurality and multiplicity of the universe and the world, they are mistaken, he believed, because no unity can generate a plurality. Heraclitus, therefore, in seeing change and flux as the essence of the universe, was wrong.

The last part of the poem, however, mocks us by ascribing to the goddess a long, traditional type of statement that suggests entirely otherwise. This is an 'Opinion' giving an account of the plurality of things *as they seem to be*. But the 'Opinion' only sets out to state an untenable case; it is not meant to be true. For Parmenides, in flat contradiction and refutation of his predecessors, had abandoned the evidence of the senses altogether. The evidence upon which he based this abandonment came, not from scientific evidence or data, but exclusively from streamlined, stringent, theoretical reasoning (*noema*). Indeed, he can be described as the earliest Greek thinker to have based his universal findings on this rational, logical argumentation – the earliest of all logicians, perhaps, pointing the way towards the creation of formal logic (Chapters 12, 31, 37), and towards the idea of what 'philosophy' means in the modern sense of the word. And the process, although austerely founded on a rigorous analysis of the verb *to be*, inspired him, his poem records, with rapture!

Parmenides had come to a conclusion that no one could believe, but he had reached it by arguments that no one could fault. The impact of these radical paradoxes was shattering. For one thing, they inflicted a lethal blow upon scientific observation, which had begun, in his day, to become more accurate and systematic, but was dismissed by him as illusory.

The Greek thinkers who came next, other than those who supported him, tried to find ways of retaining his intellectual method, while avoiding its outrageous deductions. The first answer to this dilemma was put forward by Empedocles of Acragas (*c*.493–*c*.422) – poet, orator ('inventor of rhetoric'), statesman, guru-magician and yet founder of the Sicilian medical school, and an alert philosopher. Empedocles accepted Parmenides' assertion that real, true being is permanent and everlasting. But he also accepted change: which he explained, however, as the mixture and separation of already existing things, that is to say a rearrangement of eternally undying elements. But he stressed the plurality of these elements; in other words, he denied Parmenidean homogeneity and unity. This he did by detecting, within the universe, not one basic element (as earlier Ionian philosophers had arbitrarily proposed) but no less than four – fire, air, water and earth: all primary, contrasted and combinable in a huge variety of ways.

These elements or roots are, of course, apprehensible by the senses, and in this connection Empedocles felt serious reserves about Parmenides' two-tier system of 'Truths' and 'Opinions'. Parmenides had believed that only the first, reconstructed by the pure processes of logical argument, are real, and that the 'Opinions', describing the universe seen as pluralistic and multifarious by the senses, constitute an illusion. Empedocles saw things differently. His elements came under the heading of what Parmenides would have called illusory 'Opinions'; but to Empedocles they were a valid aspect of reality. On the other hand he agreed with Parmenides that there is *also* an abstract, ideal sort of reality, and although Empedocles, unlike him, did not regard this as the *only* reality, he nevertheless saw it as an integral, eternal part of the universal system.

But he once again departed from Parmenides by suggesting that this ideal reality is not single but dual: comprising opposites, Love and Strife – attraction and repulsion – continually at work and alternately predominant. This intuitive 'twofold tale' encapsulated the antithetical opposites which figured so largely in the thought of the time (Chapter 12).

What Empedocles was above all trying to do, though somewhat impeded by his versatile metaphysical and religious preoccupations, was to provide an account of the physical world which could incorporate some of Parmenides' sweeping criticisms of old cosmologies while not rejecting root and branch all the data provided by sense perceptions. That is to say he did not meet Parmenides' logic squarely, but was determined to evade its consequences, and, with this in mind, sought to close the alarming gap between reality and appearances.

Anaxagoras of Clazomenae in Ionia (*c.*500–*c.*428) settled at Athens and became Pericles' friend, thereby incurring criminal charges though ostensibly on grounds of impiety and not for political reasons. He took the compromise of Empedocles further, rejecting all 'becoming', like Parmenides, and yet, against him, accepting the sense perceptions. For Anaxagoras, like Empedocles, envisaged a two-tier system in which these phenomena perceived by the senses were associated with an ideal, 'real' counterpart. However, he moved beyond Empedocles on to ground where the elements are not four, but innumerable, and the ideal governance is not by opposites, Love and Strife, but by a single *nous* or Mind.

As for the innumerable elements ('homoeomeries'), they are not only multiform but also infinitely divisible – a firm denial of Parmenides' unified continuity – and change, as we see it around us, is accounted for by the constant rearrangement of these particles, so that everything contains a portion of everything else: except Mind. This last Anaxagoras introduces as the initiator of cosmic motion, and the animating rational principle – a concept later much admired by Plato and Aristotle, though they were disappointed because Anaxagoras did not show that it *acts for the best* (Chapters 31, 37).[6]

Although he must still have seen Mind as corporeal and material, he was striving towards the idea of an incorporeal entity, and had, in consequence, gone even further than Empedocles in following up Parmenides' conviction of an ideal reality unidentical with the objects of sense perception. However, the pluralism of Empedocles' and Anaxagoras' reactions (carried to an extreme by the latter) was quite contrary to Parmenides' intention. That is to say, Anaxagoras, like Empedocles, conceded part of the Parmenidean arguments, but by no means all of them, seeking instead to save cosmology from their most damaging criticisms.

Another attempt to escape from the Parmenidean impasse was made by the atomists, Leucippus of Miletus (or Elea or Abdera) and the prolific and many-sided Democritus of Abdera (born 460/457; said to have died more than a century later). But endeavours to distinguish between the respective contributions of the two men have not yielded satisfactory results.

Parmenides had argued that what is real is one and motionless; that void or empty space (without which motion is unable to take place) cannot exist – nor can plurality. Now, the atomists tried even harder than Empedocles or Anaxagoras to reconcile these Parmenidean conclusions with some acceptance of the senses.[7] What they did in the first place – and here there is a distinct reminiscence of Anaxagoras – was to concede Parmenides' contention that reality is unchanging and homogeneous, while nevertheless arguing that it consists not of Parmenides' single plenum but of a huge number of invisibly small atoms. Each one of these many atoms was held to possess the unchanging, indestructible and homogeneous character of Parmenides' single reality. *But* the atoms were ascribed movement – producing the compounds and changes of the world as we know it – since the atomists drastically allowed, as Parmenides would not, the existence of empty space or void, which made it possible for this motion to take place, in the universe, the world and the soul (which is likewise made of fine atoms).

Unlike Empedocles and Anaxagoras, however, the atomists saw no need for a two-tier system leaving room not only for material but also for ideal entities (such as Love and Strife, or Mind), since the universe, despite its infinite variety, seemed to them to be governed by the orderly regularity of blindly mechanical, 'necessary' laws. Thus Leucippus and Democritus were the first explicit, thoroughgoing materialists – something that did not hinder, or even enhanced, their interest in how human beings have behaved, and ought to behave, freed from divine oppression, and somehow (how?) able, up to a point, to manipulate mechanical necessity.

But once again, in this last and most original attempt to revive the type of physical speculation in which the earlier Milesian scientist-philosophers, from Thales onwards, had indulged, the combination of debts to the views of Parmenides, and reactions from those views, is manifest.

And from now on, too, his influence continued to be overwhelming. His followers Zeno and Melissus had rammed his paradoxes home. Plato, however (Chapter 31), returned to ambivalence about these destructive conclusions. He liked the idea of a two-tier system of ideal reality on the one hand and the material products of sense-perception on the other, although his doctrine of transcendental ideal Forms, for all its extensive debts to Parmenides, did not spurn the material objects as Parmenides had done but claimed that Forms were the ideal originals and causes of those products. Yet Plato's dialogues, the *Sophist* and *Parmenides*, whatever else they were trying to do, suggested that his predecessor's logical reasoning was not as invulnerable as it had sounded. That was true enough; indeed for all their bracing, cold-water effect Parmenides' anti-commonsense paradoxes, explaining nature by shutting our eyes to it, sound unreasonably perverse today. And yet his logical method and the impact it made on other people's thinking have earned him comparisons with Descartes.

CHAPTER 9

THE OLYMPIA MASTER: EARLY CLASSICAL TEMPLE SCULPTURE

In the evolution of Greek sculpture, a large part was played by the adornment of temple pediments with reliefs and figures in the round. This was an art which made demands on the skill and ingenuity of sculptors because of the triangular shape of the pediments, tapering off narrowly to the points of their extremities, which had, therefore, to be occupied by crouching or reclining figures. For a time, however, artists ignored these difficult extremities, by concentrating all their efforts upon the central design. For example, a Gorgon appeared in this central position on the pediment of the Temple of Artemis at Corcyra (Corfu), probably designed by Corinthians (who were regarded as the inaugurators of Greek sculpture).

Far greater elaboration is shown by the well-preserved pediments of the Doric Temple of Aphaea (a local divinity of pre-Greek origin) on Cape Colonna upon the island of Aegina. The sculptures exhibit two styles, both of which are datable within the years 500–480. From this temple, the oldest in Greece proper of which the colonnade still stands today, there are remains of both the east and west pediments, now in the Munich and Athens museums. They include parts of *two* east pediments, the second (*c.*490) replacing the first when it underwent damage soon after it was made. Executed in marble, which wealthy Aegina (close to the marble quarries of Paros) could afford, both pediments represented battle scenes from the two Trojan Wars. The eastern reliefs showed Heracles' expedition against Priam's father Laomedon, in which Aegina's hero Telamon took part; whereas the west pediment depicted Agamemnon's campaign against Priam, in which Telamon's son Ajax was a heroic participant. In both scenes the goddess Athena stood at the centre, flanked on the eastern pediment by crouching Heracles shooting with his bow, and, at the other end, by a recumbent, perishing fighter, whereas its western counterpart shows warriors engaged in combat on either side of the goddess, once again flanked by dying figures at both of two angles. Myth is employed to express cosmic conflict in the manner of Aeschylus (Chapter 7), to whose work such sculptures are often compared.

The later of the two eastern pediments – even allowing for misleading restorations by Thorwaldsen – shows a move in the direction of naturalism, revealing the evolutionary process that was taking place during these decisive moments of transition to classical styles. The 'archaic smile' is now repudiated, and figures are seen in the round, and separated from one another, exemplifying a growing (though not yet complete) awareness and acceptance of the third dimension. There is a subtle balance between Peloponnesian solidity and Ionic-Attic sinewy grace, and the new appearance of the latter characteristic, in contrast with early pedimental sculptures elsewhere, is probably a legacy from bronzework, for which Aeginetan sculptors were famous.

Though labels are not very valuable, the 480s may be said to have witnessed the origin of the Early Classical (Severe) style; next displayed by the substantially surviving sculptures of the Doric temple of Zeus at Olympia (470–457), larger than any shrine previously erected in mainland Greece. These works of art, the outstanding monuments of their generation, reveal that changes have occurred, expressed in novel, harmoniously contoured groupings of two and three figures.

The contents and treatments of the two Olympian pediments are sharply contrasted. The western reliefs, of which the subject-matter appears to be derived from a wall-painting in a shrine of Theseus at Athens, built in *c.*475 to house his alleged bones brought from Scyros, depicts violent mythological combat between the Lapiths of Thessaly and their half-horse neighbours the Centaurs, who at the wedding of the Lapith King Pirithous became drunk and tried to abduct Lapith women. The theme is a heroic challenge to bestial aggression, the pitting of right against wrong. The exact disposition of the rhythmical, broadly balanced groups is still disputable, but the static figure of the ever-youthful Apollo at the centre, like a rock, it has been said, rising out of an angry sea, makes an extraordinary impact. As the god calms the interlocked combatants with outstretched arm, his idealized countenance displays no expression. Nor, curiously, do the faces of other figures, despite the extreme violence in which they are engaged – though a Lapith bitten by a Centaur at least wrinkles his forehead; and the Centaurs' faces show a certain limited amount of pain.

The extremely different east pediment depicts no fighting or action at all, but reflects an expectant, foreboding calm before the storm, like contemporary paintings by Polygnotus (Chapter 10). The subject is the mythical chariot-race between the invading Pelops (after whom the Peloponnese was named) and the local ruler Oenomaus, king of Pisa, the contest which would decide upon Pelops' demand that Oenomaus' daughter should become his bride – following upon similar applications by earlier suitors, who had lost the race and forfeited their lives as a penalty.

In the present instance, however, Hippodamia had fallen in love with Pelops, and bribed her father's charioteer to sabotage the chariot in which he was going to race against her admirer; so the marriage is going to take place, and Pelops will become master of Elis. Illustrating this situation, familiar to viewers since they knew their local mythology, this east pediment shows the frozen, tensely immobile, waiting scene just before the race begins, as the contestants, Oenomaus accompanied by his queen and Pelops with Hippodamia at his side, swear at the altar of Zeus to abide by the result. The god towers between them, though they cannot see him; the chariot-teams are drawn up on either side of the two protagonists, and spectators appear in the angles, including a seated seer, an unidentifiable seated youth, and the local river-god Cladeus.

Their forms are plain and uncluttered, because sculpture fifty-five feet above the ground, although originally painted red and blue to bring out its sharply carved highlights, could not be seen in detail. But the seer's chest is flabby, in keeping with his age – here is a figure which illustrated incipient classical approaches to realism. Moreover, the seated youth, too, strikes a distinctive and difficult pose, and Cladeus leans forward animatedly to watch what is going on, in a subtle analysis of personality and mood.

The sculptural decoration of the temple included not only the pediments but metopes (cf. p. 91), of which the visitor, passing through the outer columns, could see six at either end of the *cella*, above the inner porches. Employing a blend of high and low relief, which recalls the novel spatial ideas exploited by painters (Chapter 10), the sculptors depict the Labours of Heracles. And indeed it may have been these very carvings, in the most revered of Greek sanctuaries, which determined the eventual canon of the Twelve Labours imposed upon Heracles by Eurystheus. One of the best preserved of these reliefs shows the hero bearing the weight of the world for Atlas, who is bringing him the golden apples of the Hesperides. Athena, gracefully clothed, stands by, ready to return Atlas's burden to him; and meanwhile she effortlessly prevents the universe from collapsing.

The same goddess also appears in two further Olympian metopes, both with Peloponnesian settings. In one, which stood at the west end, Heracles brings her the man-eating birds of Stymphalus. In a moment of tranquillity *after* the action (just as the east pediment showed a quiet pause before it), this metope shows her seated on a rock, and reaching out with one arm to receive the birds from Heracles. Although the lines of the metopes are firm, simple and concentrated, this is nevertheless an unusual, complex composition, displaying the two figures at oblique angles. The last metope, from the east end, depicts the Elian episode of Heracles using a crowbar to break down the walls of the stable of Augeas, in order to flood it and clean it out, while Athena stands behind him and faces us, her right hand extended; it originally held a spear, to guide what he is doing.

The architect of the temple was Libon, a local man – in order to satisfy the new claims of democratic Elis (in charge of the Olympic Games), which became, after an amalgamation of smaller communities in 471, one of the largest cities in the Peloponnese. But the identification of the man or men who designed and executed these sculptures presents an insoluble problem. While not identifying the maker of the metopes, the travel-writer Pausanias records that the east pediment was designed by Paeonius, and the west by Alcamenes.[8] We have a statue that is certainly by the former of these well-known sculptors, and another that is probably the work of the latter. But both stylistic and chronological considerations make it improbable that Pausanias was right – unless he is referring to other, older sculptors of the same names. That has now been argued persuasively in respect of Alcamenes.

On the other hand Pausanias' assumption that there were two principal masters at work is still, at first sight, worth considering, since the pediment sculptures display a stylistic duality – a duality which, incidentally, is repeated in the metopes, so that if there were two principal sculptors of the pediments the same two men may well have designed the metopes as well. If so, they must have operated in close collaboration, and presumably shared the team of skilful carvers and technicians who carried out the actual work under their orders. But this conclusion that there were two chief designers is contested, probably with justice, on the grounds that the grand concept (notably the theme of Zeus and his children running through both pediments) was surely due to a single master whose orders all the various executants (perhaps falling into two groups) carried out.

His origins, if so, are once again a subject for dispute; Ionia, the Cyclades, the Peloponnese and northern Greece have all been suggested. But wherever he came from, he had to subordinate his local styles and tastes to the universal Panhellenism for which the Olympian sanctuary stood.

CHAPTER 10

POLYGNOTUS: THE PAINTING REVOLUTION

Greek wall-painting presents a deplorable situation. It was one of the great Greek arts – perhaps many Greeks would have called it the greatest – and yet until the latter half of the fourth century, towards the very end of the classical period, not more than an exceedingly few and fragmentary examples of paintings on walls (or painted panels or plaques) have come down to us.

For the earlier development of the art we have to go to Etruria, and particularly to its city-state of Tarquinii (Tarquinia), where a number of wall-paintings of sixth- and fifth-century date have survived in tombs. If we want to use them as evidence for the major lost art of wall-painting among the Greeks, there are arguments for and against this course. The argument in favour points out that the artists who painted the Etruscan graves, whether Etruscans or Greeks, were strongly influenced by successive Greek styles, Corinthian, Ionian and Attic, with which numerous Greek immigrants, and flourishing trade relations, made Etruria familiar. The arguments, on the other hand, against endeavouring to extrapolate Greek wall-painting from what the Etruscans have left us are as follows. First, it was not the work of Greeks, and they manifestly added modifications and quirks of their own to their imitations or adaptations of Greek models; and, secondly, these Etruscan pictures are tomb-paintings, whereas we have no evidence that the Greeks, up to near the end of the classical period, habitually decorated their tombs in this way, their principal wall-paintings having been composed instead to adorn the walls of public buildings or temples. The Greek models, therefore, which the Etruscans utilized were not by any means always wall-paintings at all (or even the sketches or copies of such paintings, which were all that they could have seen), but pictures on the Greek vases that came to Etruria in such abundance.

The oldest painted grave so far discovered at Tarquinii is probably the Tomb of the Bulls, of about 550–540. It depicts a Greek, Homeric scene – Achilles lying in wait for the young Trojan horseman Troilus – and the treatment displays Corinthian and other Greek and near-eastern analogies, although these imported features are amended by local Etruscan themes and motifs. Ionian or other Greek treatments are to be seen in the Tombs of the Jugglers, Augurs (though its gladiatorial scene is very Etruscan), Lionesses (*c*.540–530), the Baron, and Hunting and Fishing (*c*.520–510; this last-named including a diving scene adapted a decade or two later by an artist, possibly Greek but possibly also Etruscan, for the Tomb of the Diver at Posidonia (Paestum) in south-west Italy). Then the Tomb of the Two Horse Chariots at Tarquinii, of early fifth-century date, displays an interest in the human form that reflects similar tendencies in mainland Greece. The Tomb of the Dining Room in the same cemetery (*c*.460–455) is painted in a fluent and refined style which strives for the sort of effect seen on Athenian vases of the epoch (see below).

But how far can we supplement this peripheral and oblique evidence for Greek wall-paintings from what we find on Greek vases?

We have countless Greek vases, but their utility for reconstructing the lost Greek wall-paintings remains limited. For one thing, agreement as to which vase-paintings do in fact echo or copy lost Greek wall-pictures is curiously hard to come by. But in any case, even the finest Greek vase-paintings, and many are very beautiful indeed, are able to cast only a restricted light upon any wall-paintings which their artists may happen to have copied or adapted, because the two media are so different.

And when we try to reconstruct the early history of wall-painting from internal evidence, derived from such pieces of wall-painting that survive, there is very little indeed to be found. Some fragments of painted metopes belonged to seventh-century temples at Calydon and Thermum in Aetolia, which was under Corinthian domination, and small segments of painted plaster come from the exterior of an early temple of Poseidon on the Corinthian Isthmus. There are also remains of wooden panels – small easel pictures – of *c*.530 found at Pitsa between Corinth and Sicyon (both of which cities were said to have 'discovered' painting or line-drawing). They depict a sacrificial scene and procession of votaries, in a polychrome pattern of red, brown, blue, black and white.

In *c*.520, under the auspices of Athens, vase-paintings begin to display the red-figure technique (as we shall see later on): and so presumably, no doubt at a slightly earlier date, did pictures on walls, although not a fragment of them remains.

And once again, when we come, or hope to come, to later manifestations of the wall-painter's art in the early fifth century, it is tantalizing that the artist who was, by general agreement, not only the supreme master of the Early Classical (Severe) Style (Chapter 9), but also the first painter to become memorable in his own right, and on his own merits, and who seems to have been the greatest and most innovative, indeed revolutionary, of all the wall-painters of his age, has likewise left not a trace behind.

He was Polygnotus of Thasos (*c.*500–440). Polygnotus moved to Athens, where he obtained citizenship and became a friend of Cimon, and reputedly the lover of Cimon's half-sister Elpinice – that is to say, he was no mere craftsman (*technites*) but a man of a social position that no previous painter is likely to have achieved. From about the 470s onwards he painted major pictures for various cities, but most of all for Athens, where his works included 'The Sack of Troy' in the Painted Portico (Stoa Poikile), 'Achilles on Scyros' and 'Odysseus and Nausicaa' in the Picture Gallery (Pinakotheke) in the Propylaea (Chapter 15) and 'The Rape of the Daughters of Leucippus' in the Anakeion (Temple of the Dioscuri).

Employing four basic colours, black, white, red and ochre, it was Polygnotus, we are told by Pausanias,[9] who not only abandoned his predecessors' exclusive insistence on profile stances but also admitted spatial depth, dispensing with a single base-line and distributing his figures freely up and down the field. Unifying perspective, in the modern sense, did not yet exist, but Polygnotus' easily moving figures could thrust forwards or backwards out of the plane, so that pictures, it has been suggested, were beginning to be seen not simply as narratives decorating the surface but as windows on the world.

Later critics also noted Polygnotus' novel combination of *ethos* ('character' and high moral purpose) and *pathos* (spontaneous reaction to experience, expressed by emotion). It is characteristic of Greek classical art that, although praised for his 'naturalistic' or mimetic approach, Polygnotus endeavoured to represent human beings not as they are but as 'better than they are',[10] by which he apparently meant not that he 'made people more beautiful' but that he 'tried to get the best out of them'.

His techniques for this delineation of ideal character were evidently varied. His draughtsmanship must have been firm and accurate, capable of depicting the nuances of pose and gesture and facial expression needed to convey feeling and atmosphere; and he also showed a special concern for women (Appendix II), displaying their delicate headdresses and diaphanous draperies. His abandonment of the base-line meant that elaborate groupings could be introduced, and that the psychological relationships between one figure and another could be explored with greater effectiveness.

It seems, however, that Polygnotus, for all his interest in these exciting complexities, nevertheless had a special preference for quiet, intense, contemplative scenes, reminiscent of the withdrawn, inward character of the east pediment of Olympia (Chapter 9): he liked to display static figures sunk in their own deliberations and reflections just before or after the moment of action, of which the causes or consequences are depicted, rather than the instantaneous event itself. Polygnotus' religious feeling was evidently heroic and profound, and we may conjecture that his battle-pieces showed awareness of the pathos of defeat, like literary descriptions by contemporary tragedians.

The loss of all these masterpieces, which made wall-painting an outstanding Greek art, is perhaps the gravest artistic disaster that the ancient world has inflicted upon us.

Out of the numerous Greek vases of various shapes and forms and purposes which, in sharp contrast to wall-paintings, have survived, a large proportion are Attic of the classical period, displaying the red-figure technique. This had been introduced in *c.*520, perpetuating and increasing the ceramic supremacy that Athens had been able to take over from the Corinthians, by virtue of the quality of its black-figure pottery.

Using the fine Ceramicus clay – of which the iron ingredient produced an attractive red colour – and developing a complex three-stage process of firing, the Athenian potters and the painters who worked with them (though sometimes the two were identical) reversed the methods of their black-figure predecessors, leaving the figures and other designs that decorated their pots in the natural red surface tint and covering the backgrounds with a black paint instead. At the same time, the incisions that had outlined the earlier pictures were superseded by brush-drawing. The long, fluent sweeps which characterized this new type of work led to more accurate and flexible portrayals of bodies and poses, and provided opportunities for more realistic depiction of clothing.

We have enough surviving vases to enable us to trace this development from its beginnings, through the work of the 'Andocides Painter' (that is to say, one of the painters who collaborated with the potter Andocides) into the climactic epoch of the 'Pioneers', Euphronius, Euthymides and the Cleophrades Painter (*c.*510–500). Thereafter evolution continued without any visible break, and without any indication that the Persian Wars (490–479) provided a turning point or landmark.

Thus the finicky but expressive Duris – in whose activity three successive phases can be distinguished – spanned the entire period between *c.*500 and *c.*470. The Berlin painter, too, a pupil of Euthymides, worked during the first two decades of the century, helping to inaugurate the Early Classical (Severe) Style (Chapter 9) with the flowing lines of his spacious compositions, which displayed lithe, long-limbed, languid figures in increasing anatomical detail. And most gifted of all, perhaps, was the Brygos painter, who in *c.*490–480 decorated cups with tense, dramatic, Dionysiac scenes featuring fleshily realistic figures in the grip of drunken excitement and weariness, which were expressed by means of elaborate cross-rhythms and elementary shading.

Most of the red-figure painters of the period that followed appear to have sought to recapture the monumental style of the great wall-painters, notably Polygnotus, by a simple but intelligible representation of spatial depth. This can be seen in the work of the Niobid Painter, who sometimes placed his figures not on a single base-line but at different levels, in the manner supposedly invented by Polygnotus. The Niobid Painter's scenes are full of silent concentration (once again bringing the east pediment of Olympia to mind), whereas, by way of contrast, the Pan Painter reverts in deliberately archaistic fashion to the liveliness of thirty years previously.

The Achilles Painter, on the other hand, returns to a calm, serene, balanced, reflective style, revived, in his day, by the sculptures of the Parthenon (Chapter 15). He is also the supreme master of a delicate alternative technique, that of painting and figure-drawing on a white ground, which had been developed towards the end of the previous century and was especially employed for *lekythoi*, oil-flasks offered to the dead.

PART III
The Periclean Age

LIST OF EVENTS

469–427	Archidamus II joint king at Sparta
460–445	'First Peloponnesian War': Athens against Corinth (and later Sparta and Thebes)
460–454	Athenian expedition to Egypt ends in disaster
458	Aegina subject to Athens
458–456	Long Walls built round Athens and Piraeus
*c.*458/453	Athens makes treaties with Segesta, Halicyae and Leontini (Sicily) and Rhegium (south-west Italy)
457	Athenians defeated by Spartans at Tanagra but defeat Boeotians at Oenophyta
454/453	Pericles one of the *strategoi* (generals)
*c.*454	Treasury of Delian League transferred to Athens
454/453	Athenian Tribute Lists begin
453	Syracusans raid Aethalia (Elba), Cyrnus (Corsica) and Etruria and fight the Sicel leader Ducetius (451/450; Chapter 6)
451	Five Years' Truce between Athens and Sparta. Thirty Years' Peace between Sparta and Argos
451/450	Pericles' law restricting citizenship
*c.*450	The Riace bronzes and Myron's *Discobolus*
*c.*450(?)	Prosecution of Anaxagoras (Chapter 8)
*c.*450/425	Polyclitus' *Doryphorus*
449/448	Peace of Callias between Greeks and Persians
447/446–438/432	The Parthenon on the Acropolis. Temple of Athena Nike and Erechtheum planned (built in 420s and *c.*420–409/408 respectively)
447	Boeotians defeat Athenians at Coronea, and reconstitute their League
446/445	Revolt in Euboea
445	Thirty Years' Peace between Athens and Sparta

444/443	Athens' 'Panhellenic' colony at Thurii (south-east Italy); Protagoras draws up its code of laws
443	Ostracism of Thucydides the son of Melesias leaves Pericles supreme
442/441	Sophocles' *Antigone*
441–439	Revolt of Samos against Athens, assisted (unofficially?) by Pissuthnes, satrap of Sardis
438	Euripides' *Alcestis*
438/7	Spartocid rulers in Cimmerian Bosphorus (Panticapaeum; Chapter 27)
*c.*437	Pericles' expedition to the Black Sea
437	Athenian colony at Amphipolis
*c.*435	The Propylaea at Athens
435–432	Preliminaries to the Peloponnesian War: Megara, Corcyra, Potidaea
*c.*434(?)	Callias Decrees regulating the grain route
431	Beginning of the Peloponnesian War (the Archidamian war, 431–421; Peloponnesian War ended 404)
431	Euripides' *Medea*
430	Outbreak of plague at Athens. Pericles tried and fined, but reinstated (429), and then dies

CHAPTER 11

PERICLES: IMPERIAL DEMOCRACY

Unsurprisingly, the Spartan leaders were shocked when they heard of the reforms which Ephialtes had introduced at Athens in 462/461 (as we saw in Chapter 5, the news caused them to send Cimon's Athenian force unceremoniously back home). For Ephialtes had stripped the conservative, pro-Spartan Council of the Areopagus of nearly all its political power, eliminating its 'guardianship of the laws' and circumscribing its jurisdiction, so that the government of the state had been shifted a substantial distance towards democracy, which the Spartans feared. From now onwards the Athenian government depended more completely and solidly upon the popular Assembly (*Ecclesia*) and Council (*Boule*), although room for individuality remained in the ten generals (*strategoi*), who continued to be annually elected and were not only military commanders but in some cases political leaders as well.

Cimon had been one of several early examples of this phenomenon; but Cimon had been a friend of Sparta, and now a rift had opened up between the two states, so that his policy was no longer in the ascendant at Athens. However, he still had supporters in the city, and Ephialtes' reform aroused resentful feelings among them – so resentful that, in 462/461, Ephialtes himself was assassinated (a rare event in the city) at the hands of a Boeotian visitor, though almost certainly at the instigation of Cimon's partisans among the Athenian oligarchs. Ephialtes' reform, however, did not die with him, and the leadership of the pro-democratic elements in the state, stressing the sovereignty of the people, passed into the hands of one of his supporters, Pericles (*c.*495–429).

This was no doubt a gradual development, and did not at once place Pericles in a dominant position. But during the remaining thirty-three years of his life, with increasing regularity, he held repeated generalships, and, in spite of always sharing them with nine colleagues, it was he who decided policy more often than not. 'In name democracy, but in fact the rule of one man,' observed Thucydides.[1] But this was, nevertheless, free democracy in action, since Pericles, although a member of the relatively small stratum that monopolized the political leadership, remained in his supreme position through a constant series of electoral votes.

The Greeks were abnormally susceptible to oratory, and the oratorical talents of Pericles must have persuaded the Assembly with remarkable effectiveness and frequency; indeed ancient writers confirm that this was so. But to discover what happened during his 'reign' is difficult. For a Periclean myth, the myth of a Periclean Golden Age, came into existence, and, on the other side, marked hostility developed. As for ourselves, we have relatively few means of counter-checking the data and dicta provided to us by Thucydides' great brain (Chapter 23), and are left with a feeling that his version of Pericles' Funeral Speech, for example, may bear little relation to anything that was actually said.

Pericles was the son of Xanthippus, member of an eminent Attic clan, and had become prominent in the period of the Persian Wars. His mother was Agariste, niece of Cleisthenes of the Alcmaeonid family, who at the end of the sixth century had instituted a major democratizing reform of the constitution, and always hated and suspected Sparta. Pericles inherited both these policies. He had appeared on the political scene as a leading state prosecutor of Cimon (for alleged bribery), and then backed Ephialtes' reforms of 462/461; so that after the latter's murder it was natural enough that he should begin to take the lead.

Soon afterwards relations between Athens and Sparta broke down, and desultory hostilities followed (460–448), in which not Sparta but Corinth, out of motives of maritime rivalry, was Athens' most determined enemy. While Pericles initiated or completed the Long Walls from Athens to its enlarged port of the Piraeus, making the enclosed area almost impregnable, Aegina, which he had described as 'the eyesore of the Piraeus',[2] at long last became a thoroughgoing Athenian dependency.

Nevertheless, in the following year, despite a preliminary battle in which Pericles distinguished himself, a victory by the Spartans at Tanagra in Boeotia showed that Athens had no hope of getting the better of the Spartan hoplite phalanx (heavy infantry) on land. And yet very soon afterwards the Athenians were able to defeat Sparta's Boeotian (Theban) allies at Oenophyta, thus gaining control, for the time being, over central Greece – and securing direct access to the Corinthian Gulf, so that pressure could be brought to bear upon Corinth.

At the same time, however, Athens had plunged into a war against the Persians in Egypt (460–454). Probably Pericles instigated this adventure or at least went along with it. To engage in such a distant large-scale enterprise, while heavily committed on the Greek mainland, was stretching Athens' resources to an intolerable degree, and smacks of imperialistic mania, warranting a Corinthian spokesman's alleged observation that the Athenians just could not keep quiet, or allow anyone else to do so either.[3] When they attacked Egypt, however, a specific material consideration must also have been in their minds, namely access to Egyptian trade, in order to supplement their (sometimes precarious) importation of grain from the Black Sea area (Chapter 27). What happened was that a Libyan prince, Inarus, rebelling against the Persians in Egypt, appealed to Athens, which duly sent a Delian League flotilla of 200 ships (already in Cyprus) to help him. After this fleet, however, had gained an initial victory on the Nile, the Persians – goaded into action – overwhelmed the Athenian force, which was almost totally destroyed.

This catastrophe, which shook Athens' domination of the sea and even raised the menace of a new Persian invasion of Greece, may well have been used by Pericles as an argument for transferring the League's treasury from Delos to Athens (if this occurred in *c.*454, as most believe, rather than earlier), where it would be safer – and under direct Athenian control. The transfer, which must have been ill received by some of the allies, has sometimes been taken as a moment of transition from Delian League to Athenian empire. In fact, as practice hardened into precedent, this imperialistic process (inimitably and brutally defined by Thucydides, in the mouth of an Athenian envoy)[4] had been, and continued to be, gradual. We can learn much about its successive, unremitting stages from a series of inscriptions, the Tribute Lists.[5]

Military operations in Greece were brought to an end, and – now that the pro-Spartan Cimon had been allowed back from ostracism – a Five Years' Truce was concluded with Sparta (451). Two years later, Athens also concluded an agreement with Persia, though whether a formal 'Peace of Callias' was signed, as later authorities maintained, has been a matter of lasting dispute. At all events, each party recognized the other's sphere of influence, with more or less even honours, since although the Athenians undertook not to interfere with Persian possessions (a decision which later evoked shamefaced denials among their politicians), Artaxerxes I, too, guaranteed the Greek cities of Asia their autonomy, and freedom from any Persian naval presence, though not, probably, from Persian tribute.

This agreement, which wound up the Persian Wars (of nearly half a century earlier) in a spirit of compromise, prompted many of Athens' allies to suspend their payments to the League – on the grounds that the Persian danger was over; though Pericles soon compelled them to comply. However, the treaty also saved Athens from the danger of a Persian flank attack, when disaster threatened soon afterwards in the vicinity of its own borders. For following a victory over the Athenians at Coronea (447) the Boeotians reasserted their independence, reconstituting their own confederacy, and the cities of Euboea, too, launched a revolt (446/445), expelling the much disliked Athenian colonists (cleruchs) at Carystus and on neighbouring islands.

But Pericles stamped the rebellion out. Sparta, although its Five Years' Truce with Athens was now at an end, had helped the Euboean insurrection only half-heartedly (Pericles was believed to have bribed Pleistoanax, one of its kings, to keep quiet), and now concluded a Thirty Years' Peace with the Athenians, based on mutual recognition of each other's interests and power zones. Athens had to sacrifice central Greece, but kept Euboea and Aegina. Pericles' diplomacy in arranging the Treaty was dexterous, and the substantial Athenian manpower losses during the previous decades had not been entirely wasted after all.

Undeterred, therefore, he showed no signs of abandoning his expansionist policies, and in 444/443 sponsored a colony at Thurii (the former Sybaris) in far-off southern Italy, ostensibly Panhellenic in character but in reality designed to secure economic advantages for Athens, notably a supply of western grain. Then, in 440/439, a rebellion against Athens broke out on the allied island of Samos. Refusing to accept Athenian arbitration in a dispute with Miletus, the Samians had made pacts with Byzantium and with Pissuthnes, the Persian satrap of Sardis. But Pericles attacked them with 200 ships, and after a nine months' siege forced their city to capitulate, whereupon they were made to suffer heavily for their disobedience.

Then, in 437/436, Pericles successfully revived the project of colonizing Amphipolis in Macedonia – to help secure access to Thracian metals and timber, and to grain from the regions bordering the Black Sea, into which, probably at about the same time, he led an expedition aimed at establishing Athenian influence.

In 431 came the Peloponnesian War between the Athenian (Delian) League and the Peloponnesian Confederacy dominated by Sparta. There were various incidents which led to the war, and Thucydides expertly analysed them (Chapter 23).[6] Nor can his assessment of the underlying cause be faulted: namely, suspicion of Athens, which was widespread, because of its aggressive attitude to city-state autonomies. For example, Corinth, hemmed in on both sides, and on several occasions directly provoked, felt serious alarm. Its complaints were, not without reluctance, supported by the Spartans, whose jealousy and fear of Athenian power were basic factors in the events that now developed. Pericles, although seeing war ahead, advised the Athenian Assembly against drawing back, and so the die was cast, and this war began. It was not such a vast or unitary affair as Thucydides declared. Yet it was the largest war between Greeks to date, unprecedented in every respect, and leading, eventually, to the ruin of Athens – and of city-state Hellenism as a potent force (Chapters 24, 35).

Neither side had any chance of winning the war, at any rate without external (that is to say, Persian) support. The Athenians were supreme at sea, and were able to sail where they liked – importing supplies, and keeping them from the enemy. The Spartans, on the other hand, were equally unchallengeable by land, and could even ravage Attica every year, when its extensive rural population had to abandon their farms to destruction and take refuge behind the Long Walls of their city.

And so the war started, without either side displaying many efficient initiatives. In 430, however, an unforeseen horror occurred at Athens. A devastating pestilence, of which, despite Thucydides' vivid description,[7] the definition escapes us, broke out among the crowded, poorly housed Athenians within the Long Walls, and the city lost more than a quarter of its inhabitants and a third of its best troops. They included two of Pericles' sons; and Pericles himself was driven from his generalship by his desperate fellow-citizens, and accused of embezzlement, and fined. Soon afterwards, in spring 429, he was restored to office. But he, too, had been attacked by the plague, and six months later he died.

The war went on and was destined to continue, with one intermission, for another twenty-five years. Pericles' calculations did not prevail, since Athens proved the loser.

His demotion, at the hands of his fellow citizens, during the last year of his life, was not the only challenge he had faced during the long period of his power, in which, as we saw, he had had to persuade the Assembly to re-elect him, and do as he wished, year after year.

The most serious of his opponents had been a conservative leader, Thucydides, the son of Melesias, who objected to what he considered Pericles' immoral use of League funds for the construction of magnificent buildings at Athens – a practice for which the historian of the same name (Chapter 23) furnished Pericles with an eloquent justification, on the grounds that the allies ought to be proud to have their money employed for what amounted to the education of Greece.[8]

The attitude of the allies to the empire, however, was – as one might expect – mixed, and more sympathetic on the part of their democrats than among those who were oligarchically minded and did not, therefore, care for the Athenian system. The allied cities had to put up with

Athenian tribute, officials, colonists, jurisdiction and coinage. Yet, on the other hand, they gained security and prosperity (for Athenians, it was simpler: the empire benefited every class).

The challenge offered by Thucydides, the son of Melesias, failed to prevail, and he was ostracized in 443. But he had been right to consider Pericles responsible for the unique building programme – the most important scheme of state patronage ever to have been seen among the Greeks – which included the construction of the Parthenon (Chapter 15). Pericles' political enemies (whose personal attacks on himself, however scurrilous, failed to dent his power) had accused his building commissioner Phidias of corruption. They also charged another member of the Periclean circle, the philosopher Anaxagoras (Chapter 8), with impiety, as well as prosecuting Pericles' learned mistress, Aspasia. The calibre of this group – and Protagoras (likewise attacked) and Sophocles were also among them – reflects favourably upon the statesman's own intelligence or, at least, his appreciation of culture.

He liked this intellectual company; and there was nothing democratic about his manner. Although careful to avoid Themistocles' and Cimon's taint of luxurious splendour, he remained remote and reserved and even haughty, in the old-fashioned style, manipulating individuals with what was described as an 'Olympian' detachment.

Yet, paradoxically, he took decisive steps to continue and develop the process which had made, and was making, Athens into a thoroughgoing democracy. The poorer citizens had gained importance in the community because they rowed in the fleet, on which everything depended. And Pericles introduced state pay (*misthosis*). This first made its appearance in the various law-courts (*dikasteria*), among which the duties of the earlier court known as the Heliaea had been divided and distributed. The 'jurors' (dicasts) on these courts were selected by lot from a panel of 6,000 citizens more than thirty years of age. To encourage applications for this *demos* in action Pericles introduced a daily payment, or subsistence allowance, of 2 obols (raised to 3 not later than 425). It seems to have been Pericles, too, who arranged for members of the Council (*Boule*) to receive similar payments (in the later fourth century the sum was 5 obols); and probably all officials appointed by lot were receiving state payments before 439 BC.

In the democratic view these payments were justified and essential, because they utilized the prosperity of the state to benefit the citizens, and seemed to give every one of them an equal opportunity to serve the state – which, according to Thucydides, was Pericles' proud boast[9] – as well as subsidizing those who were poorest among them. However, the relative smallness of the payment (less than the rate for an ordinary day's work) meant that many of the volunteers for the services in question were old, retired men. A more serious objection, voiced by critics such as Plato, was that state pay made the Athenians 'idle, cowardly, garrulous and grasping'.[10]

Opinions were likewise divided about another, related measure put forward by Pericles. In the past the son of an Athenian citizen and a foreign woman had been eligible for citizenship. From 451/450, however, the franchise of Athens was restricted to those who were of citizen birth on both sides. This looked like narrow-minded chauvinism, and the Roman Emperor Claudius, together with some modern historians, believed that it fatally prevented the Athenian state from attaining a viable size.[11] And, indeed, one of Pericles' motives was probably elitist: he did not want the citizenship of his imperial Athens to become too diluted and less valuable. Yet his law could also be made to look democratic: the imposition of the social norms of the peasant. But the principal reason for the measure was financial, and linked to the institution of state pay. For between 454 and 440 the number of citizens who received this sort of subsidy had risen to a total of about 20,000, and there was a point beyond which this could no longer be afforded.

As for the foreign relations of Pericles, the historian Thucydides records, or more probably invents, speeches in which the leader himself purports to describe and illustrate these policies in eloquent terms. Yet at the same time he was aware of the perilous risks involved in the courses of action he proposed: though he did believe, balancing one thing against another, that he would eventually win the Peloponnesian War. Whether, however, he would ever have done so, if he had lived, remains more than doubtful, despite all the allurements of the Periclean ideal.

Nor is it possible to exonerate him completely from responsibility for the outbreak of the war. The Spartans, it is true, were also partly to blame, because fears of Athens made them, in the end, ready to fight. Their fears, however, were not wholly unjustified – owing to the aggressive activities of the Athenians. And these had largely been instigated by Pericles.

CHAPTER 12

PROTAGORAS: UNSETTLING SOPHISTS

The term sophist (*sophistes*), when it first came into use during the fifth century BC, at first meant simply a wise man (*sophos*) or expert, or a sage such as a diviner or a poet. Gradually, however, the word came to be applied to a new profession, which may be described roughly as higher education. The sophists who performed this task were doing something that had been almost lacking in Greek communities before. Their achievement is hard to assess, first because it is only recorded in literary fragments and obscure, unreliable summaries, and secondly because conservative opponents soon ensured that the term 'sophist' should bear a derogatory, pejorative significance. Yet the men who were thus described fulfilled an enormous role, virtually transforming contemporary society.

It would be wrong, however, to generalize about them as a group, since they included men of markedly different characteristics. The profession, in the main, consisted of teachers who spent their lives travelling from place to place giving instruction in return for a fee. This instruction covered a wide range of subjects – rhetoric, logic, grammar, ethics, politics, physics, metaphysics, even military matters. These subjects were taught with the object of helping the pupils to get on in life, and become successful; and the sophists concentrated on imparting techniques directed towards that end.

Some of them also claimed, with what now seems excessive optimism, to be able to teach 'virtue' or excellence (*arete*). This was regarded by themselves and their public, not as the moral goodness emphasized by Socrates (Chapter 21) but as almost synonymous with practical success. And one of the principal methods of achieving such 'excellence' was held to be oratory – rightly enough, because this was the chief path to a public, political reputation among the Greeks, who attached such great importance to articulate speech. And nowhere was this more emphatically the case than in democratic Athens, where public discussion was continuous and intense, and guided events. This being so, it was at Athens that the sophists were in keenest demand – and amassed the most substantial fortunes.

The training which they provided offered a deliberate study of the function of words, and the means of using them. For the object was to show men how to speak and to persuade – to teach them the art (*techne*) of persuasion – and to indicate what arguments to employ in public debate and discussion. As time went on this activity operated in favour of relativistic and therefore sceptical attitudes, since a well-trained thinker and orator tended to pride himself on his capacity to argue for any point of view regardless of whether it was true or not.

One central aspect of this growing scepticism was a constantly emphasized contrast between *physis*, nature, and *nomos*, the law of the land – or rather the laws and customs of each city-state. This contrast could be seen in various ways, but the increasingly dominant view was that, whereas nature is absolute and right, the legal and social systems operating in the various states were inevitably arbitrary, and conformed with no natural norm: so that they might, indeed, be wrong, and there was no obligation for anyone to obey them.

Such nihilistic deductions aroused the distaste of traditionalists, and, conversely, fascinated the increasingly individualistic and cynical young. They were conscious of a yawning generation gap, and the higher education offered by the more daring among the sophists seemed to provide just the establishment-bashing opportunities that young people wanted.

This destructive element was already just hinted at by the earliest and most renowned of the Greek sophists, and the first to describe himself by such a designation. This was Protagoras of Abdera in Thrace (*c.*490/485–after 421/411).

For four decades Protagoras travelled around the Greek states dispensing instruction, in return for substantial fees; he went to Sicily, but probably conducted a large part of his activity at Athens (from *c.*460?). On occasion, he delivered meticulously prepared lectures or orations, often as features of verbal contests – a speciality of the sophists which he himself may have introduced. But more frequently he conducted private courses.

Establishing, more than anyone else, the sophistic tradition of teaching 'virtue' – 'young man,' he is supposed to have said to one potential client, 'if you come to me you will go home a better man'[12] – he had much to say about politics, the principal expression of 'virtue' and of the success in life with which this seemed largely synonymous. He became an influential friend of Pericles, who selected him to draw up the code of laws for Thurii (444/443), the 'Panhellenic' colony in south-eastern Italy dominated by Athens. Like others among Pericles' friends, Protagoras incurred personal attacks and prosecutions from the leader's political enemies, on the grounds of impiety, though the anecdotes relating these tribulations are contradictory and at least partly fictitious.

However, it may have been because of animosities which thus arose that the written prose works of Protagoras, who was author as well as teacher, did not survive. A treatise *On the Gods*, which was reportedly the first of his works to be read before a public audience, started off with a statement which showed his lack of sympathy for the unpractical cosmic speculation of the earlier type of Ionian philosopher (Chapter 8); 'I know nothing about the gods, either that they are or they are not, or what are their shapes. For many things make certain knowledge impossible – the obscurity of the theme and the shortness of human life.'[13]

Although reflecting an agnostic suspension of judgment which queried the truthfulness of all Greek mythology, these words do not necessarily indicate that Protagoras was an atheist. If he was, he would scarcely have said so categorically, which would have caused offence. But in any case this quoted observation about the gods, whether atheistic or not, was enough to enable his critics to bring forward a charge of impiety; and enough, too, to prompt all the tales that centred round that accusation.

Protagoras is especially famous, however, for another statement, declaring that 'the human being is the measure of all things: of things that are, that they are; and of things that are not, that they are not'.[14] There has been endless discussion about what he meant by this dictum. But what he intended to assert was, surely, not only the central position of human beings in the universe but also the relativity of all perceptions and judgments emanating from each individual person, or any person you choose.

This view also, implicitly, involved scepticism about the claims of any and every philosophy or science to universal validity. And so Protagoras' disciples forced this attitude to its logical conclusion by declaring that the whole range of orthodox opinions must be subject to fundamental re-examination and re-assessment.

Whether he himself went so far as to offer this radical declaration we do not know. Yet he did prepare the way for such revolutionary doctrines, in his work known as the *Antilogiae* (*Contradictions*). Its two books are lost, but we are told by Diogenes Laertius what they contained.[15] On every subject, Protagoras indicated – with a keen eye for grammatical analysis, which he virtually invented – there are two potential antithetical arguments, one in favour and the other against. This conviction, explored more fully by his followers, inspired a widespread opinion, already mentioned, that Protagoras and the sophists were willing enough to make the weaker statement the stronger and interpret the worse case as the better – to make wrong into right.

Protagoras himself did not, however, care to extend such scepticism into the field of morality. For, in this field, he seems to have espoused conventional ethical conceptions without hesitation, believing that a moral sense has been implanted in every one of us: but that this innate tendency in the right direction needs to be developed and strengthened by education – which it was his own duty to provide.

And the form of morality to which he was referring included, in his view, the laws and customs of a city-state: it is the duty of a citizen, seeing that he is imbued with ethical instincts, to respect and obey these laws and customs. That is to say, when participating in the current (or incipient) discussions about the contrast between *nomos* (law) and *physis* (nature), Protagoras did not, despite 'man is the measure' and his democratic inclinations, adopt anything like a subversive view. On the contrary, he believed that human beings are moral, and that morality meant conformity with the legislation and customs of one's state (which was no doubt why Pericles chose him to draw up the laws of Thurii).

But Protagoras felt that this attitude needed explaining, and he explained it in a work entitled *On the Original Condition of Humankind*. In this study, in so far as we can reconstruct its contents, he offered an optimistic outline of what he took to have been the origins of civilization, explaining what he wanted to say in the form of a myth.[16] Since primitive human beings, he suggested, were worse equipped than wild beasts in the struggle for survival, Zeus had commanded Hermes to bring them morality and a sense of justice, which started them along the path to political, social and cultural evolution. Here, then, was a very early, perhaps the earliest, rational theory of progress.

We owe this account to Plato (Chapter 31). In his *Protagoras* he shows us Socrates going with a young friend to visit the distinguished sophist – who was on a visit to Athens – in order to enquire into the nature of the wisdom which Protagoras so expensively claimed to impart. The dialogue is a brilliant piece of writing, and more respect is accorded to the great man than to any other sophist ever mentioned by Plato.

Nevertheless, the mockeries, parodies and cheating arguments attributed to Socrates do not allow us to forget that Plato felt an extreme distaste for the sophists, not merely because their acceptance of fees for the teaching of virtue seemed to him degrading but because he felt that they were more interested in intellectual and oratorical acrobatics than in the truth itself, confusing the force of reason with the power of the spoken word. Protagoras' espousal of democracy seemed to him an example of this. And, in particular, Plato deplored their relativism, which was contrary to his own belief in absolute ideals. Thus his *Theaetetus*, too, attempts to refute and undermine the relativistic view that man is the measure of all things.

Nevertheless, Protagoras' outstanding intellect, and his success in Athens, had won him a profound influence on contemporary thought, inspiring progressives and conservatives alike. For he was a noteworthy transitional phenomenon between the one group and the other, in whom advanced intellectual scepticism clashed with a staunch belief in ethical and social tradition.

Other sophists developed various aspects of Protagoras' work, not always by direct debt but also independently, and carried them further, often finding his assumptions too traditional and tolerant.

Thus the versatile, exhibitionistic Hippias of Elis (*c*.485–415) stressed the sophist's role as educator, claiming encyclopaedic competence throughout the entire field of human knowledge. He addressed the *physis* (nature) *-nomos* (law and custom) controversy by declaring that *physis* binds human beings together, making them fellow citizens in a true sense, while *nomos*, in the manner of a tyrant, often exercises forms of coercion that are contrary to nature.[17]

Gorgias of Leontini in Sicily (*c*.483–376), influenced by two other Sicilians (Corax and Tisias) who wrote the first textbook on rhetoric (Tisias came with him to Athens in 427) fastened on the importance of public speaking, as a means of ensuring a successful career. To this end he created an antithetical, rhythmical, flowery, exciting prose-style that for all its extravagances served as a model for generations to come. Gorgias also (being sceptical about the chances of acquiring personal knowledge) displayed how arguments could be pursued to outrageous conclusions – of which his use of the *physis-nomos* antithesis to espouse Panhellenism, as opposed to city-state patriotism, seemed to be one.[18]

Prodicus of Iulis (Ceos), a slightly younger man with a booming voice, defined the sophist as halfway between philosopher and politician. Here, once again, was a man who concentrated on language, meticulously defining and differentiating correct and incorrect employments of terms. Prodicus also horrified conservatives by suggesting that religion is not natural, but had only come into existence as the response of human beings to their environment, the gods being man-made expressions of gratitude for the gifts that nature had provided to the human race.

Prominent among the 'younger' and even more radical sophists was Antiphon (already in ancient times distinguished, it would seem wrongly, from an 'orator' of the same name). Antiphon reverted once again to the *nomos-physis* contrast by pursuing it to both a liberal and an illiberal conclusion. The liberal conclusion was that, whereas *nomoi* are purely arbitrary and artificial, not only all Greeks but all human beings, Greeks and barbarians alike, are equal by nature (*physis*) – so that political organization should be based on their consent and co-operation – plus the shocking corollary, however, that moral restraints form part of this unnatural artificiality, with the implication that one had better ignore them when one can get away with it, and act with entire selfishness, which is what one's own natural interest demands.

This subversive point of view was pursued further by Callicles, who, according to Plato, declared that it was natural for the stronger man to prevail over the weaker (and indulge his desires to the full).[19] Another late-fifth-century sophist, too, Thrasymachus of Calchedon, is quoted as maintaining that justice is merely the interest of the superior and stronger[20] – so that might is right, a doctrine enthusiastically adopted by the tougher kind of politicians.

This, then, was what the sophists' arguments led to. Protagoras, intellectually, had paved the way to such a conclusion, although, as we saw, he shrank from the deduction that it should apply to morals and politics. Now, however, that deduction had been unabashedly made, and relativism was rampant.

CHAPTER 13

HERODOTUS: THE NEW ART OF HISTORY

With the proviso that important advances had already been made in the Middle East and especially in Israel, the writing of history was one of the major innovations of fifth-century Greece.

To Hecataeus of Miletus on Ionia, who was born before 525 BC, two works are attributable, though neither, apart from fragments, has survived. One of them was known as *Histories* (*historiai*, enquiries) or *Heroology* (study of heroes) or *Genealogy*. Mindful of the traditions of Homeric, Ionic epic, but writing in the prose medium that had been devised by Ionian philosophers (Chapter 8), Hecataeus was one of the first of the *logographoi*, tellers of tales, who with the assistance of family trees described places and customs. In this process, he dedicated a novel kind of critical analysis to the myths and legends whose massive influence upon current interpretations of the physical universe and world the philosophers had gradually sought to dispel.

Hecataeus' attempts to trace back the origins of leading Milesian families (including his own) blended reasoned criticism with gullible refusal to brush the myths aside altogether. This dilemma was displayed in an attempt to rationalize them instead, and force them into a pseudo-historical chronology, for all Hecataeus' brave assertion that he was trying to tell the truth.[21] That is to say, there was no authentic historiography yet; he did not invent or create it, but prepared the way.

His second pioneer book was a *Journey Round the World* (*Periegesis Ges*), the first work ever to record in systematic fashion the geography, topography and customs of cities throughout the Greek world.

The 'father of history', Herodotus (*c.*480–425), likewise came from the western coastlands of Asia Minor, his home being Halicarnassus in Caria, at that time controlled by Persia (Chapter 28). His mother was from Cos, but his father Lyxes (a Carian name) belonged to a distinguished Halicarnassian family. Panyassis, an epic poet, was probably his uncle; and when Panyassis perished in a civil war (461), Herodotus withdrew to the island of Samos.

After Halicarnassus became a member of Athens' Delian League (454/453) he may have returned home for a time, but did not remain. Henceforward (if not earlier) he travelled extensively – perhaps over a period of a dozen years – residing, above all, at Athens, his second home, where his contacts with the city's intellectual life decisively influenced his writing. He joined the 'Panhellenic' colony led by the Athenians at Thurii in southern Italy (444/443), where his tomb and epitaph were shown.

Divided into nine books by a scholarly editor long after his death, Herodotus' *History* had been subdivided by the author himself into two main parts. The first of them, the Prelude, describes and discusses the origins of the strife between Greece and Persia, and the rise of the Persian empire, together with relevant background events in Greece, and especially at Athens and Sparta. The second, and principal, portion of the work is concerned with the Persian Wars: the invasions of the Greek mainland by the forces of Darius I (490) and Xerxes I (480–479) (Chapters 1–3).

These wars were seen by Herodotus as the most important events that had ever happened, imposing their decisive overall influence upon the entire story of the ancient world. In particular, he saw the successful Greek resistance as a unique example of something approaching Panhellenic co-operation.

Because of this novel choice of theme, Herodotus became the prototype of all the many (perhaps too many) subsequent historians who have concentrated on military events. Yet he himself did not limit himself to the campaigns in any narrow or exclusive fashion, since his wider and more general purpose was to 'place on record the wonderful achievements both of our own and of the barbarian (Asian) peoples'.[22] This conjunction of Greeks and Persians, indicating an emancipation from narrow Greek chauvinism, mirrors not only his own liberally inclusive intellectual attitude but also his origins from the marginal and ambivalent area where Greece and Asia met – while reflecting, in addition the circumstances of his exile, which helped him to collect impartial material. True, Herodotus had derived from the Homeric poems the basic theme of a struggle between east and west: now renewed, it appeared to him, in the contrast between Greek liberty and Persian despotism. Yet he did not hesitate to praise Persian customs when he saw fit – thus incurring subsequent criticism as 'barbarian-lover' and pro-Persian.[23]

The wideness of these aims means that Herodotus not only gives us something approaching a continuous history of the Greek world for some two centuries past – an unprecedented chronological feat – but also places this tale on a canvas large enough to accommodate a mighty range of information. Although critical of his predecessor Hecataeus, Herodotus owes him structural elements and geographical interests. Hecataeus had written not only *Histories* but a *Journey Round the World*, and Herodotus may first have planned a geographical work on the lines of Hecataeus' *Journey*. If this was so, his ultimate plan, centring upon the Persian Wars, was only arrived at later.

For that eventual decision, to write about the wars, was probably formed under the influence of the Athenians whom he came to know during his residence at their city. This influence is also detectable in his admiration for Athens' moderate democracy (though not necessarily, or entirely, combined with an admiration for Pericles) and above all in his conviction (not universally acceptable elsewhere) that Athens had played the dominant part in the triumph over the Persians.

He gives Sparta some credit for these victories – but not enough. For although a lot of his geographical data had been collected by the middle of the century, he wrote much or most of his work during the subsequent Peloponnesian War (from 431) – in its early phase, when Spartan armies were devastating Attica year by year (Chapter 11).

The end of the work (concerned with an anecdote about Cyrus II the Great) is strange and abrupt: which may mean that Herodotus died before his book was complete.

His collection and presentation of material is as astonishing a feat as anything else that was achieved by anyone during the century. The mass of evidence that he provides contains a great deal that is accurate, since his determination to get at the truth, in the Ionian spirit of enquiry, impelled him to make enormous journeys.

The stories that he gathered together on these journeys, through personal contacts, hearsay and oral tradition (if possible derived from eyewitnesses), supplementing whatever inadequate documentation was available (archives, chronicles, land surveys, sparse literary sources), entitle him to be called the pioneer, not only of history, but also of comparative anthropology and archaeology – subjects already suggested, but not apparently followed up in great detail, by Hecataeus. Modern investigations have, on occasion, confirmed Herodotus' claims in these fields, even though his claims to autopsy and personal investigation have sometimes been queried. Agriculture and geology were also among his almost limitless interests.

The absence, however, of any previous historiographical tradition meant that he had to invent and impose entirely new standards. Thus his narrative, for all its brilliance, falls short of what we today would regard as a satisfying description of the Persian Wars. Those happenings, even if justifying the description of Herodotus as the first 'near contemporary' historian, were a generation past, and solid facts about them were already scarce – and often encrusted by heroic, chauvinistic, competitive legends, which offered every incentive to depart from even incontrovertible facts. Herodotus' battle-pieces, for example, are patchy and subject to error. In his desire, moreover, to be as comprehensible as possible, he too easily believes what his friends and contacts have told him, or includes what they have said even when he has reason to doubt its veracity ('my job is to write what has been said, but I do not have to believe it').[24]

Thus the speeches he includes throughout the work (reminiscent of Homeric practice, and inaugurating a historiographical custom that prevailed throughout antiquity) must not be regarded as authentic – and indeed Herodotus would have been surprised by anyone who took such a view. No one, for instance, could have reproduced discourses that took place at the Persian court, and when Herodotus offers them he is not claiming to record what was said but seeking to provide a backcloth depicting probable attitudes and patterns of behaviour.

The most serious obstacle, however, to accepting at its face value all that Herodotus tells us is his belief in divine causation and intervention, which limits and invalidates arguments based on human causes and effects. True, he fully realized that important individuals, both men and women – whom he regards with fascination and a good deal of sometimes shocked respect – are the driving forces behind history, so that their personal ambitions, hatreds and vengeances require careful biographical attention – at the very least as exemplars, or necessary illustrations of the narrative: an attitude which deserves praise, though it is somewhat unfashionable today (see Introduction). True, also, under the influence of the sophists who were so active at Athens (Chapter 12), he overlaid the divine pattern, on occasion, by modern rational explanations – and usually (though not quite always) refused to accept what is physically impossible.

Nevertheless, like Homer, and like the contemporary Athenian tragedians, whose poetical techniques he at times seems to be adapting to prose (among them those of Sophocles (Chapter 17), who celebrated him with an ode), he was dominated by the unhistorical belief that men who soared high and were arrogant, like Xerxes I or King Croesus of Lydia, must eventually provoke the gods to destroy them. This conviction meant that his approach was imbued by a moral and didactic tone, which he left as a legacy to almost all later historians of ancient times.

All this, together with the breadth of his theme, meant that subsequent authors – Ctesias, Aristotle, Manetho – could find some occasion to censure his methods, and Plutarch and Lucian felt able to call him a liar. Modern students, too, when they want historical insight into the period Herodotus is dealing with, are sometimes left at a loss by his lack of solid criteria for establishing the facts. That is all the more tantalizing because we all too often have no second account against which we can check what he tells us.

Yet he is a powerful thinker, behind whose cheerful façade lies a certain measure of pessimism and sadness. Viewed as a writer, rather than as an historian, he is nothing short of a genius, and can only win awed admiration in our own time when, so frequently, little attempt is made to make history sound attractive. For Herodotus' wide-ranging interest and curiosity expressed itself in a prolific flair for spicy, humorous tales and picturesque digressions, which make him second to none as an entertainer.

And this, indeed, must have been clear when he read his work aloud, to admiring Athenian and other audiences. For the *History* was composed with a view to such readings, which may also account for its episodic structure. Employing a literary form of the Ionic dialect, Herodotus transfigured the style he had inherited from his forerunners and converted Greek prose into a fine art. His control of this medium was perfect, and he wrote with a fluent and relaxed expansiveness that was incomparable and inimitable.

CHAPTER 14

TO THE RIACE MASTER AND POLYCLITUS: THE MALE NUDE

The distinction between temple reliefs, discussed in Chapter 9, and free-standing statues, which will be considered here, sometimes becomes blurred, because the figures on temple pediments were, on occasion, represented in the round (although not, obviously, intended to be viewed from every angle). Nevertheless, the rendering of free-standing statues had already had a long and remarkable history in Greece, independent of the adornment of temples. Yet the two media, or two branches of the same medium, had one thing in common: both were working all the time in the direction of greater naturalism (as artists continued to do until the present century), although, in the interests of idealism, this fell short of completely realistic portrayal.

The two main themes of free-standing statuary were the nude male (*kouros*) – god or ideal young man – characteristic of Greek athletic society (with its strong homosexual trends, Appendix 11), and the draped female (*kore*), representing a goddess or a votary. These figures were often designed for religious purposes (notably as grave-markers) and for dedications in temples, though they did not form part of the architectural decoration of those shrines.

The representation of the male nude seems to have originated from Naxos and Paros, where the transition from limestone to marble, in which the islands were rich, had marked the creation of large-scale images (*c*.650–600). But then it was at Athens that the genre achieved its major and rapid evolution, notably in the subtle, complex marble Moschophorus (Calf-Bearer) of *c*.570/560, perhaps dedicated to Athena.

The art of the marble maidens, *korai*, too, flourished at Athens. Once again many of the early examples found in the city had originated from the islands. But thereafter Athenian artists had their own essential contribution to make, first during a phase of Ionian influence (following the flight of Ionians from Persian rule after 546) and then by a specifically Attic style. This replaces archaic, Ionian, voluptuous elegance by the solid serenity of the Early Classical or Severe manner, which has already been encountered in temple sculpture.

During the early part of the fifth century both male and female statuary decisively progressed. As regards the former, a pair of bronze images of the 'tyrannicides' Harmodius and Aristogeiton, slayers of the joint dictator Hipparchus (514), was made for the Athenian agora by Critius and Nesiotes (477/476), to replace an earlier group removed by Xerxes I during his occupation of the city in 480 (Chapter 2). The statues of Critius and Nesiotes are lost, and their surviving Roman marble copies display the inadequacy and insensitiveness which so often defeats attempts to reconstruct the ancient Greek art which they sought to reproduce. The young Athenian Harmodius is seen to be moving forward with raised sword, while his old lover Aristogeiton protectively extends an arm, upon which his cloak hangs. Although the exact poses remain disputable, this was evidently a group with more than a single viewing point, representing an advance on earlier purely frontal compositions.

Another full-length marble statue (an original work from the Acropolis, now to be seen in its museum) is known as the 'Critian Boy', because of its resemblance to the figures of the tyrannicides by Critius and Nesiotes. It marks a breakthrough from the square, stiff-limbed stance of earlier *kouroi*, since although the figure is still at rest it is now more relaxed, with the weight shifted on to its back leg, a hip raised, the body and head slightly turned. In his search for a blend of human and divine beauty, the sculptor, whoever he was, has founded his solution upon physical fact, observed, comprehended and imitated, while at the same time endeavouring to refine that phenomenon by injecting what be believed to be perfect balance and proportion. After this figure, nothing is any longer impossible. Inspired by the growing triumph of this new 'classical' vision, the artist has moved further along the millennial path towards realism. The face displays a serious, unsmiling expression, characteristic of its epoch, and contrasting with the optimistic archaic smile of earlier days.

The head of the Fair-Haired Boy (once again in the Acropolis Museum) belonged to a statue which seems to have been of about the same date but was less symmetrical than the figure of the Critian Boy – to judge by its gently tilting angle. The expression is still solemn, indeed moody, its open-eyed stare veiled by the shadows of the eyelids, heavy like the jaw (and this tendency is mirrored in the nearly contemporary *kore* dedicated by Euthydicus, again broodingly unsmiling), and without any of the extrovert elegance of archaic times. Yet these are still not portraits but ideal portrayals, of what ought to exist and not what is actually existent, and it is only the ideal that has changed, in this epoch of serious, grave exertion that created the Athenian democratic empire.

The spirit of the times, however, and its finest artistic expression, can best be discerned in the original bronzes that the half-century following the Persian Wars has left us. Since so many bronze statues were melted down, the surviving examples are few. But they have not entirely vanished, and are relics of an art which was regarded as superior to statuary in marble.

The earliest-known example of these scarce, fine, fifth-century bronzes is the Delphi charioteer, in the museum of that town. The draped statue, with its long tunic (we have here departed momentarily from the male nude) and its eyes, lips and headband inlaid with glass, copper and silver respectively, belonged to a bronze group (of which the rest is now lost) dedicated by Polyzalus, brother of the Syracusan ruler Hiero I, to celebrate his victory in the chariot-race of the Pythian Games in 478 or 474. The proud charioteer, formerly carrying reins, appeared standing within his chariot (of which fragments, and fragments of the horses, have survived), in a quiet parade before or after the race.

His serious, taut, competent self-control has evoked comparisons with the poet Pindar (Chapter 6). But the identity, and even place of origin, of the designer and bronze-worker are uncertain. At a time when sculptural schools were beginning to lose their regional character, he has been variously ascribed to the Peloponnese or, perhaps with greater probability, to Sicily, to which the dedicator, Polyzalus, belonged; by analogy with other works from Magna Graecia, the charioteer's full features favour this Sicilian attribution.

These features are blank and ideal, and display none of the personal characteristics of portraiture: the sculptor's aim was impersonal and idealistic – and in any case individuals should not shine too brightly in city-state life. All the more remarkable, then, that what appears to be a portrait now makes its appearance elsewhere. A Roman copy – much better than most – of what must originally have been a whole marble statue, this head is in the Ostia museum, and is said (the label is ancient) to represent Themistocles. Such a portrait, with its distinctive, individual features, is out of keeping with the impersonality of the Delphi charioteer. Nevertheless, the simplified planes of the surface, and its rather abrupt divisions – displaying certain analogies with the head of the tyrannicide Aristogeiton (described above) – suggest that the original did indeed date from Themistocles' lifetime.

The explanation probably lies in his departure, in the 460s, for the Persian empire, where King Artaxerxes I made him prince or governor of Magnesia on the Maeander and other cities (Chapter 2). For the Persians, though employing Greek artists to carry out their requirements, lacked the Greeks' artistic, religious and political objections to portraiture, as is shown by the heads on coins of Cyzicus, later in the century, showing the satrap of Dascylium, Pharnabazus, and a satrap of Sardis, Tissaphernes (after Lycian monarchs, too, had been similarly depicted). In Greek territory, on the other hand – with the single exception of a coin from distant Abdera in Thrace, and a self-portrayal with which Phidias was charged (Chapter 15) – authentic portraits are not seen again for a very long time (making their first reappearance, it would seem, upon gems – in which a Graeco-Persian series can again be traced).

The Themistocles portrait then is an isolated curiosity, a flash in the pan. The future still lay with idealized figures, conceived, it is true, with a measure of increasing naturalism, as well as with increasing skill and refinement. One such figure, anatomically sophisticated but facially blank, was the marble Apollo dominating the west pediment of the shrine of Zeus at Olympia, a temple sculpture (and therefore described in Chapter 9), yet free-standing within its complex group. Another example is a muscular bronze god from Artemisium in the National Museum at Athens. It is once again uncertain who the sculptor was. He may have been Calamis, perhaps from Boeotia, though Argos and Sicyon have been suggested as alternative places of his origin. The figure stands vigorously but lightly poised, with legs apart and with one arm extended forward and the other lifted backwards. He is probably Zeus, originally carrying and preparing to hurl a thunderbolt, rather than Poseidon with a trident (or an athlete with a javelin). Though the moment is the pause before action, and the figure is still meant to be seen in profile, upon one vertical plane as though in a relief thus making a certain retrogression from a Tyrannicide group, stiff archaism, in many respects, has been left behind.

This figure brings us to the most famous sculptor of the middle of the century, who was Myron of Eleutherae, on the border between Attica and Boeotia. He was the outstanding experimenter in Greek sculpture, seeking out novel bodily postures and concentrating on the motion of men engaged, or about to engage, in violent action – falling, about to run, drawing a bow.

Myron is exclusively cited as working in bronze. But his renowned masterpiece, the Discus-Thrower (Discobolus) – which probably formed part of a dramatic group – has survived only in marble copies of Roman date, of which the least unsatisfactory, found on Rome's Esquiline Hill and now in the Museo Nazionale delle Terme, has made it possible, with ancient literary assistance, to offer a reconstruction. Once again, the tense instant immediately before vigorous action and physical exertion has been captured; the athlete is about to make his complex move, wheeling right-about upon the pivot of his right foot – but just for the moment time is suspended.

Yet despite the Discus-Thrower's realistic musculature, and the virtuosity of his pose – which testifies to Myron's acknowledged mastery of 'rhythm' – the Early Classical (Severe) Style has not yet come to an end. Facial expression is still unemotionally frozen, and the figure has been cut in one plane, to be seen mainly – like the Zeus of Artemisium – from a single viewpoint; although (as in the Tyrannicides of Critius and Nesiotes) the possibility of viewing the statue from other angles, as a third-dimensional figure, has not been wholly excluded.

The Roman novelist Petronius declared that Myron was 'able almost to imprison the life of men and beasts in stone', but the elder Pliny more accurately saw him as only *standing on the threshold* of realism.[25] In the continuing desire to unite the transitory with the timeless and permanent, and to reconcile patterned proportion with increasedly accurate representation of natural forms, yet another new stage has been reached.

The climax of classical Greek sculpture is represented by the two bronze statues discovered in 1972 in the sea off Riace in Calabria (south-western Italy), and now on view, after years of restoration, in the museum at nearby Reggio (the ancient Rhegium). The two figures are about six feet tall, and both faces are bearded.

'Statue A', the younger man, stands with his left foot forward, and his weight on his right leg. His hair is long and luxuriant, with curling locks round his ears and on his chin. His head is encircled by a band which was probably coated with a gold or silver layer, possibly in the form of a wreath. His parted lips and nipples are made of copper, and perhaps his eyelashes were too. His eyes were of ivory and glass paste, which is lost. His teeth, just visible, are of inlaid silver. He is strong, with expanded chest and large, drawn-back shoulders and powerful muscles. His arrogant turn of head, with a far-off, resolute, somewhat swaggering or even menacing gaze, approaches a theatricality that is little known in other fifth-century sculpture.

'Statue B', once again with copper lips, nipples and eyelashes, and eyes (of which one survives) of ivory and glass paste, adopts a somewhat similar stance; but the man is older, with a fuller beard. Examination with gamma rays reveals that the right arm and lower part of the left arm are of a different composition from the rest of the figure; that is to say, they are ancient replacements of the original limbs, which must have been lost or broken off. This dignified personage makes a less assertive impact than its counterpart; some even see in its posture and expression a hint of pathos.

'Statue B' originally wore a helmet, most of which has disappeared; and both men display the remains of shield-straps upon their left arms (there have been rumours, unconfirmed, that the shields were found, and subsequently vanished). Each may also have held, in his right hand, not a spear, as has sometimes been maintained, but a short sword. It would seem, therefore, that they are not athletes but warriors.

These are bronzes of such superb artistic quality that most marble statues, even when not blundering copies, look almost inane beside them. Despite arguments to the contrary, technical details suggest that the two masterpieces were made in the same workshop, and possibly in the same short period of time, or at least not a great distance of time apart. It has been suggested that the two works are by different sculptors, but this seems, on balance, unlikely. The statues, still 'Severe' in stance though their accurate anatomy and easier poses have advanced beyond the 'Severe' stage, represent the beginnings of what is described as the 'High Classical' style – although total realism is still inhibited by idealistic considerations. On such grounds both figures are attributable to *c.*450 BC.

Who are the two warriors intended to be? The sculptor Phidias (Chapter 15) is known to have executed a group for the Athenian Treasury at Delphi (*c.*465), commemorating Marathon and including Miltiades and Themistocles, but it is scarcely one chance in fifty or a hundred that the Riace statues should have happened to form part of that particular ensemble. Nor, indeed, can the hand of Phidias (or of his students) be plausibly detected in both or either of the statues at all. They have also been ascribed to another bronze group in the Achaean Treasury at Olympia, designed by Onatas of Aegina to represent the Greek heroes of the Trojan War, but that, likewise, is conjectural, and long odds. So, too, is attribution to Corinth, Sicyon, Argos and Boeotia – and to an eminent sculptor Pythagoras, described by Pliny as the 'first to represent such anatomical details as sinews and veins and hair', and by Diogenes Laertius as the 'first to aim at rhythm and proportion'.[26] But that guess is slightly more tempting, since Pythagoras' native town was Rhegium itself, so close to where the Riace bronzes were found; and it is easy to underestimate the artistic capabilities of these regions so far from the Greek mainland, because we know so little about them. Nevertheless, that, too, is little more than a surmise, and we must be content to conclude that we do not know who made these statues – or where they came from.

Nor do we know how, or when, they came to be in the sea where they were found. Perhaps a Roman despoiler or art collector was transporting them, centuries after their creation, from somewhere to somewhere else, but it is impossible to tell. All we can say is that they are as fine as any other sculptures that the classical world has yielded: and, to those who gaze upon them, more illuminating about the spirit of that world.

The theory that detects an Argive origin in the Riace figures ascribes them to Polyclitus – who was born at Sicyon but studied and worked at Argos – because of the way the figures stand. On chronological grounds this would have been possible, and it is true that Polyclitus worked chiefly in bronze (although his other media included marble, gold, ivory and embossed metalwork), but the physical proportions of the Riace warriors are less broad and burly than those favoured by Polyclitus (see below).

None of the original work that he undertook during his more than forty years of activity (*c.*464–420) has come down to us. But two of his most famous bronze statues are known from marble copies, as many as thirty in number. Like most imitations of the kind, they are of mediocre execution – and offer no idea of the careful finish of detail for which Polyclitus was famous. This is tantalizing because the bronze originals must have been of a superlative quality not inferior to that of their Riace counterparts. However, the copies of the two statues reproduce the poses and general characteristics of what we should expect of Polyclitean originals.

One of them is the Doryphorus, 'Youth Holding a Spear', of which the bronze original was nearly seven feet high. The most complete of its marble copies is in the National Archaeological Museum at Naples. Anatomically accurate, Polyclitus' figure was stockier and thicker and heavier than those executed by earlier sculptors and by Phidias. It also illustrates other features noted by ancient writers as characteristic of his style. For example, the Doryphorus is walking forward with one leg advanced, and the positions of the tense arm on the side of the relaxed leg, and vice versa – contrasting taut and slack muscles – display a studied, harmonious ease of balance marking a departure from the rigidity of earlier work.

The Doryphorus was known as 'the Canon' or Model, because it embodied Polyclitus' view of what the ideal proportions of the human form should be. 'People derive their artistic outlines from it,' remarks Pliny the elder, 'as from a sort of standard; he alone of humankind is deemed to have embodied the principles of his art in a single work.'[27] And indeed Polyclitus, to whom aesthetic theory appealed, wrote a book entitled the *Canon*, making it clear that the Doryphorus was the deliberate, programmatic expression of his general overall conclusions.

Only a few citations from the *Canon* have survived, but they confirm that the essay exemplified the Greek desire to conceptualize and idealize art, especially in mathematical terms. Beauty, to Polyclitus, was a philosophical matter of *symmetria*, which does not mean symmetry but ratio and proportion; and in his book the sculptor, viewing the human body as a supreme demonstration of mathematical principle, went on to indicate the particular set of corporeal proportions which he regarded as perfect – and which were incorporated in his Doryphorus. Other marble figures, representing specific individuals who had won contests in the Olympic Games, have likewise been identified as copies of bronze originals by Polyclitus, which no doubt likewise embodied his concepts of idealized form.

The second of his renowned statues to have come down to us in numerous (though very varying) copies is his Diadumenus, 'Youth Binding a Fillet Round his Head'. Its resemblance to the Doryphorus is clear at the first glance, but the *Canon* was flexible enough to accommodate variety, for here is a more youthful athlete, with less conspicuous muscles. The Diadumenus has been attributed to the final stage of Polyclitus' career (*c.*420).

By this time he had already designed and executed his most famous masterpiece, which was a colossal gold and ivory seated image of Hera for the Heraeum (Temple of Hera) at his native Argos. We can only reconstruct this colossal work from sketches on Argive coins of Roman date, some of which show the whole figure and others its head, while Pausanias describes the objects in Hera's hands as a sceptre and a pomegranate. The figure invited comparison with Phidias' Zeus at Olympia, of which something will be said in the next chapter, and Strabo considered Polyclitus' Hera, though not quite so large or magnificent, as the more beautifully executed of the two.[28]

His rivalry with Phidias assumed practical shape in the formal competition for the statue of an Amazon for the Temple of Artemis at Ephesus. Among five competitors, Polyclitus was placed first, Phidias second, and Cresilas third (he was also the sculptor of an ideal bust of Pericles). The Polyclitean Amazon can be identified in a copy at the Metropolitan Museum of Art, New York, which shows her suffering from a wound, in a pose reminiscent of one of the athletes ascribed to the same sculptor.

Polyclitus exercised a more profound effect than Phidias upon artistic developments of the immediately ensuing period, partly because, it was said, Phidias sculpted gods (but godlike human beings too) whereas Polyclitus depicted men. Furthermore, Polyclitus left an Argive school, which produced three generations of pupils. After 400 it was dominated by the sons of a certain Patrocles, who may have been his brother; and there was also a younger Polyclitus later in the same century, an architect as well as a sculptor.

However, despite this massive influence exerted by the older man of the same name, subsequent ancient critics noted a certain monotony in his compositions; thus Varro complained that they were square and almost all of the same configuration. Yet his system exercised a persistent and prolonged steadying influence on later sculptors: for it stamped a meaningful pattern on the chaotic flux of nature.

CHAPTER 15

ICTINUS AND PHIDIAS: THE PARTHENON

When Phidias the Athenian competed with Polyclitus for the statue of an Amazon at Ephesus, his version, as we saw, was not placed first by the judges. Yet Phidias had already, in Cimon's time, gained an early reputation, on the strength of two memorials to the battle of Marathon. These were a bronze group at Delphi (*c.*465) – of which the Riace warriors have been believed, too conjecturally, to form part – and the thirty-foot-high bronze statue of Athena Promachos, Athens' protector in battle, made from Persian weapons captured at Marathon, and designed for the Acropolis, where her spear-tip and helmet were visible from far out to sea. Later, in 451/448, Phidias' 'Lemnian Athena' was set up on the same hill.

Next, when Pericles, annually re-elected to power, planned an imposing construction programme for Athens (447/446; Chapter 11), he placed Phidias in charge of the whole architectural and sculptural undertaking, thus conferring upon him a status which no member of his profession had ever attained before. 'The great buildings', observed Plutarch, 'are what chiefly show that the record of Athens' greatness is no mere legend.'[29]

Their outstanding feature was the Temple of Athena Parthenos (the Maiden) – the Parthenon. Its erection was largely paid for by the financial contributions of Athens' subject allies, despite objections from Pericles' political opponent Thucydides the son of Melesias, who maintained that this was an immoral seizure of their funds. But in 444/443 he was silenced by ostracism, followed by exile.

The building, made of Attic, Pentelic marble upon a site where a temple had already been begun before the Persian invasion of 480 (when it was destroyed; Chapter 2), served not only, or not even mainly, as a religious shrine, but as a sensational piece of architecture crowning the Acropolis, and, above all, as one of the principal monuments to Athenian power and piety as Plutarch later appreciated.

Before the battle of Plataea (479), the Greeks had supposedly sworn that they would not rebuild the shrines demolished by the Persians, but later the Athenians, once they had concluded the Peace of Callias with the Persian monarch in 449/448, considered that this peace freed them from the oath.[30] The story was already questioned by Theopompus[31] and may or may not be true – it is not even certain whether, formally speaking, such a peace treaty ever existed (Chapter 11). But at all events work on this largest Doric temple on the Greek mainland, measuring 228 by 101 feet, was now begun.

Designed by the architect Ictinus (known also for his temple at Bassae in Arcadia), and constructed under contract by the master-builder Callicrates, it was of the Doric Order, but incorporated certain amendments. Eight columns instead of the customary six appeared at front and rear, providing a novel breadth and grandeur; and 'refinements' were introduced. These include a swelling (*entasis*) of the columns, such as had already been seen in the archaic temples of Magna Graecia but was now revived in subtler form. Moreover, the columns lean slightly inwards, and the upper portions of the building incline gently outwards. In addition, the entire platform of the temple descends in a just perceptible curve from the centre to the corners. These deviations from the horizontal norm throughout the whole of the exterior, though in some cases almost subliminal, served to soften the impact of the uncompromisingly and mathematically unresilient Doric pattern upon the eye.

The Greeks inextricably blended religion and architecture and sculpture; and the reliefs that adorned the Parthenon are the only extensive and representative body of first-class original work that any temple has handed down to us. They are much too numerous and varied to have been the work of Phidias and no one else: the project may have required the services of no less than seventy or eighty sculptors, who probably came from many different regions of the Greek world. Yet the more or less co-ordinated themes of the various compositions confirm that they were all carried out in accordance with Phidias' overall plan; and he may well have executed or perhaps sketched some of them himself (in addition to making the statue of Athena Parthenos, of which something will be said below).

The ninety-two metopes – an unprecedented number – sculptured in high relief between 446 and 400, were aligned over the architrave on the exterior of the building, between the triglyphs (blocks with vertical channels). Their reconstruction is not certain, because many are fragmentary and poorly preserved. But on the north and south sides of the temple, the subject matter included the battle between Lapiths and Centaurs (already depicted at Olympia (Chapter 9), but now in more detail), as well as various Trojan scenes. The metopes at the two ends of the temple depicted the struggles between gods and giants, and probably between Greeks and Amazons, in which the Athenian King Theseus defeated an Amazon invasion.

All these themes told of the victory of Hellenism over barbarism – of rational order over arbitrary irrationality – which had been signalized by the triumph of the Greeks in the Persian Wars (with the Athenians, local tradition maintained, in the forefront), and had now been once again, it was intended to say, reproduced by the role of Periclean Athens as the leader of Greek civilization (Chapter 11). The standard of execution varies in quality, the struggle between Lapiths and Centaurs providing the finest examples.

By the time the frieze was undertaken (from *c.*440), a more uniformly brilliant team of sculptors had been brought together. Their success can be estimated by the inspection of the more than 420 feet of the frieze – out of the original 520 – that survive, not all in particularly good condition; the greater part to be seen in the British Museum, to which many pieces were brought by Lord Elgin in 1801–4 (much to the indignation of the present Greek government).

Situated over the architrave, not of the outer colonnade but of the *cella* or interior chamber of the temple (as at Olympia), though in this case extending over the end porches as well as the sides, the frieze formed a continuous relief, depicting a single unified action. Its theme is the procession which was the principal feature of the city's most famous festival, the annual Great Panathenaea. This was celebrated with lavish ceremonial every four years, and played a prominent part in the festival policy encouraged and financed by Pericles as part of his glorification of Athens.

The identification of the *exact* occasion depicted by the frieze has produced some puzzlement. It has been suggested that some specific, individual happening may be represented, either, perhaps, the earliest of all the Panathenaic festivals, instituted by King Erechtheus in legendary times, or a commemoration of the heroic Athenian warriors who met their deaths at Marathon (Chapter 1), totalling 192, it was said; and the same number of human participants has been counted in the procession upon the frieze. But it remains more likely that these impersonal-looking figures are generalized, and do not participate in any specific scene.

The Panathenaea was a religious festival, but although this was so, and despite the appearance of certain divinities upon the frieze, its tone is predominantly secular – a feature which may have shocked pious contemporaries. The task of the procession was to bring the robe of the goddess, woven by citizens' daughters for her ancient image, up from the city to the Acropolis. But here we are shown, in a series of subtly diversified moving groups and individuals, human aspects of the scene, namely the preparatory marshalling stages of the cavalcade, down in the Outer Ceramicus. First, the old robe is being folded away, and then we see the men on horseback moving through the streets, headed by citizens and attendants leading animals for sacrifice or bearing sacrificial offerings. The procession culminates in the presentation of the sacred robe.

The high, interior location of these reliefs raised problems of visibility, but also created an interesting interplay of indirect light and shade, assisted by the colouring which such sculptures habitually displayed. Indeed, the frieze enables the art of the Parthenon to be judged at its best. Even if Greek marble sculpture never quite rises (as was appreciated at the time) to the supreme standards made possible by working in bronze, the technical skilfulness of this High Classical style marks a considerable advance beyond the Olympian sculptures (Chapter 9).

Yet in one respect there is also what might be regarded as a regression, though an entirely deliberate one. For no attempt is made to develop or increase the portrayal of emotion and mood which had been seen in its beginnings at Olympia and in a more developed form in painting on vases (Chapter 10). On the Parthenon frieze, there has been something of a return to unmodified idealism. The sculptors, it is true, displaying the utmost precision of workmanship, understand the construction of the human anatomy very well indeed, but its rendering is elevated on to an ideal plane, and these willowy figures do not reflect or embody the technical calculations and proportional scrutinies of Polyclitus.

As for the faces on the Parthenon friezes, they are reserved and tranquil, without the gleams of aggression or pathos at which the Olympian and Riace sculptors had permitted themselves to hint a few years earlier. These beings, approaching as near as a human can to the felicity of the gods, are a glorious but impossible race, rising aloof and disengaged above human passions and disturbances. That is to say Phidias, and those who worked with him, sought to harmonize (in the spirit of so many philosophers) the transience of everyday phenomena with a timeless, absolute, perfect state of being, while at the same time endeavouring to give symbolic, visual shape to the Periclean vision of Athens which the entire building embodied.

The two wide pediments of the Parthenon, the last sculptural work to be done on the temple (*c.*438/432), have only come down to us in fragmentary fashion, owing to severe damage during the seventeenth century. Their themes, which can be partly reconstructed from earlier drawings, dealt with decisive moments in the mythical story of Athens and its patron divinity Athena.

Thus the eastern pediment depicted her birth, in the presence of the other divinities. According to the story, the god Hephaestus was seen cleaving the head of Zeus with an axe, and from it emerged Athena, fully armed. This central miraculous group on the pediment was framed by the rising of the sun's chariot on the left and, on the right, by the setting of the chariot of the moon (from which a splendid horse's head has survived). On the left, too, were Dionysus or Heracles, Persephone, Demeter, and perhaps Hebe, the cup-bearer of Zeus. Their lateral figures, recumbent, seated and standing, have survived, but the goddesses have lost their heads. Their poses and gestures, however, display their excitement at the great event that is taking place at the centre. On the right, too, are three unidentified goddesses, likewise headless today.

The theme of the west pediment is the conflict between Athena and Poseidon, the sea-god, for the domination of Athens and its territory. Poseidon had caused a salt spring to gush from the Acropolis, and Athena, in response, made an olive tree grow; and it was she who proved victorious in the confrontation, though Poseidon, too, remained a patron. These superhuman acts, displaying the two deities recoiling from one another's formidable grandeur, occupied the centre of the pediment, which has survived only in fragments (divided between London and Athens), while the remainder of the space displayed their chariots and supporters. On one side, an anatomically superb, twisted, recumbent male figure, identified with one of Athens' river-gods, Ilissus or Cephisus, was shown raising himself on his arm and turning his (now vanished) head in order to secure a better view of the central conflict. These fragmentary pieces of the Parthenon pediments are enough to show how far Greek sculpture had advanced, notably in the depiction of movement in depth, since their counterparts at Olympia had been made not so very much earlier (Chapter 9).

In these pediments, moreover, bodily forms and poses reflect progress beyond the metopes and frieze of the same temple. The goddesses, for example, wear a newly fashionable type of clinging, shape-revealing drapery, with deep and restlessly multiplying razor-edge folds that catch the shadows and – like the horses' wind-blown manes – open up novel optical possibilities which would be further exploited before very long.

The principal sacred statue of the Acropolis had long been the revered Athena Promáchos – standing outside the Parthenon – of which, as we saw, a new version had been one of Phidias' early works.

But in *c.*447/439 he crowned his work on the Parthenon itself by creating a further statue, of Athena Parthenos, for its interior. This renowned figure was forty feet high, and made (perhaps unprecedentedly) of gold and ivory – or rather of wood veneered with gold for the drapery, and ivory for the head, hands and feet. It was not primarily intended as a magical cult-image, since the Athena Promachos already fulfilled this role. The purpose of the Athena Parthenos, on the other hand, was to emphasize still further the position of the goddess as the patron of Athens' greatness, within the shrine created, by Pericles' initiative, to glorify the city.

The Athena Parthenos, like the Athena Promachos, no longer exists, but we can reconstruct its appearance from Pausanias' description,[32] assisted by diminutive copies and coins. Robed in heavy, solemnly folded drapery – intricate detail was not needed on this scale – she was armed, and wore about her shoulders her miracle-working short goatskin cloak, the *aegis*. Upon her head was a helmet with three crests, which were worked in the shape of a sphinx and two winged horses. Her left hand, holding a vertical lance, rested upon the rim of a shield, within which her holy snake was coiled. The shield was engraved with reliefs depicting (like the temple's metopes) the struggle between the Greeks and Amazons. These reliefs reputedly included not only a 'portrait' of Pericles fighting an Amazon, but a figure of a bald old man lifting up a stone in both hands, who was identified with the sculptor himself (the figure is represented on a later copy of the shield, which is partly preserved).

Such a self-portrait, on this sacred statue, was held to be sacrilegious – indeed any self-portrait, or any portrait, still seemed an affront to democratic equality as well – and together with a charge of embezzlement it involved Phidias in legal proceedings. He was by no means the first Greek, or first Athenian, to be penalized for too great success, although his real crime, no doubt (magnified by the blatant extravagance of the Athena Parthenos), was to have been a friend of Pericles, whose political enemies, unable to get at the great man himself, brought the charge against his protégé, just as they also prosecuted Anaxagoras and Protagoras (Chapters 8 and 12).

Contradictory legend obscures our knowledge of these events, but it appears that Phidias fled to Olympia, where remains of his workshop have, surprisingly, come to light. There he designed and executed the huge gold and ivory seated image of Zeus, for the god's temple. Once again, we can obtain some idea of what it looked like from Pausanias,[33] and from small reproductions, as well as from terracotta moulds employed for the drapery. The figure, its expression so sublime and gentle, people said, that it could console the deepest sorrow, was regarded by ancient opinion as the sculptor's finest work, the greatest statue in Greece (although Strabo in some respects preferred Polyclitus' Hera) and one of the Seven Wonders of the World. In Roman times, Quintilian declared that 'it can be said to have added something to traditional religion'.[34]

According to modern taste these bedecked, colossal sculptures do not, for all their calm majesty, represent a very elevated form of art. Nevertheless, Phidias' statues of Olympian Zeus and Athena Parthenos must have conveyed a strong sense of awe as one entered the shrine and confronted their vast forms and rich decorations, gleaming through the dim light of the interior.

Phidias made other famous statues too, and was also a painter (in early life), an engraver and a maker of decorative metalwork. The date of his death is uncertain. It may have been in *c*.430.

The Parthenon was only one of four significant buildings which adorned the Athenian Acropolis in the second half of the fifth century, and broke in various decisive ways with traditional precedent. The others were the Propylaea and Temple of Athena Nike and Erechtheum. Despite their very different appearances they are in close enough proximity to one another, and close enough also in scale and level, to suggest deliberate, dramatic co-ordination. This is presumably attributable to the overall plan of Phidias, although no direct evidence to that effect exists.

Phidian origin, at least on the drawing-board, is more than likely in the case of the Propylaea, which was probably erected while he was still at Athens, working as the director of the building projects of Pericles; though the architect of the edifice was Mnesicles. 'Propylaea' was the designation given to porches or other monumental entrances to sacred or secular enclosures in Greek lands, and, in particular, it was the name by which the complex entrance structure of the Athenian Acropolis was known. This stands obliquely to the Parthenon which rises above and beyond it (but the approaches to ancient temples were often oblique in order not to disturb ancient ritual locations). The Propylaea was built in 437/432 of Pentelic marble, with details in black limestone from Eleusis. Its plan was a version of the traditional gateway with a porch on either side, modified, however, by elaborate and original variations.

The building consisted of a large square three-aisled hall, pierced by five gateways reached by five steps, with the exception of the central gateway, which was approached by an inclined ramp. The Propylaea blends the traditional, solid Doric Order of architecture with the more slender delicate Ionic. The new amalgam was not without contemporary significance, since whereas the Doric was still reminiscent of the Peloponnese, of which Sparta was the leader, the Ionic – which had hardly ever been seen before to the west of the Aegean – recalled Athens' claim to be founder and leader of all the Greek cities of Ionia in western Asia Minor. The blend of the two Orders was introduced by retaining Doric for the six-column porticoes that face inwards and outwards, whereas the columns dividing the hall were Ionic, and the outer porch of the avenue spanned by the central gateway was flanked by colonnades of the same Order.

Mnesicles also added wings projecting from the front, faced with Doric columns. The north wing contained a square chamber which served as a picture-gallery (*pinakotheke*), its walls painted by Polygnotus (Chapter 10) and other artists, but the south wing included no corresponding chamber, and its design was asymmetrically curtailed to avoid encroachment on existing or planned adjoining temples.

One of these buildings was the miniature shrine of Athena Nike (Victory), on the bastion of the hill.

This was the traditional location of a sanctuary in her honour (destroyed by the Persians in 480), but the adjustment of the design of the Propylaea indicates that the reconstructed temple of Athena Nike, too, formed part of Phidias' original plan. This is confirmed by the recorded existence of a priestess of Athena Nike before *c.*445, and by the name of the temple's architect, Callicrates, who is probably identifiable with the master-builder working for Ictinus, architect of the Parthenon. (The design and construction of the shrine of Athena Nike, however, belong to the 420s, after Phidias' departure and death; see Chapter 22.)

The Erechtheum, too, must have been planned, in some form or other, by Phidias and his colleagues when they determined the future configuration of the Acropolis, although, once more, its construction did not take place until about 420, and then again, after interruption, in 409/408. The temple was designed to replace a sixth-century shrine of Athena Polias a little to the south (another building burned down by the Persians in 480), and was intended to house her ancient, venerated, olive-wood image, but was also employed to enshrine and honour a number of other objects and locations sacred to Athenian myth and legend and prehistory. It is this multiple intention which, together with an uneven terrain, accounts for the complicated, irregular, tripartite layout of the Erechtheum, as mysterious as the antique cults which it was built to harbour and perpetuate.

PART IV
The Peloponnesian War

LIST OF EVENTS

*c.*433	Satyrus I becomes king of the Cimmerian Bosphorus at Panticapaeum (d.389; Chapter 27)
431–421	Archidamian War (first phase of Peloponnesian War)
429	Death of Pericles (Chapter 11)
*c.*429/427	Sophocles' *Oedipus the King*
428	Euripides' *Hippolytus*
427	Gorgias sent by Leontini to Athens
427–424	First Athenian expedition to Sicily ends with Conference of Gela, dominated by Hermocrates of Syracuse
425	Athenians capture Sphacteria and its Spartan garrison
425	Aristophanes' *Acharnians* (424 *Knights*, 423 *Clouds*, 422 *Wasps*)
425/424	Euripides' *Hecuba* (*c.*422/421 *Suppliant Women*)
424	Death of Persian King Artaxerxes I and accession of Darius II (423)
424	Thebans defeat Athenians at Delium
424	Brasidas captures Amphipolis from the Athenians. The historian Thucydides exiled
424/423	Treaty of Epilycus between Athens and Persia
420s	Temple of Athena Nike on the Acropolis
422	Brasidas and Cleon killed outside Amphipolis
421	Aristophanes' *Peace*
421	The Peace of Nicias: twenty years' treaty between Athens and Sparta
Before 420	Death of Herodotus at Thurii
*c.*420	Polyclitus' statue of Hera at Argos
*c.*420–409/408	Construction of the Erechtheum on the Acropolis

420	Alliance between Athens, Argos, Mantinea and Elis; destroyed by Spartan victory at Mantinea (418)
416	Melos capitulates to Athens
415–413	Syracuse under Hermocrates and then Gylippus resists Athenian expedition which ends in disaster
415	Euripides' *Trojan Women*
414	Aristophanes' *Birds*
*c.*414–412	Athens sends aid to Persian dissident Amorges in Caria
413	Spartans fortify Decelea
413/412	Revolt of Athens' subject allies
412	First treaties between Spartans and Tissaphernes and Pharnabazus, Persian satraps of Sardis and Dascylium
412	Hermocrates exiled from Syracuse *in absentia*
411	Oligarchic revolution at Athens. Governments of Four Hundred and Five Thousand
411	Aristophanes' *Lysistrata* and *Thesmophoriazusae* (or 410)
410	Athens win victory at Cyzicus but refuse Spartan peace offer
*c.*410	Euripides' *Phoenician Women*
409	Sophocles' *Philoctetes*
409	Carthaginian expedition to Sicily under Hannibal (Chapter 25)
409/406	Completion of the Erechtheum on the Acropolis
408	Euripides at the court of King Archelaus of Macedonia (*c.*433–399), whose palace was decorated by the painter Zeuxis
408/407	Cyrus the younger becomes Persian governor-general of Asia Minor and forms alliance with Lysander
*c.*407(?)	Cos, home of the physician Hippocrates, occupied by Lysander
407	Alcibiades returns from exile and is appointed *strategos* (general)
407	Death of Hermocrates after attempted coup at Syracuse
406	Spartan victory at Notium. Alcibiades withdraws
406	Hannibal's second Carthaginian expedition to Sicily. Supremacy of Dionysius I of Syracuse (405; Chapter 25)
406	Deaths of Euripides and Sophocles

406	Athenians win victory at Arginusae but execute generals (despite opposition by Socrates) and refuse Spartan peace offer
405	*Frogs* of Aristophanes (d.*c*.385) and Euripides' posthumous *Bacchae*
405	Victory of Lysander at Aegospotami followed by siege, capitulation and oligarchic revolution (Thirty Tyrants) at Athens (404), and establishment of 'decarchies' by Sparta elsewhere
c.405(?)	Philosophical work of Democritus
405/404	Death of Persian King Darius II and accession of Artaxerxes II Mnemon (d.359/358)
404	Alcibiades (seeking refuge with Pharnabazus) murdered in Phrygia
403	Restoration of Athenian democracy by Spartan King Pausanias against policy of Lysander who is discarded and killed (395)
401	Sophocles' posthumous *Oedipus at Colonus*
c.400(?)	Death of Thucydides

CHAPTER 16

HERMOCRATES: SAVIOUR OF THE WESTERN GREEKS

During the fifth century Sicily, enjoying so many natural advantages, remained one of the principal conglomerations of rich, powerful and prosperous Greek states, despite abrupt changes in their political patterns. After the expulsion of Thrasybulus, the brother of Hiero I (Chapter 4), from Syracuse (466) – followed by the loss of its empire, though it still remained the island's leading city – most of the Sicilian dictatorships came to an end within the next few years, and the states where they had existed set up more or less democratic constitutions.

Thus the government of Syracuse was conducted by an Assembly and a Council (not chosen by lot as at Athens but annually elected), while fifteen generals, appointed in the same way, comprised the chief executive. For a time *petalismos*, a device resembling the Athenian ostracism, was introduced in an attempt to check abuses of power. But although this discouraged many prominent citizens from engaging in public life, the privileges of the prosperous agricultural class – descendants or successors of the aristocratic, land-owning *gamoroi* – were hard to eliminate, as the results of elections made clear; and in Syracuse, as in other Sicilian cities, years of mass exile, deportation and transplantation left a turbulent factional inheritance. For example, the new 'democratic' regime declared some 7,000 mercenary soldiers, imported by the dictators, ineligible for full citizenship and therefore for public office, whereupon they revolted and were, with difficulty, expelled (461).

Yet Syracuse was still strong enough to launch a fresh assault against potentially menacing Etruscan city-states. Their fleet had been defeated off Cumae in 474, and in 453 sixty Syracusan triremes attacked Aethalia (Elba) and Cyrnus (Corsica), and returned with extensive plunder from the coastlands of Etruria. Two years later, a native Sicel leader Ducetius, who had organized a threatening federation within Sicily itself, defeated a combined army sent against him by Syracuse and Acragas, the second city in the island. But in the following year their joint force put him out of action at Nomae (which has not been identified) whereupon Syracuse turned against their Acragantine allies and defeated them with heavy loss (445), taking the subsequent precaution, however, of considerably augmenting its own infantry, cavalry and navy.

But most of the events that took place in Sicily during and after this period, as so often, are known to us only in so far as they impinged on the history of Athens. During the 450s, if not before, the imperial Athenians had begun to display an interest in Sicily, either as part of their general, megalomaniac aim of interfering wherever they could, or more particularly (as in Egypt) in order to secure a new source of grain in case the lifeline to Black Sea supplies (Chapter 27) was cut. And so by making treaties with the Sicilian city of Segesta in 458/457 or 454/453 and with Halicyae and Leontini and Rhegium (across the strait) in *c.*454/453 or a little later, Athens seemed to the Syracusans to be issuing a deliberate challenge to their political power on the island. This meant that in the following decade and a half they felt impelled to expand their armed services and strategic resources still further.

When the Peloponnesian War broke out between Athens and Sparta (431), Syracuse took the side of the Spartans, and sent them considerable supplies of grain. In 427 rich Ionian Leontini, attacked by Dorian Syracuse, requested assistance from the Athenians under the terms of the alliance between the two states, and Athens sent twenty ships under Laches and two other generals: because, remarks Thucydides, 'it wanted to prevent grain from being sent to the Peloponnese, and also to test whether it was capable of conquering Sicily'.[1] The historian was no doubt right to detect the first of these two motives, since this grain was important to the Spartans, and Athens would have liked to lay hands on it instead. And even if the second motive looks like hindsight, the Athenians were no doubt suspected, already, of cherishing such ambitions – particularly after they had sent out forty additional ships in 425. By this time much of Sicily had been drawn into the Peloponnesian War, which threatened many of the island city-states with internal factional convulsions. But then in the following year their representatives met at the Conference of Gela (which, in conjunction with Camarina, had taken the initiative in arranging this meeting).

One of the speakers at the Gela conference was Hermocrates, the son of Hermon, a leading Syracusan aristocrat and land-owner, the city's most important statesman of the post-dictatorial age, and a man who (if we knew more about him) would probably prove to have justified the unusual admiration of Thucydides.

The main argument of Hermocrates at Gela, we are told, was that the Sicilian city-states must cease fighting against one another, otherwise they would be swallowed up by the Athenians – who should not be appealed to by any of the island's cities for assistance, but must be excluded from their affairs altogether.[2] Once again Thucydides could be injecting an element of hindsight, after the great Athenian invasion of Sicily during the following decade (see below). Nevertheless, Hermocrates may very well have argued more or less as Thucydides recorded; though his Pan-Sicilian sentiments need not have been purely idealistic, since what he wanted was Syracusan rather than Athenian predominance – and predominance, at Syracuse, by his own group or faction, the oligarchical land-owners.

At all events, Hermocrates succeeded in creating a fragile and temporary Sicilian unity, and this First Sicilian expedition of the Athenians was a failure: for which they punished all the three generals concerned.

Meanwhile upon the Greek mainland and in the Aegean, the first phase of the Peloponnesian War, known as the Archidamian War, had continued to take its course. Pericles was dead (429), and the leaders who competed to take his place, exploiting the ambitions, fears and prejudices of the Assembly and lawcourts, included the financial expert Cleon, who was hated and reviled by the historian Thucydides and other conservatives – mainly because, although wealthy, he did not belong to the traditional, aristocratic governing circle.

In the war, both sides scored encouraging, though inconclusive, successes. The Athenians crushed a revolt by Mytilene on the island of Lesbos (428/427), and in 425 captured the island of Sphacteria (off the fortress-peninsula of Pylos), with the result that 292 prisoners were taken, including the spectacular figure of 120 Spartiates.

But then a misconceived attempt by the Athenians to subdue Sparta's ally Boeotia was heavily defeated at Delium (424). And in the same year a Spartan of unusual talents, Brasidas – general, diplomat, honest man – carried the war into Macedonia and Thrace, capturing Amphipolis and threatening Athens' imports of metals and timber and Black Sea grain.

When, however, both the war-leaders Brasidas and Cleon were killed (422), the two sides felt prompted by exhaustion, in the next year, to agree to the indecisive 'Peace of Nicias'. During the subsequent chaotic and inglorious period a flashy, unreliable Athenian politician, Alcibiades, intrigued against the Spartans (whose principal allies Corinth and Boeotia had indignantly rejected the Peace) and formed a coalition against them, which was defeated, however, at Mantinea (418). So Athens had squandered an unusual opportunity.

The Athenians then launched their massive expedition to Sicily (415–413), made famous by the dramatic and tragic account of Thucydides.[3] The chief motive of the invasion, once again, was their desire to have Sicilian grain and to deny it to Sparta; but a wider ambition to seize the whole of Sicily and enrol its city-states as tributary allies must also by now have become more clearly defined than in 427. As to ostensible pretexts for intervention, the Syracusans' close alliance with Athens' enemy Corinth was sufficient.

During the winer of 416/415, then, the Athenians sent envoys to Sicily at the invitation of their allies at Segesta (a native Elymian city), who were hard pressed in a war against Doric Selinus, an ally of Syracuse. When the envoys returned home (bringing, it was later said, erroneous reports that Segesta had plenty of money to pay for an Athenian expeditionary force), it was decided to send a flotilla under the joint command of three generals. They were Alcibiades (who showed enthusiasm for the enterprise), the rich, pious, indecisive Nicias (who showed better sense than usual in regarding this Second Front as a rash dispersal of forces), and Lamachus (who was what was needed – a professional soldier – and produced the best operational plan).

The allied Athenian force that was finally dispatched, supported by financial resources that mirrored a remarkable recovery from wartime depletions, included 134 triremes, many support vessels and 5,100 hoplites, in addition to numerous troops of other kinds. It was the most formidable fleet and army that had ever left the shores of Greece, and presented the most deadly threat that had ever been offered to the independence and survival of the western Greeks.

The natural leader of the Syracusans was Hermocrates, although as representative of the oligarchic faction he was handicapped by the rival existence of a powerful democratic group, led by Athenagoras, which together with similar parties in other Sicilian cities was suspected of sympathy with the Athenian democracy. Indeed, Athenagoras' party was even believed willing to do a deal with the invaders, in the hope that the riches of the Syracusan oligarchs could be redistributed.

Hermocrates was delighted, however, by the Athenians' recall of Alcibiades soon after their expedition had reached Sicily (charged with impiety, he jumped ship, during his return journey, at Thurii, and joined the Spartans, to whom he thereafter offered invaluable traitorous advice). The death of his colleague Lamachus in 414 virtually paralysed the Athenian expedition, and Hermocrates was further encouraged by the unenterprising conduct of Nicias, who after an initial victory ordered his army back to Catana, leaving Syracuse time to make its preparations for resistance.

Both sides spent the winter seeking allies in the region. Thucydides pictures a meeting in neutral Camarina at which, while an Athenian envoy blatantly asserted his own state's naked self-interest, Hermocrates put forward his Pan-Sicilian policy which involved the total exclusion of Athens from the island; whether or not he had already formulated this proposition in 424 he did so now. 'When', he is reported as saying, 'fellow Sicilians who live at a distance from us are destroyed first, do we imagine that the danger will not subsequently come to each of us in our turn?'[4] And he was also at pains (as on previous occasions) to dispel the suspicion that what he was really after was the supremacy of Syracuse, by which he still meant, said his political enemies, the dominance of the Syracusan oligarchs – and of himself.

Hampered by these internal frictions, Hermocrates was not able to do as much as he should have to prepare for the inevitable siege of his city, although he made some progress in the badly needed tasks of equipping and training the Syracusan hoplites and navy. Moreover, he also succeeded in reforming the city's system of military command, so that the board of fifteen annually elected generals was replaced by himself and two others, entrusted with full powers, which were, in fact, largely concentrated in his own hands.

But he also performed a remarkable task of self-denial – realizing that his own gifts as a general were not unlimited – by urging Sparta to provide the Syracusans with a new commander-in-chief. This they did, sending Gylippus, a short, undistinguished-looking man of dubious antecedents, but a competent and energetic officer. Gylippus brought with him a small Spartan contingent (later strengthened by picked helots (Appendix IV) and freedmen), and other elements of his force came from Corinth and Boeotia. Athens, too, reinforced its invading army by ten triremes, under Eurymedon, at the end of the year, and then dispatched its ablest general Demosthenes, bringing sixty-five more triremes and a hoplite reinforcement.

The siege of Syracuse involved three separate though interconnected issues: the domination of the Great Harbour, the control of the overlooking heights of Epipolae, and a circumvallation which both sides were laboriously endeavouring to erect round the city, in accordance with standard military procedure. But as the year 413 wore on, it became clear that the Syracusans were gaining the advantage, both on sea and on land. They were on their home ground and their own shores, whereas the army of the Athenians (and the same would have applied to the forces of any other Greek city-state) did not possess the equipment or supply organization or morale to pursue prolonged campaigns abroad. As their spirits seriously flagged, and epidemics incapacitated them still further, the Syracusans won decisive victories.

In the end the Athenian generals, no longer able to escape by sea, decided (too late) to retreat by land. The result was a total disaster. Many soldiers were slaughtered, in or beside the River Assinarus; and the two generals Nicias and Demosthenes became prisoners of war and – against the advice of Gylippus and Hermocrates – were put to death. Seven thousand of their men, captured at the same time, were confined in the limestone quarries of Syracuse, where many perished during the winer. Only a very few managed to get home.

'This', declared Thucydides, 'was the greatest Hellenic action that took place during this war, and, in my opinion, the greatest action that we know of in Hellenic history.'[5] And he went on to say that to the victors it was the most brilliant of successes, and to the vanquished the most calamitous of defeats. Amid epic and tragic overtones (Chapter 23), he stresses the total nature of the catastrophe that had overtaken the Athenians. Through the mediocre incompetence both of Nicias in the field and of the Assembly at home, they had lost one-third of their total military potential, and most of their navy.

Yet, even after this shattering defeat, their resources still did not prove to be exhausted nor their resilience undermined, since the weakness and poverty of Sparta made it possible for them to go on fighting the Peloponnesian War for another nine years.

Moreover, writing as he does from the Athenian standpoint (like many a historian after him), Thucydides does not lay sufficient weight on his other assertion: that to the winning, Sicilian side this was the most brilliant of successes. Together with the victory over the Persians at Himera (480), it was the outstanding military triumph in the history of Syracuse. Just as Himera had saved the city, and all western Greeks, from the domination of Carthage, so these events of 415–413 had rescued them and their rich good life from forcible domination by Athens.

Whether it would have been better for them, in the long run, and for humankind in general, if they had succumbed to the invaders and suffered incorporation in the empire of Athens (which could then, with the help of Sicilian grain and money, have won the Peloponnesian War) is, like other historical might-have-beens, too hypothetical to be worth exploring. What the Syracusan victory had achieved, however, was something very concrete: that the western Greeks and their cities would continue upon their vivid, turbulent history, without any further effective interference from the Greek mainland states.

Hermocrates, the most influential citizen of Syracuse, whose share in the victorious process had been so essential, came to the sordid end that so often awaited Greek saviours. True, after the Spartan Gylippus had disappeared into the anonymity from which he had come (subsequently to be convicted of embezzlement, and dying in exile), Syracuse expressed its gratitude to the Spartans by sending a squadron under Hermocrates to help them against Athens. But while he was away, his political enemies, now under Diocles – swept into power by the triumphant Syracusan rowers, who had won the war against the Athenians – pushed through radical democratic reforms, including the use of the lot (reforms, ironically enough, of an Athenian character) and sentenced Hermocrates to banishment.

Not long afterwards, taking advantage of a Carthaginian invasion of Sicily – which caused the destruction of Himera and Selinus and enabled pan-Greek feelings to be whipped up against the invaders – Hermocrates returned to Sicily on his own initiative, bringing five triremes and 1,000 mercenaries, and earned wealth and popularity by plundering Carthaginian territory on the island.

Although, however, the Syracusans banished Diocles, they did not recall or reinstate Hermocrates, who tried to force his way into the city and was killed. Despite his uncompromising patriotism in earlier times, Syracusan charges asserting that, in the end, he was aiming at the establishment of a personal dictatorship cannot be dismissed as entirely implausible. But it was a shabby end for a man who seems to have been, as Thucydides believed, one of the outstanding personages of fifth-century Greek life.

CHAPTER 17

SOPHOCLES: HARROWED HEROES AND HEROINES

The son of Sophilus, a rich weapon manufacturer from Colonus outside Athens, Sophocles (*c*.496–406) learned music from Lampros, the most renowned musician of the time, and possibly studied tragic drama under Aeschylus (Chapter 7). Good-looking and courteous, he was a friend of Pericles, and served in a series of important public posts: *Hellenotamias* (collector of allied tribute) in 443/442, general in 440 (sharing the command against insurgent Samos) and again later, commissioner (*proboulos*) to deal with the emergency after the Syracusan expedition (Chapter 16). He was also a priest, and served as envoy to other Greek states.

A hundred and thirty plays (of which seven later ceased to be regarded as authentic) were attributed to his long career. In dramatic competitions twenty-four of his tetralogies (groups of four plays) were victorious. Each tetralogy consisted of three tragic dramas and a satyr-play. But Sophocles abandoned Aeschylus' custom (Chapter 7) of presenting three connected, serial tragedies at a time, instead envisaging each of the three plays, which he presented on a single occasion, as an artistic unit in itself.

Seven of his tragedies (as well as a large part of one satyr-play, the *Ichneutae* or Searching Satyrs) have survived. They extend over a period of four decades of his life, but are all relatively late, representing the maturer phases of his art.

His *Ajax* was written in the 440s. When Achilles was killed towards the end of the Trojan War, the play recalls, there was competition for his weapons and armour. Ajax claimed them, on the grounds that he was the bravest fighter in the Greek army. But they were awarded to Odysseus instead, and Ajax vowed vengeance against him and against those who had chosen him for the prize. However, the goddess Athena, angered (although she was his patron) by his rejection of divine help, afflicted him with madness, so that he mistook cattle for his enemies and attacked them.

When Ajax recovered from these hallucinations, he insisted on committing suicide, out of shame. His captive and mistress Tecmessa, and the chorus consisting of his sailors from Salamis, failed to dissuade him, and after summoning his son Eurysaces he prepared to die. Then, however, a messenger brought a report from the seer Calchas that if only Ajax will stay in his tent for one day all may still be well. But it was too late, and Tecmessa found him already dead. Menelaus, with the support of his brother, the commander-in-chief Agamemnon, refused to allow the body to be buried. Yet Odysseus persuaded them to relent, and Ajax was carried by his sailors to his grave.

Athena's gloating attitude causes a shock, and Agamemnon and Menelaus show distasteful vindictiveness, though Tecmessa is an appealing figure. Everything centres, however, on the personality of Ajax, confronted with a typical Sophoclean issue. His excessive strength, ruined by his own limitations and ignorance, destroys him; though his grandeur is acknowledged and ratified, his presumptuous self-assertion means that there can be no escape from the fatal blow.

Sophocles, in his own way, is tracing the transition from a primitive code towards the *polis* ethic of his own day. For Ajax had been a hero in the ancient meaning of the word, belonging to an age that has passed away – and Ajax himself came to realize that in this new epoch there was no room for a heroic personage like himself any longer.

In 441 Sophocles wrote the *Antigone*, the earliest of his three great surviving tragedies taken from the Theban mythological cycle.

After the abdication of Oedipus from the throne of Thebes, his son Polynices, one of the Seven Against Thebes (the title of one of Aeschylus' plays), had endeavoured, with the help of the Argives, to capture the city from his brother Eteocles. The two brothers, however, slew one another in single combat, and their uncle Creon, who succeeded to the throne, forbade anyone to bury the corpse of Polynices under pain of death. As in Aeschylus' *Seven*, however, the dead man's sister Antigone is determined to defy the order and carry out his funeral rites.

But she is caught in the act and taken before Creon, to whom she justifies her action on the grounds of sacred natural law overriding mere human enactments. Yet the king condemns her, and she is sentenced to be walled into a cave until she dies. Her sister Ismene, who had refused to participate in her defiant deed, nevertheless now demands to share her penalty. Creon's son Haemon, too, who is betrothed to Antigone, after pleading vainly with his father rushes out to perish beside her. The blind seer Tiresias warns Creon of the heavy consequences of contravening the divine law. Impressed by this admonition Creon reverses his attitude, and hastens to the cave where Antigone is immured. But he finds that she has already hanged herself. Haemon, discovered embracing her dead body, strikes out at his father with his sword, and then he, too, takes his own life. Then Creon, returning to the palace, finds that his wife, Eurydice, has committed suicide as well.

Although the specific issue involved, the rites of burial, meant more to the ancient Athenians than it means to us, this remains an ever-memorable confrontation between the requirements of state or society and the superior claims of universal morality. In the terms used by contemporary sophists (Chapter 12), whose thinking was well-known to Sophocles, the confrontation is between the limited claims of man-made law and custom (*nomos*) and the transcendent demands of eternally valid natural principle (*physis*). Both Antigone and Creon have cases to make, and make them with passionate, eloquent conviction. But Creon, flawed by expediency and over-confident *hubris* (see below), is trying to correct a moral standard that is beyond his control, and Antigone, though harsh, impetuous and ferociously stubborn, is not only self-sacrificing but right. This play is a hymn to humanity: 'Many wonders there are,' declares the chorus, 'but nothing more wonderful than a human being.'[6]

All this questioning of public authority against private conscience gave the Athenians much to ponder upon, at a time when multitudinous issues of legitimacy and obligation were raised year after year as the Athenian democratic empire went its heady, confident way; and each issue had to be measured against the yardstick of right and wrong. Not that Sophocles is equating Creon with Athens or Pericles – he is too subtle for that: it is only obliquely, though forcefully, that the play tackles the issues of the time.

Oedipus the King (staged shortly after 430) deals with an earlier epoch in the same Theban family's history. Oedipus had departed from his earlier home at Corinth, where everyone supposed him to be King Polybus' son, in order to avoid fulfilling an oracle that declared he would slay his father and marry his mother. He went to Thebes, and there, after solving the riddle of the Sphinx – which had defeated everyone else – made himself ruler of the city.

After a number of years, however, impelled by the need to ward off a divinely inspired pestilence, he becomes convinced that its cause was the murder of his predecessor, Laius, struck down at a crossroads, and that he must therefore find out who had killed him. By gradual degrees, and particularly through the blind seer Tiresias (whose warnings Oedipus at first angrily rejects), it is revealed to him that he himself is the murderer of Laius, that Laius, and not as he believed Polybus, had been his father, and that by making Jocasta his wife he had married his own mother. What had been prophesied by the oracle has come about after all. Jocasta hangs herself; Oedipus puts out his own eyes, bids farewell to his two daughters, and is led away out of the city.

Oedipus is the foremost of all searchers after the truth. A self-made absolute ruler, who unaided had mastered seemingly insuperable obstacles, he moves with gradual, terrible inevitability from ignorant misconceived assurance to recognition, shattering knowledge and despair. Aristotle believed that this play was the model of what a tragic drama ought to be. It is the *hubris* of the courageous, resolute, iron-willed, hot-tempered Oedipus which causes his fault (the *hamartia* discussed by Aristotle; Chapter 37), and, despite all his attempts to shake and tug at the net, brings about a classic reversal of his condition, and overwhelms him in utter ruin – while conducting an investigation he had believed he ought not to shirk.

This demonstration of human fragility is conducted through an intricate plot possessing a uniquely lucid and concise structure, and leading through persistent imagery of light and darkness (truth and delusion) to its harrowing climax. This was the play that gave birth to Sigmund Freud's Oedipus Complex, the theory that love of mother and jealousy of father are the most potent of human instincts.

Sophocles' *Women of Trachis* (early 420s) is named after the chorus, who come from that region of central Greece. Deianira, its queen, is distressed by the prolonged absence of her husband Heracles, and plans to send their son Hyllus to look for him. But a messenger arrives to announce that Heracles is safe and sound, and on his way back to Trachis; after accomplishing mighty deeds, his herald Lichas reports, the hero is at present on the island of Euboea, gratefully dedicating an altar to Zeus. Lichas has brought captive women from Oechalia, and it becomes known to Deianira that one of them, Iole, is Heracles' mistress.

Deianira plans to win his love back by sending him a robe supposedly smeared with an aphrodisiac left her by the centaur Nessus when he died. But this substance is really a lethal poison, and Hyllus arrives to bring the news that Heracles has put the robe on and is perishing in agony. Deianira, in remorse, commits suicide, after commanding Hyllus to cremate his father's body and take Iole for himself.

Hyllus, in conclusion, vehemently blames the gods, who overwhelm even the greatest men with misfortunes, by which they themselves, however, remain unconcerned. Or worse: for this is a play in which the immortals, acting upon their own inscrutable, undetectable plans, have ensured that every step Heracles takes to escape his destiny brings him closer to its fulfilment. As for himself, he has shown himself to be too heroically self-centred; and Deianira is wrong-headed, because she believes that her magic can not only deceive men but frustrate the gods. It is a bleak, grim landscape, in which fierce emotions rage close beneath the surface and sometimes break through.

In the *Electra*, staged between 418 and 410, Orestes, of the House of Atreus, in the company of his friend Pylades, is approaching his native city of Mycenae (Argos), at the command of Apollo's Delphic oracle, in order to avenge his father Agamemnon's assassination by his mother Clytemnestra, the theme of Aeschylus' *Oresteia*.

The young men plan to visit Clytemnestra in disguise, inventing a story that Orestes is dead and that they are bringing his ashes. The queen and her daughter Electra are reviling one another when a messenger comes to bring the false information of Orestes' death. But Clytemnestra's other daughter Chrysothemis – who has tried to moderate Electra's bitterness – informs her sister that flowers and a lock of hair, which she has just seen at Agamemnon's grave, prove their brother is still alive. Electra remains unconvinced. But then Clytemnestra's dying shriek rings out, for Orestes and Pylades have struck her down, and, next, her lover Aegisthus, who has usurped the throne as her partner, is butchered in his turn. The women of Mycenae, who form the chorus of the play, welcome the upstart's murder, and hope it will mean that the curse on the House of Atreus comes to an end.

Sophocles does not allow himself to be too greatly disturbed by the matricide, which, though painful, is just and necessary. There is a lot of cruelty in the play, and courage, and suffering, and extremities both of hate and of love. The plot is excellently constructed. Among a group of characters who no longer seem remote creatures of myth but show human strengths and weaknesses, Electra may not always look like the central figure, but she is skilfully portrayed, all the same, from several different angles.

The hero who gave his name to the *Philoctetes* (409) had been left behind on the island of Lemnos by the Greek army on its way to Troy, nine years before the play began, because a snakebite had put him out of action; and only his possession of Heracles' bow and arrows had saved him from starving to death. But a seer foretold that Troy would fall only when Neoptolemus, Achilles' son, and Philoctetes – with the bow of Heracles – joined the expedition. Odysseus, therefore, was sent by the Greek army to Lemnos, accompanied reluctantly by Neoptolemus, who then obtained possession of Philoctetes' weapons by a trick – which he subsequently confessed to his stricken victim in remorse, insisting that he himself, by way of compensation, will take him back to Greece. At this juncture, however, Heracles, now a god, made his appearance, with orders from Zeus that they should both instead proceed to Troy, where the bow would, indeed, bring the Greeks victory; and so Philoctetes, assured that his wound would be cured, complied with the divine command.

The *Philoctetes* is the most dramatically complex of all Sophocles' tragedies, and its psychological accuracy and sympathy make it appealing to modern readers and audiences. The play shows human beings going through their motions, and attempting to plan the future, upon the basis of inadequate knowledge, amid an atmosphere of persuasion, deception and violence that must have made Athenian spectators reflect upon the degradations of their own war-convulsed world.

Philoctetes is torn between his longing to rejoin his own comrades and his bitterness at having been cast away from them. The dilemma of the young Neoptolemus, on the other hand, is between a noble aim and ignoble means; and he witnesses the death of his ideals, at the hands of Odysseus, whose amoral dishonesty recalled the worst sort of contemporary sophist (Chapter 12). The chorus, composed of Neoptolemus' sailors, is unusually involved in the play's action.

The *Oedipus at Colonus*, the last play of Sophocles, was performed in 401 after his death. The story is a sequel of *Oedipus the King*, at the end of which he had blinded himself and departed from Thebes. Now, a ragged beggar, after years of wandering from place to place, he arrives at Colonus, near Athens, led by his daughter Antigone. The elders of Colonus, the chorus of the play, go to see him, but are horror-struck when they learn who he is, and order him to leave, though when he appeals to Athenian hospitality they agree to await the decision of King Theseus. Theseus promises to help him, and frustrates Creon, who has arrived from Thebes to seize both the blind former monarch and Antigone (her sister Ismene has already been captured). Next comes Oedipus' son Polynices (whose subsequent history had been the background of the *Antigone*) to seek his father's blessing, but Oedipus rejects him and curses both his grasping sons.

Thunderclaps tell Oedipus that his hour has come, and attended by Theseus and his daughters he leads the way to the place where he will depart from the land of the living. Halfway he bids Antigone and Ismene farewell, and what happened next no one but Theseus knew; but, according to a messenger's report, Oedipus was taken by the gods.

Their justice has the last word; but we are not in a position to understand how it works. For this, the last testament of Sophocles, is the most mysterious of his plays. Oedipus is far from a saint, as his continuing vindictiveness towards his sons confirms. Yet the story of *Oedipus the King* has been modified, so that now he can declare he is sinned against and not sinning: his tragic suffering justified and made meaningful by nobility of character, he has moved onwards from utter isolation to ultimate divine acceptance.

At the time of Athens' downfall the dramatist makes Theseus utter these poignantly nostalgic words to Creon: 'You have come into a *polis* that cultivates justice and sanctions nothing without law.'[7] And this new, monstrous Creon comes from Thebes, which, in real life, was still the bitter enemy of defeated Athens (Chapter 24).

Stage spectacle must have played an important part in Sophocles' technique. He also introduced a third actor on to the stage, which presented the opportunity to develop more complex situations and plots than Aeschylus had been able to provide. These plots display rapid development and taut, economic, succinct unity; and Sophocles' style and diction displayed an infinitely flexible versatility.

Athenian audiences knew the myths that he handled, and were aware, therefore, of the likely progress of events – in contrast to the personages on the stage. The plays, therefore, operated on two levels of meaning summed up by the term 'tragic irony' – illustrating the gulfs and contradictions between the apparent and the real – for which Sophocles is supremely notable. The chorus, much more than the dramatist's mouthpiece, and more, too, than a negative or detached observer, often arrives on the stage in a mood of agitated uncertainty or questioning. Its lyrical, prodigally inventive odes are employed to offer wider, profounder perspectives, to fuse action and emotion together, and to display the traditional myths as frameworks of human strivings and confrontations.

As for the mythical characters who live out these strenuous endeavours, they are not depicted with elaborate subtlety but present stark contrasts that accord primacy to action rather than to character. When character, however, is stressed, it is stressed in order to delineate the ethical qualities and principles that prompt these personages to work out their terrible dilemmas between the demands of their states, their families, their own aspirations – and the will of the gods.

Calamities such as the downfalls of Deianira and Oedipus come when the divine order has somehow been flouted, by mulish fixity of human purpose or self-seeking violence, or even by involuntary, injudicious action. In contexts full of arbitrary unawareness, we cannot always detect when or why this fault has been committed, or whether or why its unbearable divine punishment is just. Yet, whatever the answers to these desperate questions, the will of the gods has to be accepted, because, although its expression may seem morally neutral or, even menacingly worse, it nevertheless embodies the ineluctable, however puzzling, order of events.

The helpless suffering thus caused, Sophocles believed, is ultimately beneficial, because it teaches how things are, and how they take their course. And besides, the sufferer's virtues – even if they have contributed disastrously to his downfall – can exhibit tragic dignity and glorious heroism, larger than life. All too often there is no consolation or redemption or escape. Yet there can also be an eventual, solemn reconciliation, as in the conclusion of the *Oedipus at Colonus*, embodying the latest and last of Sophocles' lifelong hard thinking.

Two types of portrait-bust supposedly representing the playwright date from later periods of antiquity, and are represented by copies. Both versions, however, are imaginary. The 'Farnese type' is exemplified by a fine bronze head from Asia Minor, probably of the second century BC, in the British Museum. The 'Lateran type' is represented by a full-length marble statue, of Roman times, which goes back to a bronze set up in the Athenian theatre in *c*.340, over sixty years after Sophocles' death.

These heads form part of a tradition that has been misleading. For they depict him as tranquil and serene, the dramatic poet as it was felt that a dramatic poet ought to look, a man seeing life steadily and seeing it whole, in the words of Matthew Arnold. But this sort of outdated appraisal of Sophocles pays too little attention to the bleak and tortured pain which his view of the universe reflects, mirroring agonized conflicts that have evoked deeply felt reinterpretations in our own troubled times.

CHAPTER 18

EURIPIDES: DRAMATIC CHALLENGER

Euripides (485/480–406) belonged to a family of hereditary priests which owned a property on the island of Salamis. In sharp contrast to Sophocles (Chapter 17), he was a loner who played no part in public Athenian affairs, apart from once, perhaps, going to Syracuse as a member of a delegation. He was said to have written eighty-eight or ninety plays, of which seventeen or eighteen complete tragedies and one satyr-play (the *Cyclops*) survive. But he won very few dramatic victories – only four in his lifetime, and one after his death. That may have been partly why, shortly before he died, he went to live at the court of Archelaus, King of Macedonia (408).

In the *Alcestis* (438) Apollo, temporarily banished from Olympus and working as a shepherd for King Admetus of Pherae in Thessaly – whose elders form the chorus of the play – has induced the Fates to promise that Admetus may escape death, when the time comes, if a substitute will volunteer to die in his place. His wife Alcestis offers this sacrifice, and Thanatos (Death) arrives to claim his victim. But Heracles, visiting Pherae, goes off to rescue her, and when she and Admetus have been reunited he leaves them, and proceeds on his way.

The *Alcestis*, which was substituted for a satyr-play but can, with some difficulty, be classified as a tragedy, links the themes of two fairy-tales into a bold and exciting whole.

Heracles is exploited both for tragic and comic material. But the human characters show that a new playwright has arrived. The magnanimous courage and devotion of Alcestis lead the way to many of Euripides' later psychological studies of strong-minded women, good and bad. As for Admetus, he seems scandalously unheroic – until we realize that, in the ancient Greek view, the survival of the family took precedence over any single woman's fate; and besides, at the end, he sees his weakness shatteringly laid bare.

The *Medea* is named after the daughter of King Aeetes of Colchis in the Caucasus, who in order to help Jason of Iolcus in Thessaly, leader of the Argonaut expedition, to gain possession of the Golden Fleece, has left her father and murdered her brother. After Jason seized the Fleece, she accompanied him on his homeward journey – and arranged the death of his hostile uncle Pelias, king of Iolcus. Since then, she had continued to be a loyal wife to Jason, and had borne him two sons. But now, at Corinth (whose women provide the play's chorus), he intends to cast her aside – pointing out that she is only a foreigner – in favour of Creusa, daughter of the Corinthian King Creon.

Fearing her powers as a witch, Creon orders her to be banished, but she persuades him to let her stay until the following morning. After assailing Jason with devastating abuse, she is offered refuge by a visitor, the Athenian King Aegeus. Instead of leaving Corinth, however, she assassinates Creusa with a poisoned robe, puts Creon to death in the same way, and kills her children with her own hands. At the end of the play, she miraculously appears above the stage, in a fiery chariot sent by her grandfather Helios the Sun-god; and Jason, who has been swearing vengeance, is left vainly lamenting her cruelty.

The *Medea*, like the *Alcestis*, is a play of simple construction, with its principal scenes astutely balanced. It deals with a novel theme, the power of passion, in the heart of a woman transformed into a fiend by an intolerable wrong. Medea, before her bloodthirsty actions, undergoes a dramatic internal conflict – one of the first of such psychological dilemmas ever to have been so fully and harrowingly described. She knows exactly what she is doing, so we may assume that Euripides, as part of his habitual discussion of ideas, is contesting Socrates' assertion that 'no one does wrong willingly' (Chapter 21).

Or was she really doing wrong? To what extent can violent personal retaliation against gross social injustice be justified? And what pride can one take in being a civilized Greek like Jason, when, although he is constantly pointing out how foreign Medea is, his own behaviour is what has brought out her savagery? He is a smug, snobbish and ungrateful character, a good deal worse than Admetus in the *Alcestis*.

The *Heraclidae* (*c*.429/427) is named after the children of Heracles who are persecuted, as their father had been, by King Eurystheus of Argos and Mycenae. Together with Heracles' mother Alcmena they have taken refuge at the temple of Zeus at Marathon, where Demophon, king of Athens, grants them sanctuary. Eurystheus, whom Demophon will not allow to see them, threatens war against the Athenians, and an oracle declares that, to avoid defeat at his hands, a noble maiden must be sacrificed to the underworld goddess Persephone. Heracles' daughter Macaria dedicates herself to this destiny, and the Athenians repulse and capture Eurystheus, whom, despite remonstrations from the chorus of old men of Marathon, they then put to death, on Alcmena's insistence. The *Children of Heracles* seems hastily written, since its various themes are not knitted together into a coherent whole. The heroes do not make a favourable showing, but the self-sacrifice of Macaria (like that of Alcestis in the earlier play) is moving, and, as in the *Medea*, there is heartfelt praise of Athens, in these early years of the Peloponnesian War.

The *Hippolytus* (428) takes its name from the son of King Theseus of Athens and the Amazon Hippolyte, who has rejected the overtures of Aphrodite and admires only Artemis, virgin goddess of the chase. The chorus of the play are huntsmen. Aphrodite, vengefully, makes his stepmother, Phaedra, fall in love with him, though Phaedra keeps her passion secret, until, by accident, she lets her nurse know how she feels. The nurse informs Hippolytus, and when Phaedra learns that she has told him, she hangs herself. To get her own back, however, against him, she leaves a statement that he had raped her. This was untrue, but his father Theseus banishes him, and prays for his death. Thereupon Hippolytus, setting out into exile, is dragged by his horses – frightened by Poseidon coming out of the sea – and suffers grave injuries. But now Artemis appears and reveals to Theseus the innocence of his son, who dies reconciled with his father.

In this tragedy, two virtuous people, Hippolytus and Phaedra, perish largely because of their virtue. Hippolytus has remained fastidiously, even priggishly, chaste; and Phaedra dies of shame when her feelings are known. The message she leaves behind her does great evil, and this and her sexual obsession have contributed largely to Euripides' reputation as a misogynist: though he is neither attacking nor defending her infatuation but clinically recording its dire results. And her dying message has another significance for the playwright as well, for it shows what damage is done by misinformation, causing Theseus to decide upon a fatal act – out of ignorance – that proves to have disastrous effects.

The play is also full of debate and colouring that owe debts to the sophists (Chapter 12). 'My tongue has sworn, but my brain has not' earned especially scathing satire from the comic dramatist Aristophanes (Chapter 19), as an illustration of how speakers could argue a wrong cause and make it sound right.[8]

In the *Andromache* (430/424) Hermione and her father Menelaus, King of Sparta, plan to murder Molossus, the child of her absent husband Neoptolemus (son of Achilles) by the captured Trojan Princess Andromache. Andromache flees for sanctuary to the altar of Thetis (mother of Achilles and grandmother of Neoptolemus) beside Neoptolemus' palace at Phthia in Thessaly, of which the maidens comprise the play's chorus. Tricked by the would-be murderers of Molossus into leaving the sanctuary, Andromache and her child are condemned to death. But Peleus, the husband of Thetis, comes to rescue them, despite the arrival of Menelaus, who offers unfeeling objections. Hermione, in despair, is afraid of her husband Neoptolemus' anger, and plans to commit suicide, but her cousin Orestes dissuades and reassures her, and plots Neoptolemus' death – which, however, a messenger reports, has already come about at Delphi. The play ends with a divine epiphany of Thetis, who foretells a royal future for the descendants of Andromache and Molossus in Epirus.

The *Andromache* is by no means a well-constructed tragedy because it displays a triptych of successive and more or less separate themes, which are not resolved into a unity, while each of the main characters receive examination in turn, at critical junctures. But even if it lacks dramatic unity, the *Andromache* concentrates on a single idea, very welcome during the Peloponnesian War: and that idea is the nastiness of Sparta, exemplified by Menelaus, who is portrayed as a disagreeable stage villain.

The beginning of the *Hecuba* (*Hecabe*, *c*.425/424), named after the Trojan monarch Priam's wife and queen – now a captive of the Greeks – witnesses the appearance of the ghost of their son Polydorus, assassinated by Polymestor of Thrace, to whom he had been dispatched for safety. This phantom Polydorus discloses that the victorious Greek fleet can sail away from Troy only if his sister Polyxena is sacrificed on his grave; and Odysseus leads her off to her death. But Hecabe entices Polymestor to her tent, where she and her attendant women (the chorus) put out his eyes and assassinate his two sons. Agamemnon, the Greek commander-in-chief, pronounces that justice has been done, and the blinded Polymestor is cast off on a desert island, but not before prophesying that both Agamemnon and Hecabe will come to a bad end.

The *Hecuba*, like the *Andromache*, has been criticized for lack of unity, since one episode follows another in a more or less disconnected fashion. But once again, amid all the sophisticated discussion, there is a single persistent theme, and this time it is psychological. For the play is dominated by the figure of Hecabe, whose character we see disintegrating under the pressure of disaster – disaster brought about by the harsh necessities of war, destroying the habits (*nomoi*) of decent behaviour: so that her suffering is transformed into bestial, murderous fury.

The *Suppliant Women* (*c*.422/421) reverts to the mythical stories of the Theban cycle, immortalized by Aeschylus' *Seven Against Thebes* and by

Sophocles' *Antigone*. The attack on the city and its ruler Eteocles (Oedipus' son) by his brother Polynices, supported by his Argive allies, has failed, and the Theban leadership has refused burial to the bodies of its assailants. Their mothers, the suppliants who give the play its title and form its (very active) chorus, come to Athens, led by King Adrastus of Argos – the father-in-law of Polynices – in order to beg Theseus, the ruler of Athens, to induce Thebes to relent and allow the burials. Theseus finally agrees to place their plea before the Athenian Assembly. When, however, he requests the Thebans to hand over the corpses, they refuse, and tell him to expel Adrastus from his kingdom. Theseus will not do so, and wins the war that follows. The Seven are ceremonially cremated, and Adrastus, by order of Athena, swears that Argos will never fight Athens again.

This was topical, for whereas Thebes was the Athenians' enemy, Argos had not joined Sparta against them, and the Peace of Nicias (421) was soon to be followed by an alliance between the Argives and Athenians. The Peace, although shortlived, was evidently in the playwright's mind, for the play contains a good deal of pacifism. No tragedy is so full of political and ethical discussion. Aethra, the mother of Theseus, agrees with Sophocles' Antigone that burial rites form a supreme obligation imposed by nature (*physis*), but Theseus himself eloquently defends the laws and customs (*nomoi*) of Athens, which ensure equality and freedom of speech.

Heracles or *Mad Heracles* (*Hercules Furens*) was performed in *c.*420. While Heracles is absent, Lycus, King of the Thebans (whose elders supply the chorus of the play), plans to slaughter the hero's family, using fire to force them out of the sanctuary to which they have fled. Heracles returns in time to save them, and puts Lycus to death. Now, however, Iris (the messenger of the gods) and Lyssa (Madness) appear, ordered by the goddess Hera, Heracles' foe since his birth, to drive her heroic enemy insane so that he will slay his own wife and children. This he does, only sparing his father Amphitryon, because Athena hurled a stone which knocked Heracles out just in time. When he recovers consciousness, his mental balance has returned, and he is persuaded not to commit suicide by Theseus, who offers him a home at Athens.

Once again constructed in the form of a triptych, the *Mad Heracles* presents a pathological study of madness. The tragic vulnerability of all human achievement, which, in historical fact, had so often caused the jealous Athenians to cut their own eminent citizens down, is all too clear, and a series of shocking reversals illustrate the fluctuations of the noble but flawed Heracles' destiny. Viewing the end of the play, moreover, just after the Peace of Nicias, Athenians may well have detected a hoped-for reconciliation between Athens (Theseus) and its historic Peloponnesian foes (Heracles).

The *Trojan Women* (415) is named after the chorus of the play, comprising the fellow prisoners of Queen Hecabe (see the *Hecuba* above); the herald Talthybius arrives to name the Greek leaders to whom they have been assigned as slaves. But Astyanax, whose father was the queen's dead son Hector, is torn from the arms of his mother Andromache and slain, and Menelaus, king of Sparta, comes to take back Helen, whose elopement with Paris had caused the war. The city of Troy goes up in flames, into which Hecabe despairingly, but vainly, attempts to hurl herself. Then the lamenting captive women move down to the Greek ships. Yet their prospects of a safe journey to their victors' land remain precarious, since Athena has engaged the help of Poseidon – who, like her, is angry with the Greeks – to wreck their homeward journey.

The emotional and lyrical power of the *Trojan Women* has ranked it among Euripides' masterpieces. It was performed in the very year when Athens was so confidently launching its Syracusan expedition, but does not contain the deliberate topicalities that hindsight might lead us to expect. Euripides' indictment is more general: the play's unrelieved portrayal of intense and agonized feeling adds up to a devastating attack on war and on the human cruelty and misery that come in its wake.

Greeks are not made to seem inferior to foreign 'barbarians' – on the contrary (as in the *Medea*). Moreover, it is a foreign figure, Hecabe, who provides the unifying element: and it is she who shows that among these horrors of war it is women who suffer worst. A meaningless and pitiless destiny seems to be at work. No wonder Hecabe describes Zeus as 'past our finding out – whether you are the necessity of nature or the mind of human beings'.[9] In her downfall, the gods had seemed indifferent, and had not listened to her.

In Euripides' *Electra* (413), the woman this drama is named after, following the murder of her father Agamemnon, King of Argos, by her mother Clytemnestra, had been obliged to marry a peasant. But her brother Orestes in disguise, back from banishment with his friend Pylades, overhears her bemoaning her fate: and, after he has been recognized by an old servant, he and she are happily reunited. Orestes and Pylades slaughter Aegisthus, Clytemnestra's lover and joint ruler, while Clytemnestra, not yet knowing that this has happened, attempts to justify her slaying of Agamemnon to Electra, but in vain. Then her daughter escorts her into her hut, where the two young men put her to death.

But Orestes feels remorseful horror, and so do Electra and the chorus of Argive women. Clytemnestra's divine brothers, the Dioscuri (Castor and Polydeuces), proclaim that the deed itself had been just, but that Orestes should not have killed his own mother. For this, they foretell, he will suffer prolonged harassment from the Furies (Erinyes), before eventually attaining his freedom.

Whether Euripides' *Electra* was written before or after Sophocles' play of the same name is uncertain. But the play of Euripides lowers its story firmly from mythological unreality into the seediness of an all too painful human situation. Like Sophocles' heroine, Electra is ravaged with grief, but whereas Sophocles had invested her matricidal vengeance with a spiritual exaltation, it is now abased to an unglamorous domestic level, thus deftly enabling Euripides to indulge his taste for realism to the full. Clytemnestra is weary and regretful, Aegisthus opportunistic and vicious. This unrelievedly disagreeable analysis of warped minds seemed to Schlegel a piece of 'monumental poetic perversity'. Yet the playwright has a purpose in thus degrading his characters. It is not so much, as some have believed, to blame the gods, as to show how the human personality degenerates and falls to pieces under the pressures of mutual, retaliatory hatreds.

According to this *Electra*, and many other tragedies, Clytemnestra had murdered Agamemnon because he sacrificed their daughter Iphigenia at Aulis, so that the gods should permit the Greek fleet to sail to Troy. In Euripides' more or less contemporary *Iphigenia in Tauris* (414/412), however, Iphigenia, accompanied by captive girls (the chorus of the play), explains that this had never happened at all, but that Artemis had magically removed her to Tauris (the Tauric Chersonese), where King Thoas had given her the task of massacring every visiting stranger as a sacrifice to the goddess.

Her brother Orestes arrives, with Pylades, to purloin Artemis' statue for Athens, by order of Apollo. They are caught, however, and handed over to Iphigenia, who recognizes them; and they all escape. Thoas orders their capture, but Athena appears, declares to him that it was by the divine aid of Poseidon that they had been able to depart, and bids them go on their way to Attica, where they shall each be linked with a sacred cult.

With this beautifully constructed play, replete with suspense and dramatic irony, Euripides has entered a phase in which we are regaled with intricate, romantic intrigues, and surprises, and recognitions, and touches of sentiment, that seem closer to Menander's New Comedy of the next century than to classical tragedy. Despite the reminder of the faraway Trojan War, and reminders, also, of Athenian patriotic feeling, the dominant theme of the *Iphigenia in Tauris* is pure escapism, remote from the contemporary grimness of the Peloponnesian War. For we are far away, in an exotic foreign land, where the hero and heroine, amid the mysteries of divine guidance, excitingly triumph over every obstacle to arrive at a happy ending. The dramatist depicts his chosen course of events in characteristically realistic detail, and yet he is also performing what had become, at this period of his life, his favourite trick, the counterbalancing of realism by illusion. Iphigenia's destiny had not been what we thought it was; and so perhaps Euripides is reassuring his fellow citizens, amid wartime anxieties and austerities, that things need not always be as bad as they seem.

In the *Helen* (412), by the same token, that heroine explains that she had never left for Troy with Paris after all; it was only a phantom that he carried off, while she herself had been escorted to Egypt by the god Hermes. There, accompanied by captive Greek maidens (once again the chorus of the play), she sought sanctuary at the tomb of the late Egyptian King Proteus, to escape the lecherous attentions of his son, the present monarch Theoclymenus. Her husband Menelaus, shipwrecked, totters on to the stage, and eventually accepts that she is the real Helen (whereupon the false one, whom he believed that he had rescued from Troy, vanishes into thin air). He and Helen, reunited after so many years, escape on a ship Helen has borrowed. Theoclymenus tries to stop them, but her brothers Castor and Polydeuces, the Dioscuri, appear and command him to bow to fate, foretelling that Helen will become a divinity like themselves.

The play named after her is another piece of fairy-tale gaiety and illusion, imaginatively pitted against realistic excitements. Once again the heroine has not fared as we thought she had, although in this case the variation, distancing her from the Trojan War, goes back to the sixth-century poet Stesichorus of Himera, whose *Recantation* had supplied this more respectable version of what happened to Helen, so as not to give offence to those who revered her as a goddess. Once again, too, the heroine tricks a barbarous king and escapes from him into eventual salvation. This is an amusing work; and it has even been suggested that Euripides is parodying his own *Iphigenia in Tauris*.

Ion, from whom another play (*c.*411?) takes its name, is the son of Apollo and the Athenian Princess Creusa, who gave birth to him secretly in a cave. The god Hermes takes the infant to Apollo's priest at Delphi, where he grows up and works as an acolyte in the temple. Creusa and her husband Xuthus come to Delphi and meet Ion. They do not know who he is, but Xuthus acclaims him because, according to Apollo's oracle, the first person whom he is going to encounter upon leaving the shrine will be his own son. Creusa, however, resenting this introduction of a strange youth (as she believes) into the family, speaks critically of Apollo. Then, however, she notices a chest she had left with Ion as a baby, and understands who he really is. Athena, too, tells Ion that Apollo is his father, and orders him and Xuthus and Creusa to depart for Athens, where the Ionians will be his descendants. His mother, and her husband Xuthus, will become the ancestors of those other main branches of the Greek people, the Dorians and Achaeans.

The *Ion* is another elaborately complicated drama, containing a recognition theme which again seems more akin to the New Comedy of the next century than to the classical tragic theatre – like the subject matter of the *Iphigenia in Tauris*, although here we have left its distant scenes (and those of the *Helen*) behind, and are back in Greece itself. Indeed, we are at its holiest place, Apollo's Delphi. And yet this is one of the plays which caused Euripides to be regarded as sceptical about the gods, for Apollo, although Creusa managed to praise him in the end, had behaved, and she thought so herself, extremely shabbily. Or are we to take the more elevated view that his seduction of Creusa was ultimately a beneficial and ennobling act, since it infused humanity, and the Ionians of the future, with the glory of a divine origin?

The *Phoenician Women* (*c*.410) is named after its Tyrian chorus, who are once again connected to Delphi, since they are on the way to Apollo's service there. The play, however, reverts to the Theban mythological cycle, already the theme of the *Suppliant Women*.

Here we are at an earlier stage of the story, when, as Jocasta, the wife of the blinded Oedipus, recounts, her sons Eteocles and Polynices are at war. Polynices, with an army from Argos, has launched an assault – despite Jocasta's attempts to reconcile the pair of them, and the willingness of Menoeceus, King Creon's son, to offer himself as a propitiatory sacrifice. Eteocles and Polynices fall at each other's hands, and Jocasta commits suicide. Creon decrees that whoever grants burial rites to Polynices shall be executed. But the dead man's sister Antigone declares she will defy this order, as in Aeschylus' *Seven Against Thebes* and Sophocles' tragedy named after her, and at the end of the *Phoenician Women* she decides to lead her father into exile.

The *Phoenician Women* symbolizes better than any other of Euripides' dramas a period in which he packs increasingly abundant, indeed over-abundant, subject matter into vigorous and rapidly moving plots. No central figure is to be seen, but the various characters are sharply differentiated, the rival qualities of despotism and democracy are keenly debated, and the play's broad sweep encompasses a comprehensive, continuous stretch of Theban legend. Its narrative is exciting, but not tragic; a sort of mythical pageant, which continued to be popular throughout ancient times.

The *Orestes* (408) goes back to the theme of the *Electra*. After slaying his mother Clytemnestra and her lover Aegisthus, Orestes is tormented by the Furies (Erinyes), and his Argive (Mycenaean) compatriots have decided that he and his sister Electra must die. But now King Menelaus arrives at Argos, on his way back to Sparta, and when he fails to help them the pair plan to kill his wife Helen and kidnap their daughter Hermione – or put her to death as well – unless Menelaus changes his mind. However, Apollo makes his appearance, rescues Helen, and declares that Orestes, after suffering exile, will be tried and acquitted (with divine help) at Athens, and is then destined to marry Hermione and become the king of Argos. The chorus are Argive women.

The *Orestes* is Euripides' most melodramatic and exuberant *tour de force*, replete with novel theatrical effects and, in its later scenes, crammed with violence and crime. In antiquity it surpassed all other tragedies in popular esteem. Traditional mythology is stood on its head to display an all too human world steeped in venality and pitiless malice, where the interplay between one degenerate individual and another, and between their competitive wickednesses and demented loyalties, creates a debased squalor from which only divine intervention can bring release. What has seemed meaningless evil is woven into a significant pattern, so that the destiny of retribution is not, indeed, abandoned but integrated into a larger whole.

The *Iphigenia at Aulis* (performed in 406/405, after the dramatist's death) revives the theme of Iphigenia's sacrifice by her father Agamemnon, king of Argos (Mycenae), at Aulis in Boeotia, in order to assuage divine wrath and thus permit the Greek fleet to sail off to Troy – the story which Euripides himself, in his *Iphigenia in Tauris*, had declared to be fictitious.

In this new play, Agamemnon has written home to his wife Clytemnestra, ordering that their daughter be sent to him at Aulis. But now he has changed his mind, deciding that the girl's sacrifice would be intolerable. At this point, however, Iphigenia arrives with her mother, who is naturally appalled to hear of the plan. Yet that must be the maiden's end after all, Agamemnon explains, because the army insists on its necessity. So Iphigenia courageously goes to her death. But the messenger who comes to report the event adds that at the fatal moment she was no longer to be seen: nothing remained on the altar but a doe, bleeding to death.

Although a finely constructed theatrical piece, the *Iphigenia at Aulis* is nevertheless, and is meant to be, complex and confusing. Epic heroism is piquantly interwoven with modern human muddle, in which every character is enmeshed. A bewildering array of doubts and reversals is laced by alternations of pitying pathos and light-hearted entertainment.

This confirms the reader's impression, already suggested by earlier Euripidean productions, that tragedy is on the way out. Although censured by Aristotle,[10] the personality of Iphigenia is skilfully drawn. The chorus is composed of women from Chalcis in Euboea, who have come over to Aulis to see the fleet.

The *Bacchants* (*Bacchae*, shown posthumously in 405) are Asian Maenad women who form the chorus. They are attendants of the god Dionysus (Bacchus), who has returned from Asia to his native Thebes. Agave, the mother of King Pentheus, and her sisters had at first refused to acknowledge his divinity, but now instead, overwhelmed by the frenzy he inspired, they have become his devotees and departed for Mount Cithaeron, where he, too, intends to join them. Meanwhile, however, two old men make their somewhat comic appearance: Cadmus, Thebes' founder monarch, and Tiresias the prophet, who conclude that refusal to acknowledge Dionysus would be injudicious.

Then a servant of Pentheus arrives with a man he has captured, who is Dionysus himself, although nobody realizes this. Pentheus demands that the prisoner be locked up in his stables. But the whole palace suddenly crashes down, as though struck by an earthquake, and the captive, returning, treats Pentheus' further menaces with disdain. However, the king's wits are now fuddled, and Dionysus persuades him to disguise himself and go to spy on the women, in order to find out about certain strange happenings that are reported from the mountain. But when Pentheus arrives there, we are told, the Maenads seize him and rend his gory body apart. They are led by his own mother Agave, who has gone mad, and arrives on the stage carrying his head, believing it to be a lion's. Cadmus restores her sanity, and amid their lamentations Dionysus reappears, discloses who he really is, and explains and justifies his revenge upon those who had failed to accept him.

Poetical and dramatic and compact, the *Bacchae* chooses as its subject the ancient worship of Dionysus, which had inspired the earliest attempts at Greek tragedy. But this well-worn theme has been transformed in order to construct the most terrible and moving play that has come down to us from antiquity; and it is a play that speaks directly to ourselves today.

Euripides is neither for nor against Dionysus: the god is devilish and holy, beyond any moral categories of good and evil, representing the incomprehensible, unreachable quality of nature. But civilized man is being warned that he ignores the darker orgiastic forces of his nature at his own peril. And he is also being told that inspired religious emotion is immensely powerful and dangerous – an elemental force that has to be lived with, but menaces and dissolves the bonds of society, and conflicts with the order of the *polis*. King Pentheus is offered a variety of guises which he might assume when he goes to contact the god. But his earthbound common sense makes it impossible for him to take this imaginative leap, typifying the fatal inability of human beings to come to terms with the irrational.

The Maenads of the chorus (known from the Brygos Painter's vases; Chapter 10) play an active part. The ecstatic irresponsibility that Dionysus offered to women was unique in Greek religion, and confirmed the belief that they were volatile, unreliable creatures, and that to allow them to escape from modest confinement presented peril (cf. Appendix II).

Amid the convulsive events of the epoch in which Euripides was writing, community values were being called increasingly into question, notably by the second generation of sophists, whose hair-splitting, acrobatic advocacies and antithetical polarities as we saw in the *Hippolytus*, so greatly fascinated Euripides, despite one of his character's warnings against the 'art of over-subtle words'.[11] The questioning and crumbling of social norms that such definitions encouraged meant that the individual assumed larger importance than before; here was a playwright who conducted novel explorations of personality.

He knew all too well the lethal forces ever ready to constrain and overwhelm the human spirit, and the strivings of men and women inspired him to analytical, clinical observation, not unmixed with compassion. Happy endings alternate with gloomy and comfortless *dénouements*, brought about by chaotic successions of happenings that exemplify no moral or rational pattern. Mythical or legendary 'heroes' are often portrayed by Euripides in an unattractive light, brought down to earth and transformed into the sort of inferior personage who could be encountered, in real life, during the bleak years of the Peloponnesian War when so many of Euripides' tragedies were performed.

His characters, therefore, have become all too familiar to modern psychologists. So is his treatment of love, which he, above all other tragedians, made the central theme of drama and narrative. The varied situations that we encounter in his plays are sometimes deliberately farcical but more often violent and passionate, and their treatment contains a great deal of realism, even when this is expressed in stylized forms. Athenian patriotism shows itself again and again, and yet these works reflect a profound hatred of war, and horror at the miseries it produced. Women were among its worst sufferers, as the *Hecuba* and *Trojan Women* made clear, and Euripides felt great pity for them, and admired their self-immolations, although he also, and more often, portrayed murderous, terrifying women, which earned him, as we saw, the name of misogynist – an unreasonable appellation since so many of his male characters were equally flawed.

His gods and goddesses emerge as demonic psychological forces – which the application of human reason cannot possibly overcome – or as nasty seducers, or figures of fun. Not surprisingly, the playwright was denounced as impious and atheistic, and it was true that under his scrutiny the plain man's religion crumbled to pieces. Yet, first, it is his characters who are speaking, and not Euripides himself; and secondly, in so far as his own views are detectable in the utterances of his characters, he is speaking not as an atheist but as a questioning agnostic, who distrusted facile answers, at a time when their validity had so often become eroded by the bitter experiences of war.

A curious feature of some of Euripides' tragedies, perhaps mirroring some fundamental religious irresolution, is the *deus ex machina*: the god or goddess who appears and intervenes at the conclusion, clearing up all the loose ends – to the accompaniment, very often, of antiquarian religious erudition – and at the same time, no doubt, providing an additional opportunity for the spectacular theatrical staging for which Euripides was famous. At the beginning of each drama, on the other hand, there are explanatory prologues or introductions. They helped to weave together the internal structure of his plays, which tends to be looser and more episodic than that of Sophocles.

His diction is clear and natural, abounding in clever quotable ideas: not far from ordinary life, but interspersed by vividly contrasted, increasingly dazzling and fantastic choral and monodic lyrics – enhanced, it was said, by the latest and most original whirling and trilling music.

Despite the continuing absence of official recognition, Euripides was already famous in his lifetime. Socrates found his skill and insight deeply impressive; Aristotle believed him 'the most tragic of poets',[12] and he became the most admired of the tragedians, his plays being constantly revived.

CHAPTER 19

ARISTOPHANES: COMEDY OF PROTEST

The origins of Attic Old Comedy are as ancient and mixed as those of tragedy; disguised or masked figures on Athenian vases of *c.*500 already reflect some crude predecessor of comic drama. But the provision of comic plays at the annual City Dionysia did not begin until 488/487 or 487/486, and they were first included at the Lenaea in the 440s. Before the Peloponnesian War five comic plays were licensed by the chief archon at each festival. Later the figure varied.

Known writers of Athenian comedy included Cratinus, and Eupolis who was younger, and Aristophanes (457/445–before 385). From the plays of Cratinus and Eupolis only fragments survive; Aristophanes has left us forty-three titles, and eleven complete plays. He was regarded as the greatest of the three, and his writings provide extensive information about many aspects of fifth-century Athens.

The Acharnians (425) is named after Acharnae in Attica, where Dicaeopolis ('just government') is trying to induce the local Assembly to initiate discussions with the Spartans so that the Peloponnesian War can be brought to an end. Amphitheus is not allowed to go to Sparta and conclude a peace treaty, but Dicaeopolis nevertheless dispatches him there to make a private peace for himself and his family.

After Amphitheus has come back – bringing various proposals – Dicaeopolis seizes upon the suggestion of a thirty-year truce, and is preparing to celebrate the Rural Dionysia (vintage festival) when he is assaulted by Acharnian charcoal-burners (the play's chorus), who want the war to go on. He convinces some of them that they are wrong, but the rest mobilize the general Lamachus to lead them against him. Dicaeopolis offers to trade with anyone, and a Megarian and a Boeotian respond (the former with two starving daughters, to be sold as pigs). However, heralds arrive to order Lamachus to go out and fight against the Boeotians; and we see him limping back wounded from the battle. Dicaeopolis, on the other hand, the man of peace, goes off to an enjoyable party, from which he staggers away happily, with a girl on each arm.

The *Acharnians*, which won the first prize at the Lenaea, already reflects Aristophanes' characteristic, moderate attitudes: his liking for honest country people and peace, and his hatred of glib warmongers and 'hawks'. This was a sharp political statement, at the height of the Peloponnesian War: a war which never ought to have been fought, the dramatist believed, and could now be ended on favourable terms. That is the message which Aristophanes mobilizes all his ebullient powers of burlesque and fantasy to convey.

The *Hippeis* (*Knights*) are the chorus of the comedy named after them (424). Bad-tempered old Demos ('the people') has two slaves who, pretending to be the generals Nicias and Demosthenes (Chapter 16), protest against the deplorable conduct of Demos' favourite new slave, a Paphlagonian tanner (who is meant to be the politician Cleon, the most prominent among the successors of Pericles). But an oracle has told the generals that a sausage-seller will soon supersede the tanner, and so they back the claims of Agoracritus ('choice of the market-place'), who seems ignorant and brash enough to direct the city's affairs.

He and the tanner launch into competitive mutual abuse, in which the tanner recalls his leadership in the recent Athenian victory at Sphacteria (Pylos), but Agoracritus wins the day. He puts Demos into a pot and boils him in order to restore his youth, and the old man, when he gets out, announces that he is going to cancel all innovations and revive traditional customs, rejecting guileful politicians who offer the people fraudulent inducements.

The Knights was the first play to be produced under Aristophanes' own name, and provided him with one of his greatest successes, winning the first prize at the Lenaea. His principal message, however, was not accepted. For although the angry young dramatist, without any of the attractive variety or lyricism he customarily displays, delivers a virulent attack on Cleon – seen as typical of the pretentious politicians (demagogues) whom he hated – that politician was, nevertheless, re-elected as one of the Athenian generals later in the same year.

Cleon had recently prosecuted Aristophanes for criticizing him in *The Banqueters* (which is lost) – on grounds of alien birth and high treason – and the playwright is hitting back hard, and at the same time subjecting the whole process of Athenian democracy to scathing criticism. Indeed, after Cleon, he says, somebody even worse is sure to appear – namely, the sausage-seller. We are being given a comic version of the old cyclical view of a succession of ages, each worse than the last, until things finally reach their nadir, when a Golden Age can be hoped for once again.

In *The Clouds* (423), old Strepsiades ('twister') has lost all his money, because of his son Pheidippides' obsessive addiction to horseracing. So he proposes to enrol Pheidippides in the Phrontisterion ('think school') conducted by Socrates and Chaerephon next door. Among the various subjects the school offers is the sophistical form of argumentation which can make false, wrong ways of thinking seem more plausible than the truth (Chapter 12).

Strepsiades likes the look of this idea, thinking it will enable him to evade his creditors; and so he wants to join the school in place of his son. Socrates, climbing down from a flying basket, enrols him as a student, calling upon Air (Aether) and the Clouds (the chorus of the play), the only divinities he is prepared to acknowledge. Strepsiades persuades his son to become his fellow pupil, and two rival disputants, the Just and Unjust Cause, argue about which of them shall become Pheidippides' instructor. The latter prevails, and equipped with this teaching the youth beats his father up, on 'logical' grounds; whereupon Strepsiades, with the help of his slaves, launches an assault on the school and burns it to the ground.

What we have is a second, rewritten version of *The Clouds*; the first version had secured only third place at the City Dionysia, a failure for which Aristophanes records his disappointment, blaming the audience for not being able to appreciate his cleverest comedy. What is particularly interesting about the play is the attack on Socrates, who is blamed for all the faults of the new education launched by the sophists and detested by Aristophanes as constituting an irresponsible threat to traditional religion and social morality (cf. Chapter 21).

The result is an outrageous parody in which Socrates is invested with all manner of alien, ludicrous characteristics and no attempt is made to distinguish him from the sophists – as Plato later was so anxious to do (Chapter 31) – except that he is shown as a wretched starveling, while they become rich. It is Socrates whom the comic dramatists singled out as the scapegoat because he alone was known to the ordinary people who could be relied upon to distrust and ridicule intellectuals. The dispute between the Just and Unjust Cause is the most brilliant of the 'contests' (*agones*) characteristic of Aristophanes' theatrical construction, and the choruses contain some of his finest poetry.

In *The Wasps* (422) the elderly Athenian Philocleon ('Cleon-lover') so greatly enjoys sitting on juries that his son Bdelycleon ('Cleon-hater') has shut him up so that he cannot get to the courts. But Philocleon is nevertheless determined to join a group of old jurymen, dressed as wasps (the chorus of the play), who denounce Bdelycleon as an atheist and collaborator with the Spartans.

After father and son have ludicrously debated the juror's social role, Philocleon is horrified to find that (for the first time in his life) he has voted in favour of an acquittal. Henceforward, however, Bdelycleon promises that his father will be able to abandon himself to unrestricted pleasure. But Philocleon gets drunk at a feast and misbehaves, speaking rudely to his fellow guests and scuffling with passers-by on the way home. His son pushes him into the house, but the old man comes out again and joins the chorus in a dance.

The Wasps was awarded second prize in the Lenaean competition. The most formally constructed of Aristophanes' plays, it satirizes the legal system that was creating an epidemic of litigation in Athenian democratic society (Chapter 36). *The Wasps* also follows up *The Clouds* by an amusing new presentation of the generation gap – a serious problem in later-fifth-century Athens – in which Philocleon, transformed from a cantankerous juror into a uninhibited party-goer, is one of the best depicted literary rascals.

In *The Peace*, performed in 421, two slaves are found feeding a huge beetle with dung cakes. Their master Trygaeus proposes to climb up to heaven upon its back, in order to pray Zeus for peace. On his way there, however, Trygaeus is informed by Hermes that the gods no longer take an interest in the Greeks, who have repeatedly been offered opportunities for peace but have always turned them down.

War has incarcerated Peace and her female attendants Holiday (Theoria, i.e. watcher of Games and Festivals) and Harvest in a cave. But now a group of farmers (the play's chorus), encouraged by Trygaeus, manages to get them out. Trygaeus flies down to the earth again, with Harvest, whom he is told he can marry. But the sacrifice to Peace before the wedding is held up by a soothsayer who declares that the time for Peace to be set free has not arrived after all. After begging for some meat, however, the soothsayer is hustled away, and so is a manufacturer of weapons, but a peaceful sickle-maker secures permission to attend the marriage banquet that follows.

The Peace, which gained a second prize at the Dionysia, displays an optimistic spirit – which is unusual for Aristophanes – because Athens and Sparta were planning the Peace of Nicias, which temporarily put a stop to the Peloponnesian War. Or perhaps the play was begun in order to urge that such an agreement should be reached, and was concluded to commemorate its termination – later, it seems, Aristophanes produced a second and no doubt more celebratory version, unless that was another comedy altogether, his lost *Farmer*. The chorus of farmers who comprise the chorus of *The Peace* reflects Aristophanes' sympathy with such men, upon whom the war inflicted so much hardship; at one point, they join Trygaeus in a hymn to the land and its beneficial uses. The play also, in some passages, shows a concern for the allies of Athens, and the bad treatment they sometimes suffered from the city's representatives.

The Birds (414) are the chorus, composed of jackdaws and ravens who guide Peithetaerus ('Persuader') and Euelpides ('Hopeful') away from Attica – which has become unendurable – in the hope of finding somewhere better. Peithetaerus' idea is to establish a utopian community of birds in the middle of the sky, Nephelococcygia (Cloud-cuckoo-land), immune from attacks either by gods or by human beings. A poet, bureaucrats and other undesirable busybodies are shooed away from the site, but when Poseidon and Heracles and Triballus (a farcical barbarian) arrive as envoys from heaven, Peithetaerus agrees that the birds will establish amicable relations with the powers that be, on the condition that he is given Basileia (Sovereignty) as his bride; and a festive wedding procession concludes the play.

Often regarded as Aristophanes' masterpiece – though it won only a second prize – *The Birds* is his longest and most spectacular production, composed of a variety of closely knit scenes, and crammed with comic inventions and charming lyrics. It is a satire on utopianism, but a satire not unmixed with hankering, since Nephelococcygia serves to show up, by way of contrast, the faults and fads of contemporary Athens. They seemed numerous and damaging, and the play, for all its gaiety, was written at a critical and nervous period of the city's fortunes, when the Syracusan expedition had been perilously launched and could well be headed for catastrophe, as indeed it was (Chapter 16). It is also a striking commentary on the freedom of the Athenian comic stage that Aristophanes can ridicule and humiliate the gods, during the very year in which death sentences were passed for mutilating holy statues and parodying the Mysteries.

In the *Lysistrata*, 'Demobilize the Army' (411), the woman of that name summons other women who want an end to the war from all over Greece, for she has thought up a scheme to restore peace to Athens. Her plan is to deny sex to their husbands until the fighting stops.

Some of the women occupy the Acropolis, where old men try to smoke them out, but are prevented from doing so by old women who bring their besieged juniors water supplies (the two groups comprise the chorus of the *Lysistrata*). A magistrate endeavouring, with the help of four Scythian policemen, to take money from the treasury in order to hire rowers for the fleet is repelled, and Myrrhine teasingly frustrates the sexual advances of her husband Cinesias, while male envoys from

Sparta report similar hardship stories. Lysistrata censures Spartans and Athenians alike for fighting one another when the armies of Greece's foreign foe (Persia) are close at hand, and invites them all to the Acropolis to join a party with the women. After enjoying good food and drink, the Athenians and Spartans dance together to celebrate the end of the war.

Produced under the name of Aristophanes' friend Lysistratus, this comedy was written at a period of even deeper anxiety than the time of *The Birds*, when the Syracusan expedition had disastrously failed, and the Athenian constitution had been overthrown by revolutionary oligarchs (Chapters 16, 24). One of the dramatist's principal messages is the need for internal unity at Athens. But the need is placed in a Panhellenic context, and Aristophanes warns that only the Persians could win if the war is prolonged (though what was actually happening, and about to happen, was that Persian gold would make Sparta the winner).

The thought that women, to whom the war had caused such misery, could make peace by keeping the men at bay must have caused amused surprise to the Athenians, who were far from seeing females in a dominant or governmental role (Appendix II). The idea is cleverly worked out, but despite the underlying seriousness of such a message it is the play's unrestrained sexuality and obscenity that has assured its permanent popularity.

The *Thesmophoriazusae* (411 or 410), the chorus, are the women attending the Thesmophoria, the autumn festival of Demeter and Persephone celebrated by members of their sex. They are planning vengeance against Euripides for his alleged anti-feminism (Chapter 18): as another poet, Agathon, reports to his father-in-law Mnesilochus.

Euripides hopes that Agathon, suitable for the purpose because of his effeminate appearance, will agree to slip into the women's meeting and spy on what happens, but Agathon is too afraid to do so. Mnesilochus, therefore, wearing drag, goes in instead – but is detected. Then Euripides arrives (providing an opportunity to mock a number of his dramatic techniques), and finally brings in a Flute Girl and Dancing Girl who entice the attendant policeman away. Euripides, who has meanwhile consented to call a halt to his unfriendly attitude to women, hastily escapes with Mnesilochus, but the policeman, discovering he has been tricked, reappears, whereupon the chorus give him misleading directions, showing that their hostility to Euripides has been abandoned.

In the *Thesmophoriazusae*, then, women are in the forefront once again, but this time in the context of the religious activities which were the only public life, or safety valve, that Athenian males allowed them (Appendix II). But the main purpose of the comedy is to make fun of Euripides, who was at this period occupied with his plays balancing illusion and realism, notably the *Iphigenia in Tauris* and the *Helen*. Euripides was telling the Athenians that they could get away from the dismal reality of the war, at least in their minds; but Aristophanes, amid a good deal of sparkling literary foolery, concludes that this will not do, since he and his war-torn compatriots had to live their lives, in a real physical world which they must improve instead of pretending it does not exist.

In *The Frogs* (spring 405), the god Dionysus is proceeding to the land of the dead, accompanied by his slave Xanthias, who is loaded with baggage and mounted on a donkey. Dionysus, the god of the theatre, informs Heracles – at whose house they have stopped to ask the way – that his object is to bring back Euripides, who has just died.

The ferryman Charon conveys Dionysus across the Great Lake (making him row), but Xanthias, being a slave, is told to go round the shore on foot. The frogs, who form the chorus, croak 'Brekekekek koax koax', and stop singing only when Dionysus joins in. They arrive, after a series of incidents, at Pluto's palace in the underworld, where the doorkeeper Aeacus offers them physical violence. Aeschylus and Euripides, who challenges his predecessor's right to the throne of tragedy, then hold a poetic contest, arranged by Pluto. Finally, Dionysus decides to take Aeschylus rather than Euripides back to the upper world – and Aeschylus appoints Sophocles to succeed him as king of tragedy.

Writing *The Frogs* when the military and political power of Athens was on the verge of collapse, Aristophanes prefers to send Dionysus away from the world altogether, to the other realm below: thus sadly indulging in the escapism that the *Thesmophoriazusae* had censured in Euripides. Or rather, the world is not completely escaped from, since the god's task is to bring back a poet who will rejuvenate Athenian society.

This is the background of the contest between the two dramatists in Hades. During this confrontation Aeschylus accuses Euripides of a sceptical attitude that undermines the morality, and future, of the Athenian city-state. Aristophanes admires both of them, however – and allows Euripides to accuse Aeschylus of theatrical gimmicks and bombast. Yet he evidently agrees that Euripides' influence had been harmful, at this critical juncture in the fortunes of Athens, since it is the more conservative and high-principled Aeschylus whom he bids accompany him back to the earth, in the hope of saving the state.

The play won the first prize, though whether this was because of its political message or the amusing literary contest, or both, we cannot tell.

In the *Ecclesiazusae* (the Assemblywomen forming the chorus), the female sex is still to the fore. These women have disguised themselves in their husbands' clothes, and are wearing false beards, in order to attend the Assembly, where Praxagora is going to propose that the government should be handed over to women; and this motion wins a majority vote.

Her husband Blepyrus (dressed as a woman because he cannot find his own clothing) is informed of what has happened, and when he tells Praxagora – after catching her creeping into the house – she boldly outlines her plan for national reform. It is this: all possessions shall become common property – including spouses – and it shall become obligatory for men to have sex with unattractive women, and vice versa, before they are allowed to take a more alluring partner. In accordance with this new edict three old women fight over a young man, and finally tear him away from his girl. In conclusion, everyone walks away to a banquet, to which a herald has summoned them, dancing and singing as they go.

The central theme of the *Ecclesiazusae* is at first, once again, woman's rule, of which the *Lysistrata* had had so much to say; but then interest shifts to Praxagora's utopianism, which echoes Nephelococcygia of *The Birds*, with communistic trimmings. This is a whimsical parody of the sort of state which we shall find later in Plato's *Republic* (Chapter 31), but was already, no doubt, a fashionable talking point.

Aristophanes seems to have become rather weary (the play has a feeble end), but both he and Athens were two decades older than when his earlier plays on these subjects had been performed.

In *Plutus* (388), Chremylus, accompanied by his slave Cario, has gone to Delphi to consult Apollo's oracle about how he can turn his son into a villainous character, so as to ensure that he can make a success of his life at Athens.

Commanded by the oracle to befriend the first person he meets after leaving the shrine, he does so, accosting a ragged, blind old man, who turns out to be Plutus, the god of wealth. Chremylus conducts Plutus to the temple of the god of healing, Asclepius, driving away the massive, formidable Penia (Poverty). Plutus recovers his sight, declares that he will never abandon good people again, and goes into Chremylus' house, filling it up with desirable objects.

Five persons now enter whose lives have been transformed by this sudden influx of prosperity. A just man offers gratitude, an informer complains that he has been deprived of his profession, an old woman laments the loss of her lover (who has become rich and left her), and Hermes (god of luck) and a priest grumble that they are starving, because no one offers sacrifices any more. Chremylus promises he will do what he can to be of help, and the play ends with a procession to Athena's treasury in the inner cell of the Parthenon, where Plutus is going to live from now on.

The comedy named after him seems to be a revised version of a play originally written two decades earlier (although the two compositions may have been entirely different). In this changed epoch, sixteen years after the Peloponnesian War was over, Aristophanes has moved from political preoccupations to social concern with poverty and wealth. Such satire as remains is watered down, and the dramatist's long lyric choruses of the past have given way to mere interludes (marked in the script) which were occupied by song-and-dance acts. In other words we have left Old Comedy behind, and have passed into the mild and somewhat indeterminate, though apparently very varied, Middle Comedy which followed (on the way to the New Comedy; see below) and is otherwise nearly all lost. Despite its rather uninteresting characters, the *Plutus* had a long career as a favourite schoolbook, because it is pleasant, easy and free from obscenity.

Aristophanes' style displays inexhaustibly dazzling powers of invention, deriving exuberant images, similes and metaphors from any and every aspect of life. As for his characters, they do little, for the most part, but symbolize one or another of the conflicting points of view that the playwright is presenting – in the form, very often, merely of a simple, impudent caricature. After all, these characters had to impress themselves on spectators, not on readers who might have been able to study them at leisure. And yet these characters are also frequently and deliberately taken from contemporary life, and represent real, prominent personages of the day, whom Aristophanes loads with unrestrained abuse and ridicule.

One of the most remarkable features of his plays is that, although the great majority of those that have come down to us were performed at festivals – state occasions – during the Peloponnesian War, they nevertheless contain violent assaults against leading members of the Athenian government – and eloquent pleas for peace. The pro-war politician Cleon was a special target of Aristophanes' scurrilous attacks, and retaliated, as we saw in connection with *The Knights*, by bringing him into the courts. Undeterred, and no doubt encouraged by audience reaction – since the public evidently enjoyed what he said, even if they failed to vote for the policies he favoured – the playwright pursued his effervescent satire, surviving two oligarchic coups and the democratic revolutions that followed them.

He was evidently a man of staunch and solid and old-fashioned opinions, founded, as we have seen, upon a blend of common sense, humaneness, moderation and conservatism. Poets (Euripides), philosophers (Socrates), scientists and musicians were at the receiving end of his caustic mockery and parody. Cultural innovators (although he was one himself) continue to be seen as pretentious charlatans and pseudo-reformers, whereas the persons he likes best are ordinary Athenians, who just want to live quietly and have a pleasant time in traditional, conventional ways. Prominent among these people with whom the dramatist sympathizes are the shrewd, coarse, independently minded 'little men' on the Attic land. It is largely because of their wartime tribulations – including annual invasions by the Spartans – that Aristophanes, for all his patriotism, espouses such markedly pacifist views, which no country engaged in a war would tolerate in modern times.

Can, or will, the gods be of any help? Here Aristophanes' attitude, once again, is hard for modern readers to comprehend. For on the one hand he agrees, without question, that the community should offer them due worship, and yet at the same time he often depicts these same deities as ridiculous and dishonest. His spectators evidently regarded this irreverence as acceptable and funny – even though his plays were performed at religious festivals.

The female parts in Aristophanic comedy, as well as the male, were acted by men, as in tragedy. There were usually four actors, though additional persons could be introduced as well. They wore gargoyle-like masks and padded robes, including exaggerated stomachs (and over-sized penises for men). There were twenty-four members of the chorus, and in addition to its dancing and choral or solo singing, which were vital ingredients in the plays, it fulfilled an important role in the development of the story, sometimes acting as the mouthpiece of the dramatist – and eventually taking the 'hero's' side. The chorus's songs often possess an attractive, light, lyrical quality, in contrast to the uproarious pornography to be found elsewhere in most of these plays.

Structurally speaking, Aristophanes' comedies tend to adopt a more or less conventional sequence: prologue or exposition; entry of the chorus (*parodos*); contest between two characters (*agon*), containing the main gist of the plot; elaborate address by the chorus to the audience; further episodes divided by choral songs; joyful concluding scene (*exodos*), leading up to a banquet or a wedding or both. As was noted, his last plays, the *Ecclesiazusae* and particularly the *Plutus*, abandoned many of the traditional features of Old Comedy. This is apparent in their structure as well as their content. For in the Middle Comedy, which these plays heralded, the *parabasis* disappeared, and the dramatist's own choral lyrics were replaced by pieces taken from other writers.

The drama of Aristophanes remained an object of unceasing study and admiration in ancient times, and elaborate commentaries were written about it. With the New Comedy of Menander and its Latin adapters Plautus and Terence as intermediaries, the entire comic drama of Europe can be traced back to Aristophanes' art.

CHAPTER 20
HIPPOCRATES: SCIENTIFIC PHYSICIAN

Although progress in Greek science was delayed because empirical observation, on the whole, fell behind theory, medicine, following some of the early Ionian scientist-philosophers' reliance on observed phenomena, had gradually established itself as something of an exception. During the sixth century, as the popularity of athletics encouraged greater understanding of the human body, medical schools began to be established at Croton, Cos, Cnidus, Rhodes and Cyrene.

The idea of justice (*dike*) – to which political thinkers ascribed the origins of the city-state – was prominent in the minds of physicians, who identified the 'just law' with natural bodily processes. Thus Alcmaeon of Croton (*c.*500?), possibly the founder of that city's school of medicine, ascribed bodily conditions to the interplay of opposites. Indeed Alcmaeon, who was deeply interested in nature and especially in human nature, appears to have been the first thinker to have applied such antitheses to medical theory, insisting that health depends on the balanced 'equal rights' (*isonomia*, again a familiar political term) of opposites, in contrast to the *monarchia*, or 'tyranny', of disease.

Such concepts, drawing analogies between the human body and the community, were borrowed from philosophers, notably Pythagoras (Appendix 1), to whose followers Alcmaeon, said to be Pythagoras' younger contemporary, addressed his book. Yet the approach of Alcmaeon was pragmatic. For he based these abstractions not only on the theoretical, inferential kind of argument that Greek thinkers tended to favour, but also on surgical practice – thus converting medicine into something not too far removed from a scientific discipline.

By all accounts, however, the marathon step forward, enabling medicine to reach a far higher level than any other Greek science, was taken by the physician Hippocrates of Cos, a contemporary of Socrates (469–399) or slightly his junior. Although the son of a physician who belonged to the Aesclepiad guild (or family?), the religious cult of the healing god Asclepius does not seem to have been prominent in his upbringing, since its principal development at Cos came later on (providing the temple-medicine of the mid-fourth century). He was rather the heir of Ionia's philosophers; and his teachers (or so tradition reports) included the Ionian philosopher Democritus, as well as the sophists Prodicus and Gorgias (Chapters 8, 12).

Hippocrates travelled widely, practising medicine in various Greek cities; and then he died at Larissa in Thessaly, after acquiring extraordinary fame. Our imperfect sources, however, make it hard, or impossible, to conclude just what he himself actually thought and said. But according to Plato, he appears – if this is the correct interpretation of the passage in question – to have interpreted the human frame as an interrelated organism, and to have founded his medical theories and activities on the combination of all its diverse elements into a single, coherent unity.[13]

That may well be so, but when we come to the fifty-eight works (in seventy-three books) known as the *Corpus Hippocraticum* our problems continue. The *Corpus*, despite its inevitable limitations, contains the most determined of all Greek attacks on pre-rational, non-rational ways of thinking. Yet the difficulty of tracing any of these works back to Hippocrates himself remains acute – as was already recognized in ancient times.

Varying from meticulously composed medical lectures to less technical demonstrations indebted to the methods of the sophists (including Gorgias, whose brother was a physician), the treatises cover an enormous range of medical themes and topics. Moreover, the originators of these studies did not by any means all come from Cos, the home of Hippocrates, but belonged to other eastern Greek medical schools as well, notably that of Cnidus, which was more interested in science, it was said, while Cos laid greater emphasis on humanity. Furthermore, the gathering together of these essays into a single 'Hippocratic' Corpus cannot be traced back earlier than the third or second centuries BC, when its compilation probably took place at Alexandria.

Yet on grounds of language and style certain of the pieces the corpus contains must be regarded as dating right back to Hippocrates' own lifetime. One is *Airs, Waters and Places* – now often entitled *On Environment*. The study consists of two parts. The first weighs up, in an original manner, the different respects in which various environmental conditions affect the human body. The second part (owing debts to earlier Ionian scientist-philosophers) notes the different and contrasted geographical, climatic and demographic conditions of Europe and Asia.

Another early 'Hippocratic' essay is *On the Sacred Disease*, that is to say, epilepsy. Its writer is prepared to concede that, ultimately, everything goes back to a divine origin. But he shows that epilepsy is not more 'sacred' (as was supposed) than any other sickness – and this gives him an opportunity to attack demonological beliefs and other superstitions cherished by charlatans.

A late-fifth- or early-fourth-century authorship can also be ascribed to a further category of writings, including *On Diet* and *Epidemics* (Books I and III, full of empirical, systematic observation), *On Ancient Medicine* (declaring war, in the practical spirit of a craftsman or technician, against hypothetical, philosophical methods) and the *Prognosticum* (illustrating the elevation of prognosis over diagnosis which was typical of Cos). None of these works are attributable to Hippocrates himself, but any or all of them may have been written by physicians who knew him and were influenced by his teachings. For he left many pupils, in addition to two sons.

The famous Medical Oath associated with his name, which once again illustrates progress in this field, was not composed, in its existing form, before the fourth century BC. Moreover, it may have been intended only for a restricted group of physicians, namely a Pythagorean brotherhood (Appendix I). This would account for certain features which can be paralleled in Pythagorean thought, such as the prohibition of suicide and abortion, and the command that physicians should not practise surgery (which is not specifically condemned, but regarded as outside their sphere).

The Oath is notable for its covenant to respect, and if necessary teach, other members of the physicians' profession, emphasizing close bonds between pupil and teacher, father and son, that could well go back to Hippocrates himself, who may, like the Oath, have depicted medicine as a craft learnable by apprenticeship and heredity. The Oath is sworn 'by Apollo, Asclepius, Hygiea (Health) and all the powers of healing', mirroring, it would seem, a transitional stage between revering these figures as divinities and interpreting them, instead, as abstract forces. But the Oath's most notable and permanent feature is its insistence upon standards of medical ethics, and upon the physician's responsibility to his patients and their families and to the community he serves.

It was not long before the fame of Hippocrates had become so pre-eminent that his career – like those, for example, of Pythagoras and Socrates – attracted a multitude of non-historical legends. But he also came to be seen as the virtual creator of medical science. Galen, in the second century AD, venerated him both as a practical physician and as a medical and biological theorist. From the 800s onward Arabic scholars examined, translated and adapted the *Hippocratic Corpus*, and after the turn of the millennium there were Latin versions (taken from the Arabic and perhaps, to some extent, from the original Greek), which later formed part of the teaching programmes of European universities.

Yet despite this the contribution originally made by Hippocrates himself remains mysterious, though he must have done something to justify his enormous renown – and what he probably did was to lay the foundations not merely of the knowledge but of the *attitude* from which later medical studies grew.

CHAPTER 21

SOCRATES: IRONICAL QUESTIONER

Socrates (*c*.470–399) exercised a gigantic influence on younger Athenian thinkers, and on men of later generations. And yet we know practically nothing about him, because he wrote nothing himself, and because the historical truthfulness of those who wrote about him is gravely suspect. Indeed they would have been surprised if one had reproached them with this, since they were aiming at something rather different: namely, the presentation of a stock personality from whose career and opinions, depicted with literary imagination and licence, lessons could be drawn.

Thus the *Clouds* of Aristophanes, written in Socrates' lifetime (Chapter 19), made him a figure of fun, embodying, unfairly and arbitrarily, all the features of the current higher educational movements sponsored by sophists and scientist-philosophers of whom the playwright disapproved. Yet his choice of Socrates as figurehead for this role shows how famous the philosopher already was in the 420s. Then, once again, he makes his appearance in Aristophanes' *Frogs* (405), as someone quite dangerous; and another comic dramatist, Eupolis, had likewise singled him out for attack, as a seedy, beggarly chatterer.

Next, after Socrates' death – which caught people's fancy even more than his life – he provided the subject matter for a host of propaganda pamphlets, both for and against him. The pamphlets attacking him have vanished, but lengthy discourses survive from his junior pupils Xenophon and Plato which are strongly in his favour (Chapters 30, 31). The two writers, however, differ in what they say and think about Socrates. Xenophon makes him a commonsensical, humdrum plaster saint purveying wise views and adages, while Plato, in a massive series of supposed 'dialogues', builds him up as the founder of his own elaborate idealistic philosophy.

Few people think that Xenophon grasped more than a small part of the true picture, but the historical reliability, or otherwise, of Plato's descriptions of Socrates has been disputed for centuries. Surely, however, except when Plato points to a trait or saying of Socrates that is confirmed elsewhere, his depiction of the sage can claim no historical reliability at all, but is, rather, a depiction of Plato's own mental processes, inspired by the general recollection of what an extraordinary and thought-provoking man Socrates had been. Plato himself virtually warns us to adopt this cautious conclusion when he introduces obvious anachronisms into a dialogue or its setting (p. 209).

Socrates' father was an Athenian sculptor or stonemason, and apparently not badly off. Socrates himself married in later life, perhaps for the second time; his wife Xanthippe subsequently became notorious for her bad temper, whether rightly or wrongly we cannot tell. He served in the army as an infantryman (hoplite), apparently on several occasions.

He was on close terms, it would appear, with members of the inner Periclean circle (Chapter 11), and seems, when young, to have been an associate of Archelaus, an Athenian pupil of the philosopher-scientist Anaxagoras (Chapter 8). But then (claiming, it was said, that Anaxagoras' Mind (*nous*) did not 'plan the universe for the best') he turned away from these cosmological interests and spent the rest of his life enquiring into right and wrong human behaviour.

The most important of his opinions was the conviction that there is an eternal and unchanging *absolute standard*. In conformity with this, the achievement of 'as good as possible' a condition for one's own soul – which Socrates, perhaps unprecedentedly, saw as commanding the body – must be the end-product (*telos*) of all one's endeavours. Socrates seems to have been, in this respect at least, the creator of the 'teleological' approach, the belief that all nature works towards a purpose, which is later so clearly detectable in Plato and played such a dominant part in Aristotle's thought (Chapter 37).

Socrates' insistence on an absolute standard meant that he rejected the view that standards were relative, proposed by the sophists (Chapter 12; with whom he was often equated). He also believed that one must work hard if one wants to discover what is right and wrong – in other words, one must acquire knowledge; *virtue (moral goodness) is knowledge*, though one cannot be sure that he himself expressed it in precisely that provocative way. And Socrates went on to maintain, first, that knowledge means, above all, *self-knowledge* ('know thyself'), and secondly that *no one does wrong willingly*, which was another perverse, paradoxical idea. His insistence upon knowledge, his pioneer championship of the supremacy of the intellect, harmonizes with Aristotle's further assertion that he innovated by seeking to arrive at definitions: even though he himself continued to insist that he knew nothing himself – that he was only a 'midwife' who gave birth to knowledge in others.[14]

This assertion was partly, no doubt, ironical mock-modesty, but it also conformed with his philosophical method. For instead of writing, or teaching (he allegedly claimed never to have taught anyone, or to have imparted any information at all), he adopted the famous 'Socratic method' of cross-questioning everyone with whom he came into contact, particularly young men, as Aristophanes pointed out.[15] Guiding these companions, he sought to arrive at the truth through rational enquiry, since 'an unexamined life is not worth living'[16] – though this technique must have proved irritating, especially when he pulled the legs of his acquaintances, as seems to have been his habit.

His religious views were outwardly orthodox, for Socrates was scrupulous in his observances, according to 'the usage of the city'. All the same, like Euripides (Chapter 18), he evidently applied his critical methods to some of the traditional beliefs of his time, notably foolish or immoral myths about the gods (as Plato's *Euthyphro* indicates). Moreover, he claimed, on occasion, to be guided by a divine sign or voice (*daimonion*). Whether this should be interpreted as an inner conscience or intuition (as Plato implies) or a mystic phenomenon (for Socrates sometimes went into spellbound trances), it was this sign that compelled him so urgently to philosophize. The sign also meant that he was one of those uncomfortable persons who believe that they have God up their sleeve, so that, despite his modest irony, whatever he said or did must be right.

His physical appearance, we feel, is well known to us, although this may be a mistaken impression, because his numerous, whimsical portrait-busts are merely later reflections of how it was thought that a man of such a kind ought to have looked – with some added influence from the old comic satyr-Silenus type. His powers of physical endurance were remarkable, but so were his geniality and kindliness (despite that taste for ironical mockery); and among other aspects of his personality were self-control and curiosity and charm. This blend of qualities gained him a devoted circle of friends and followers of varying types, ranging from respectable serious thinkers to more alarmingly spectacular figures such as Alcibiades and the destructive intellectual, Critias.

Critias was one of the most fanatical extremists among the leaders who, after the final Athenian defeat of 404, engineered a successful revolution (which echoed the similar coup of 411), installing the oligarchic government of the 'Thirty Tyrants', with the help of the victorious Spartan General Lysander (Chapter 24). But when Lysander's influence and policies were undermined by Agiad King Pausanias in the following year, the Athenian democracy was restored, largely through the heroic efforts of an admiral with a distinguished war record, Thrasybulus. The revived democracy was (for the first time) given a regular constitution, and another of its achievements (authorized by Pausanias) was a comprehensive, and again apparently unprecedented, amnesty. Only the surviving leaders of the oligarchic party were outlawed; the amnesty applied to everyone else, and was enforced by penalties against private vengeance. But feelings remained tense and bitter, as the evidence of lawsuits from the period confirms.

By far the most famous of these lawsuits was the trial of Socrates (399). Socrates, who admitted that the upper class provided many of his followers,[17] had never thought highly of the democratic form of Athenian government, observing that its use of the lot, for example, was stupid – and that most would-be politicans did not know what they were talking about. Moreover, in 406, he had openly opposed the popular will, when, as a member of the Council of Five Hundred (Boule), he tried, unsuccessfully, to prevent the execution of the generals after the battle of Arginusae.

In 404, the Thirty Tyrants, led by his friend and pupil Critias, considered him favourable to their regime, making him a member of the oligarchic 3,000 whom they created as a political elite; and then they ordered him to make an arrest on their behalf. True, he refused. Yet, all the same, the subsequently reinstated democracy can scarcely have regarded him as its friend – at a time when a united Athenian front, purged of destructive, subversive, 'free' thinking, seemed essential, so that Sparta should not have a pretext to intervene again.

And so the responsible, moderate, democratic general Anytus brought Socrates to trial for his life – employing a certain Meletus, 'a young man with a sparse beard and beaky nose',[18] perhaps a religious bigot, as his figurehead to launch the accusations. They were: 'That Socrates does not believe in the gods in whom the city believes, but introduces other and new deities; also that he corrupts the young'.[19]

What does the first charge, relating to impiety, mean? It can scarcely refer, literally, to the introduction of foreign gods, since these were quite often introduced into Athens, without incurring penalties – and in any case there had never been suggestions that Socrates had had anything to do with such a matter. Was the accusation intended to refer to his 'divine sign', as some of his friends believed? That was hardly a new deity, though perhaps the talk of Socrates' pupils made it sound like one, or at least like a guardian spirit, which could be described as a god. Aristophanes had made fun of Socrates as a believer that Vortex, not Zeus, was the chief god, and had mocked him as a gazer into the sky – so that it might be possible to link him with the allegedly impious astronomy of the scientist-philosopher Anaxagoras, whose pupil Archelaus Socrates had befriended, but that had been a long time ago, and it was a long shot. Probably the point lies elsewhere. Socrates was a devout man, but his questioning methods, as we saw, covered religious institutions and mythical beliefs – and Anytus may have made such queries sound blasphemous.

But the real force of the indictment lay in the second charge, that Socrates 'corrupted the young'. For some of his younger friends and pupils seemed highly corrupt in the eyes of the current government: the unreliable Alcibiades (d.404), and, worst of all, Critias and Charmides, both members of the oligarchic Thirty Tyrants, and both killed while democratic rule was being forcibly restored.

Moreover, Socrates himself had not been sympathetic to democracy. However, the existence of the amnesty made it impossible to bring him to trial as an oligarch; hence, perhaps, the cryptic wording of the charge. And in general, too, his famous style of questioning may well have seemed subversive to the precarious and sensitive new regime. Besides, Anytus himself, Xenophon tells us, had a son who ought, as Socrates told the young man's father, to have a higher education: much to the fury of Anytus, who sent his boy into business instead (whereupon the youth took to drink).[20]

The accounts of the trial, and its speeches, are fictitious, but Socrates was found guilty by 281 votes to 220. At this point, as earlier, he could have escaped from Athens. But he declared that any such step would have been contrary to his civic duty. As to the penalty, when, as here, the law provided no specific guidance, a condemned man had the right to propose an alternative to whatever the prosecution demanded. In this case, its demand had been death, but if Socrates had proposed banishment as an alternative, the jury would not have demurred – indeed (now that ostracism was no longer practised) this may well have been what the prosecutors wanted, desiring merely to silence him. But Socrates refused to offer any such proposal, and instead made a speech suggesting that he should be maintained for life as a public benefactor – or, failing that, merely fined. The jury felt insulted by what sounded like flippancy, and voted for the death penalty by a larger majority than had originally decided upon his guilt. Thirty days after the verdict he died, by drinking hemlock.

Eternally significant because he seemed to have perished in the cause of freedom of conscience, he summoned up, through his death, the Socratic legend. There were, it is true, those who defended his condemnation – amid a welter of *Apologies* from those who deplored it among these many 'Socratics' who leapt to his defence and immortalized his last days. Plato was outstanding: to such a degree that, among the outburst of never-to-be-forgotten scenes and doctrines in his dialogues the personality of Socrates himself is almost lost beyond recall behind the brilliant figure of Plato himself.

But although the view, held in later antiquity, that Socrates was the first man ever to make people think about ethical questions and human behaviour does less than justice to his predecessors, it does appear to have been he who subjected these problems to critical analysis of an unprecedented quality and intensity, placing man at the centre of philosophical enquiry, and thus enlarging the horizons of the human spirit as few others have ever done before or since. And his meticulous examination, too, of the assumptions and definitions on which such analyses should be based showed equally formidable originality.

He was not, of course, the first Greek questioner; and there were other questioners of a searching kind in his own lifetime – Euripides, for example, and Protagoras and other sophists. But the supreme questioner of all, although his tone remained light, was evidently Socrates. His questioning, moreover, although he never left a written word, assumed a peculiarly urgent character – and produced endless later interpretations, follow-ups and reinterpretations – because, as noted earlier, he would not accept the relativism of the sophists, but believed that if one questioned hard enough there was an absolute truth somewhere to be found: and he was indifferent to everything except that.

CHAPTER 22

ZEUXIS AND PARRHASIUS: A NEW LOOK AT ART

The years following 450 BC witnessed a second technical revolution in wall-painting – the art to which Polygnotus had given the lead (Chapter 10) – although, once again, not a single example of these novel developments has come down to us.

At about this date, Agatharchus of Samos seems to have been the earliest painter to employ perspective as an important element in his method. That is to say, in depicting buildings, he evolved a system of perspectival diminution to denote the spatial depth that some of his predecessors had already attempted to represent. His method, like theirs, still displayed limitations, for Greek and Roman artists, although they foreshortened individual objects, never achieved a unitary viewpoint for entire scenes. However, it was supposedly Agatharchus who took at least the first step towards basing a picture upon a single vanishing point. Moreover, this innovation was founded on deliberate theoretical considerations, since he was the author of a commentary on 'scene-painting' (*skenographia*), which prompted the philosophers Anaxagoras and Democritus to write studies propounding optical perspective as a scientific theory.

Agatharchus' innovation was probably suggested by the requirements of theatrical scene-painting, since he designed the scenery for a tragedy of Aeschylus – probably a revival in the late 430s or early 420s. Moreover, he broke new ground by executing the mural paintings for a private house, the mansion of Alcibiades, who no doubt got into trouble among his egalitarian fellow Athenians for such a luxurious indulgence.

The second decisive figure in this artistic revolution, attempting to improve on the innovations of Agatharchus, was Apollodorus of Athens, about whom Pliny the elder writes:

> Apollodorus was the first artist to offer realistic presentation of objects, and the first to confer glory as of right upon the paint-brush.

> His works include the Priest at Prayer and Ajax struck by Lightning, the latter to be seen at Pergamum at the present day. There is no painting now on view by any artist before Apollodorus that arrests the attention of the eyes. He threw open the gates of art.[21]

This is high praise, but as artistic criticism it is vague. From elsewhere, however, we learn what Apollodorus achieved. The first to win a reputation in easel as well as wall-painting, he was known as *skiagraphos*, painter of shadow, which means that (improving on the elementary attempts by some of his forerunners) he developed realistic shading, that is to say the modulation of light and shade. This involved a novel employment of colour gradation and hatching to suggest mass, so that in a sense it might be said that Apollodorus had created, or given a new direction to, the art of painting, whereas previously there had only been outline drawing, with flat washes of colour.

This employment of shading produced lively discussion. Things could now be portrayed by artists as the eye saw them, which was why Apollodorus was regarded as the first painter to represent 'appearance', that is to say the appearance of reality – and Plato employed the term *skiagraphia* to mean illusionistic painting.[22] (But should we not rather – he also suggested – be looking at the matter from a philosopher's point of view: seeing things, not by this illusionary conjuring trick, but as they truly are?)

Pliny dates Apollodorus to 408 BC, but he must already have been painting by 430 if Zeuxis, as the same writer declares, 'entered' the gates of art that Apollodorus had thrown open.[23]

Zeuxis and Parrhasius are grouped together as members of the 'Asiatic school', since Parrhasius at least came from Asia Minor (Ephesus), though Zeuxis described himself as a man of Heraclea (Lucania, south-east Italy), and each of the two centred his activities upon Athens, where they were metics (Appendix III), working at the time of the Peloponnesian War. Both artists became the subjects of stories illustrating their skilful *trompe l'oeil* illusionism, which was what got painters talked about.

Zeuxis, who is described in Plato's *Protagoras* (dramatic date *c.*430) as a young man who had recently arrived at Athens, not only, as Pliny observed, went one better than Apollodorus, but was generously recognized by that artist as having 'robbed his masters of their art and carried it off with him'.[24] A large number of Zeuxis' works is recorded, including scenes of an unusual character; and his pictures were often, it was said, small compositions, frequently including only a single figure. While adopting and refining Apollodorus' methods of shading, his principal innovation, apparently, was to lend them additional vividness by the employment of highlights which gave an impression of three-dimensional volume. Moreover, he specialized in expressing strong emotion, notably in portrayals of the weeping Menelaus, and wild Boreas. But his most famous picture was a naked Helen, painted for Croton: an ideal, ethical interpretation derived from an amalgam of different human models.

Zeuxis received his share of criticism; for example he was censured for giving his figures too large heads, and too large fingers and toes as well (if that is what *articuli* means). He deserved credit, however, for securing a new recognition and more exalted status for the artistic profession. That he achieved by decorating the palace of King Archelaus of Macedonia (*c.*413–399) at Pella (Chapter 35) – and acquiring substantial wealth. 'This wealth', records Pliny the elder, 'he advertised at Olympia by displaying his own name embroidered in gold lettering on the checked pattern of his robes. Afterwards he set about giving away his works as presents, saying that it was impossible for them to be sold at any price adequate to their value'[25] – a theme he developed further in an epigram.

His rivalry with his contemporary Parrhasius was notorious, centring upon their competing claims to achieve total realism. Pliny makes an attempt to explain where Parrhasius' excellence lay, from which it emerges that he was an outstandingly skilful draughtsman, famous for his subtlety of outline and contour rather than for shading. He employed these techniques 'to reveal even what was concealed',[26] and to make facial expressions more lively, mouths more beautiful and hair more graceful. A prolific artist, not averse to painting an occasional obscene picture, he gained special renown from his colourful 'Theseus' (which later adorned the Roman Capitol) and from his 'Demos', which offered a complex psychological study of the People of Athens. In self-laudatory arrogance, Parrhasius put even Zeuxis in the shade, describing himself as the perfect prince of painters, of divine lineage.

Efforts to reconstruct elements of some of these lost wall-paintings from the designs on vases do not work out very well. At most one can say that perspective experiments reached vase-painting late in the century, and that certain white-ground grave-vases (*lekythoi*) show (unshaded) figures with taut, expressive contours which seem to echo the innovations of Parrhasius and could, indeed, conceivably be his own work. By this time, however, the enhanced pre-eminence of wall- and panel-painters had drawn off much of the talent previously devoted to vase-painting, which no longer, therefore, appears anywhere near the forefront of artistic development, and sinks back into a merely decorative craft.

Or, at best, large showy pieces, or domestic boudoir scenes, echo, in their own way, versions of the escapist day-dreaming that people seemed to want in these last phases of the Peloponnesian War. The Midias Painter is the most spectacular representative of the new style. He employs line, like Parrhasius, to suggest volume. But his style – which impressed Winckelmann in the eighteenth century – conveys animated feeling by means of a new, elaborately mannered ornateness, expressed in a sensuous treatment of bodies (sometimes seen in three-quarter views). These figures pose theatrically in idyllic, nostalgic attitudes within Elysian gardens replete with over-sweet delights; and their transparent draperies are depicted with care and skill.

What these vase-painters were doing was to reflect, in an exaggerated fashion permitted by their medium, certain tendencies that had already become apparent not only in Greek wall-painting (though Zeuxis and Parrhasius must surely have been better than the Midias Painter) but also in sculpture during the last quarter of the fifth century BC. For the sculptors of that period had already begun to distance themselves from the serene classicism of the previous epoch, and they, too, had started to experiment in clinging, wind-blown female robes that went beyond the endeavours of Phidias in the same direction (Chapter 15). If labels must be used, these are still High Classical artists, but they represent the ultimate phase of that style.

One of the earliest surviving statues in the new manner is a damaged figure of Nike (Victory) by Paeonius of Mende (now in the Olympia museum), set up by the people of Messenia and Naupactus to celebrate a part they had played in the Athenian victory over the Spartans at Sphacteria (Pylos, 425). The goddess displays her body almost naked against a torrent of clothing that billows out behind her.

Further examples of the style are provided by panels from the low stone balustrade of the temple of Athena Nike on the Athenian Acropolis. This was a building which had probably been envisaged by Phidias (Chapter 15) as part of his original design of the hill-top in the 440s – when the shrine's eventual architect Callicrates seems to have worked with Ictinus on the Parthenon – but was only built in 420 and equipped with its balustrade in *c*.410–407. Upon these panels, now in the Acropolis Museum, at least half-a-dozen artists, depicting seated figures of Athena and winged Victories, exploit the novel possibilities of drapery with animation, assisted by the use of the running drill.

Such works, in the fields of sculpture and painting alike, have prompted the suggestion that these final years of the fifth century witnessed the true inauguration of 'later Greek art', turning away from the classical severity of public affairs to a soft, sympathetic insight which no longer saw every male and female personage as an element in a civic communal situation.

Another sign of this tendency towards delicate gracefulness is the same temple's abandonment of the sturdy Doric in favour of the more slender Ionic architectural Order, despite Callicrates' link with the Doric master Ictinus. This change must have been introduced largely because of the contemporary Peloponnesian War, in which Doric stood for Sparta and Ionic for Athens.

For the same reason the Ionic Order was selected for the Erechtheum, which had likewise seemingly formed part of Phidias' original plan but once again was not designed in detail, and constructed, until later on (*c*.420, and then after interruption in 409/408). The east and north sides of the building have Ionic porticoes that have earned high praise. To the south projects the unique 'porch of the maidens' (Caryatids), figures clothed in deeply cut and folded drapery which serve as columns and support the architrave.

Viewed as architecture the Erechtheum is asymmetrical and irrational, a rare example of radical originality, the antithesis of the tautly unified, rectangular Parthenon near by. The Erechtheum's lavish mouldings, too, including capitals and bases originally gilt and inlaid with polychrome glass, give it something of the character of a luxurious jewel-box or reliquary, once again in contrast to the solid splendours of the Parthenon.

CHAPTER 23

THUCYDIDES: HISTORIAN OF THE WAR

The historian Thucydides (*c*.460/455–*c*.400) was the son of an Athenian who bore the Thracian name of Olorus (suggesting a family relationship with the early-fifth-century statesman Cimon (Chapter 5), who was the grandson of another Olorus). Thucydides possessed an estate at Scapte Hyle in Thrace, from which the neighbouring gold and silver mines of Mount Pangaeum could be exploited. It was no doubt because of this Thracian connection that, as one of Athens' ten annually elected generals (*strategoi*) in 424, he was placed in command of the city's fleet in the northern Aegean. His failure, however, to save Amphipolis from capture by the Spartan Brasidas (Chapter 16) earned him banishment, which ended only after Athens' final defeat in 404.

His *History of the Peloponnesian War (431–404)*, or rather of its first two decades down to 411, is now divided into the following eight books. Book I provides motives for writing the work, a summary of early Greek history (*Archaiologia*), and preliminaries of the Peloponnesian War, set against the Pentekontaeteia (fifty years leading up to the war, i.e. since the Persian invasions). Then come the principal happenings of the opening period of hostilities, known as the Archidamian War (431–421), including the plague and Funeral Speech of Pericles (II; Chapter 11), the revolt of Mytilene and its suppression by the Athenians (III), the capture of the Spartan garrison on Sphacteria (Pylos, 425) and the loss of Amphipolis (IV), the deaths of Brasidas and Cleon in battle and the Peace of Nicias (V). Book V continues with the confused events that followed the peace, down to Athens' ruthless subjugation of a recalcitrant ally Melos (416). Books VI and VII describe the catastrophic Athenian expedition to Sicily (415–413) and Book VIII tells of the rebellion of Athens' allies, followed by the oligarchic revolution in the city (411).

But this last book remains incomplete, and the story of the remaining seven years of the war, culminating in the Athenians' final defeat and surrender (Chapter 24), is lacking. Presumably Thucydides died before he was able to finish it. He was still at work, we can see, at the time of

Athens' final defeat, although he had starting writing, as he tells us himself, when hostilities first broke out twenty-seven years earlier.

Like Herodotus (Chapter 13), he selected a war as a theme, but he innovated – and a vastly influential innovation it was – by choosing a war of his own time: by writing contemporary history (or rather, one should say, *very nearly* contemporary history, because events only a decade or two past were already hard to reconstruct). And he justified this decision by explaining that the Peloponnesian War was the greatest event of all time[27] – thus endeavouring to supersede Herodotus, who had seen the Persian Wars in a similar light.

This pronouncement by Thucydides can be criticized on the grounds that the Peloponnesian War's military operations were mostly not only small-scale but intermittent – it took him time to conclude, even, that the war was a single unit, and not a succession of different, smaller wars. If the war was 'great', this is partly because it had no less a man than Thucydides as its historian. And yet his conclusion can, all the same, be justified on a long-term view, because the war, and the widespread degradation that accompanied it, so severely disabled the city-states that it caused the eventual ruin of their independence, and so, also, of their distinctive civilization.

As and when the different parts of his history came to be completed (at various dates that remain the subject of argument), the successive portions of his masterpiece were no doubt read out aloud to Athenian audiences, as Herodotus' work had been, though Thucydides also wrote, unusually or unprecedentedly, to be read. He concedes that his refusal to admit a romantic element (so much to the fore in Herodotus) made his *History* less pleasing to the ear, but he stresses that it was designed to be 'a possession for all time'.[28]

The work is the product of a powerful brain, probably the most powerful that has ever addressed itself to historical writing. Unsurprisingly, therefore, he himself attaches primary importance to the intelligence, or otherwise, of the characters he describes. The word *gnome*, meaning understanding or judgment, appears more than three hundred times in the course of the *History*, and intelligent men are singled out for praise, notably Themistocles (whose reputation had otherwise not fared very well), and Pericles (who, despite implied reservations, inspired the historian with nostalgic fascination), and a later politician, Theramenes (who although a trimmer was unmistakably clever).

The outstanding acuteness of Thucydides' own intellect has both favourable and unfavourable effects on his work. To take the former first, no one can fail to be impressed by the iron, cerebral objectivity and restraint with which he describes his own dismissal by Athens for military failure. And, in more general terms, his intellectual powers reveal themselves in a passionate desire to transcend individual events and attain to universals, by searching below the surface in order to find underlying causes.

Here the spirit of the contemporary physician Hippocrates (Chapter 20) (to whose desire to seek out causes and effects Thucydides' analysis of the plague must also owe a debt) is applied, unprecedentedly, to history. The historian's explanations of the origins of the Peloponnesian War that emerges is divided into two parts, the immediate grievances of the two sides (relating to Corcyra and Potidaea), and the real underlying motivation, which he identified as Sparta's fear of Athenian expansion. Such a distinction between immediate 'causes', or occasions of friction, and the basic underlying realities of power represented progress in political thinking. Indeed, for such reasons, Thucydides must be described as the creator of political history – for good and also for evil, since it is partly due to him that western civilization has regarded politics as the central concern and study of the human race, to its dubious benefit.

No less decisive was his persistent refusal, in contrast with Herodotus, to blame human failures on divine intervention. Certainly oracles are still given prominence, because human behaviour is influenced by them, but the causes and effects of what men do and say are seen to be more essentially and fundamentally the products of their own human natures. Speak of the operations of Fate or Necessity, if you like, but those are merely names for the unavoidable results of human beings' own actions, results which they have brought upon themselves. This is not always the case, however, since room must also be allowed for the irrational, and some things are a matter of Chance, mere inexplicable coincidence, the unpredictable in an otherwise predictable world. Certainly, it is slack thinking to see Chance as a sufficient explanation everywhere, since (as Pericles is made to say) 'we commonly blame Chance for whatever makes nonsense of our calculations'.[29] Yet Chance does have a devastating effect, especially in wartime; and the Athenian plague manifested its workings.

These messages are conveyed in language which, in contrast to the relaxed expansiveness of Herodotus, is grave, intense and crammed with meaning. Thucydides' language is equipped to present the most incisive analyses of the shifting, deteriorating attitudes of states, councils and armies, capable of investigating internal strife (*stasis*, notably at Corcyra) with devastating skill, and able to portray battle-scenes (for example at Syracuse) by more than Tolstoyan pictures of soldiers' collective psychologies and high hopes and miserable despairs.

Before turning to the unfavourable effects of Thucydides' massive brain-power, it is desirable to mention two factors that do *not* deserve to be regarded as pejorative. The first is his attitude to economic affairs. He knows they are important (noting, for example, the early significance of navigation and commerce), but he says much less about them than some of us would like him to. That is partly because the statistics were just not available, but also because, even when they could be found (for example in the Athenian Tribute Lists), he was not interested in using them since he saw the real motivation and significance of the war as political, with economic motives only ancillary. Given his selectiveness (of which more will be said below) this was legitimate.

The second factor that should not count against Thucydides as a historian was his educative, instructional purpose. He was writing, he said, for those who wanted 'a clear record of what had happened in the past and will, in due course, tend to be repeated with some degree of similarity':[30] a knowledge of the past will be a useful guide to the future. These are unfashionable assertions today, when we hear (and must agree) that since past history does not repeat itself we ought to study it for its own content and not for its analogies to our own and future times. True, history does not repeat itself, and Thucydides was well aware of this, but in answer to the second point he maintained that history, in addition to the intrinsic, self-contained interest of what happened, *should* be studied because of the instruction it offers to our own lives and times. And to exclude that possibility would mean depriving ourselves of something of great value.

However, there are more damaging things that can be said against Thucydides as a historian in any of the senses in which we employ the term. His summary of very early Greek history, the *Archaiologia*, though a *tour de force* which established a new, unsentimental way of investing the past with rational continuity, is flawed by the belief that myth, by critical attention, can be converted into historical narrative – take away what is impossible, and what is left will be true (p. 76). Then, to come down to the fifty years before the Peloponnesian War (*Pentekontaeteia*), this leaves out a great deal – including dates – that we would like to know: because his survey is not meant to be an even-handed history at all, but an account of the rise of Athenian power which brought about the Peloponnesian War.

And it is a rigorously selective account at that. At every stage Thucydides, quoting few sources, reserves the Olympian right to select as he thinks fit. He offers no alternatives to his choice of facts, which are punctuated by gaps and silences, or to his biased character-sketches and other value judgments – and it is impossible for us, very often, to supply them from other authors.

One example is his excessive minimization of the Persian factor. The Peace of Callias (449/448; Chapter 11) is omitted altogether (thus, wrongly, inspiring doubts whether it ever happened). Thucydides, it has been argued, does reveal indirectly that the treaty was not unknown to him. Whether he does or not it was too important an event to deserve omission. And nothing is said of the Treaty of Epilycus between Athens and Persia in 424/423. Furthermore, the Athenians' assistance to the Persian rebel Amorges, which more than anything else brought Persia, fatefully and fatally, into the Peloponnesian War on the other side, does not receive the emphasis it ought to have (Chapter 24). Was this, once again, because Thucydides, at the time of writing, did not believe this Athenian decision relevant to his story? – although it eventually proved very relevant indeed. Or is there an element of Greek chauvinism here, making it impossible for him to admit Persia's continuing decisive role? Or a fear that, if he did so, he would be seeming to justify Herodotus' exaltation of that role, exhibited in his account of the Persian War?

But what places us most of all on the alert is Thucydides' employment of speeches. Herodotus, too, had included them, but Thucydides offers us as many as forty, constituting a quarter of his entire history. This would have caused no surprise to his Athenian hearers or readers, who were connoisseurs of public eloquence. But Thucydides admits that these 'speeches' are only 'as near as possible' to what each speaker said, and do not reproduce his actual words.[31] Obviously they do not, in view of their single unindividual, uniformly Thucydidean style (a special unvarying variant of his normal manner, adopted for speeches and set-piece analyses); and in any case these orations had not, when delivered, been put into writing, and no one could be expected to remember their entire text.

Thucydides was aware of all this – for no one knew better than he did how quickly and easily the truth is distorted by contradictory witnesses; and, when recording alleged speeches, he explicitly declared his intention, not of attempting to reproduce them verbatim, but of making the orator say what, in his opinion, was called for by each situation. Thus they fulfil psychological and philosophical purposes, offering universally valid truths and suggesting how decisions may have been arrived at. But they are not what any speaker said. All too often Pericles' 'Funeral Speech' is treated as if Pericles actually delivered it. He did not; it is Thucydides' own personal interpretation and reconstruction and epitaph of the Periclean state, a state that was imperialistic and yet productive of a brilliant civilization – only a 'nominal democracy', but Thucydides did not think democracy was intelligent. No fault can be found with his assumption that words were as important as deeds in Greek and Athenian history. But these orations consisted of *his* words, not those of the alleged speakers.

Their diction and their frequently balanced, antithetical placing (in pairs), reveal the influence of the sophists (especially Gorgias; Chapter 12), whose methods thus contributed to Thucydides' fictional treatment.

And the elaborate employment of these orations as an indirect vehicle of his own communicative purpose is reminiscent, also, of the tragedians, who again guided many of Thucydides' methods. For example, they prompted his view of Athenian imperialism. Thus the Sicilian expedition is shown to be replete with all the infatuated, misinformed arrogance (*hubris*), the reversals, the Nemesis and the irony of tragic drama. This makes splendid writing, but is scarcely history. The same applies, again, to the dramatic dialogue form in which the debate about the fate of insurgent Melos is presented. This method is reminiscent of the contemporary tragedies of Euripides; but once again, it is not history.

Although, then, fifth-century Athens produced one of the most important civilizations the world has ever known, for large chunks of its story we are almost solely dependent on very personal, and uncheckable, judgments and selections: those offered to us, so potently, by Thucydides. This is perhaps the most tantalizing of all the challenges that the period presents to us. For Thucydides, despite his giant steps forward and his unique cleverness, was not, as Macaulay believed, the 'greatest historian who has ever lived', since he is too insistent upon giving his own views of what happened – upon telling us, that is to say, what we have to believe.

CHAPTER 24

LYSANDER: CONQUEROR OF ATHENS

Before the Athenian expeditionary force was destroyed at Syracuse, Sparta and its allies had resumed the war against Athens (414). On the traitorous advice, it was said, of Alcibiades – who had eluded the Athenian officials conducting him back from Sicily to answer charges of blasphemy, and taken refuge at Sparta – the Spartans established a fortified base at Decelea in northern Attica. This denied the Athenians their Laurium silver-mines (from which hosts of slaves deserted) and greatly increased their already perilous dependence on imported grain (413). Then the catastrophe that overwhelmed the Athenians in Sicily, although it did not cause them to collapse straightaway – indeed, despite a shortage of trained crews, they began to rebuild their fleet – encouraged the Spartans to hope, for the first time, that they themselves might win the war at sea; so they, too, ordered as many new ships as they could.

These Spartan hopes were enhanced by the behaviour of the Athenians, who lent their support to a Persian dissident Amorges in Caria (the bastard son of another rebel, Pissuthnes, satrap of Sardis), when he revolted against King Darius II Ochus in *c*.414/412. This Athenian decision was both ineffective and suicidal, since, although Thucydides (perhaps out of Greek pride) does not acknowledge the fact and says too little about Amorges (Chapter 23), the outcome of the Peloponnesian War depended on the attitude of Persia, which could finance either side's fleet as it wished, and blockade the Athenians' access to their Black Sea grain supplies (Chapter 27).

During earlier phases of the war both the Athenians and the Spartans had made overtures to Persia – without durable success, since Artaxerxes I and then Darius II preferred to stand aloof and allow the two contestants to weaken and destroy one another. Now, however, in 412, with Alcibiades' help, Sparta entered into an agreement with Tissaphernes (who had taken over Pissuthnes' satrapy of Sardis) and Pharnabazus, the satrap of Dascylium in north-western Asia Minor. The Spartans had only won the Persians' support at a humiliating

price, by having to abandon their professed 'liberation' of the Greek states on the Asian mainland (though this may not have become clear until later). Nevertheless the new Persian backing for their cause was at first only intermittent and half-hearted: since what the satraps still hoped for was the exhaustion of Sparta and Athens alike.

All the same, this Persian support for the Spartans, such as it was, proved enough to encourage Byzantium, Chios, Miletus and other subject-allies of the Athenians to rebel against their control (413/412), with the help of a small Peloponnesian fleet which crossed the Aegean and established itself at Miletus. Athenian grain supplies from the Black Sea (as well as Egypt) were now indeed imperilled, and the danger became more urgent still when Abydus in the Hellespont, assisted by the Spartans and Persians, joined the revolt; and so did the city-states on the island of Euboea (411).

At Athens itself, too, a group of oligarchs staged an insurrection, and set up a government of the Four Hundred, who inspired terror, and tried both to negotiate financial support from Persia (with the help of Alcibiades) and to arrange peace with Sparta at one and the same time. But when their hopes in both these directions were disappointed, they in turn were overthrown by a more moderate administration, halfway between oligarchy and democracy. This regime of the 'Five Thousand' co-operated with the Athenian navy at Samos, which had become an outpost of democracy under the command of Alcibiades (following various reversals of attitude on his part).

Then, late in 411, the Athenians defeated the fleet of the blundering Spartan Mindarus at Cynossema, and in the following year – under three generals including Alcibiades – won another victory at Cyzicus, so that the route to the Black Sea was now out of danger, the enemy fleet incapacitated for two years, and insurgent allies brought to heel. The Five Thousand was replaced by a revived full democracy, the Athenian politician Cleophon refused official or unofficial Spartan offers of peace, and Alcibiades returned to Athens in triumph, to be elected as general and commander-in-chief (407).

Now, however, came one of the major turning points in Greek history, as a result of an unforeseeable accident.

This chance event was an intimate personal understanding that sprang up between the Persian Prince Cyrus the younger, who was a son of Darius II and, at the age of about eighteen, had just been given an overriding command in Asia Minor, and the Spartan Lysander.

Lysander's father was a certain Aristocritus; his own early career is unknown – stories of his humble birth can be viewed with suspicion – but the Spartans appointed him admiral in 408/407: at last, it has been

said, the right man in the right place at the right moment. His rapidly formed friendship with Cyrus, silencing any sections of Spartan opinion that were uneasy about collaboration with Persia, meant that for the first time adequate Persian money was available to equip and maintain the Spartan fleet. And this proved decisive for the Peloponnesian War just as similar Persian aid (for either side) would likewise have been on earlier occasions, if it had only been provided.

By means of subsidies from this Persian source, Lysander mobilized ninety ships and defeated an Athenian fleet at Notium (407). Alcibiades was not present – one of his subordinates Antiochus, a skilled steersman but nothing more, was in command – but he was disgraced, as a result of this reverse, by his political enemies (an unfortunate development, since for all his faults he was the Athenians' best hope), and eventually took refuge in fortified residences he possessed in Thrace.

Athens rallied, contrived to man 150 more ships, and won a costly sea-battle at Arginusae (406), foolishly executing six generals afterwards, by a vote of the Assembly, bcause they had failed, in stormy weather, to rescue drowning Athenian seamen. The by no means pro-Persian Spartan general Callicratidas, who had succeeded Lysander, also perished in the battle, and Lysander's partisans demanded his reappointment in the dead man's place. A second term as commander-in-chief, however, was impossible under the Spartan constitution, so Lysander crossed the Aegean in 405 in the nominal position of second-in-command (*epistoleus*), although, as his specialized naval experience warranted, he was recognized as the effective commander.

Cyrus gave him the money to build two hundred new vessels, and the decisive moment was now approaching. Lysander sailed to the Hellespont and seized Lampsacus, where he established his base. This renewed threat to their grain route from the Black Sea caused the Athenians to send a fleet of scarcely inferior size (raised with great difficulty) to the area, and it took up its position at Aegospotami, across the straits from Lampsacus. In order to deter Greeks from serving in Lysander's well-paid crews the Athenian Assembly passed a decree ordering that every seaman, captured from the other side, should have one of his hands amputated.

The Athenians were determined to compel Lysander to fight, and every day they sailed across to Lampsacus to offer battle. Every day too, after the challenge had been declined, they returned to Aegospotami, disembarked on its open beach, and foraged for food. On the fifth day (perhaps 1 September) Lysander waited until the Athenians, after offering their habitual challenge, had made their way back to Aegospotami, and then suddenly launched an attack on their ships. Scarcely any battle developed, since nearly all the Athenian soldiers and sailors were away looking for food. A few of their triremes escaped, but because of this one day's carelessness 170 were captured; and three or four thousand Athenian prisoners taken on board them were executed in cold blood. Only one Athenian general got back home (and this earned him accusations of treason). The Black Sea route was lost to the Athenians, so they could no longer be fed; and the war was therefore over.

Lysander had achieved one of the outstanding feats in Greek history; by Persian money and his own naval skill, and through the tenacity of the Spartan fighting man under a government which, even if unimaginative, made futile military decisions less frequently than its enemies, he had won the Peloponnesian War. Although Thucydides, as we saw, may have magnified the dimensions of the struggle, its outcome was nevertheless a landmark, because the civilization of the city-states could never be the same again. Under the strain of the war many of them had displayed ominous internal instabilities – the period of hostilities witnessed at least twenty-seven betrayals or attempted betrayals of cities from within – and, as for their external relations, a simple balance of power (as would soon become clear) had been superseded by a complex and shifting pattern, replete with uncertainties which eventually proved lethal (Chapters 29, 35).

But at first Sparta was in charge. Lysander threatened any Athenians caught outside Athens with death, and refugees streamed into the city, where food soon ran short. Even then, the citizens resisted a Spartan blockade, fearing the same vengeance that they themselves had imposed on enemies and defectors, and seeking desperately, and vainly, to make terms that would leave them, not indeed their empire and fleet, but at least their Long Walls. Yet by spring 404 there was nothing to eat any longer, and they offered unconditional surrender.

Their offer was accepted; and Lysander proceeded to Athens. However, he refused to agree with Sparta's allies Corinth and Thebes that the city should be destroyed and its inhabitants annihilated. For he wanted instead to keep them as loyal puppets and watchdogs against Theban expansion. With this in mind, he set up an oligarchic government at Athens, the Thirty, who before the year 404 was over had executed 1,500 Athenians and banished 5,000 more. Enforced by the presence of a Spartan garrison, this reign of terror was directed by the clever but sinister Critias, who put his more moderate, opportunistic colleague Theramenes to death for opposing the bloodbath.

Moreover, Lysander set up similar oligarchic Boards of Ten (decarchies) in other cities that had hitherto been subject-allies of Athens. These boards were composed of his collaborators, and once again, in many cases, propped up by Spartan troops, under a harmost (governor). This was an attempt to replace an Athenian empire by a Spartan counterpart, under tighter control. And it proved a dismal failure. Yet Lysander was an able man, who had earlier shown not only expert generalship but astute diplomacy and organizational skill; and his decision not to obliterate Athens had been prudent – or at least fortunate for humanity. Nevertheless, when he was finally in a positon to exercise power – greater power than had come the way of any Spartan before him, and widely recognized abroad, for example by his religious veneration as a living hero at Samos – a streak of self-seeking arrogance and brutality in his character ensured that his political endeavours henceforward came to nothing.

But the fault was also Sparta's. For the subsequent imperial efforts of the Spartan state, transformed abruptly from a backward, isolationist military community into a world power, were not only hampered by an acute shortage of manpower but also displayed corrupt, heavy-handed ineptitude – partly caused by a sudden influx of wealth with which the Spartans did not know how to cope.

Initially, however, their government at least had the good sense to reverse Lysander's unworkable arrangements at Athens, when the Agiad King Pausanias (409–395) persuaded a majority of the ephors (now more powerful than they had been in earlier times) to promote a settlement which permitted the restoration of democracy in that city. In other Greek states, too, many of the decarchies proved unable to govern, and had to be modified or abolished (*c.*403/402). Lysander's position was thus weakened, and it may have been at this time that he considered launching a *putsch* which would make the joint monarchy elective, so that its power would have been reduced in his own favour.[32] But if so, the plan came to nothing.

However, on the death of Pausanias' colleague King Agis II (427–399), of the Eurypontid royal house, Lysander saw an opportunity to regain his authority by supporting the claims of the late king's half-brother Agesilaus (II) to the throne. Sparta, by this time, had become alienated from the new Persian monarch Artaxerxes II Mnemon (405/404–359/358), owing to its unofficial support for an unsuccessful rebellion by Lysander's friend Cyrus the younger (the theme of Xenophon's *March Up Country* (*Anabasis*); Chapter 30). In 395 Agesilaus, faced with the hostility of the Persians, launched an invasion of their dominions in Asia Minor. Lysander headed the thirty Spartan officers who accompanied him, and displayed his intention of once again becoming the decision-maker of his state. But Agesilaus proved unwilling to tolerate this elevation of one of his subjects to any such role, and discarded Lysander, who returned home (395).

In the same year Corinth and Thebes, supported by Argos and even by recently defeated Athens (which must have enjoyed a considerable recovery), launched the 'Corinthian War' against the tyrannical rule of Sparta. Lysander led a force of Sparta's allies against the coalition, moving from Phocis into Boeotia, where he captured Orchomenus. Then he marched on to Haliartus, where he was to join Pausanias and the main Spartan army. But before it arrived he attacked the town alone, and was killed.

PART V

First Half of the Fourth Century: West and East

LIST OF EVENTS

	Dionysius I *strategos autokrator* (commander-in-chief):
405	Makes peace with the Carthaginian Hannibal
403	Captures Sicilian cities of Aetna, Naxos, Catana and Leontini
398/397–396	First Carthaginian War, against Himilco's expedition
394/393	Athenian inscription calls him 'archon of Sicily' (also 369/368 and 368/367)
392	Second Carthaginian War, against Mago I
390–387/386	Invades south Italy; defeats a Greek coalition at the River Elleporus (388) and destroys Rhegium (387/386)
388	Syracusan delegation to the Olympic Games, under his brother Thearidas
387	Plato's first visit to Syracuse (second and third visits in 367 and 361)
c.386	In north-eastern Italy and the Adriatic and the Balkans
383	Third Carthaginian War; defeat at Cronium (*c*.378 or *c*.375)
368/367	Fourth Carthaginian War
368/367	Alliance with Athens; his tragedy *The Ransoming of Hector* wins first prize at the Lenaean Festival
367	His death; succeeded by Dionysius II (displaced in 357/356 by Dion (d.354) and in 343/342 by Timoleon)

CHAPTER 25

DIONYSIUS I: EMPIRE BUILDER

The Syracusan Hermocrates, who had played such a historic part in the repulse of the Athenian expedition (415–413; Chapter 16), was sentenced to exile by the radical democrats of his city under Diocles, who took advantage of his absence while he was fighting for Sparta. Hermocrates lost his life while attempting, illegally and forcibly, to return (408).

Meanwhile, after prolonged quiescence since 480 (Chapter 4), the Carthaginians had decided to invade Sicily. They had not tried to take advantage of the Athenian expedition, but now, following shifts in their own internal balance of power, they moved to the attack. They were encouraged, no doubt, by war-weariness and internal dissension among the Syracusans, and provoked by the fear that, the Athenian threat to their existence having been removed, they would endeavour to conquer the territory in the west of the island which had been colonized by the Phoenicians, and was now dependent on Carthage.

The first Carthaginian army, led by a certain Hannibal, invaded Sicily in 409, and a second force, again under Hannibal (with his young relative Himilco as his deputy), arrived in 406. When the Syracusans failed to relieve Acragas, Dionysius, who had been the son-in-law and supporter of Hermocrates – ignoring his own partial responsibility for the military failure – seized the opportunity to induce the city's Assembly to elect a new set of generals, including himself. Then, however, he got rid of his colleagues, and with the help of a bodyguard (and encouragement from Sparta) had himself elected commander-in-chief (*strategos autokrator*) with dictatorial powers. And that was how Dionysius inaugurated a second wave of military autocracy in Sicily, of which Gelon and Hiero I had represented the first phase at Syracuse (Chapter 4).

However, Dionysius was not successful in halting the Carthaginians' advance, and, when confronted by a rebellion among the nobility and former ruling class (*gamoroi*) of Syracuse itself, felt it advisable to make peace with them (405). The treaty's terms were not favourable, since for the first time they recognized a Carthaginian dominion (*epikrateia*) in Sicily – comprising three-fifths of the island. Nevertheless, the agreement gave him the opportunity to suppress opposition at home and build up his power.

Like Gelon and Hiero I, he did not assume the title of king, preferring instead to maintain a semblance of democratic government – in which the principal appointments, however, went to members of his family, and to friends. (But whether it was also true that he later dressed himself like the Persian Great King, and allowed the erection of statues that identified him with the god Dionysus, we cannot tell.)

His position was largely based on mercenary soldiers from numerous Greek territories. Warriors of this kind had long constituted a part of Sicilian armies, but never before had they formed such a formidable body, comprising many thousand men, among whom were numerous freed slaves. Weapon manufacturers (*technitai*), too, had been brought to Syracuse from many Mediterranean lands, and with their help Dionysius developed the catapult, thus transforming the tactics of siegecraft which he learnt from his Carthaginian enemies. He also increased his fleet from 100 to 300 warships, including, it was said, quadriremes and quinqueremes, with four and five men to a single oar – an idea once again borrowed from Carthage (and only revived in the Greek world half a century later).

A new type of trained professional warlord who regarded warfare as a science, Dionysius excelled in amphibious operations, and was an expert in the co-ordinated employment of specialist arms. He realized the need to ensure the safety of Syracuse itself, and, with this as his aim, converted the city's island of Ortygia into an impregnable fortress. Moreover, warned by the Athenian expedition, he mobilized 60,000 free workers to fortify the adjoining heights of Epipolae, where his walls remained impregnable for centuries.

Then he was ready to turn against other Sicilian Greek states. Aetna, Naxos, Catana and Leontini were all ruthlessly captured (403), and their citizens displaced (and usually moved to Syracuse) in favour of mercenaries and native Sicels, as part of a policy of large-scale human transplantations.

Thus he was fully prepared when a new Carthaginian invasion took place in 398/397, under Himilco. This First Carthaginian War of Dionysius, said to have been popular among his people who were shocked by the attack,[1] was signalized by a bloody massacre of Carthaginian merchants on the island. And a memorable Syracusan victory soon followed, for Dionysius employed his new siege engines and techniques, with revolutionary success, to blockade and capture Motya, the enemy's principal centre in the west of the island.

In the following year, however, Himilco reconquered the whole north coast of Sicily, repelling Dionysius' brother Leptines off Catana, with severe losses, and blockading Syracuse itself. But the city was saved by a combination of Spartan reinforcements and a plague that struck the besieging Carthaginian troops, who became demoralized and were totally defeated. However, Himilco was able to preserve the lives of his surviving soldiers – apparently by agreement with Dionysius who may not have wanted the complete destruction of Carthaginian power on the island, since this 'foreign threat' not only rallied Syracusan public opinion but gave him an excuse to extend his authority over other Sicilian city-states.

Nevertheless Himilco, on his return to Carthage, was so badly received by his fellow citizens that he killed himself (during a revolt). In 392 Mago (I), who had been his deputy and now held the Carthaginian command in Sicily, was directed to launch a further attack on the Greek parts of the island. However, this Second Carthaginian War of Dionysius once again ended in a peace that was favourable to himself, according to which the Carthaginian sphere of influence was limited to a relatively small territory west of the River Mazarus, and Dionysius' authority over other Greeks, and over native Sicels, was recognized by Carthage.

The consequent strengthening of his regional position emboldened him to look further afield, and in 390 he intervened in southern Italy, against Rhegium and its Greek associates. Allied with native Lucanians, he devastated his enemies' territory far and wide, defeated a coalition force at the River Elleporus (388), and attacked Rhegium itself (387), of which the subsequent capture and destruction, after an eleven months' siege, was a landmark of his reign.

Such successes, backed by amicable relations with Taras (Chapter 26), made Syracuse the principal power in south Italy as well as in Sicily itself. Not content with this, however, Dionysius sent a fleet into the Adriatic, where he built a canal (*fossa Philistina*) at the mouth of the Eridanus (Po), settled colonists not only at Italian Ancona and Hadria but across the sea at Issa and Pharos, and reduced King Alcetas of the Molossi in Epirus to the status of a subject ally.

These incursions into the Balkans attracted notice among the city-states of Greece – which were aware that they, too, might become targets of Dionysius' apparently unlimited ambitions. At Athens his expansionist activities, not to speak of his frequently displayed sympathy with Sparta (which had helped his enterprises, and received help from him in turn), provoked alarm, by no means dispelled either by political negotiations or by Plato's first visit to Syracuse (387), which proved a dismal failure. In the previous year (it would seem) Dionysius had dispatched a grandiose delegation, led by his brother Thearidas, to the Olympic Games. There the Athenian orator Lysias attacked him in his *Olympic Speech* (*Olympiacus*) – part of which is still extant – and his envoys' tents were looted by the crowd.

The year 383 witnessed the outbreak of Dionysius' Third Carthaginian War, which he himself provoked; he won a battle in which Mago (I) was killed. But after his crushing defeat by Mago's son at Cronium near Panormus (*c.*378 or 375?) he was obliged to pay heavy reparations, and had to retract his frontier, ceding all Sicilian territory west of the River Halycus.

In 373 Sparta once again secured his support, but subsequently his relations with Athens improved. We do not know when it was that Isocrates (Chapter 32) wrote him an open letter, praising his championship of Hellenism.[2] But Athenian inscriptions of 369/368 and 368/367, describing him as 'Archon of Sicily' – a title which he may or may not have employed himself – record a treaty and an alliance between the two states.[3]

Despite opposition from radical Athenian democrats, which made such contacts somewhat precarious, these official links with Athens enabled Dionysius to satisfy one of his most ardent desires, which was to gain renown as a tragic poet. Hitherto his possession of Aeschylus' writing table and the pen and harp and tablets of Euripides had not been enough to procure success in this direction. But in 367 his play *The Ransoming of Hector* won the first prize at the Athenian festival of the Lenaea. This victory, the story goes, so greatly excited him that at the ensuing celebrations he drank too much and died.

At this time he was engaged in his Fourth Carthaginian War, once again begun by his own initiative, and involving large forces on either side. He gained control of Selinus and Eryx, but failed to take Lilybaeum (which had succeeded Motya as Carthage's principal stronghold in western Sicily); and after his death his son Dionysius II made peace on the same terms that had been agreed after his father's third war.

So much of the reign of Dionysius I had been dedicated to fighting wars against the Carthaginians (in obvious recollection and emulation of the victory of Gelon at Himera) that his record must, to a large extent, be assessed in terms of their results. On the one hand, he had not allowed Carthage to extend its control over the whole of the island – and his endeavours meant that in the future, too, it was never able to do so. Nevertheless, as his ancient critics did not refrain from pointing out, his military and organizational skills had failed to drive the Carthaginians out of Sicily (it remained for the Romans to achieve this, a century and a half later).

In any attempt to judge the other aspects of Dionysius' protracted rule – the strongest and longest tyranny, it was said, recorded by history – no such neat estimate can be offered, with any degree of confidence. This is because of the predominantly hostile tradition that gathered round his name. The hostility was partly due to the recriminations arising out of Plato's failed mission (the power-mad dictator in the ninth book of his *Republic* may well be Dionysius), but it is more particularly owed to the hostility of the influential and popular historian Timaeus of Tauromenium (*c*.356–260). His work, which put Sicily and Magna Graecia in the centre of the historical map, has survived only in fragments, but it gave birth to a mass of ancient moralizing lierature about the evil ways of tyrants – an old, Herodotean folklore theme which he now brought up to date by attacks on Dionysius, embroidered by numerous fictitious tales.

True, Dionysius himself also had propagandist writers at his own court, including the historian Philistus, one of his principal advisers. But Philistus' works, once again, are almost entirely lost, and so are those of Theopompus of Chios, who although moralistically inclined could not find too much (except luxury) to complain of in Dionysius' regime.

What of Dionysius then? An exponent of military rulership on a scale the Greeks had never seen before, he was the most magnificent figure in their whole world, and made Syracuse, housing a population not far short of half a million, the capital of the most powerful among all the Greek states. The heir of Gelon and Hiero I, Dionysius was also the advance guard of the Hellenistic monarchs and their military skills and empires – and the forerunner of their contempt for autonomous city-states.

Apart from his literary and dramatic ambitions, his character displayed few features that were attractive or humane. Anecdotes tell of his obsessive concern for his own personal security – and such a preoccupation may well have been justified. For he was a ruler whom many hated for his unflinchingly despotic measures – murders, destructions, aggressions, enslavements, compulsory exchanges of population, forced labour, severe and multiple financial oppressions and confiscations (to pay for his mercenaries), not to speak of marriage broking and polygamy on the most high-handed scale. It was difficult to behave like that without making numerous enemies, and their existence prevented him from exploiting his empire's manpower with the maximum effect.

On the other hand his astute, indomitable, resilient regime not only extended the dominions of Syracuse but also, in order to secure money for his mercenaries, greatly enlarged its commercial activities – with the help of the strongest currency in the west, designed by exceptional numismatic artists, notably Cimon and Euaenetus.

Although Dionysius was willing enough to encourage class war, when it suited him, he must have enriched Syracusans of all classes, who did not get in his way. These beneficiaries, and supporters, included not only members of the aristocracy, who had helped to create his power and were united to him by complex marriage ties, but also (as Aristotle and others pointed out) the bulk of the ordinary people of Syracuse, in addition no doubt – although of this we have no direct knowledge – to many Greek and non-Greek peoples in his various dependencies.

And there was, indeed, something to be said, on a longer view, for his attempts to weld the city-states of Sicily and south Italy into a coherent political unit, so as to avoid the eventually fatal inter-city bickerings of the Greek mainland. But Dionysius' tyrannical methods failed, ultimately, to produce the desired results; in the end he did not so much consolidate Hellenism as undo it. For the new citizenries and new classes, brought into being by all his demographic convulsions, created a society which was more bitterly faction-ridden than ever before, so that the future history of Sicily became a series of lethal civil wars and conspiracies and dynastic carnages, in which the populations of the cities were shoved mercilessly this way and that by one unscrupulous adventurer after another, and the mercenaries upon whom they relied.

CHAPTER 26

ARCHYTAS: PHILOSOPHICAL RULER

The regions of southern Italy settled by the Greeks had come to be known as 'Great Greece' (Magna Graecia). This may have been because the hot, dry summers and mild winters, and characteristic interplay of land and sea and vegetation of their coastal areas offered a familiar and welcoming environment. The settlers could embark on their agricultural and other activities with little or no modification – although often on a larger scale than they had been accustomed to back in the homeland.

Before the eighth century BC was over, the Greeks had established colonies in two sectors of south Italy, first Campania (Cumae (*c.*730/725), preceded by a trading station, and an earlier post on the island of Pithecusae), and then in the 'instep' of Italy, upon the Ionian Sea.

In this latter area the Gulf of Taras was named after a city founded, according to Eusebius, in 706 BC. The colonists, led by Phalanthus, were Spartans, known as 'Partheniai' (sons of unmarried women), allegedly because they were the illegitimate children of Spartan mothers by helots (Appendix IV), born while the women's husbands were away fighting; although the story was, and is, regarded with scepticism.

The first of these immigrants chose a site seven miles to the south-east of the later Taras, to which, however, they soon transferred themselves, joining (or more probably subjecting) a population of native Iapygians. The fortified city which Taras then became stood on a promontory almost cut off from the mainland and crowned by a virtually impregnable acropolis which overlooked, to the east, an inner lagoon harbour, and, to the west, its external counterpart, which was protected from the sea by two small islands and formed the largest and safest port on the Italian peninsula.

In *c.*500 Taras was ruled by a monarch, Aristophilides, whose kingship, Herodotus reported, followed the Spartan model.[4] The city's territory and crops were threatened by tribes in the hinterland, but in the early years of the fifth century the Tarantines won a series of military successes against these peoples, which caused them to dedicate two victory monuments at Delphi. In *c.*475/473, however, in alliance with Rhegium, they suffered a severe defeat from the adjacent Iapygian confederacy. As a result, the aristocratic government of the city was dismissed, and replaced by a relatively stable, if somewhat undisciplined, democracy, which after *c.*450, profiting from the decline of neighbouring Croton, converted Taras into the principal Greek centre of southern Italy.

Its citizens successfully fought the new Panhellenic foundation of Thurii, sponsored by Athens, for the possession of Siris, and then established a colony of their own at Heraclea in Lucania, which became the meeting-place of a League of Italian Greek (Italiot) cities, formed to protect them against the tribes of the interior. This confederacy was dominated by Taras, which possessed the largest fleet and an army fifteen thousand strong.

The income of the Tarantines was derived from wool (which many people preferred to the well-known Milesian product) and *murex* (purple dye from a sea-shell, employed to colour a woman's garment known as the *tarantinon*), as well as from agricultural produce, and horses, and trading (which extended as far as northern Adriatic waters). The prosperity derived from these enterprises was reflected in the production of a renowned silver coinage depicting a horseman, the most prolific currency of the region, which continued to be issued for two hundred years. During the Peloponnesian War the city, jealous of interference from the Greek mainland, opposed the Athenian expedition against the Syracusans (415–413), to whose fleet it contributed ships.

In keeping with a longstanding artistic tradition, Taras was now well known for its own school of Apulian pottery, as well as for its jewellery, which was as distinguished and varied as any in the Greek world; and the popular theatre (*hilarotragoedia*) for which the city became famous had by this time already established itself.

It was under the leadership of Archytas, in *c.*380–*c.*345(?) that the city – its regional supremacy confirmed by the ravages that Dionysius I of Syracuse inflicted on other south Italian city-states (Chapter 25) – attained the height of its power and wealth.

Although the constitution of Taras did not permit a man to serve more than two terms as general, Archytas was elected to the office on no less than seven occasions – during which, according to his biographer Aristoxenus, he never lost a battle;[5] and he must have dominated the political life of the Italiot federation. His career became encrusted with legends, centring upon his lofty morals, gentle kindness, self-control, and rigorous asceticism (contrasted with the luxury that surrounded

The 'Temple of Neptune' – it was, in fact, dedicated to Hera – at Posidonia (Paestum), a colony Sybaris, in south-western Italy. *c.* 450 BC; it is the latest in date of a group of three surviving temples.

The so-called Temple of Concord, *c.* 430 BC (its correct title is uncertain), one of a remarkable oup of shrines at the Rhodian and Cretan colony of Acragas (Agrigento) in southern Sicily, the thplace of Empedocles. Mid-fifth century BC.

3. The Propylaea, the monumental gateway of the Athenian Acropolis, designed by Mnesicles in 437–432 BC.

4. The Parthenon, Temple of Athena 'the Maiden' on the Acropolis at Athens, erected between 447 and 438 BC. The architect was Ictinus and his master-builder Callicrates, working in accordance with Phidias' general plan.

. Temple at the Elymian city of Segesta
north-western Sicily). Work on the
building was probably started after the
own's alliance with Athens in 426 BC, and
t was left uncompleted when Segesta
uarrelled with Selinus in 416.

. The Ionic Temple of Athena Nike
Victory) on the Athenian Acropolis,
onstructed in the 420s beside the Propylaea,
lthough Phidias must already have
lanned some building on the site at an
arlier date.

. The Caryatid porch of the complex,
symmetrical Erechtheum, constructed in
. 420 and from *c.* 409–408 BC, although, as
n the case of the Temple of Athena Nike,
ome building on the venerated site was
robably envisaged in Phidias' earlier plan.

8. The latest of many proposed reconstructions of the Mausoleum a Halicarnassus (Bodrum), the tomb of Mausolus (d. 353 BC), satrap and independent ruler of Caria (south-western Asia Minor). The Mausoleum ranked as one of the Seven Wonders of the World.

9. Heracles shooting an arrow, at the corner of the east pediment of the Temple of Aphaea, Aegina, designed at the outset of the Severe Early Classical style (490–480 BC).

11. (*Above*) Fair-Haired Boy (480s BC). The solemn, pensive expression of this head, possibly by the sculptor of the Euthydicus *kore* (see no. 10), contrasts with the archaic smiles of previous sculptures. Yellow paint is still faintly visible on the hair.

12. (*Below left*) The bronze Delphi charioteer, part of a group dedicated by Polyzalus, brother of Hiero I of Syracuse, to celebrate a victory in the Pythian Games of 478 or 474.

13. (*Below*) Roman copies of the statues of the 'tyrannicides' Harmodius and Aristogeiton, who slew the joint dictator of Athens, Hipparchus, in 514 BC. This group was sculpted in 477/476 by Critius and Nesiotes, to replace an earlier version removed in 480 by the Persians.

). (*Above*) *Kore* (maiden) edicated by Euthydicus. Marble atue from the Athenian Acropolis 80s BC). An Early Classical evelopment from the long series archaic *korai*. 'Prettiness, egance, virtuosity are out' (C. M. obertson).

14. The front of the 'Ludovisi throne', which may have been a balustrade surrounding the sacred pit of Persephone at Locri Epizephyrii in south-eastern Italy (*c.* 475–450). Aphrodite is assisted from the sea by two nymphs.

15. (*Above left*) Metope from the Temple of Zeus at Olympia, showing Heracles carrying the world for Atlas, who is bringing him the apples of the Hesperides. Athena stands behind Heracles (*c.* 470–457 BC). 16. (*Above right*) Copy of head of Themistocles. In Greece in his time, such an approximation to individual portraiture would not have been possible, but the original head was probably made in Asia Minor, where, in the later 460s, the Persians gave the ostracized and exiled Athenian a princedom.

17. Reclining god from the east pediment of the Temple of Zeus at Olympia, occupying the narrow ends of the pediment. The body of the god shows an ageing physique.

18. (*Above left*) Bronze statue of Zeus, found in a wrecked ship off Artemisium. The brows and lips were originally inlaid with other metal, and the eyes inset. The figure, which is more than lifesize, originally, it seems, brandished a thunderbolt (*c.* 460 BC). 19. (*Above right*) Pericles: Roman copy of an original by Cresilas of Cydonia in Crete (*c.* 450–430 BC), which is not a realistic portrait but an ideal conception of an enlightened soldier-statesman. 'The wonder of this art', said Pliny the elder, 'is that it makes noble men nobler.'

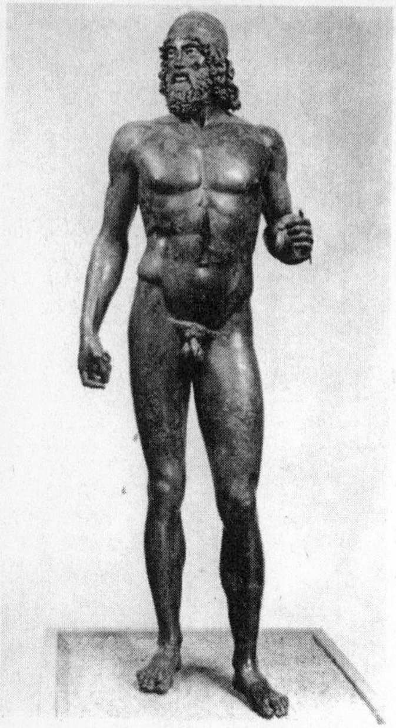

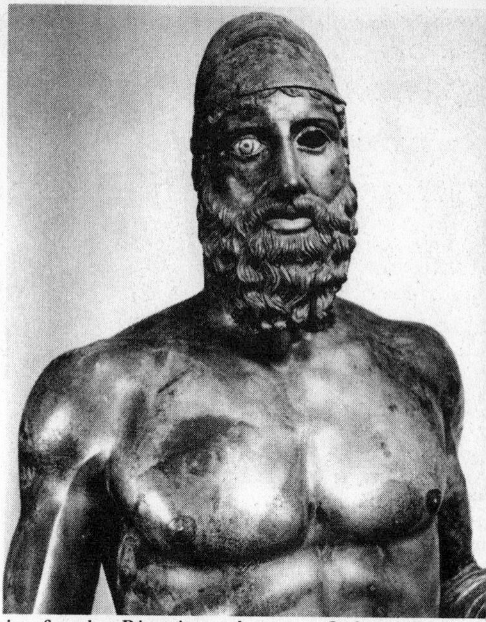

20a and 20b. The two bronze statues of warriors found at Riace in south-western Italy, *c.* 450 BC. These masterpieces mark the development of the High Classical style from its Severe (Early Classical) forerunner.

21. (*Above left*) Modern reconstruction, from imperfect copies, of the bronze Discobolus (Discus-Thrower) of Myron, the outstanding mid-fifth-century sculptural experimenter, 'on the threshold of realism' (Pliny). Time is suspended at the tense moment before the discus is hurled.
22. (*Above right*) Marble Roman copy of the bronze Doryphorus (youth with spear, which is missing) by Polyclitus of Argos (*c.* 440 BC). The statue embodies his *Canon*, incorporating ideal proportions as he saw them. The weight is carried on one leg (the supporting tree-trunk is the copyist's addition).

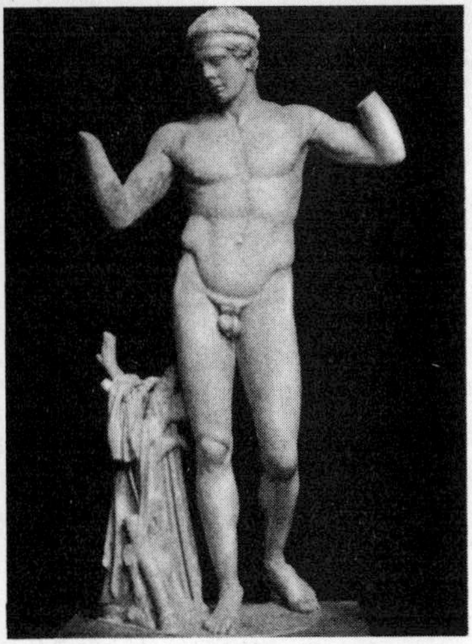

23. (*Above left*) Marble copy of the bronze Diadumenus (youth tying victor's fillet round his head) of Polyclitus, a work dating from the end of his career (*c.* 420 BC).

24. (*Above right*) Metope from the Parthenon, showing battle between Lapith and Centaur, *c.* 447–438 BC. The extensive and varied sculptures of the Parthenon were executed by a team under the general direction of Phidias.

25. Part of the Parthenon frieze showing a procession of the Great Panathenaea, celebrated every summer on Athena's birthday (*c.* 440 BC).

26. (*Above*) Goddesses on the east pediment of the Parthenon (*c.* 438–432), attending the birth of Athena. The figures wear swirling drapery deeply cut into shadow-catching folds.

27. (*Left*) The 'Varvakion statuette', a Roman copy of the colossal Athena Parthenos by Phidias. The original, set up in the Parthenon, was chryselephantine (gold and ivory), i.e. made of wood covered by a gold veneer, with an ivory head (surely much superior to the copy's).

28. A good Roman marble copy of the head of Phidias' Athena Lemnia, a bronze statue dedicated on the Athenian Acropolis by colonists departing for the island of Lemnos.

9. Roman copy of Praxiteles' Aphrodite of nidus, shown leaving her bath. The original . 340 BC) established a new epoch in the ensuous depiction of the female nude – a point ard to appreciate from this dismal copy.

30. The Hermes of Praxiteles, with the infant Dionysus. This epoch-making figure is either an original by Praxiteles (*c*. 343 BC) or an exceptionally fine near-contemporary or Hellenistic copy.

1. Roman copy of one of the fourth-century nterpretations of Socrates (*c*. 399 BC), combining eminiscences of his satyr-Silenus appearance vith the idea of a homespun philosopher.

32. Roman copy of a head of Aristotle (d. 322 BC). 'Portraits' of philosophers are usually generic and unindividual, but some heads of Artistotle may show more authentically personal characteristics.

34. (*Above*) Miniature ivory head of Philip II of Macedonia. Found in the 'Royal Tomb' at Aegae (Vergina).

33. (*Left*) Demosthenes, portrayed more than four decades after his death by Polyeuctus (280–279 BC), whose rendering may be partly, or largely, imaginary – intended to show how the grim and pensive orator ought to have looked.

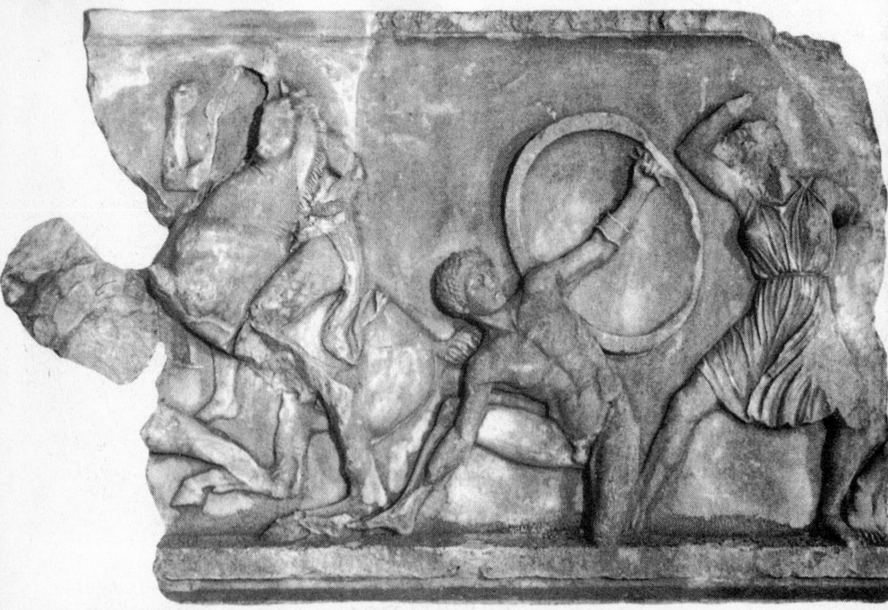

35. Part of frieze from the Mausoleum at Halicarnassus. A battle between the Greeks and the Amazons

a (*Above left*) and 36b (*Above*
ht). Ancient copy and modern
construction of the Apoxyomenus
Lysippus; an athlete scraping the
l from his forearm with a strigil.
ne original (*c.* 320 BC) marked the
ansition from the late Classical to
e Hellenistic style.

. (*Right*) Red-figure oil-jar
tributed to the Midias painter,
ade at a time when this Athenian
t acquired a mannered, theatrical
aracter, during the last decades of
e fifth century BC.

. (*Far right*) Red-figure Apulian
nphora from Taras (Taranto) in
uth Italy, one of the leading
ntres of this art in the fourth
ntury BC.

39. An Athenian dinner-party. Painted by the prolific Duris, who regularly signed his vases. First quarter of the fifth century BC.

40. White-ground oil-jar (*lekythos*) by the Achilles painter showing a Muse playing the lyre on Mount Helicon, with a nightingale beside her. The inscription above praises the beauty of the youth Axiopeithes (*c.* 440 BC).

41. Red-figure amphora ascribed to the Berli painter, showing Heracles with tripod. (On th other side of the vase appears Apollo, pursuin him.) Early fifth century BC.

42a. (*Above left*) Jasper scaraboid gem (seal-stone) from Kara (Attica) by the supreme master Dexamenus of Chios (late fifth century BC). This is an approximation to a portrait (of some unknown person) such as was still very rare in other media.

42b. (*Above right*) Chalcedony by Dexamenus, showing a woman and her maid.

43. (*Right*) Inscription of 425/4 or 424/3 BC, during the Peloponnesian War, giving a list of Athenian war casualties. Epigraphy is one of the principal tools by which the information provided by the ancient historians can be supplemented and checked.

44. (*Below*) Necklace of the fourth century BC from Taras (Taranto), which was one of the outstanding centres of Greek goldwork.

45. (*Below right*) Bronze Etruscan helmet, found at Olympia, dedicated by Hiero I of Syracuse to celebrate his naval victory over a fleet from Etruscan city-states off Cumae (Campania) in 474 BC.

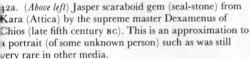

46a

46b

47b

48a

48b

49a

49b

50a

50b

46a and 46b. Silver tetradrachm of western Asia Min showing a portrait of Tissaphernes, the Persian satrap Sardis, by a Greek artist. The coin is on the Attic standard but was intended for the payment of Sparta troops (*c.* 412–408 BC).

47a and 47b. Silver decadrachms of Syracuse signed Cimon (a), and Euaenetus (b), depicting the water-nymph Arethusa, with dolphins, and a four-horse chariot (with trophies beneath). The coins were probably issued by Dionysius I (405–367 BC) to accompany the Assinarian Games celebrating the victory over the Athenian expedition (413).

48a and 48b. Gold coin of Panticapaeum (Kerch), capital of the state of the Cimmerian Bosphorus, whic possessed abundant supplies of gold and provided Athens with much of its grain. This coin, showing an Iranian horned and lion-headed griffin, is of exceptionally fine style.

49a and 49b. Silver coin of Mausolus (377–353 BC), who succeeded his father Hecatomnus as dynast of Cari (cf. his Mausoleum, of which a reconstruction is illustrated above, no. 8), and fomented the revolts which dissolved the Second Athenian League (357–354). The coin shows a head of Apollo and figure of Zeus stratios.

50a and 50b. Tetradrachm of Philip II of Macedonia (359–336 BC). These issues, made of silver from Moun Pangaeum which he had conquered, enjoyed very extensive circulation.

him). Yet even from this sentimental picture he emerges as an outstandingly versatile person, such as few other periods of world history could have produced: and as a man whose talents warn us how wrong it would be to limit our search for classical Greece to the Greek mainland, and to look no further.

In particular, he was among the most prominent and gifted leaders of the philosophical school named after Pythagoras, the semi-legendary sage who had emigrated from Samos to Croton in *c.*531 (Appendix I). Archytas, who revived and rejuvenated the school, wrote a life of the master, and by uniting this philosophical activity with political leadership followed a tradition which went back to Pythagoras himself, and had also been a feature of other south Italian city-states that likewise came under the influence of Pythagorean secret societies.

Archytas was also a mathematician of outstanding distinction – described as the founder of mathematical mechanics, and teacher of the famous Eudoxus of Cnidus: mathematical calculation alone, Archytas allegedly remarked (in Pythagorean vein), is able to breed confidence among men and prevent strife. Acoustic and musical theory were other fields to which he made major contributions, no doubt accorded special notice in the biography of Aristoxenus, who was a leading musicologist himself.

Archytas' most widely known claim to fame, however, was to earn the deep admiration of Plato, whose introduction to the Syracusan court he arranged – according to the *Seventh Letter* of dubious Platonic authorship; and this is likely enough, whether the letter is authentic or not (Chapter 31). On the occasion of Plato's first visit to the west, when he saw Dionysius I (387), he also called on Archytas – indeed, this was perhaps the principal object of his entire journey – and later it was Archytas, once again, who promoted his third visit, and was said, when Plato received bad treatment from Dionysius II, to have intervened to secure his return home (360).

The mathematical writings of Archytas were made use of by Plato, who appreciated their application to ethics and the social order; and Plato's indications of other Pythagorean influences (notably in respect of the immortality of the soul) almost certainly once again bear witness to doctrines he had learnt of from Archytas (Appendix I). It may well have been the Tarantine, too, who gave him the idea of founding the Academy. Moreover, the ideal ruler in Plato's *Republic*, the 'philosopher-king', was probably based on Archytas (just as the 'tyrant' was Dionysius I of Syracuse). Aristotle, too, wrote about him on a number of occasions.

After Archytas' death, Taras maintained and continued to diversify its cultural traditions. Yet in the politico-military field, owing to the absence of any real cohesion within the Italiot League, renewed pressure from the hinterland tribes prompted the Tarantines to call in mercenary leaders from other Greek lands, a thing Archytas had advised them never to do.

CHAPTER 27

LEUCON I: THE GRAIN ROUTE

The northern (Scythian) hinterland of the Euxine (Black) Sea provided abundant exports, which made the adjoining coastal regions a significant part of the Greek world. Yet the ancient writers' preferred concentration on the mainland of Greece itself, together with the fact that the modern archaeological reports on the area are written in Russian, have meant that this whole territory and its importance tend to be ignored by students of the classics.

We know, however, of the massive grain supplies dispatched, already at an early date, from the inexhaustibly fertile 'Black Earth' territory of the Ukrainian and Moldavian and Crimean (Tauric) plains and deltas. Nor was this their only product. It we may extrapolate (as indeed we must) from the writings of various later periods, there were also abundant fisheries, producing herring, sturgeon and tunny, for which increasingly elaborate salting facilities had to be locally provided. Pickled meat and honey and wax and furs were also available, and crowds of men and women found themselves sent away as slaves.

Timber was transported to the region from forests in the interior, and metals (notably iron) were mined in the Black Sea area itself, or brought from Transylvania by river and sea. All these goods could then be passed on to the Mediterranean city-states, in exchange for wine (to supplement the presumably inferior Bosphoran product), olive oil, ceramics, utensils, weapons, medical supplies and luxury items – once the Greeks, who were capable of carrying out these operations, had settled on the Black Sea coast.

This Greek initiative was first taken by the seamen of Miletus. Only ten years, it was said, after they had first planted a settlement on the west coast of the Black Sea, at Istrus in what is now the Rumanian Dobrogea (657), they joined equally intrepid adventurers from other parts of the Greek world in colonizing the same sea's furthermost extremity, at Olbia near the estuary gulf (*liman*) of the River Hypanis, twenty-three miles west of another great river, the Borysthenes (Danapris)*. These Olbians, controlling a territory thirty miles deep and forty miles across, became the rulers or suzerains of numerous other Greek settlements or trading posts, and enjoyed, as a result of their exports, a prolonged period of prosperity.

The Scythian expedition of the Persian King Darius I (*c*.513–512) caused the Olbians anxiety, because it cut off their contacts with the Transylvanian mines and meant that henceforward Persian territory was dangerously near. Nevertheless, when Herodotus visited the place in the middle of the next century, he found a thriving community, and learnt that a Philhellenic Scythian King Scyles frequently resided at Olbia, so that we can deduce, perhaps, that the city existed and prospered only by grace of the protection of the Scythians. These were people whose wealth and luxurious artistic tastes are displayed by goldwork unequalled in other parts of the Greek world (where the metal was far scarcer). These pieces were executed mainly by Greek artists, though the motifs they employed were often indigenous.

It must have been partly to get away from this Scythian proximity or predominance that, by the start of the fifth century, the most influential centre of Greek life in the northern Black Sea region was shifting to another and more distant point. South-east of Olbia lay the peninsula of the Tauric Chersonese. Although its interior, inhabited by potentially hostile tribes, was perilous to the Greeks – despite the presence of rich grain-lands – the eastern end of Tauris, looking out over the Cimmerian Bosphorus – as well as the shore on the opposite side of that strait – seemed inviting to the seamen and colonists. This was because the narrows led into Lake Maeotis, which, although its waters were often rough, contained abundant fish. So a number of Greek colonies clustered round the Bosphorus, on both banks.

The most important of these settlements was Panticapaeum on the western side of the strait, founded by Milesians in *c*.600 on the site of an earlier Scythian settlement. Protected by an impressive acropolis, Panticapaeum owed its significance to two advantages: its access by sea to the major passage and fisheries of the Bosphorus, and by land to the extensive grain-fields in the south-eastern regions of the Tauric Chersonese.

Good contacts with Panticapaeum were vital to the Athenians, whose prosperity and very survival depended upon the importation of Black Sea grain, since supplies from other sources (Egypt and the west) were so unreliable: a dependence that was confirmed by the countless occasions, from the seventh or even eighth century onwards, when

*For modern equivalents see the Index.

Athens endeavoured to secure control of the Hellespont which led to the Black Sea through the Propontis. Between these two seas lay another strait, the Thracian Bosphorus, dominated by Byzantium, and it must have been a relief to the Athenians when they were able to expel the Spartan commander Pausanias from that city (Chapter 3) and enrol it in their own Delian League (478), thus adequately protecting, at last, the transit of Black Sea grain, which they by now had a sufficient balance of trade to import in the large quantities that they so urgently needed.

All this time their eyes were turned towards Panticapaeum and its neighbours, from which their grain must come. A significant stage was reached in *c.*480, when a new dynasty of rulers of Panticapaeum – the Archaeanactids, perhaps of Milesian or Mytilenean origin – unified the Greek states on either bank of the Cimmerian Bosphorus. This protected them against their non-Greek neighbours, some of whom they absorbed, thus laying the foundations of the Bosphoran state. This half-century of its rule by the Archaeanactids, however, remains more or less a historical blank, except that we know them to have been notable, in good and bad times alike, for their friendly attitude towards the Athenians, who continued to show a lively interest in Panticapaeum and its capacity and willingness to export grain.

Then in 438/437 Spartocus I, a mercenary general, created a second and even more powerful and wealthy state of the Bosphorus, which proved durable. He himself may have been a Thracian, or more probably partly Thracian and partly Maeotian (from the shores of Lake Maeotis). His ruling class, dominating the local (mainly Maeotian) population, was of mixed Thracian, Greek, Scythian and Sindian blood (the Sindians being a group of Maeotian tribes in and behind the Taman peninsula, on the eastern shore of the Cimmerian Bosphorus, beside the lower reaches of the copper-rich River Anticeites (Kuban) beneath the Caucasus mountains).

This Spartocid regime was an autocratic hereditary monarchy, supported by an army and navy consisting mainly of mercenaries, who included native 'allies', and were costly, but the Bosphorus could afford them – and needed them, to keep down Black Sea pirates. The co-operation of foreign merchants, too, was enlisted with success. Bronze foundries and jewellers' shops show that Scythian metalworking skills were taken over and adapted. The state still depended, to some extent, on fisheries but more especially, as always, on the export of grain, which came partly from its own large and increasing dominions, partly from the territories of its subjects and vassals, and partly, again, by purchase or confiscation, from the peoples of the hinterland.

Athenian interest in this grain, far from lessening, became intenser still during the opening years of Spartocus I's reign, as the population of Attica increased, and the military commitments of Athens made it essential to ensure a supply of foodstuffs. It has been questioned whether Spartocus I established himself on the Cimmerian Bosphorus with or without the approval of Athens, but at all events when Pericles, during the 430s, led an Athenian naval expedition into the Black Sea, this may well have been intended not merely to colonize ports on its southern shore, as we are told, but also to reduce Spartocus to the status of an obedient Athenian commercial agent.

It is in this connection, too, no doubt, that we hear of Athenian military fortresses and colonies in the immediate neighbourhood of Panticapaeum.[6] A series of edicts, the 'Callias decrees' (*c.*434),[7] show how tightly Athens controlled the Black Sea grain route, under the control of a special board of inspectors known as Guardians of the Hellespont (Hellespontophylakes). The Athenians claimed the sole right to dispose of Black Sea commodities, and then to collect them at Athens, and to distribute them afterwards among their allies as they wished.

Nevertheless, the Bosphoran state enjoyed no very great prosperity, as yet, under Spartocus I or during the early years of Satyrus I (*c.*433–389). True, the latter appears to have induced or compelled the three Sindian tribes of the Taman peninsula to accept his sovereignty and perhaps recognize him as 'king'. But a jealous Athenian monopoly of Bosphoran grain hampered economic development.

After Athens' defeat in the Peloponnesian War, however – caused precisely because the defeat at Aegospotami (405) cut off its Black Sea grain route – the Bosphorans were able to use adjacent cities, which had formerly belonged to Athens, as their bases. But their greatest success was to incorporate the Chersonesian city of Theodosia, a natural harbour for grain exports, which was captured – despite assistance from Heraclea Pontica in northern Asia Minor, the Bosphorans' principal enemy – and became their main exporting centre. The closest overseas link of the Bosphorus was with Athens' port the Piraeus, for Satyrus I took the long view, and, even if suspicious of the Athenians, continued to collaborate with them, granting their city favourable priorities from time to time, and then, after their recovery of naval power (394), making a treaty with them. Under this agreement, the Athenians were exempted from Bosphoran export duties, or rather, since similar exemptions had no doubt been granted at an earlier date, such previous privileges were confirmed or revived.

These arrangements were strengthened by Leucon I (*c*.389–*c*.349/346), to whom, instead of Satyrus, some would prefer to attribute the first kingship over the Sindians and the reduction of Theodosia (unless he had to annex Theodosia for a second time, in 364, after another war with Heraclea). At all events Leucon was archon of the Cimmerian Bosphorus and Theodosia, and was the king of the Sindian tribes, and extended the Bosphoran kingdom to the east and north until it reached all the way from the Caucasus Mountains to the River Tanais. He also developed the agriculture of the huge flat lands of Russia, by means of serf labour, until they had become the granary of the Greeks to an even greater degree than before; fourth-century inscriptions record Bosphoran exports to many Greek cities, and this activity is confirmed by the kingdom's remarkable coinage. It was made of gold – which was exceptional in Greek states – so that Panticapaeum, of which the name appears on the coins, was evidently the receiving point for bullion from Ural or Siberian mines, utilized to create this currency.

The stylistic quality of the pieces is first-rate, and confirms the tradition that Leucon encouraged the arts. Many other stories, too, centred around him: telling, for example, of his successful devices to foil conspiracies, and of how he stopped his soldiers' pay when vice or gambling plunged them into debt. The Bosphorus was, at this time, the largest state in the whole Greek world, and Leucon was its outstanding king. He was described as one of the most enlightened of rulers, the 'virtuous tyrant', as good a man as any autocrat can be, and admissible to the gallery of famous Greek statesmen.

This favourable characterization was due not only to his own propagandists but to praise from the Athenians, with whom, carrying on and completing the work of Satyrus I, he established close ties. These were not only beneficial to himself, but to Athens as well, as Demosthenes explained to his fellow citizens in 355/354.[8] So Leucon was granted Athenian citizenship, and a golden crown, and immunity from civil burdens; and a decree to this effect was set up at Athens in triplicate.[9] For the Athenians, who lost many of their allies at just about that time, now needed Black Sea grain more than ever before, being compelled to import perhaps eighty per cent of their needs – during an epoch when there was a shortage of cereals throughout the Greek world – and stringent laws and conditions were imposed in an endeavour to ensure that this inflow was maintained without interruption.

Then, in *c*.349/346, the Athenians were visited by envoys from Leucon's sons Spartocus II and Paerisades (Berisades) I, to announce that their father was dead.[10] Thereupon Athens granted the young co-rulers honours equal to his, once again in response to privileges which the

Bosphorus had granted, or would grant, to the Athenians – though Athens nowadays, seeing that imperial force had to give way to diplomacy, was obliged to renounce its exclusive, monopolistic, right to purchase Bosphoran grain.

The two brothers reigned jointly for five years, after which Spartocus II died, and Paerisades I continued to rule as archon until 311/309. It has been suggested that the earlier part of Paerisades' reign, at least, witnessed prosperity as great as any that the Bosphorus had ever enjoyed before; and he himself – perhaps before his death – was said to have been worshipped as a god.[11]

Described as a mild and capable man, he was, like his father, a patron of the arts – or at least he welcomed at his court the Athenian harp-player Stratonicus (whom he tried to prevent from leaving). Paerisades dealt diplomatically with the Sindians by marrying Komosarye, daughter of their prince Gorgippus. Against the Scythians, on the other hand, he was engaged in a prolonged war, which must have damaged his trade. However, following a period in which they had possessed formidable power, their tribes in the Tauric Chersonese, under pressure from other peoples (the Sauromatae or Sarmatae), were slowly retreating into the interior of the peninsula, and may have been compelled, for a time, to accept Paerisades' suzerainty. He also claimed to be 'King of all the Maeotians'.

The Bosphoran state was a remarkable example of inter-racialism, and showed the capacity of the Greeks, on occasion, to adapt themselves to unfamiliar conditions, incorporating native elements with fruitful effects. Despite ups and downs, the kingdom was fortunate in the strength and longevity of many of its rulers; and it had an extended and on the whole settled and stable life ahead of it, continuing to issue coinage until the fourth century AD.

CHAPTER 28

MAUSOLUS AND PYTHIUS: THE MAUSOLEUM

Caria was a region in the extreme south-west of Asia Minor. It was occupied by a people who claimed to be indigenous, and retained their non-Indo-European language (recently deciphered) throughout ancient times, although Greeks established important colonies on the coast as early as *c.*900 BC, notably at Halicarnassus and Cnidus, from the Dorian cities of Troezen and Sparta respectively.

The Carians became subject to King Croesus of Lydia (d.546) and then to King Cyrus II the Great of Persia, but many of their men went abroad (especially to Egypt) to serve as mercenaries. Under Persian suzerainty – restored after the failure of the Ionian revolt against Darius I, which the Carians had joined – Halicarnassus was the capital of a princely house, numbering among its rulers the semi-legendary Queen Regent Artemisia I, who thus occupied a position to which Greek women could scarcely have aspired. She fought on the Persian side at Salamis, and according to Herodotus (who was partial, since he came from the city and was her grandson) enjoyed Xerxes' special esteem.[12]

A subsequent member of her dynasty, however, was expelled in favour of a republican government, with the backing, it was said, of Herodotus himself. Halicarnassus was at that time a member of the Athenians' Delian League and empire, providing them with an important naval base during the Peloponnesian War. During the course of the War, the Athenians imprudently supported an insurrection against the Persians in Caria, led by Amorges (Chapter 16; his equally rebellious father, the satrap Pissuthnes, had first made Caria clearly visible as a regional entity, rather than merely an appendix of Lydia). Amorges was crushed by Tissaphernes, viceroy of the coastal provinces of Asia Minor. But Tissaphernes was relegated to Caria by Darius II in 408, and murdered in 395.

His successor, promoted to the new rank of satrap of Caria (*c.*392/391), was a local hereditary prince Hecatomnus, who subsequently assumed joint command of the Persian fleet in operations against King Euagoras of Salamis in Cyprus (390). Establishing his capital at his home town Mylasa – the religious meeting-place of a loosely organized Carian League – Hecatomnus gained greater autonomy for his Carians, and founded a dynasty which sponsored Greek, Iranian and Anatolian culture, presiding over an equally mixed bureaucracy.

Hecatomnus' son Mausolus (*c*.377–353) transferred his residence to Halicarnassus, where he ruled as a virtually independent sovereign, conceding formal obeisance to the Persian court at Susa, but taking advantage of revolts against Artaxerxes II Mnemon (d.358), and extorting recognition from Artaxerxes III Ochus (d.338/337).

With the help of a fleet of a hundred ships and a standing army, he temporarily elevated Caria to a central role in the political and military life of the eastern Mediterranean area, annexing parts of the neighbouring territories (in Lydia and Lycia), and assuming control of Greek city-states on the coast and adjoining islands (notably Rhodes, in order to harass the Athenian grain supply from Egypt). At the same time, he pursued an intensified policy of Hellenization, supported by prosperous agriculture and manufacturing, and by widespread commercial activity, including a flourishing slave trade.

Mausolus was a vigorous founder of new towns, formed by the forcible amalgamation of native communities; and he transformed Halicarnassus by this means, moving the population of six or eight Carian towns or villages into the reconstructed city (*c*.367). Vitruvius described the layout of the site, a spectacular example of urbanization. 'The front of Halicarnassus', he observed,

> is like the curved shape of a theatre. In the first row of the seats by the harbour was the market-place. About halfway up the concave slope, at the point where the main cross-gangway is in a theatre, a wide piazza was laid out, in the middle of which was built the Mausoleum.... At the top of the hill in the centre is the temple of Mars (Ares); on the extreme right the temple of Venus (Aphrodite) and Mercury (Hermes) ... and, corresponding to it on the extreme left, the royal palace which Mausolus built in accordance with a plan all his own. To the right it commands a view of the market-place, the harbour and the entire line of fortifications, while just below it to the left there is a concealed harbour hidden under the walls in such a way that nobody would see or know what was going on in it. Only the king himself could, in case of need, give orders from his own palace to the oarsmen and soldiers, without the knowledge of anyone else.[13]

The fortress-like palace, built of materials from many different places and surfaced with marble from the island of Proconnesus in the Hellespont, echoed the styles of Achaemenid Persian royal residences and anticipated the palaces of Hellenistic monarchs.

As for the Mausoleum, even though it was not actually a 'hero's shrine' (*heroon*), as has been suggested, Lucian was right to point out that it exalted the ruler to an extent that had never been seen before.[14] Gleaming with white marble and stucco veneering, this building was the visual centre of the waterfront of Halicarnassus, and dominated the entire city; it was subsequently acclaimed as one of the Seven Wonders of the World. The Mausoleum was constructed, according to Pliny the elder, after Mausolus' death (353), by his sister, widow and successor Artemisia II. But Vitruvius' account, confirmed by other writers, indicates that it had formed part of the original overall layout of the city, designed during the lifetime of Mausolus himself – and probably at the outset of his planning of Halicarnassus.

Pliny's description of the edifice contains a number of obscurities, which have led to differing modern reconstructions. We can deduce, however, with the assistance of excavations, that it was a rectangular structure, with a height of 140 feet and a breadth, on the long sides, of 63, surrounded by an Ionic colonnade of thirty-six columns 34 feet in height (perhaps arranged in double rows). The Mausoleum's lofty substructure or podium seems to have receded upwards from the ground to the foot of the colonnade in three mighty steps: this being the reason why Pliny implies that the building was pyramidal.[15] Its roof was another 'pyramid' or stepped cone; we do not know how steeply it was angled, but upon its apex stood an enormous marble four-horse chariot, driven by Apollo as the sun-god Helios – a symbol of the passing of the dead, familiar from earlier Greek tombs.

This chariot, Pliny indicates, was the work of the architect, who was Pythius (designer, also, of a temple of Athena at his home town Priene). The carefully thought out, three-dimensional stage setting of the Mausoleum recalls that Pythius had studied architectural theory deeply enough to write books about his creations. These works are not extant, but he not only insisted, we are told, that architects should be well informed about the arts in general, but also expressed a preference for the Ionic Order over the Doric, on the technical grounds that the latter raised difficulties about the spacing of the frieze.

Vitruvius also mentions a second architect of the Mausoleum, and co-author of the book on the subject, Satyrus of Paros, who was probably identical with a sculptor of the same name. It is not possible to determine the two men's relative roles in the building's design, although apparently Pythius played the more important part, since a papyrus mentions his name alone in this connection.[16]

At all events the Mausoleum turned out to be unprecedented, integrating architecture and sculpture in a highly sophisticated and intricate fashion. It was also multi-racial, blending Greek motifs and styles with non-Greek forms, since the tall podium was of Persian or Lycian origin, and the pyramidal roof seems to have echoed Egyptian prototypes.

Parts of the chariot designed by Pythius as the crown of this roof, and fragments of its colossal horses, have been found, as well as lions – guardians of the tomb – which stood along a ledge above the cornice, apparently in two rows. There was a mass of other sculptured figures as well, adding up to more than three hundred (enough for ten temples). Among them were statues between the columns and on the second and third steps of the podium, and battle groups on the other steps.

A few of all these numerous figures, nine or ten feet high, have come to light in various states of incompleteness, and are to be seen in the British Museum. The best-preserved of them, representing a male, has a distinctive face which, although to some extent idealized, must all the same be intended as a personal likeness – looking ahead to Hellenistic times – and has been thought to represent Mausolus himself. Since it bears a certain resemblance to heads of Heracles (or Mausolus as Heracles) on the coinage of Cos, which was one of the King's dependencies, this identification is possible. But it remains likelier that one of his ancestors, real or fictitious, is depicted. This colossus originally carried a sword, or sacrificial bowl and knife. A woman's statue, too, has survived, except for the head; it has been identified as Artemisia II, but once again this remains doubtful.

Considerable fragments of sculptural friezes have also been unearthed. Originally coloured – with blue backgrounds and reddish-brown masculine flesh – these were executed, we are informed, by the most eminent artists of the time. Who they all were, however, and who sculptured each section, remains problematical. Pliny names them as Scopas, Bryaxis, Timotheus and Leochares,[17] joined subsequently by 'a fifth artist', and Vitruvius offers a somewhat different list, in which Timotheus is only mentioned as a possibility ('some think' he participated), but Praxiteles also appears.

All these sculptors were famous, but apart from Praxiteles (Chapter 33) the outstanding name on the list is Scopas of Paros, who made statues for various other cities as well, and was the architect of the temple of Athena Alea at Tegea (360/340) and creator of two of its statues. He was also, probably, responsible for its swirling pedimental reliefs, since heads that have survived from these groups display restlessly emotional, painful, distorted expressions and poses – characterized by deeply sunken eye-sockets and low, lowering brows, on square massive heads – which have been interpreted as characteristic (and deliberately 'anti-classical') features of Scopas' work: and they reappear in the anguished, unrestrained movements of the Mausoleum friezes, foreshadowing Hellenistic compositions of the future. Scopas was no stranger to the region, since he also undertook commissions for other places in Caria (as well as Ionia).[18] Moreover, a sculpture he made at Tegea was dedicated to Mausolus' sister Ada and her husband Idrieus.[19]

Pliny indicates that the four sculptors whom he mentioned by name worked on the east, north, south and west sides of the Mausoleum respectively. But they (or they and Praxiteles) cannot have done *all* this work, because it was far too extensive for four or five men to undertake (and, besides, some of the surviving pieces are clearly not by artists of such oustanding talent). Vitruvius remarks that the sculptors, in competition with one another, 'decorated and gave approvals',[20] which presumably means that each sketched out the overall treatment of his side and then entrusted the carving to a team of assistants, whose work he subsequently checked. The overall designs, it would seem, must have been prepared at an early stage, that is to say when the new city of Halicarnassus itself was planned by Mausolus, with his Mausoleum as an integral part of the design.

Three of the Mausoleum's friezes have been partially preserved. They represent a chariot-race, a battle between Lapiths and Centaurs, and a battle between male Greeks and Amazons.

The chariot-race scenes may have been located high up within the colonnade, like the Parthenon friezes, and it might be these which Pliny and Vitruvius divide among their various sculptors, according to the points of the compass. The horses are shown galloping with all four legs extended, a pose which does not exist in real life, but reflects the eye's registration of how a race is run. The surviving head of a charioteer is executed with particular delicacy. The Centaur-Lapith frieze, on heavy slabs which have only survived in poor condition, is likely to have served as a support for the chariot on the apex of the building.

The Amazonomachy, on the other hand, which is the best preserved of the three sets of reliefs, seems to have extended round the top edge of the substructure(podium), that is to say at a height of about thirty feet above the ground; and its posturing figures, some in high and some in low relief, are widely spaced in order to suit this elevated position, far from the eye. The diagonal lines of the design are rhythmical and audacious, and the torso of a dying Amazon has been especially admired.

The subject matter of this frieze, as of the battle between Lapiths and Centaurs, dealt with the traditional theme of civilization pitted against its enemies. True, this could only by a propagandist effort be thought appropriate to the wars of Mausolus, a non-Greek (although enthusiastically Hellenized) who fought many of his battles against Greeks. But the choice of the Amazons could have been motivated by a further consideration, the possession by Halicarnassus of two exceptional warrior queens, representing an Anatolian tradition that may go back to the Hittites – the first Artemisia who had fought at Salamis and the second who was equally formidable, and had now completed the tomb of her late husband Mausolus. (But this, too, was not a wholly satisfactory comparison, since the mythical Amazons had not been winners.)

Artemisia II died in 351/350, and was succeeded as ruler of Caria and Lycia by Idrieus, who shared his princely status with her sister Ada, whom he married. Idrieus died in 344/343, and in 341/340 Ada was deposed and expelled by Pixodarus, who ruled jointly with the Persian satrap Orontobates. But when Alexander the Great captured Halicarnassus, after an arduous and damaging siege, he restored Ada to the throne. However, the short period of Caria's power had now ended, and henceforward (with only brief intervals of freedom) the region and the city became subjected to one Hellenistic state after another, and eventually to Rome.

PART VI

First Half of the Fourth Century: The Greek Mainland

LIST OF EVENTS

399	Trial and death of Socrates
396–394	Campaigns of King Agesilaus II of Sparta against the Persian empire
395–387	'Corinthian War': Athens, Boeotian League, Corinth and Argos against Sparta: battles of Cnidus, Coronea (394), Lechaeum (390)
*c.*390	Isocrates' *Against the Sophists*; and founds school
387	Plato's first visit to Syracuse (also 367, 361)
387/386	Peace of Antalcidas or King's Peace, imposed by Persia
*c.*386	Plato's Academy
*c.*385	Jason dictator of Pherae (ruler of Thessaly 374, d.370)
*c.*384	Plato's *Symposium*, Xenophon's *Apology*; 380s/370s Plato's *Republic*
382	The Spartan Phoebidas seizes Thebes (liberated by Pelopidas in 379)
382–380	Spartans besiege and reduce Olynthus in Chalcidice (Macedonia)
380	Isocrates' *Panegyricus*
378	The Spartan Sphodrias raids Attica, and Agesilaus II invades Boeotia (now allied with Athens)
377	Second Athenian League
*c.*377	Xenophon's *March Up Country* (*Anabasis*)
374	Peace between Athens and Sparta
373	Thebes seizes Plataea (attacked by Isocrates' *Plataicus*)
370s	Xenophon's *Education of Cyrus* (*Cyropaedia*)
371	Abortive (second) 'Peace of Callias', with Persian support. Thebans under Epaminondas defeat

	Spartans at Leuctra. Athenians attempt Common Peace, again with Persian support
370	Epaminondas' first invasion of the Peloponnese: Arcadians and Messenians liberated from Sparta. (Subsequent invasions in 369 and 366)
c.370	Plato's *Parmenides* (c.368 *Theaetetus*)
367/366	Pelopidas and envoys from other Greek states visit Persian King Artaxerxes II Mnemon at Susa
366	Peloponnesian League dissolved
c.365	Isocrates' *Euagoras*
c.365	Xenophon returns to Athens
364	Epaminondas wins over Byzantium from the Athenians
364/361(?)	Praxiteles' statue of Aphrodite of Cnidus (Hermes of Olympia c.343?)
362	Battle of Mantinea between Thebans (and allies) and Spartans: Epaminondas killed
360	Death of Agesilaus II on way back from mercenary service in Egypt
359	Accession of King Philip II of Macedonia; captures Amphipolis (357, see Chapter 35)
357–355	Revolts from Second Athenian League: the 'Social War', prompted by Mausolus of Caria (see Chapter 28)

CHAPTER 29

EPAMINONDAS: THE END OF THE POLITICAL ROAD

After the Persian viceroy in Asia Minor, Cyrus the younger, had provided the funds which enabled Sparta to win the Peloponnesian War against Athens (404; Chapter 24), Cyrus decided to contest the Persian throne with his brother Artaxerxes II Mnemon, and mobilized 13,000 Greek mercenaries.

He also asked for Spartan help (401); and, in response, Sparta furnished naval support and a military commander Clearchus. This aid was only unofficial; all the same, it represented a grave and rash step, since it meant that the Spartans were jettisoning the Persian alliance – which had won them the Peloponnesian War – at a time when their own control over their newly acquired 'empire' was maladroit and precarious. The hand of Lysander, their victorious general, may be seen in the intervention, for he was Cyrus' intimate friend, and this consideration evidently prevailed, in his mind, over the undesirability of breaking with the Great King. Besides, Spartans had a bad conscience, and an awareness of unfavourable publicity, because they had relinquished the Asian Greeks to Persian intervention and control.

Cyrus was killed at Cunaxa, as Xenophon's *March Up Country* (*Anabasis*) so brilliantly recounts (Chapter 30), but Sparta nevertheless made an alliance with Egypt (in revolt against Persia), and raided Persian territory. In 399 there was an open state of war between the Spartans and Persians, and in 396, amid Panhellenic propaganda (if that is not a later embellishment), the new Spartan King Agesilaus II arrived with reinforcements. In spite of two effective campaigns, however, he failed to check the increasing Persian naval menace.

Meanwhile, in the homeland, a coalition comprising the Boeotian League (Thebes), Athens, Corinth and Argos rebelled against the heavy-handed conduct of Sparta, and launched the 'Corinthian War' (395). Persia, with pleasure, financed the confederates, and in the following year the Athenian Conon, sharing the command with Pharnabazus, the satrap of Dascylium, inflicted a naval defeat on the

Spartans at Cnidus. Meanwhile, however, Agesilaus had been recalled, and proceeded overland to Boeotia, but although victorious at Coronea (394) was obliged to return to the Peloponnese.

The Persians allowed Conon to rebuild the Long Walls at Athens – which thus achieved a rapid recovery from the Peloponnesian War, accelerated by an inventive commander of light-armed troops, Iphicrates. Next, however, because this renovated Athens had ventured to help the rebellious Euagoras of Salamis in Cyprus, Persia changed sides, transferred its support to Sparta after all, and in 387/386 compelled all Greek contestants to adhere to the King's Peace or Peace of Antalcidas, a 'Common', general agreement of a type that from now on became recurrent.

Athens was willing to make peace because of threats to its grain supply (blocked by a Spartan, Persian and Syracusan fleet), and Spartan supremacy was confirmed; but only on the condition that, whereas other Greek city-states would remain 'autonomous', those in Asia Minor and Cyprus were to be subject to the Great King. This was not a new requirement, but its formal inclusion in the treaty meant that the subordination of those Greek states to Persia had been underlined with humiliating clarity – as if the Persian Wars (Chapters 1–3) had never happened.

Convinced, however, of the backing of the Persians, Sparta flagrantly interfered with other city-states of the Greek mainland. Phoebidas was sent to capture Thebes by treachery and install an oligarchic regime. This new government was backed by a Spartan garrison, and others were planted at Thespiae, and Plataea, and Heraclea in Trachis. But Thebes fought back in 379, when seven exiles, led by Pelopidas, returned by night and led a successful revolt against Spartan control. This moment can be seen, in retrospect, as a historical landmark, marking the approaching end of Sparta's hegemony and the inauguration of a brief period during which the Boeotian League in central Greece, dominated by the Thebans, took its place as the principal mainland power.

The strategically located, relatively fertile Boeotian heartland consisted of the flat lands of Thebes and Orchomenus (on Lake Copais, now drained), which produced grain and olives and bred horses. In classical times the independent Boeotian cities numbered about a dozen, dominated in varying degrees by Thebes, which had become the administrative centre of a regional league, not later than *c.*550, when the coins of a number of cities began to display a uniform type – a round or oval Boeotian shield – reflecting a federal organization. During the Persian Wars, because of its hatred of Athens (which was far too close for comfort) this Boeotian League (with the exception of Plataea and Thespiae) submitted to the invaders: after which it suffered dissolution.

But the confederacy was reconstituted in 447/446, on an oligarchic basis. There was no federal citizenship, but a system of proportional representation, in which the states were grouped in seven wards, each returning sixty members to a sovereign federal council. This move towards Boeotian unification was a significant experiment in a type of inter-state union which generally eluded the Greeks of the classical period, with ultimately fatal results. But the new League could not – except perhaps theoretically – be regarded as an association of equals, since the Thebans, who became more prosperous and numerous after the Peloponnesian War, were always dominant; and after the King's Peace of 387/386 Sparta's fear of Thebes meant that this League, too, like its forerunner, was temporarily dissolved.

Soon afterwards, however, following Sparta's coup at Thebes (382) and the ejection of its garrison three years later, it was decided that the League should once again be revived. And there was a time, too, when the Athenian recovery from the Peloponnesian War assumed a concrete form. First, the Spartans repeated their Theban gesture by dispatching Sphodrias to make an unsuccessful attack on Athens (378). The Athenians, although no longer the political leaders of the Greek world, were still a power to be reckoned with (for example, their city was the Greeks' chief banking centre: cf. Appendix III). And now Sphodrias' stupid action so greatly infuriated and alarmed them that they founded a Second Athenian League of maritime cities, offering more tempting terms than the first (in the previous century). Moreover, they also took the unusual step of forming an alliance with the Boeotians, which Agesilaus' invasions of Boeotia in that and the following year failed to disrupt.

Seeing that the Athenians were now reviving and increasing their naval potentialities, Sparta hastened to do the same. However, the alliance between Athens and Thebes did not last after all, and a split developed between them. Greece was now in a state of complete deadlock; and Persia saw an opportunity to intervene once again. In 371, therefore, its representatives came to Sparta to meet envoys of the belligerent Greek states, and the result was the 'Peace of Callias' (a misleading title, since there had probably been another treaty of the same name sixty years earlier). The new Peace was made on the basis of 'independence', according to which no city-state should maintain a garrison on another's territory, and all should disarm.

The Spartans duly took the oath on behalf of their own city and their allies, but the delegates of Athens and other states swore separate and individual oaths. Thebes, too, did the same. But then the Theban delegates, led by Epaminondas, claimed to be recognized as acting for the Boeotian League as well; and this Sparta refused to allow. So the Thebans withdrew from the negotiations, and this second 'Peace of Callias' came to nothing.

The Theban obstruction, which nullified it, was the work of Epaminondas, the most important public figure that his city ever produced, who thus appears at the head of his city's affairs for the first time. He became the subject of many eulogies, for everyone agreed about his qualities. The nobility and uprightness of his modest, unambitious character were impressive and even Athenians had to admire his eloquence and culture, which he had acquired as a pupil of Lysis, a Pythagorean philosopher in exile.

Epaminondas was said to have assisted Spartan troops in their siege of Mantinea in 385 (although this remains doubtful), and also, perhaps, helped in the restoration of Theban power six years later. Now, in 371, he was one of the generals (Boeotarchs) elected as leaders of the Boeotian confederacy. In its new form, the earlier system of indirect government by proportional representation was abandoned in favour of a broadly democratic federal Assembly, meeting at Thebes, which took its decisions by direct vote. Three of the 'wards', however (reduced from eleven to seven), were still dominated by the Thebans, and it was this pre-eminence which prompted Epaminondas' demand that Thebes should act for the League.

The result, as he had probably hoped and intended, was immediate war against Sparta. The Spartan army, under the Agiad King Cleombrotus I, was already in the territory of the Thebans' neighbour Phocis, and now it made a rapid move – before Thebes could mobilize its allies – arriving in the middle of Boeotia by a surprise march through the glens of Mount Helicon, and forcing battle at Leuctra. The Spartans enjoyed a numerical advantage, marshalling 10,000 hoplites, including 700 Spartiates, against a total of 6,000 Thebans (though the Theban cavalry enjoyed a slight superiority).

But the decisive factor was Epaminondas himself, who was serving as one of the Theban generals – and proved more than a match for the invaders. Behind the Spartans' cavalry – drawn up, like that of their opponents, in the front line – their hoplite phalanx stood twelve deep. On the Theban side, however, Epaminondas massed hoplites fifty deep to constitute his left wing, which advanced not in the customary continuous front aligned with the rest of the army, but ahead of the other units in a slanting, oblique formation. Then, after the Thebans' cavalry had driven its enemy counterpart back on its own phalanx, this strengthened left wing, led by the Sacred Band (of devoted homosexual couples) under Pelopidas – Epaminondas' closest associate – charged forward at the double. King Cleombrotus I, attempting to oppose the charge, was struck down and killed, and four hundred Spartiates died with him. Those of his followers who survived fled in disorder, and so did the rest of his force, leaving nearly a thousand dead.

'The most famous of all victories won by Greeks over Greeks',[1] this engagement proved for the first time, and once and for all, that the Spartans' phalanx was not invincible. Their conduct as an imperial power had been inefficient and brutal, at a time when diminishing manpower had augmented their already grave social stresses; and now, this stunning reversal of their military reputation announced the end of their thirty-three-year-old predominance in Greece.

Despite Epaminondas' previous lack of experience as commander-in-chief, the battle of Leuctra had shown him to be a masterly strategic and tactical planner and commander. True, the Thebans had tried out something like this heavily weighted wing before, notably at Delium in 424 (and at Coronea in 394 a deep phalanx had fought well), so that it should not therefore have taken the Spartan king by surprise. But no doubt, like most of his compatriots, he was conservative in his military thinking, and, besides, the scheme had never before been put into effect on so formidable a scale. Epaminondas had also displayed himself as an adroit co-ordinator of infantry and cavalry, and co-ordinator, also, of the diverse forces that various states had placed under his command. He goes down to history as the most professional military genius that the Greek city-states of the mainland ever produced, and one of the mentors of Philip II and Alexander.

Thebes was now the leading land-power in Greece, though it had to keep a careful watch on a potential rival, Jason of Pherae in Thessaly, who had recently brought all the other Thessalian states under his control. After Leuctra Epaminondas diplomatically invited him to join up with the Theban forces, but Jason refused to lend his well-trained mercenaries for the purpose, and instead negotiated an armistice between the Thebans and Spartans. Athens, which Epaminondas had also asked for help, organized a conference seeking a renewed Common Peace, under the auspices of its own confederacy, and Persia sponsored the plan.

But this did not prevent Epaminondas from pressing ahead with the destruction of Sparta's hegemony, amid a chaotic outburst of factional strife in numerous cities. In 370/369 he invaded the Peloponnese, helped the Arcadians to throw off Spartan control (building Megalopolis as their new federal capital), and led the first recorded invasion of Sparta's own Eurotas valley, penetrating into the barricaded streets of the unwalled city itself. Next he liberated Messenia – where many Spartiates had owned their rich land – and founded a new fortified town of Messene beside the ancient Ithome. Before long (366), the long-lived, famous Peloponnesian League had ceased to exist. Meanwhile the envoys from various Greek states had gone to Susa to see King Artaxerxes II Mnemon of Persia (367/366); the Theban envoy, Pelopidas, succeeded better than the rest.

At some time during this period, Epaminondas' position was threatened by his political opponents in Thebes itself. However, he survived the challenge, and moved north to defeat Alexander, Jason's nephew and successor at Pherae, though Pelopidas, the architect of this diplomatic and military penetration of Thessaly, was killed in the battle. Then in 364, despite the relative inaccessibility of Boeotia's ports, Epaminondas decided, in what was for Thebes a revolutionary innovation, to challenge the Athenian supremacy at sea, leading a fleet as far as Byzantium.

However, learning that the Arcadian League had broken away from his coalition, he returned, with unprecedented speed of movement, to the Peloponnese, where his force, consisting of troops from Argos, Sicyon, Messenia, together with Arcadian dissidents, had to confront a coalition of Spartans, Athenians, Eleans and Achaeans. In the battle of Mantinea that followed (362) – the largest battle yet fought between one Greek force and another – Epaminondas, employing tactics similar to those of Leuctra, was well on the way to an overwhelming victory when he fell, mortally wounded.

After his death, the Boeotians and their allies halted in their tracks, and concluded peace. For the Greek mainland states were exhausted; and although yet another and even more ambitious Common Peace (excluding only Sparta) was attempted, Xenophon gloomily observed that, from now on, the confusion was more hopeless than ever (Chapter 30).[2] He was writing, admittedly, as a dillusioned pro-Spartan, but what he said was not far wrong.

And the Roman biographer Nepos, too, was right to say that Epaminondas counted more than his state. For Thebes and Boeotia had nothing to fall back upon once he was dead. True, whatever future eulogists might say, his successes had not been unlimited: despite his military talents, he had not achieved extensive, positive results in the political field. Certainly, he had overthrown the incompetent Spartan predominance. But the 'Panhellenic' liberation which he evidently sought to establish in its place,[3] envisaging a utopian coalition of self-governing leagues (linked somehow with a novel Boeotian overseas confederacy), came to nothing – and may, indeed, be little more than a later fiction.

Instead, all that had replaced the Spartan hegemony was a vacuum, which the Boeotian League proved unfitted to fill. True, Boeotia's agricultural economy was strong. But the manpower of the territory was insubstantial, and its professional army (once Pelopidas and Epaminondas had died) fell short of Spartan standards. Nor did Thebes (except in mythology) have a distinguished past to live up to, unlike Sparta and Athens. But Sparta was shattered, and the Second Athenian League, too, lacked sufficient strength to survive. So now there was no mainland city capable of taking the lead – and, without a lead, the Greek states were too divisive and quarrelsome to maintain any stable equilibrium, or any combined resistance to a threat from outside. That threat would very soon be presented with formidable effect, not this time by Persia, but by Philip II, who came to the Macedonian throne three years after Epaminondas had fallen at Mantinea (Chapter 35).

CHAPTER 30

XENOPHON: LITERARY LAND-OWNER

The son of an upper-class Athenian, Xenophon (*c*.428–*c*.354), as a young man, served in the cavalry during the final years of the Peloponnesian War, and may have fought at Arginusae (406; Chapter 24). He got to know and admire Socrates (Chapter 21) during this period, and shared his right-wing oligarchic tastes, which accounts for Xenophon's withdrawal from Athens after the oligarchic revolution of the Thirty had been overthrown, and democracy was restored.

In 401 his Boeotian friend Proxenus invited him to join the rebellion of Cyrus the younger against Cyrus' brother King Artaxerxes II Mnemon of Persia. After Cyrus' death at Cunaxa, he played a leading part in the evacuation of the Greek force to Trapezus (north-east Asia Minor), eventually becoming its commander-in-chief. Then he served with the Thracian (Odrysian) King Seuthes II and with two Spartan generals fighting against Persia (399–397).

At the time, however, of Socrates' execution, Xenophon was politically compromised at home because of his oligarchic views, and the Athenians sentenced him, *in absentia*, to banishment, involving the confiscation of his property. In 396–394 he served as one of the senior commanders of King Agesilaus II of Sparta, whom at this time he greatly admired, in his war against Pharnabazus, the Persian satrap of Dascylium, and returned with him to fight against his own Athenian compatriots at Coronea (394).

Next he settled at Sparta, until the Spartans gave him an estate at Scillus in Elis (north-west Peloponnese), where he spent many years hunting and writing; until the battle of Leuctra (371) removed Scillus from Sparta's control, whereupon the family moved to the Isthmus of Corinth.

In *c*.365 however, relations between the Spartans and Athenians having improved, Xenophon was able to return to Athens, which had cancelled his sentence of exile. In 362 two of his sons formed part of an Athenian contingent helping the Spartans against the Thebans at Mantinea, and one of them, Gryllus, was killed. When Xenophon died about eight years later he was apparently on a visit to Corinth.

Four works relating to Socrates (Chapter 21) fall into a special category of his writings. The *Apology* (*c*.384) describes Socrates' conduct before, during and after his trial, and endeavours to show that he was a man of great worth, who should never have been condemned to die. The *Symposium* invents discussions at an imaginary party held at the house of the younger Callias in *c*.422, at which Socrates was supposedly present. In 371 Callias, by then a man of advanced years, arranged the peace between Athens and Sparta that bears his name (Chapter 29), and Xenophon's *Symposium* may represent an attempt to ingratiate himself with the old politician.

Household Management (*Oeconomicus*), (*c*.362/361?) professes to reproduce discussions in which Socrates offered advice about household affairs and the behaviour of wives; the essay is designed to exhibit the virtues of a country gentleman. The work known since the Renaissance as the *Memoirs* (*Memorabilia*), written partly in *c*.381 (or later?) and partly in *c*.355/354, curiously combines its defence of Socrates with discussions on education, wealth and domestic management, which were subjects that, in all likelihood, had never occupied the philosopher's attention.

Xenophon was very proud to have known Socrates, although, since his philosophical capabilities fell short of his pretensions, he must have been one of the great man's more or less uncomprehending, intermittent hangers-on, rather than a serious student. What he later had to say about his hero, therefore, is just a rag-bag of second-hand hearsay and reading and invention. A mild, prosaic, prudent, robustly commonsensical, commonplace Socrates emerges, reflecting, all too often, the known tastes and limitations of Xenophon himself. Xenophon is also eager to plunge into the already abundant literary controversies about Socrates' trial and death, refuting by implication a certain Polycrates, who had asserted that Socrates only got what he deserved.

Turning to those of Xenophon's surviving writings which do not concentrate on Socrates, the earliest of these pieces seems to have been *The Spartan Constitution*, written in *c*.388 to express admiration (although some doubting afterthoughts intrude) for the stable governmental system of the Spartans, who had given him his home at Scillus. *On Hunting* (*Cynegeticus*) dates from the same period, and manages to insert an attack on the moral subversiveness of the sophists (Chapter 12); but it is not certain that Xenophon is the author.

The *March Up Country* (*Anabasis*), completed in 377 and now comprising seven books, is a vivid and beguiling account of the expedition of the Greek mercenaries to help Cyrus the younger against Artaxerxes II Mnemon (401–399). In order to answer his critics (who existed in the expeditionary force and Spartan government alike), Xenophon exaggerates the importance of his own role, so that unfairness to the other generals sometimes makes its appearance.

The *Education of Cyrus* (*Cyropaedia*) (370s), now in eight books, is in effect one of the earliest of many Greek treatises 'On Kingship'. It is a sort of historical novel, with Cyrus II the Great of Persia (559–529) as its model hero; and Xenophon, while expressing admiration for the monarch and for the other Cyrus (the younger) with whom he had served, takes the opportunity to express his own views on authority, organization, moral reform and family life. For centuries this discussion was regarded as his masterpiece, and Edmund Spenser preferred it to Plato's *Republic*, though Gibbon described the work as 'vague and languid', and Macaulay considered it 'a very wretched performance'.

The *Hiero* seems to constitute a postcript to the *Education of Cyrus*. It takes the form of a dialogue between Hiero I of Syracuse (478–467/466) and the poet Simonides of Ceos, who visited his court (Chapters 4, 6); the two men discuss whether an autocrat can lead a happy life and gain his subjects' support. This *is* possible, we are told, though the poorer a tyrant's subjects are, the more submissive they will be.[4]

Xenophon's *Hellenica*, as it stands, is a Greek history, in seven books, covering the period from 411 to 362, and professing to continue Thucydides (Chapter 23). It was written at intervals between *c.*403 and the years after 362, and its contents reflect the author's places of residence at those various epochs. Although he is not, altogether, a Spartan propagandist (the King's Peace and its aftermath shocked him), his sources and tastes exhibit a pro-Spartan bias. The Second Athenian League, for example, is omitted altogether; and his concluding gloom about the hopeless situation after the battle of Mantinea (however justified) is motivated by Sparta's downfall. Moreover there is too little emphasis on Epaminondas and too much on Agesilaus II (d. 360), although undiluted praise of the latter had to wait for Xenophon's posthumous eulogy which bore Agesilaus' name, and portrayed him as a hero in the Panhellenic cause.

On Ways and Means or *On Revenues* (*Peri Poron, De Vectigalibus*, *c.*355/354) proposes practical methods of increasing Athens' resources by the encouragement of commercial and industrial enterprises (for example, by an increase in the number of metics, Appendix III), according to a somewhat free version of the sensible, peace-orientated policies of the financier–politician Eubulus (Chapter 36). The work seems to refer to the Third Sacred War, which started in 356. Xenophon (or someone imitating him) had written earlier *On Hunting*, as we saw, and now came *On Horsemanship* (the earliest surviving study of the subject) and the *Hipparchicus* (about the duties of a cavalry commander). Both these essays are professionally competent contributions to military science, written during an epoch when that subject was developing rapidly, and when textbooks dealing with such technical themes had become fashionable.

Xenophon's versatility, then, was impressive – indeed, perhaps he spread himself too widely. A man of deep reactionary political tastes (so that Athens was no place for him, and Niebuhr called him 'a thoroughly bad citizen'), he held a simple belief in the virtues of strong leadership, which accounts for the various treatises in which he eulogizes and glorifies powerful leaders. As regards military life, he was not a soldier by training, but acquired considerable expert knowledge, especially in cavalry tactics, and this appears in the writings mentioned above. About the desirability of discipline among the troops, as might be expected, he held rigorous views, but combined them with great sympathy (too great, it was felt by some)[5] towards ordinary soldiers, to whose day-by-day existences he devoted careful attention.

After his military career was over, he lived the life of an affluent land-owner and the rural activities involved in such a position absorbed most of his interests. As a historian and continuator of Thucydides, the *Hellenica* showed Xenophon's deficiencies (notably in grasping the causes of events) all too clearly – although his eye for a good scene and story cannot be denied, and received greatly admired illustration in his *March Up Country* (*Anabasis*). But in contrast to his mediocre performance as a general historian, *On Ways and Means*, even if not wholly practical in its interpretation of Eubulus' policies, shows a reasonable assessment of what might currently be done at Athens.

Although an egotist, Xenophon was also a generous, philanthropic man with an essentially optimistic outlook, but his frequent bouts of earnest moralizing reflect a lightweight amalgam of banal prejudice and pious superstition. Nevertheless, this same popular ethical uplift, conveyed in lucid, intelligible prose and sometimes gripping narrative, made him readable, and many Romans so warmly admired his combination of an active public life with literary achievement that he became the most popular of all Athenian prose writers.

CHAPTER 31

PLATO: ETERNAL REALITY

Plato (*c*.429–347) belonged to an Athenian family that was aristocratic on both sides. After aspiring, at first, to become a poet, he became an adherent of Socrates (*c*.407?; Chapter 21) and devoted himself to philosophy. It appears that he took some part in political life during the oligarchic revolution of the Thirty (404) – whose leaders included members of his own family. But the subsequent democratic restoration, followed by the traumatic experience of Socrates' condemnation to death, inspired him with a disgust for democracy and for politics in general. So he fled, with some of his fellow students, and took refuge with the philosopher Euclides of Megara.

In 387 Plato visited the Pythagorean philosopher, mathematician and political leader Archytas at Taras in south Italy, and Dionysius I of Syracuse in Sicily (Chapters 26, 25). On his way back to Greece, he may have been detained at Aegina, and released only after paying a ransom. After returning home, he instituted his Academy outside Athens (named after the tomb of the hero Academus), and spent most of the rest of his life teaching within its precincts. However, he also made a second and third visit to Sicily.

The second followed the death of Dionysius I (367) when the late ruler's brother-in-law and son-in-law Dion invited Plato (whose friend he had become on the philosopher's earlier visit) to endeavour to make Dionysius' nephew and heir Dionysius II into the ideal philosopher-monarch – or so it was said, although some have dismissed the story as a fable. The young Dionysius II, although he was a writer himself, and invited other learned men to his court, reputedly resented this attempt to guide him, and in particular objected to Plato's insistence that statecraft began with geometry. In any case Plato had to return home.

Nevertheless, he risked a third visit in 361, aimed at securing the recall of Dion, now exiled, whom he hoped to reconcile with Dionysius II. However, all that happened was that Plato was detained by the hostile Dionysius, until the influence of Archytas secured his release. Yet members of the Academy continued to interfere in support of Dion, who knew the school well, since he had earlier taken refuge there; and indeed, when he tried to return to Sicily (357), Academicians supported his attempt. Three years later, however, one of their number, Callippus, dismayed by Dion's increasingly despotic behaviour, employed men from Zacynthus to murder him (and himself seized power for a year).

The verbose, waffling *Seventh Letter* attributed to Plato, containing a series of depressing admissions about the Syracusan mess, may well have been subsequently invented (along with the scarcely less realistic *Eighth*) by the Academy to explain its participation in these unsavoury affairs, and to seek to justify Plato's unsuccessful endeavours to match philosophical theory with political action. Some, however, still believe that these compositions were written by himself, with the same purpose in mind; though this seems less likely.

Plato's *Apology* is not a dialogue but an idealized and, for the most part, imaginative version of Socrates' defence at his trial. The actual charges are treated with satirical, contemptuous mockery, for what Socrates really intends to explain – we are told – instead of offering any serious legal defence, is that he has a divine mission to 'philosophize', to 'make his soul as good as possible' – and to induce others to do the same. That is to say, the *Apology* aims at offering a substantial, overall defence of Socrates' life work.

The *Crito* – named after one of his close friends, a kindly, practical man – asks why he is deliberately throwing his life away by refusing to escape from prison. His answer is that the capital verdict, although mistaken, has been pronounced by a legitimate court, so that to flout its decision would be to damage the Athenian system, which would be improper. This rejection of civil disobedience, in face of the superior demands of political obligation, is Plato's first attempt to deal with right and wrong in relation to the *polis*.

The *Euthyphro*, in which Socrates interrogates a religious expert (of fundamentalist views), is intended to display his attitude to conventional religion – one of the two counts in the case against him. He is quoted as spurning immoral mythology, and denying that the carrying out of any arbitrary set of demands can be true religious observance. Service to the divine holiness, we are meant to understand, means co-operation in noble activity, the tending of the soul.

The *Phaedo* defends as a rational, if improbable, hypothesis, the soul's immortality, or rather, divinity which ensures its survival after death. This is achieved by the soul freeing itself from its prison, the body, of which Plato learnt from Archytas and the Pythagoreans (Appendix 1). Socrates discusses the topic with a few friends during his last day on earth, concluding with an imposing myth about the afterlife. This doctrine of an immutable soul is linked with the Theory of Forms, of which more will be said later. A masterpiece of sublimity and pathos, the *Phaedo* is a general glorification of Socrates and all that Plato believed he had stood for.

Turning to the dialogues which do not deal directly with the trial and death of Socrates, yet display him, inventively, as the principal interlocutor, an early group is mostly concerned with questionings rather than answers: it is 'aporetic', full of puzzles.

The *Charmides* is a typical example. It seeks to define temperance or self-control (*sophrosyne*), which brings up the subject of the self-knowledge ('know thyself') that Socrates had so strongly emphasized. He is shown talking to a promising but diffident young man, Charmides, so that Plato can, indirectly, defend him against the charge of corrupting the young. (Critias, on the other hand, for whose evil conduct during the oligarchic revolution of the Thirty (404–403) Socrates, as his educator, had been particularly blamed, is shown as an aggressive, self-confident figure clearly beyond the master's control.)

The *Laches*, pursuing the same exculpatory aim by way of a debate on education (as the *Lysis* does later on, discussing friendship), tries to define another virtue, namely courage. This is a lifelike, light-hearted and approachable little piece. However, the attempt fails, merely concluding that the ordinary decent man cannot be an adequate teacher. Nor, according to the *Ion*, can the poet or poetical singer (rhapsode), since both these practitioners operate by non-rational methods, so that the conduct of life – the task of the educator – lies outside their competence.

The *Protagoras*, crammed with people and movement and subtle characterization, presents the main principles of what Plato understood to be the morality of Socrates, who meets the eminent sophist (Chapter 12) in the younger Callias' house. While Plato (like Socrates) evidently has a love-hate relationship with the sophists, Protagoras is given every opportunity to argue for the capacity of the common citizen to make decisions on public, non-technical matters. But Socrates suggests that it is doubtful whether this art can be taught at all, since the conduct of life is not teachable (Plato regarded it as dangerously democratic to say otherwise). And yet Socrates, by a convoluted, humorous *volte face* (and he cheats and parodies in this dialogue with exceptional vigour), concludes by changing places with Protagoras and asserting after all – as he had apparently asserted in real life – that virtue (meaning all virtues, for he sees them as a unity) *is* knowledge, and that no one does wrong willingly.

In the *Lesser Hippias*, which endeavours to explain and justify the same paradox, the polymath sophist of that name is treated less respectfully than Protagoras had been; indeed, he seems to find it hard to follow the subtleties of Socratic argument. And so he does in the *Greater Hippias* as well; to such an extent, in fact, that some have seen this as a clumsy caricature, not written by Plato at all. The modern application of a computer to the text, however, seems to corroborate Platonic authorship, but interprets the piece as subsequent to the *Lesser Hippias*, and forming part of a later group of dialogues. The theme of the *Greater Hippias* is 'what is the good (*kalon*)?' That looks a too ambitious question, and we reach no conclusion, except that 'good' is not the same as 'pleasant' or 'useful'.

In the *Meno* Socrates, speaking with Anytus, who later became his prosecutor, reverts once again, in a series of unfairly leading questions, to the teachability of virtue, which had been discussed in the *Protagoras* – and again concludes that there is no certain proof of this: perhaps it can only be achieved by divine providence, unless there should happen to be a statesman who could produce another statesman by his training (see the *Republic* below). The centrepiece of the dialogue is the weird doctrine of Recollection (*anamnesis*) of a previous condition, by which, as Plato had learnt from the Pythagoreans (Appendix 1) through Archytas, all knowledge is acquired. The *Euthydemus*, on the other hand, displaying Plato at his instructional best, shows the lamentable effects of hoping to acquire knowledge by the sort of education provided by the sophists, who chopped logic with a frivolity, he maintained, that sharply contrasted with the solemn mission of Socrates himself; and this is perhaps how the *Meno* and *Protagoras* can be reconciled.

The *Menexenus* (385), the funniest (and most scathing) of these dialogues, contains a certain amount of philosophy (relating to virtue and freedom), but turns aside in order to present a funeral oration allegedly learnt from Pericles' mistress Aspasia: Plato's purpose is to satirize the Periclean 'Golden Age', and mock all the patriotic commonplaces and distortions and falsifications of history that this glorified regime had stimulated. The dialogue, however, although excellently constructed, contains a manifest anachronism, since Socrates and Aspasia discuss happenings in the Corinthian War (395–387) which took place long after both of them were dead. Here is a direct warning from Plato that the scenes he enacts are fictitious, and must not be taken as reproducing discussions that had ever actually taken place.

The *Gorgias* is a long and powerful work, of a positive character missing in Plato's earlier analyses. Though the exaggerations of that sophist's opportunistic followers are comically routed, he himself is treated with some respect. However, Socrates will not allow that the rhetoric Gorgias professes (Chapter 12) is the 'art' that he claims it is, maintaining that it amounts to no more than a knack of humouring audiences and a manifestation of expediency, whereas what is instead needed in public and private life alike (and their requirements cannot be dissociated) is *absolute right* – upon which it does seem that Socrates had, authentically, insisted. Conscience must always be obeyed, and nowhere is that injunction more forcibly and passionately conveyed than in the *Gorgias*.

Amid a heavy homosexual aura (although Socrates himself, we are told, had heterosexual tastes)[6] the dramatic, subtle and at times funny *Symposium* is one of Plato's most original achievements. Professing, in accordance with an antique tradition of formal *symposia*, to record the various speeches in praise of Love (Eros) delivered at a banquet in honour of the tragic poet Agathon (caricatured in a play by Aristophanes (Chapter 19),[7] who is also present at the dinner), the purpose of the work is to show how this 'Platonic love', excited in the first instance by a beautiful body, is capable of ascending to unmaterial objects, finally becoming a rapturous 'desire to beget the Beautiful', a passion for Beauty, a supersensuous, transcendental Form (p. 217) which only the intellect can apprehend. In opposition to the somewhat inebriated Alcibiades (whose worldliness is intended to remind readers that the charge that Socrates led him astray cannot have been true), Socrates enunciated these unworldly doctrines, which he claimed to have learnt from the priestess Diotima of Mantinea; and he himself is seen as the aspirant who has achieved this mystical emotion and union.

Because of its continued preoccupation with mysticism and love, it is convenient, at this point, to mention the somewhat later *Phaedrus* (containing Plato's most vivid background, with an extended description of the landscape). However, the dialogue, named after a young pupil of the orator Lysias with whom Socrates is talking, is primarily concerned not with love but with the principles of rhetoric (prose composition), presenting new dialectical ideas and methods, and discussing the orators of the day. In the *Gorgias*, Socrates had dismissed rhetoric as a mere trick, but here he shows that it could, after all, be placed on a scientific foundation, if logic was accurately applied – and if systematic study was devoted to human desires and passions, which are now granted a substantial reality, in contrast to their dismissal by the philosopher Parmenides as part of the experiential non-reality of material phenomena (Chapter 8). As in the *Symposium* Plato goes on to speak of the Forms as objects of mystic contemplation by the immortal soul.

On the basis of its diction and style, the *Cratylus* (named after, and presenting, a follower of the philosopher Heraclitus) has to be placed in the same group as the *Symposium*, rather than later as has been supposed; but the exact chronological sequence remains uncertain. Although somewhat jocular and fanciful, the *Cratylus* is our first surviving treatise on etymology, dealing with a question of permanent interest to linguistic philosophers: whether names are significant – to use the terms of a fashionable ancient antithesis (Chapter 12) – by nature (*physis*) or by convention and social usage (*nomos*). Beware of criteria based on *nomos*, Plato says (together with any metaphysical conclusions derived from it), since Heraclitus and Parmenides, for example, had used the same words to denote quite different things. Yet language, once we can get away from such subjectivities, *is* an instrument of thought, to be judged by its power to express true thinking with accuracy; and then behind the words rise the genuine, ideal realities enshrined in the Theory of Forms, which alone are admissible as true objects of knowledge.

The *Parmenides* (*c*.370) is a good example of the puzzles (*aporiai*) which Plato continued to enjoy. The youthful Socrates is found addressing Parmenides and his follower Zeno, and defending an aspect of his own Theory of Forms, namely the doctrine that material things 'participate', have a genuine part, in the ideal Forms. Then Parmenides raises objections to this view, since although the concept of Forms fits in well with his own belief that the only authentic reality is imperishable, indivisible, immutable and non-material, he cannot, by the same token, concede that experiential material things, accessible to the senses, have any real existence at all, even on a secondary level of reality (a view which Plato had contradicted in the *Gorgias*), so that the question of their 'participation' is illusory.

Parmenides is even made to hint that Socrates would fare better if he received more training in logic. What is the purpose of this curious concession on Plato's part, if that is what it is? Is he pointing out that the thoroughgoing, exclusive non-materialism of Parmenides is in fact nonsensical logic-chopping? Or is he, on the other hand, telling us that, as the years went by, after repeated, searching enquiries, he no longer found his own Theory of Forms satisfactory? He is not, we must suppose, jettisoning the theory altogether, but attempting, sometimes playfully, to face its difficulties: Parmenides is helping to clarify and rearticulate the Platonic doctrine of Forms rather than demolishing it – though he does so, it must be admitted, with somewhat disconcerting cogency!

The *Theaetetus* (*c*.368), then, was timely, because its aim, ascribed to Socrates, was to discuss how knowledge should be defined – to decide *what* it is, not its contents or objects, or the means by which we can acquire it. The treatise has still been described, in our own century, as the best existing introduction to epistemology, the science of knowledge. Relativism, in the form of Protagoras' assertion that man is the measure of all things, is once again refuted with ingenious (and what may seem excessive) agility, and so is the concept that knowledge can be equated with sensation (*aisthesis*). But now comes another puzzle: for the problem has become so elusive and difficult that, after demolishing these theories, Plato sets nothing whatever in their place. Here indeed is an echo of Socrates' famous assertion that he knew nothing himself. But the reason, perhaps, why this negativeness appealed to Plato was that the truth, in his view, being an ultimate Form, *defies* definition: though he does not explicitly say so, since the time when he wanted to express everything in terms of Forms may already have been over – unless a later date is preferred for the *Phaedrus* (already discussed) and the *Timaeus*.

But in any case the *Timaeus*, while speaking of 'imitation' rather than 'participation' when describing the relation of perceptible, material things to Forms, does not assert this or any other such theory in any dogmatic fashion, but only as a matter of reasonable likelihood. According to this dialogue, Timaeus, an astronomer of Locri Epizephyrii (who appears as the central figure, replacing Socrates), distinguishes between eternal being and its copy – the mutable, insubstantial, temporal world. Imaginative, abstruse, unique among the writings of Plato, the *Timaeus* combines cosmology, physics and biology, so that it could almost be summed up as the Academy's encyclopaedia of current scientific research at this epoch.

The *Timaeus* begins with the origins of life as we know it, recounted as the myth of the imaginary continent of Atlantis and the Athenians' defeat of its attempt to take over the whole world (a story that was to have been completed in the unfinished *Critias*). Then Timaeus introduces God as the intelligent, effective cause of this whole providential world and moral order, operating at times, however, through an element of errant causality (*planomene aitia*) or 'necessity' (*ananke*), which functions without our being able to discern the reason why.

In the *Sophist*, formally presented as a sequel to the *Theaetetus*, Socrates is once again no longer the principal spokesman; instead, we find a stranger from Elea in south Italy. He is a follower of Parmenides, who had come from that city: but one of the purposes of the dialogue is to reiterate Plato's earlier rejection of Parmenides' theory that the temporal, material world of our sense perceptions is a mere illusion. This new criticism adopts a method which tries to fit individual ideas into some systematic, generally applicable treatment and method, and in so doing illustrates the importance of meticulous classification – thus establishing the basis of subsequent logical procedures. The dialogue bears the name that it does because the Eleatic stranger makes six successive attempts to define what a sophist really is, which offers the opportunity to distinguish between the right and wrong sort of sophist, and the differing qualities of moral education which such men provide.

Then came the *Philebus*, which summed up Plato's last thoughts on ethics and good life. The question at issue, recalling the *Greater Hippias*, is whether the good is pleasurable feeling or the exercise of intelligence, a matter, apparently, on which the Academy was divided, the hedonist faction being led by the mathematician and astronomer Eudoxus, while its principal opponent was Speusippus, who subsequently succeeded Plato as head of the Academy. In this rather untidy and difficult dialogue Socrates (who makes a final appearance as principal speaker) concludes that the best life includes both these elements, with intelligence, however, occupying the major role.

The *Republic*, *Statesman* (*Politicus*) and *Laws*, though widely separated from one another in date, can be grouped together as Plato's major statements on political matters.

The monumental, complex, intoxicating work known to the Greeks as the *Politeia* (system of the *polis* or state) and to ourselves as the *Republic*, written in the 380s or 370s or both, sums up in its ten books a great deal of the philosophy enunciated in Plato's other dialogues, amalgamating ethics and politics and metaphysics in a spirit of creative crusading passion. The ostensible theme is justice: what is it, and can we show that it is always beneficial to its possessor? Can we show, in fact, that moral distinctions are based upon a rational principle? Plato's answer is that we can.

In Book I Socrates holds a discussion on the subject with the aged Cephalus – whom he is visiting at the Piraeus – and his son Polemarchus (brother of the orator Lysias), and then with the sophist Thrasymachus of Calchedon. When Thrasymachus defines justice as the advantage of the stronger, he is refuted. But in Books IV–VI Plato's brothers Glaucus and Adeimantus take up the argument (more intelligently) on his behalf. Plato answers them by describing an imaginary state (a popular and sometimes more whimsical literary genre; cf. Chapter 19), to be regarded as the embodiment of justice, under the direction of a governing class, the guardians, presided over by a philosophical ruler, the 'philosopher-king'.

This state, which should be neither too rich nor too poor, must be based on the provision of an excellent education to the members of its dominant class, continually exposing them to the Good (the pessimism of the *Protagoras* and *Meno* about the teachability of virtue is set aside). Under Pythagorean influence (Appendix I), Plato believed that the mathematical sciences, led by arithmetic, should form the most prominent feature of this training. As regards other subjects, traditional modes of music (poetry) and gymnastical methods must be preferred to novelties, as part of a general policy of shunning cultural innovation and licence. For that leads inevitably, Plato felt, to social and political licence as well: seeing that art involves a kind of imitation, and imitation is not reality and can encourage further imitation, in the form of bad behaviour (Book III).

Justice in the state, he asserts, consists of the performance, by each of the three classes or castes of citizens, of its own proper functions. They include – in addition to the first, governing class of guardians – the auxiliaries ('the dogs who heed the guardians' voice'),[8] and the Third Class, or populace, consisting of farmers, traders, artisans and so forth. The education of this last group of people corresponds with their inferior status, since it will be restricted to the instruction that they need in order to perform their own defined tasks; and in order to induce them to accept this inferior role in society it will be necessary to tell them 'noble' lies.

And then Plato goes on to develop his familiar analogy between the state and the human soul: the state is merely the soul 'writ large', since, that is to say, ethics cannot be distinguished from politics, the soul, like the community, possesses three parts, reason, the will (spirit) and sensation (appetite, desire). And just as the guardians have the task of ruling the state, so reason ought to rule the soul.

The remaining books of the *Republic* contain elaborate analyses of residual problems. One of the subjects discussed in Book v is the position of women, who are capable of becoming guardians, although most (not all) are inferior to men in strength. The guardians will have wives and children in common, so that no parent knows his own child; indeed, they will possess no private property at all of their own (see also Appendix II).

Meanwhile, however, we return to ethical questions. What, really, is the nature of wisdom, and how should one define the person who wants to attain it – that is to say, the philosopher? He is needed to conduct the state, and in Book VII the lofty level of knowledge and reality which he is capable of achieving, and must achieve, is illustrated by the Myth of the Cave, from the shadowy darkness of which a man can be drawn out and liberated so as to become gradually accustomed to the light.

Book VIII offers us Plato's theory of history, in which, since the perfect state will experience no historical happenings whatever, all change is inevitably deterioration, and a symptom of political illness (just as he had earlier shown hostility to educational innovation). In Book IX this illness is described in its most virulent forms: tyranny, arbitrary dictatorship, conducted by unqualified persons. Book x returns to an earlier provocative suggestion: imitations are condemned again, and most notably poetic imitations, which merely obscure and hamper our understanding. Homer's mythological poetry is splendid, but must be rejected in favour of truth.

The work ends, however, with another myth of Plato's own, the Myth of Er. He is a hero who was slain in battle and returns to tell his tale, offering a vision of the destiny of the just and unjust in the afterlife, so as to show, once and for all, that justice is not merely an arbitary conception, but part of the structure of the universe.

The *Statesman* (*Politicus*), composed in the middle or late 360s, forms a bridge between the *Republic* and the *Laws*. It was written after the *Sophist*, and that dialogue's Eleatic stranger returns as the principal speaker; the technique of careful classification, which had been discussed in that dialogue, is now applied to practical problems of human government.

The *Statesman* reaffirms, in detail, that personal dictatorship is inferior to the rule of law; so that the treatise formed a basis of subsequent constitutionalism. Plato concludes, however, that where sovereign law is in existence limited monarchy is preferable to democracy (although where there is no such rule of law, a sovereign democracy is, at least, better than irresponsible autocratic rule).

The *Laws*, Plato's longest and perhaps last work (written in the 350s and early 340s, although some passages may be earlier), takes up once more his plan for the best constitution of a city, jettisoning certain of his earlier and most obviously hypothetical conclusions, in favour of a second-best state.

In this book, an Athenian stranger, addressing a Cretan and a Spartan, describes a proposed new colony 'Magnesia', and explains how he would wish to have it governed. The *Republic*'s emphasis on education is reaffirmed, and the unity achieved by communism, too, remains a theoretical ideal, but is in practice abandoned, the family and its private property (though not the individual's) being recognized, subject to stringent regulations.

Since extremes both of despotism and of freedom must be avoided, a mixed constitution is preferable. Five thousand and forty is a convenient number of citizens, each possessing an almost exactly equal piece of land, and all trained for combat (in the *Republic* only the guardians and auxiliaries had been allotted such training). A hierarchy of commissioners and superintendents, representing a meticulous system of checks and balances, will culminate in thirty-seven Guardians of the Law, whose authority, however, is shared with, or limited by, a Nocturnal Council.

This Council's members, versed in philosophy, will have the task of visiting dissidents and criminals at a House of Correction (Sophrontisterion) 'for their soul's salvation';[9] but if their arguments prove of no avail, the offenders will be put to death. One liquidation centre will be the Place of Punishment, where prisoners die in solitary confinement and are not granted burials. These delinquents will include irreligious persons, since emphasis is now laid on the rigid prescription of a state religion (of which the truthfulness can be deduced from the soul and the stars (gods)), in place of the dialectic and philosophy stressed in the *Republic* as foundations of the state.

In this later work, the guardians are called Guardians of the Law (and remain subject to its constitutional limitations), because Law, too, is valued very highly, and it is imperative that it should prevail: if an ideal monarch cannot be found, then the best we can hope for is a statesman who is also a lawgiver.

Embodying, however imperfectly, the absolute moral standards that have to be aimed at, the state's legal code should incorporate a comprehensive array of fundamental enactments, and the citizens must never attempt to modify *either* the moral ideal *or* the code of laws which expresses it, since they are unqualified to do so. They must instead maintain unwavering obedience to the regulations laid down for them by their legislators. These rules, incidentally, will take for granted a constant state of undeclared war between one state and another: 'what most people call "peace"', observes Plato, 'is only a name'.[10]

His writings are famous for their presentation of Socrates, although, as was pointed out earlier (Chapter 21), nothing they say about him can be regarded as authentic – unless independent corroboration can be found – since Plato was not trying to recount historical facts about Socrates but instead, stimulated by his acquaintance with that remarkable man and by the tragic circumstances of his death, wanted to honour his thoughts and his career as a framework and background for his own philosophical opinions. And in so doing he erected the greatest literary monument any disciple has ever dedicated to his master.

His earliest pieces were largely designed to refute the charges, put forward at Socrates' trial, that he had been guilty of impiety and had corrupted Athenian youth. But many of these early dialogues also raise philosophical issues, in a distinctively 'aporetic' (doubting, puzzle-discussing) manner, that is to say by bold, thought-provoking questions which only receive inconclusive or oblique or paradoxical answers. Plato's second group of writings ranges more widely and positively and toughly, and goes deeper into logical and metaphysical theory. In his final works, Socrates plays a smaller part or none at all, and although these studies retain a semblance of the dialogue structure they are often practically monologues.

Socrates, by his questioning methods, had attempted to demonstrate the paradox that virtue, moral goodness, is knowledge: and Plato, even though his methods too were exploratory, made it his task to try to explain what goodness is, and what kind of soul becomes good by understanding this. Socrates' insistence on absolute standards was what impressed Plato, who also absorbed the Pythagorean convictions that there is a divine and unchanging reality transcending our senses (and expressible in mathematics), and that the soul is a fallen deity imprisoned in the body but capable, eventually, of realizing its divine character after death (Appendix 1).

Such were the influences behind Plato's Theory of Forms (Ideas), which pervaded so much of his thinking – although his attitude to the concept became less clear-cut and dogmatic in later life. These Forms, apprehended by the reasoning processes of the mind, are permanent, unvarying, eternal realities, in contrast to the shifting, imperfect, material phenomena of the senses that echo and 'participate in' them, or as he subsequently said, 'imitate' them. There are Forms corresponding to every universal or general conception, but they are crowned by the Form of the Good, the supreme reality which provides the source and foundation of all the others – the objective standard by which knowledge is made possible, and men and women are enabled to govern their lives.

As we learn increasingly in Plato's later works, the Forms are apprehended by the Soul, which is their ultimate partner both in the macrocosm which is God, the cause and explanation of the universe, and in the microcosm which is the individual human soul. This human soul – first seriously discussed, it would seem, by Socrates – is far more real than the body (from which it is distinguished with a new sharpness) and, being immortal, has always existed and will continue to exist in Pythagorean transmigrations.

It is the soul which bridges the gulf Parmenides had set between true, unchanging reality (now embodied in the Forms) and the changing world we are aware of from our sense perceptions. And Plato, apparently once again developing an attitude of Socrates, maintained that the health, the well-being, of the soul is the natural end (*telos*) of all movement and endeavour, so that his work laid the foundation of the 'teleology' which plays so prominent a part in Aristotle (Chapter 37) and much subsequent European thought.

Although Plato was anxious to provide a rational, intellectual foundation for these views (thus providing categories such as substance and quality with the names that they have borne for ever afterwards), he was, above all else, the sponsor of idealism: the doctrine of a material world formed and governed by something non-material, so that behind perceived phenomena there is a true, eternal, unchanging reality. It is this idealistic conviction that has earned Plato his overwhelming influence on the philosophical and religious thought of the later western world. With him began the central tradition of metaphysics; and he was also the forerunner of analytical philosophy (of which the modern development has made some of his later dialogues less difficult to understand).

No thinker before him had undertaken such a majestically wide-ranging survey of humankind and the universe. And yet, as the bewildering diversity of his writings suggests, he was the least systematic and most exploratory of philosophers. Moreover, much of what he said or made his speakers say (not always the same thing) seems unacceptable or even preposterous; and it can never be assumed that Plato, who had inherited some of the irony of his master Socrates, failed to realize this himself. None the less, his eloquent advocacies, the climactic products of a society geared to persuasion, have compelled searchers after the truth, throughout the ages, to turn back to him again and again.

It is all the easier to do because, although he seems to have claimed never to have written down his most fundamental beliefs at all, he was a superlative master of Greek prose. He employed, and radically developed, the dramatic fruitful dialogue form, because it preserves the living relationship between teacher and student – offering us the illusion that we are taking part in the search. And in doing so he displayed a powerful, graceful, many-faceted, flexible style, ranging lucidly, with the aid of sparkling metaphors, from humorous lightness to fervid solemnity. It is easy to believe the story that, when he was young, he wanted to be a poet, because his prose rises to lofty heights of poetical lyricism, particularly in the imaginative myths and allegorical narratives in which he seeks to convey otherwise scarcely expressible profundities.

Utilitarianism, too, the theory that action is right if it achieves the greatest good of the greatest number, has claimed Plato as its founder, owing to his explicit desire to secure the welfare of the whole community. His conviction that a philosopher ought to direct state affairs was remote from what was happening in most Greek lands, but he believed he had found one such man in Archytas of Taras (Chapter 26) and he was not far wrong. Next, however, came his own alleged attempt to train Dionysius II of Syracuse to become another philosopher-king, and, if the tale is true, the abysmally unsuccessful outcome of this endeavour may be partly responsible for the somewhat greater practicability that he later displayed in the *Laws*, as against the *Republic* – though even the *Laws* contains fantasies which still make it look more like a utopian exposition of the 'logic of ideas' than a workable blueprint.

The authoritarian opinions contained in both these works are due to Plato's desire to devise a society immune from the recurrent menaces of internal subversion and external attack. This desire made him insist that people must be governed by Reason. Since, however, that is not their natural inclination, they must be induced, and if necessary compelled, to move in the required direction, by the enforcement of controls which seem to us (and would surely have seemed to Socrates) deplorable and alarming. It is not people's natural inclination, Plato realized, to obey the promptings of Reason, because they are dominated by emotion instead. In consequence of this, he sees the training of the emotions as one of the most important functions of education, a function in which the teaching of art, music and poetry has to be scrupulously regulated. This is the necessity that made him insist on the cultural censorship which has shocked so many readers.

Such coercive guidance seems, in western countries today, undemocratic, but Plato was not a democrat. Although all forms of current politics (including oligarchy) incurred his disgust – since they were based on no absolute moral standard – and although he was humane and acute enough to note that increasing contrasts between wealth and poverty breed civil strife, his basic attitude remains *opposed* to democracy, displaying an aristocratic contempt for manual workers and slaves and barbarians.

Men are irredeemably unequal, it appeared to him; so educators (except perhaps, as the *Laws* suggested, those concerned with military training) are best advised to concentrate on the training of an elite – not of the masses which made up a democracy. And he felt a powerful distaste for what he regarded as the extreme democracy that governed Athens – the evil system that had executed Socrates, although later, paradoxically enough, this same system enabled Plato himself to teach in uninhibited safety for many decades, and to teach anti-democratic doctrines at that.

CHAPTER 32

ISOCRATES: PANHELLENIC EDUCATIONALIST

Isocrates (436–338), the son of a prosperous Athenian knight (mocked by comic dramatists as an oboe-manufacturer), was said to have studied under the rhetorician Tisias, the rhetorician-sophists Prodicus and Gorgias (Chapter 12), and the moderate oligarchic politician Theramenes. And he also regarded himself as a follower of Socrates, though their relationship may not have been very close.

Twenty-one of his so-called speeches have survived. Isocrates himself tells us that some of them were written for recital (by others) to private audiences;[11] and some, too, went into circulation as pamphlets. Six early orations, however – so it would seem, though this is disputed – were composd for delivery by litigants in the lawcourts. For Isocrates' family property had been lost in the Peloponnesian War, and it was by writing such speeches on demand, for a time, that he earned his living.

In *c.*392, however, he felt able to give up this sort of activity, and instead embarked on a career as an educationalist, establishing his own school of advanced rhetoric, first on the island of Chios and then, perhaps two years later, at Athens. There his new institution offered a course of three or four years of continuous study, and soon outclassed the more informal schools established by the sophists; and he continued this work for the rest of his life.

It was during this prolonged period, lasting for the rest of his life, that he produced his large output of literary speeches. Some of them dealt primarily with educational topics, while others were concerned with political themes. The first category included *Against the Sophists* (*c.*390); of which the first part (the only section of the work to have survived) attacked not only alleged experts on forensic oratory but also those who advocated more extemporaneous methods, and philosophers as well. In the *Antidosis*, written, we are told, in *c.*353, when he was eighty-two years of age – the term refers to a process for shifting a public tax (liturgy) on to another citizen – he summed up his own views on these same subjects at greater length. The methods of rhetoricians and speakers, he repeated, were valueless, since they worked in a prosaic fashion according to sets of rules which any reasonably efficient teacher was capable of imparting, so that their instructive value was negligible.

In contrast, Isocrates pointed to his own superior system, which he identified as true 'philosophy', because it was broader and more liberal and more humane; for he insisted that his students, when engaged in the composition of speeches, should avoid narrow or trifling topics and select themes of general interest and significance. His own even later *Panathenaicus* – completed, after three years' work, in 339, when he was ninety-seven years of age – restates these views on writing and teaching. Isocrates gives prominence to morality, interpreted (in terms of enlightened self-interest) as righteousness towards gods and other human beings. But Isocrates shows little regard for scientific knowledge – which no one, he believed, was capable of achieving.

The success of his school, assisted by effective publicity, was enormous, and for half a century he attracted pupils from every part of the Greek world, including numerous future orators, politicians and historians. His school came into existence shortly before Plato's Academy, and competition between the two establishments can be discerned. Isocrates' *Helen* (390/380) obliquely depreciates Plato, and Plato's *Phaedo* contains veiled criticisms of Isocrates. Plato's objection was that his rival's system was not based on any rational, intellectually defensible method; whereas Isocrates thought that Plato's attempt to turn virtue into a science was too ridiculously idealistic to be worth including in any educational programme.

For to him, as to his teacher Gorgias and many other Greeks, education primarily meant the ability to speak. It is that ability, he maintained, which distinguishes humankind from animals, and provides a self-sufficient, creative, mental and moral culture, universally valid for any and every occasion – and therefore capable of providing the intellectual elite which Athens needed here and now. To minister to such requirements, Isocrates evolved an elaborate, mellifluous and distinctive prose style.

In this tug of war with Plato, the victor was Isocrates, in the eyes of the ancient world, which found his principles and methods easier to understand and accept. Thus it was he who provided the model for the humanism which Cicero subsequently formulated and expanded, bequeathing it as an ideal to late antiquity, Petrarch, the Italian and European Renaissance, and our own world, right up to the present century.

Isocrates, however, was not only a teacher but a man who, like Plato and Aristotle, trusted education to improve city-states and transform inter-state relations. These were subjects on which he held pronounced opinions; and the political orations he composed to give them expression shed much light on the attitudes that were being adopted in fourth-century Athens.

The *Panegyricus* (380) – which he had been composing for a whole decade, and regarded as his masterpiece – smoothly and eloquently, if somewhat conventionally, advocated the unification of the Greek city-states under the joint leadership of Athens and Sparta. Isocrates asserts, at one point, that 'Greek' means a possessor of Hellenic culture (*paideusis*) and mental attitude (*dianoia*) rather than blood (*genos*) (see Epilogue, note 3). The *Plataicus* (373) is an attack on Thebes which had seized and destroyed Plataea (and the censure is reiterated in the *Archidamus*, supposedly delivered by the Eurypontid King Archidamus III of Sparta, *c.*366).

To Nicocles (*c.*372) and the *Nicocles* (*c.*368, the name of a king of Salamis in Cyprus) and the *Euagoras* (*c.*365, named after Nicocles' father) are traditional *encomia* or eulogies, composed to illustrate Isocrates' growing conviction that the Greek city-states needed a monarch, imbued with a regal sense of duty, to knit them together. *On the Peace* (356/355), written when Athens had failed in the Social War against its allies and was almost bankrupt (Chapter 36), urged the abandonment of imperialistic ambitions in favour of a Panhellenic peace. The *Areopagiticus* (*c.*354?) voiced Isocrates' hankerings after a ludicrously idealized past, deploring the current Athenian democracy and urging a return to what he saw as the traditional, moderate system of two or more centuries ago, when the venerable Council of the Areopagus had still been in charge of the city.

In *Philip* (346), Isocrates' most important political pronouncement, he called upon King Philip II of Macedonia (Chapter 35) to unite the Greeks, and particularly their propertied classes, under his own direction, and lead them in a national struggle against Persia, a renewed but this time aggressive Persian War. (Philip is also the recipient of an ecumenically minded letter which is attributed to Isocrates, perhaps rightly, although eight other epistles ascribed to the same authorship may not be authentic.) Then, ignoring Philip who had failed to respond to these overtures, the *Panathenaicus* (339) combines its literary discussions with a long and diffuse eulogy of Athens, which is now contrasted, very much to its advantage, with Sparta.

Isocrates' political role – like his entire personality and achievement – has been variously estimated, incurring both praise and vituperation. Although he had important Athenian friends, nothing he wrote seems to have had much effect on political events. Yet, despite oscillations, he did adhere fairly consistently to the Panhellenic aim of uniting the Greek city-states against their common, and as he believed threatening and oppressive, enemies the Persians, whom he saw as barbarians and therefore natural helots or slaves – although he remained painfully conscious of their recurrent influence on Greek affairs.

To induce the Greek states to co-operate instead of fighting with one another was theoretically an excellent idea, even if, as history had shown, it was scarcely likely to become a practical proposition. And when Isocrates (like Gorgias and the orator Lysias) maintained that the best way for the Greeks to display this unity was by renewing the Persian Wars he was again asking for something which, whether sensible or not, the city-states were incapable of organizing on their own account. He had first hoped that Athens and Sparta would take the lead in this enterprise, working together, but when that aim proved illusory he appealed instead, opportunistically, to a succession of individual autocrats to take the lead, including Agesilaus II of Sparta, Dionysius I of Syracuse, Alexander of Pherae in Thessaly – and finally, as we saw, the Macedonian monarch Philip II.

To the orator Demosthenes (Chapter 36), who saw Philip as an ogre who menaced the Greeks, this last proposal appeared not only foolishly over-optimistic, but nothing less than traitorous collaboration. To Isocrates, on the other hand, it seemed the only way to rescue the city-states from their eternal bickering. The events, then, leading up to Chaeronea (338; in which Athens allied itself not with Sparta but with hated Thebes), and the traumatic battle itself (in which his hero Philip fought against Isocrates' fellow Athenians and other Greeks and crushed them), must have disillusioned him; a third Letter professing to exalt Philip's victory (and still hoping he would lead an anti-Persian crusade) may or may not be genuine. At all events, Isocrates died shortly afterwards, though probably not by starving himself to death as tradition reported.

CHAPTER 33

PRAXITELES: THE HUMANIZING OF SCULPTURE

In the later fifth century, perhaps to escape from the worries of the Peloponnesian War, sculptors (like painters) had begun to turn away from public interests to more intimate concerns, imbuing their statues and reliefs with a new softness and elegant flourish (Chapter 22). That has been described as the last phase of High Classical art, which then, in about the 370s (or some would say two or three decades earlier), was replaced by the Later Classical style, still intent upon idealism but portraying it by means of a closer imitation of nature.

This Later Classical epoch was also an increasingly individualistic age, and one of its manifestations was the appearance of more and more sculptors mentioned as individuals and not corporately as members of schools: since they were less tied down to one place, or a few places, than their predecessors had been, but, instead, often worked abroad. Outstanding among them was the Athenian Praxiteles, who was the son of another sculptor, Cephisodotus, and remained active between 370 and 330 BC.

Praxiteles' masterpiece was said to have been the nude Aphrodite which he made for Cnidus in *c.*364/361, regarded by the elder Pliny not only as his most talented achievement but as the finest statue ever made anywhere in the world.[12] Only a fragment of the figure has survived, but literary descriptions, and later coin-types, have enabled numerous copies to be identified.

These copies, for the most part, are far from distinguished, but they do make it clear that Praxiteles was adopting a revolutionary approach to the female form, displaying it naked and endeavouring to establish a new feminine physical principle – in keeping with an increased and more widespread interest in women and their characteristics, which was a feature of the age (Appendix II). Praxiteles' statue of Aphrodite, said to have been taken from a living model, was meant to be seen from the back and sides as well as from the front; despite various earlier moves away from total frontality (Chapter 14), this seems to have been an innovation.

The goddess's knees are very close together; above them swell buttocks and hips, of which the amplitude is further stressed by a stooping, drooping upper torso with immature breasts. A water-pot, with her robe draped over it, serves as a support (which marble statues needed), although she is not leaning on the pot but resting her hand upon its top, so as to lift up her garment. Her pose, with its modest gesture concealing – but drawing attention to – the genital area, and her expression, grave and calm, but said to convey a hint of invitation,[13] have been described as frankly but not vulgarly erotic (unlike the copies, which provide no erotic stimulus at all).

This Cnidian Aphrodite became one of the most influential sculptural creations in all artistic history, although it is now so tantalizingly lost. Lost, too, are nearly all the other full-length figures attributed to Praxiteles by ancient writers, many of them, evidently, embodying equally inventive deviations from recognized types.

Only one statue has survived which, if not by his own hand – as it may well be, and if so *c.*343 has been suggested as its date – is at least a contemporary, or possibly Hellenistic, copy of the utmost distinction, far removed from the dreariness of Roman imitations, reflecting with considerable accuracy (though perhaps with a little liberty as well, notably in regard to the drapery) the sensitive brilliance of the original. This is a marble statue of the god Hermes carrying the infant Dionysus. It was found in the temple of Hera at Olympia, the very place where Pausanias saw and described it.[14] The figure leans on one leg in a pronouncedly double-curved pose that was characteristic of Praxiteles. A tree trunk serves as a support, which was even more necessary than it had been for the Cnidian Aphrodite, owing to the Hermes' marked lateral inclination.

The god's eyes look into the distance with a dreamy gaze, and there is a suggestion of a remote smile. Here, once again, is a new ideal, based on an entrancement with physical beauty that had never received such intense expression before.

The material favoured by Praxiteles – unlike so many earlier sculptors – was marble, of which the smooth, soapy, shaded planes seemed to him most appropriate for the representation of skin. He excelled in the employment of this medium, imparting a fluid finish to its receptive surface, with the aid of delicate colouring, for the application of which, as Pliny the elder recorded, he liked to employ Nicias, a leading painter of the day.

The austere Phidian and Polyclitean styles, which had already undergone considerable modification in the hands of later fifth-century sculptors, were finally transformed by Praxiteles into a sophisticated, *bon vivant* manner emphasizing sensuous, graceful, gentle charm, displayed by the use of sinuous, almost indolent poses and soft, fleshy contours. These languid, pensive deities – nearer to humanity than they had ever been before – enticed the viewer to escape from his or her humdrum day-to-day anxieties into an undisturbed world. Praxiteles was said to convey the 'passions of the soul', which we should interpret as signifying not so much emotion as the subtle personal feeling, mood and temperament which is to be seen in his Hermes and a few other exquisite male heads that can also, with some probability, be identified as original works by Praxiteles himself.

Although, unlike so many of his predecessors, he derived his principal reputation from the employment of marble, he also made outstanding bronzes. None of them have survived, but a fine, complete bronze statue of the 340s, known as the Marathon boy because that was where it was found in the sea, seems to be the work of his circle, since it displays (even more markedly) the undulating pose of the Hermes; though the head, hair and face deny any supposition that the sculptor was Praxiteles himself.

He became wealthy in his lifetime (his son was especially rich), but his renown stood highest under the Roman empire, although some religious people found his portrayals of the gods too naturalistic, and preferred earlier sculptors.

PART VII
The End of Classical Greece

CHAPTER 34

TIMOLEON: SICILY AT ITS BEST

After the death of Dionysius I in 367 (Chapter 25), his son Dionysius II became ruler of Syracuse, at the age of about thirty. He immediately made peace with the Carthaginians, on the familiar basis of a frontier on the River Halycus.

A decade of peace followed, during which, at first, the young man's principal adviser was Dion (Chapter 31). Since, however, Dion's position at court was threatened by other factions, he invited Plato (of whose Academy he was regarded as a member) to make his second visit to Syracuse, in the hope that some of the philosopher's prestige would rub off on himself. Whether or not Plato hoped, as was said, that Dionysius II would become a 'philosopher-king' (an unrealizable ideal), Dion may well have wanted help in endeavouring to replace the dictatorial regime by a government of a more ostensibly constitutional character, with himself as its leader. However, Plato left without achieving anything, and through the influence of the historian Philistus (now in the ascendancy) Dion was exiled, for allegedly intriguing with Carthage (366/365). Efforts by Plato, on a third visit (361/360), to secure his restoration proved unsuccessful.

Dion remained for a while at Athens, but in 357, with the collusion of fellow members of Plato's Academy (and probably of the Carthaginians as well), he led an expedition to Sicily which captured Syracuse, though its island nucleus of Ortygia held out for two years. Dionysius II, who was in southern Italy at the time, stayed on at his mother's city Locri Epizephyrii as its ruler. But at Syracuse Dion's stringent taxation and increasingly dictatorial behaviour, in the role of commander-in-chief (*strategos autokrator*), led to his assassination by mercenaries from the island of Zacynthus, instigated by an Academy colleague, Callippus (354).

Amid the ensuing convulsions, Dionysius II returned to Sicily, and recovered Syracuse (347/346). But within two years he found himself blockaded in Ortygia by Syracusan rebels; and they obtained the support of a compatriot, Hicetas the dictator of Leontini. Hicetas was backed by a strong mercenary force; and he was also assisted by a fleet from Carthage, which had taken advantage of the disturbed situation in Sicily to revive the recurrent warfare of the time of Dionysius I, in an attempt to extend Carthaginian power from the western to the eastern part of the island.

Confronted with these threats, Hicetas' Syracusan supporters appealed to the mother city of Corinth to send a liberation force, and a Corinthian named Timoleon was dispatched for the purpose.

A man in his mid-sixties, Timoleon was known for only one thing, his killing of his own brother Timophanes, either recently (Diodorus) or twenty years earlier (Plutarch), after Timophanes had made himself dictator at Corinth; though whether this much discussed action afflicted his brother Timoleon with everlasting remorse, as was said, must remain uncertain, because his exaggerated praises from the Sicilian historian Timaeus and the derivative, moralistic Plutarch (together with Timoleon's own expert publicity) make all attempts at reconstructing his career problematical. To begin with, we cannot even tell why Corinth chose to accede to the Syracusans' request for help, or why, having done so, they selected such an obscure and elderly man, when so many vigorous adventurers are likely to have been available for such a job.

At all events Timoleon, with nine or ten ships and something like a thousand mercenaries, eluded the Carthaginian fleet, landed at Tauromenium, defeated Hicetas in two engagements, besieged Dionysius II in Ortygia, and by a blend of audacious tactics and tricky negotiation made him a virtual prisoner. Finally Dionysius was expelled from Sicily altogether (whereupon he made his home at Corinth).

Next Timoleon, reinforced at this juncture by 2,000 additional mercenaries and 200 Corinthian cavalry, assumed plenary powers at Syracuse, but gave notice that this was only a temporary measure, and not a renewed dictatorship, by demolishing the palace fortress which stood for the old autocratic order. Then, with the aid of two Corinthian lawyers, he introduced what was described as a 'democratic' constitution,[1] but was more probably oligarchical in character. Its titular head was the priest (*amphipolos*) of Olympian Zeus, nominally elected, but in fact chosen by lot from a trio of clans. And Timoleon also launched a programme of social reconstruction, importing to Syracuse no less than 60,000 settlers from other parts of Sicily and from the south Italian mainland and Greece.

At the same time, he launched a series of campaigns against the dictators of other Sicilian cities. In consequence, the most prominent among them, Hicetas, joined forces with the Carthaginians when, seeking to profit once again from the disputes among the island Greeks, they sent further expeditions. First Mago (II) mysteriously failed to attack the outnumbered Timoleon, and withdrew (*c*.343). Then Hasdrubal and Hamilcar (II) brought 70,000 men, 1,000 troop transports and 200 warships (*c*.341). This army landed at Lilybaeum but, while it was crossing the River Crimisus near Segesta, Timoleon's force of only 12,000 men, with the help of a timely or providential flooding of the river, defeated it heavily, inflicting unprecedented losses. He did not, however, follow up his success – since he was afraid of Greek threats to Syracuse. Instead, therefore, he concluded peace with Carthage, establishing the boundary between the Greek and Carthaginian territories on the River Halycus, where it had been before.

This treaty not only safeguarded the independence of Greek Sicily but gave Timoleon a free hand to resume his offensives against the various dictators in other Greek city-states of the island, including Hicetas who, after vainly attempting a reconciliation, was crushed and executed, together with his wife and family: and so were other local autocrats – actions that proved embarrassing to the eulogists who were unwilling to find blots on Timoleon's moral record.

However, this ferocious clean-up no doubt played its part in what amounted to a general rehabilitation of Sicily. For the restoration of peace encouraged agriculture, and the evidence of coin finds and new buildings and new pottery industries confirms that the impoverished island, repopulated after the model of Syracuse and interlinked by a federation of cities under its leadership, experienced a revival of prosperity.

In 337 Timoleon's eyesight was beginning to fail, and he retired into private life, although continuing to attend meetings of the Syracusan Assembly, in which his expressions of opinion (we are told) were generally acclaimed by a unanimous vote. Before long, however, he died. After a public funeral his body was buried in the agora, and a monument known as the Timoleonteum, comprising a gymnasium in a colonnaded precinct, was erected above the tomb.

His fellow citizens were right to honour him. True, his eulogists unduly glossed over the duplicity and violence which he sometimes felt obliged to employ. Moreover, he depended on mercenary soldiers just as much as the dictators whom he so harshly repressed. He commanded these mercenaries with audacious skill, knowing well how to strike when his enemy was at a disadvantage; and, besides, he was a firm, clever statesman and diplomat and propagandist. These gifts enabled him to provide Syracuse and Sicily, for all too short a period, with the most effective and beneficial regime they ever enjoyed – a regime which even, possibly, tolerated free speech, as Plutarch claimed.[2] And Timoleon's alleged, modest, mystical dependence on fortune and the gods earned him widespread admiration.[3]

After his death, however, nothing came of his Sicilian federal union. Many states, on the contrary, asserted their separateness, by overstriking Syracusan coins with their own designs. At Syracuse, too, in *c.*330, his political reforms were swept away by a revolution, which placed 600 oligarchs in power. And then in 317 they in their turn were forcibly replaced by the dictatorship of Agathocles.

CHAPTER 35

PHILIP II: THE CITY-STATE SUPPLANTED

LIST OF EVENTS

359	Accession of King Philip II of Macedonia: successes against Paeonians and Illyrians (359–358)
358	Death of King Artaxerxes II Mnemon of Persia and accession of Artaxerxes III Ochus
357	Philip II captures Amphipolis; then Pydna and Potidaea (356) and Methone (354)
357	Philip II takes Olympias (Molossian) as an additional wife (Alexander (III the Great) and Cleopatra born in 356 and 355)
357–355	Revolt of Athens' subject-allies: the 'Social War', prompted by Mausolus of Caria (Chapter 28)
356–346	Third Sacred War between Phocian and Theban coalitions
355	Isocrates' *On the Peace* (Chapter 32)
355–342	Eubulus' political leadership at Athens
352	Demosthenes' *On Symmories* (reform of the navy)
352	Philip II at Heraion Teichos, capital of the Thracian (Odrysian) King Cersobleptes
*c.*351 (or 349)	Demosthenes' *First Philippic*
349	Demosthenes' *Olynthiacs*; but Philip II captures Olynthus (348)
347	Death of Plato (his last work *The Laws*; Chapter 31)
347–345	Aristotle at Assus, then Mytilene (345–343)
346	Peace of Philocrates with Philip II. Demosthenes' *On the Peace*, Isocrates' *Philippus*
344	Demosthenes' *Second Philippic*
342/341	Philip II annexes Thrace
341	Demosthenes' *On the Chersonese* and *Third Philippic* (*Fourth*, probably authentic, in 340)
340	Philip II besieges, but fails to capture, Perinthus and

	Byzantium, and Athens declares war
339	Philip II defeats the Scythian King Ateas in the Dobrogea, and then moves south to capture Elataea in Phocis
339	Isocrates' *Panathenaicus*
338	Philip II captures Amphissa, defeats Athenians and Thebans at Chaeronea and convenes the First Congress of Corinth
338	Death of Isocrates
338	Murder of King Artaxerxes III Ochus of Persia and accession of Arses (Artaxerxes IV?)
337	Second Congress of Corinth: Philip II announces expedition against Persian empire
337	Philip II's marriage to Cleopatra, a Macedonian
336	Macedonian general Attalus lands in Asia Minor
336	Murder of Philip II and accession of Alexander III the Great (334 lands in Asia Minor, d.323)
336	Murder of King Arses of Persia and accession of Darius III Codomannus
335	Aristotle returns to Athens and founds the Lyceum
322	Suicide of Demosthenes

To the north of the continental homeland of Greece, divided from it by Mount Olympus, lay the kingdom of Macedonia. Its nucleus was the fertile Macedonian plain, formed by three substantial rivers (the Haliacmon, Lydias and Axius), flowing all the year round and debouching into the Thermaic Gulf. The northern boundaries of the country were formed by a crescent of mountains, occupied by undeveloped and potentially aggressive tribal princedoms and chieftainships of mixed Illyrian, Thracian and perhaps Greek origins.

The kings of Macedonia, whose position in the state echoed the heroic, Homeric age, called themselves Argeads because they traced their roots back to Argos and Heracles, thus claiming pure Greek descent. The Greeks of the city-states were often sceptical about these assertions, which were, indeed, fictitious – even though the court religion of Macedonia was Hellenic in character, thus reflecting very ancient Greek influences. The upper class, a strong nobility which from time to time vociferously expressed its views to monarchs, spoke a language which possessed some relationship to Greek, or was one of its branches, perhaps a primitive Aeolic dialect. The rest of the population, however, whose Assembly was more or less powerless (though the peasant soldiers might address the king individually or collectively), could lay little claim to Greek origins.

Yet the coastland, at an early date, had become the target for colonization by Greek city-states, which made profits from their exportation of Macedonian foodstuffs and metals and ship-building timber, at a time when the kingdom was not sufficiently advanced or organized to undertake this activity itself.

In *c*.640 King Perdiccas I, the first historically identified Argead monarch, expanded his territory and established its capital at Aegae. In *c*.512, however, Amyntas I, after Darius I's annexation of Thrace, became a vassal of the Persians, whose troops garrisoned his towns. In consequence, his successor Alexander I accompanied Xerxes I against Greece (480), though he claimed afterwards to have secretly helped the Greek side. Later, he was accepted – that is to say, recognized as a Greek – at the Olympic Games: and he welcomed the poets Pindar, Simonides and Bacchylides to his court. It was probably Alexander I, too, who first organized a Macedonian hoplite army.

The belligerent powers in the Peloponnesian War were played off against each other by Perdiccas II (*c*.450–*c*.413). The reign of his son Archelaus (*c*.413–399), who adopted a pronouncedly philhellenic policy (harbouring Euripides, and employing Zeuxis to paint his palace), was followed by a prolonged period of dynastic changes, under the shadow of encroachment from the temporary major power of Pherae in Thessaly, with which Amyntas III (393/392–370/369) made a treaty.

In 359 his son Perdiccas III, after working hard to improve the country's fiscal system, died in a disastrous defeat at the hands of the Illyrians (Dardanians, Paeonians), whose grip over Macedonia's northern frontier provinces he had been attempting to loosen.

This brought Perdiccas' brother Philip II into power, perhaps at first, for a brief period, as regent for an infant nephew (Amyntas IV), although this remains doubtful.

Philip was at this time a young man of twenty-three. While in his teens, he had spent three years (367–365) as a hostage in Thebes, where he admired and learnt from the military talents of Epaminondas (Chapter 29). After defeating, in the first two years of his reign, the Illyrians who had killed his brother, in 357 he captured the coastal colony of Amphipolis: to the alarm of the Athenians, who were afraid for their grain route (Chapter 27). Then in the following year he seized Crenides (renamed Philippi), which enabled him to dominate the gold and silver mines in and around Mount Pangaeum.

The massive income from this source made it possible for him to overcome the weaknesses of Macedonia with which he had been battling. He was now in a position, for example, to engage in audacious diplomacy, rammed home by massive gifts and bribes, with the aid of an excellent coinage. He was also able to transform his country's pastoral economy on to an agricultural basis.

And, above all, he personally organized the large-scale development of the Macedonian army, which became a professional, national force, enlarged by the inclusion of non-Macedonians, and displaying capabilities that had never been seen in the Balkan peninsula before. The courageous Macedonian infantrymen – small landowners or peasants – became soldiers who fought in a novel and greatly improved infantry phalanx, carrying sixteen- or thirteen-foot pikes (*sarissai*), instead of the hoplite's spear. The new phalanx was drawn up in a more mobile, flexible open order, and Philip's infantry order of battle incorporated Epaminondas' method of combining deeper and shallower contingents in the same line. The cavalry, too, which already possessed a heavy elite force of Companions (*hetairoi*) as its nucleus, likewise assumed a more formidable character. It included special units whose principal task was to protect the flanks and the rear of the infantry phalanx, in wedge formation, and this well-timed co-ordination between the two arms (another technique learnt from Epaminondas) was one of Philip's specialities. So was a revolutionary development in siegecraft, which owed debts to the engineering innovations of Dionysius I of Syracuse (Chapter 25).

But this efficient army was possible only because of the personal inspiration of Philip. He drank too much, it is true, and behaved rowdily, but was a more than competent commander (with the help of his best general, Parmenio). In addition, he showed great personal courage, sustaining wounds, we are told, which included the loss of an eye, a broken shoulder and a crippled arm and leg: a small ivory bust from the barrel-vaulted 'royal' tomb at Aegae (now in the museum at Salonica (Thessalonike)), representing, it would seem, Philip, seems to show a damaged eye – and the tomb in which it was discovered contained a pair of gilded greaves of different lengths and shapes, one of which may well have been made to fit his damaged leg. Despite these handicaps, he was tireless, and ready to campaign (his enemies complained) at any season of the year.

When he was at home, he seems to have lived at an unprecedentedly vast palace at Pella, built probably by himself, including two architectural complexes constructed side by side; while the above-mentioned grave at Aegae, and a 'small chamber tomb' at the same place, were found to contain important wall-paintings, the earliest substantial pictures of the kind to have survived in the classical world outside Etruria (Chapters 10, 22).

The Athenians' distress at the capture of Amphipolis was only the first of a number of similar shocks, at a time when they were crippled by a revolt of their allies (Social War), abetted by Mausolus of Caria (Chapter 28). Pydna, Potidaea and Methone successively fell into Philip's hands (356–354), rounding off the kingdom's supremacy beside the Thermaic Gulf without any effective check from a coalition organized by Athens, since the true, perilous significance of Philip's army reforms had not yet been sufficiently appreciated.

Meanwhile the outbreak of the Third Sacred War (356), marked by the seizure of Delphi by Phocian separatists (opposed to the Theban control of their country), who used the temple treasure to recruit a new mercenary army, prompted the Aleuadae of Larissa in Thessaly to appeal to Philip, thus providing him with an opportunity to extend his influence southwards from Thessaly into central Greece.

After initial setbacks, he defeated and killed the Phocian General Onomarchus (despite help sent to the Phocians by Athens at the Battle of the Crocus Field (352)). But when a combined Greek army blocked Philip at Thermopylae, he turned north instead, delivering a preliminary attack on Thrace – one of the largest and richest countries of the ancient world, though disunited – and subjugating one of its kings, the Odrysian Cersobleptes, after a siege of his capital Heraion Teichos. Next Philip moved against the Greek cities on the Chalcidice promontory adjoining his own homeland, namely, the members of the Chalcidian League, which, like the Boeotian Confederacy (Chapter 29), was an early example of a federal state. The League's principal centre, Olynthus – of which the excavations display a unique picture of a fourth-century city – appealed to Athens. But, despite Demosthenes' eloquent advocacy (Chapter 36), Athenian aid came too late and too sparsely, and Olynthus fell to Philip by treachery, and was destroyed (348).

Hampered further by a revolt he had fomented in Euboea, the Athenians were induced to consent to his Peace of Philocrates (346). This was the subject of many later recriminations among their politicians, because, first, the Peace incorporated Athens' acceptance that Amphipolis was lost, and, secondly, Philip emerged from it as the predominant power in the centre of Greece, with a place on the Amphictyonic Board controlling Delphi, which welcomed him as a victorious crusader and made him president of the Pythian Games in the same year.

But if Philip already had designs on Greece, as is likely enough, he did not yet feel that the time was ripe to put them into effect. For instead he now extended his power in more northern lands, notably Epirus and Thessaly, and launched massive schemes of Macedonian road-building, transplantation of local inhabitants, and colonization. Invited by Isocrates (Chapter 32) to lead a Panhellenic force against the Persian empire (so as to open up new regions for Greek settlement), he at first tried to respond by making overtures to prominent Athenians, until opposition in the city hardened under Demosthenes' leadership.

The orator's arguments became even more convincing when Philip, after finally annexing Thrace as a tributary province (amid incidents with Athenian mercenaries in the Thracian Chersonese), tried to seize Perinthus and Byzantium on the Bosphorus (340), which were vital points on Athens' grain lifeline from the Black Sea, as Philip painfully emphasized by seizing an Athenian corn-fleet. He did not succeed in capturing the two Bosphoran cities, but Athens, supported by a coalition which Demosthenes had whipped up, now confronted him with a declaration of war. Remarkably enough, too, the orator persuaded Boeotia (Thebes) to join his alliance, when Philip (after launching an attack on the Scythian King Ateas in the Dobrogea) marched a huge distance southwards to exploit a new Delphic conflict, moving during the winter (339/338) with what seemed a shocking disregard for campaigning seasons.

Then Philip confronted the Greek army at Chaeronea in Boeotia. It included about 30,000 Boeotian, Athenian and allied infantrymen. On the right wing were 12,000 Boeotian hoplites, including the Sacred Band on their extreme right flank. Ten thousand Athenian hoplites stood on the left wing; allied hoplites and 5,000 mercenaries manned the centre. Philip's force may have been slightly superior in numbers. Knowing that the Athenians lacked experience, he deliberately withdrew his right wing, that stood opposite their force, in order to tempt them to pursue, whereupon his men regrouped and took the Athenian force in front and rear, with complete success, so that every Athenian soldier was killed or put to flight. Meanwhile on the Macedonian left, the young Alexander, leading the Companion Cavalry, succeeded in breaking through the Boeotian troops, well seasoned though they were, and the victory was won. It had been gained by better training, masterly co-ordination between infantry and cavalry, and the superiority of the new Macedonian pike-phalanx over the old spear-phalanx of the Greek hoplites.

Thebes was severely punished, its Boeotian League disbanded, and a Macedonian garrison installed in the city, and in others as well. But Athens, although its divided military command provoked Philip's caustic wit, got off lightly, not only because he revered its culture, but because he thought he might need its fleet.

For he had, by now, decided to assault the Persian empire, thus taking vengeance, once and for all, upon its invasions of the previous century (Chapters 1–3), and their attendant sacrileges – as champion of the Greeks of whom he allegedly was one, and under pressure from his new army which wanted imperialistic plunder (just as he himself needed funds in order to pay them). It is uncertain whether he had already projected such an enterprise at the time when Isocrates advocated it in 346, except perhaps as a pious propagandist dream. But in 341 he had broken off relations with Artaxerxes III Ochus (for executing his ally, Hermeias of Atarneus). Then in 340 his siege of Perinthus was opposed by Persian satraps (who felt threatened by his control of the European shores of the Bosphorus and Hellespont); and by 338 his hostile intentions towards Persia were unmistakable.

Indeed, this was the principal, immediate purpose of the Panhellenic Congresses (*synedria*) which Philip, after the battle of Chaeronea, summoned at Corinth. All Greek cities south of Thermopylae – with the single notable exception of Sparta – sent their representatives: because the King was not unpopular in the smaller states, which saw him as a defender against their larger Greek counterparts – or were penetrated by his Fifth Columns and bribes. A Common Peace between the city-states was established, as in earlier years, but now with novel features; since, first, despite their proclaimed freedom and autonomy, adherence to the Peace was made compulsory (in order to exclude any recurrence of chaos), and, secondly, the representative council was presided over by a leader (*hegemon*) and monarch, namely Philip, with whose person the new 'confederacy of the Hellenes' was allied. For the first time, too, a clause was specifically directed against all forms of internal subversion within the cities, so that their propertied classes, unlikely to foment disturbances, were entrenched in power.

It was at a further Congress, in 337, that Philip announced the war against Persia, and in spring of the following year an advance force of 10,000 Macedonian troops, under the command of Parmenio and his son-in-law Attalus, crossed over into north-western Asia Minor, where the Persians' mercenary Greek general Memnon of Rhodes resisted them with initial success.

In the same summer, at Aegae, Philip fell dead, assassinated by a psychopathic homosexual courtier. The ultimate authorship, and motive, of the murder remain uncertain; but the deed may well have had something to do with Philip's complex matrimonial affairs. For one of the weapons of his inter-state diplomacy was political polygamy, which caused savage struggles for power within the royal circle. In 357 he had taken Olympias, daughter of the Molossian (Epirot) King Neoptolemus, as his wife (by no means his first), and she had borne him two children, Alexander (356) and Cleopatra (355). But now, in

337, a new marriage by Philip – possibly his sixth or seventh – to a Macedonian woman, again called Cleopatra (the niece of his general Attalus), had shattered his relations with Olympias, and she left him to go back to Epirus with her son.

In the hope, however, of reconciling the important Molossian royal family to which she belonged, he arranged for the other Cleopatra, his daughter, to marry Olympias' brother Alexander I, the reigning Molossian king; and it was at a feast to celebrate this wedding that Philip was struck down. Olympias had returned to Pella for the occasion. She was said to have been a cruel and passionate woman, and could well have instigated the murder – feeling that her brother's marriage failed to atone or compensate for her supersession by Philip's new wife, whose son, when she gave birth to one (and she may have borne a child a few days before the murder),[4] could well exclude Olympias' own child Alexander from the throne.[5]

As it happened, however, amid Philip's funeral ceremonies – a star-embossed gold casket, found at Aegae (and now in the Salonica museum), contained bones that may be his – Alexander, to the accompaniment of bloodshed, asserted his claim to the succession, and became Alexander III the Great. The success with which he subsequently pursued the invasion of the Persian empire, planned by his father, became one of history's most spectacular transformations. Yet Philip's many-sided achievement, in Europe, was perhaps no less fateful than Alexander's in the wider spaces of Asia. At all events, the historian Theopompus had some reason to assert that, despite glaring personal failings, Philip was the greatest man (man of action, that is to say) whom the continent had known up to his time.[6].

What he did, above all, was to terminate the classical age of the autonomous city-states. Some of them survived and even prospered, it is true, but by and large their epoch was ended – since they could not match his kind of professional army without ceasing to be what they were. Despite phenomenal successes in so many fields during the previous centuries, their mutually hostile fragmentation, and their internal treacheries, and their failures to produce a stable political response to economic and social changes, had effectively destroyed any real possibility that they could form an effective union or federation of independent states by themselves. So Philip had to do it for them.

A less painful solution, perhaps, would have been a union or federation under the leadership of the cities themselves. However, the attempts by Athens, Sparta and Thebes to achieve this through their own confederacies had hitherto proved ineffective and abortive; and there was no reason why they should succeed in the future. Philip, on the other hand, had triumphed where they had failed; and the Congress of Corinth was the result.

Philip's new policy of Greek unification, even if slanted in favour of local oligarchies, contrasted with his earlier exploitation of strife between Greek city-states. But it need not be regarded as wholly insincere and opportunistic, since the egotistical ambitions which had prompted him to become the national leader of Greece did not necessarily exclude considerations of statesmanship or even idealism. However, the ambitious project represented by the Congress was never given a chance to display its potentialities, since after the death of Alexander (323) the Greek world became divided within itself once again, but this time with great Hellenistic kingdoms, not city-states, as the disputants. The result of their disunity, however, was the same as the result of the city-states' earlier squabbling: that is to say, it meant that an external great power profited from their disarray and took over – namely Rome.

CHAPTER 36

DEMOSTHENES: ORATOR RESISTING THE FUTURE

During the first half of the century the Athenians' major achievement had been the creation of a new confederacy (377), intended 'to make the Spartans leave the Greeks to enjoy peace in freedom and autonomy' (Chapter 29). Its constitution, accompanied by a remodelling of the Athenian taxation system, took far more comprehensive steps to safeguard the independence of the allies than the first Athenian ('Delian') League had ever done in the previous century (Chapter 5); and after an Athenian naval victory over the Spartans off Naxos (376), about seventy city-states that had revolted from Spartan control were happy to join Athens and its new League.

But meanwhile Thebes, too – and this was part of the reason for the Athenians' rival initiative – had been building up, on land, a powerful new Boeotian confederacy which inflicted a historic defeat on the Spartans at Leuctra (371). The ensuing Athenian attempt at an international conference was frustrated by the Thebans, whose subsequent successes frightened the Athenians into converting their confederacy into an empire after all, despite earlier assurances to the contrary, so that Thebes could be opposed. At Mantinea (362) they and their allies were losing to the Thebans, when Epaminondas was killed, and a confused situation followed (Chapter 29).

In the 'Social War', or War of the Allies (357–355), who were instigated to revolt by Mausolus of Caria (Chapter 28), this Second Athenian League was ruined beyond repair, and the state not only lost its principal generals but was in danger of forfeiting its grain route, and became nearly bankrupt. At this stage, however, the leading Athenian statesman of the day, Eubulus, introduced a prudent policy of financial retrenchment. Funds were made available for public works and distribution to the poorest citizens through the Theoric Fund (introduced, it was said, by Pericles, but now redesigned to form a pool to receive all financial surpluses except in time of war). Meanwhile Athens' military resources were to be concentrated on the defence of its essential interests, and not squandered on hazardous adventures, which the poor majority of the population saw as a threat to its Theoric income.

This raised, of course, the issue of how to find funds to deal with the Macedonian King Philip II, who had started to threaten and capture key points on his coastline (and on the Athenian grain route) very soon after his accession (359), notably Amphipolis, which was always a prime object of Athens' foreign policy (Chapter 35). Eubulus and his associates were not pacifists, for they induced the Assembly to resist these Macedonian inroads on several occasions in the late 350s. But they soon came up against Demosthenes, who had formerly supported their decisions, but now, instead, advocated a more forward policy in many areas, and from about 352 (not perhaps earlier, as he subsequently maintained)[7] came to see Philip as the supreme menace to Athens and Greece.

Not a member of a wealthy family like most earlier Athenian statesmen, Demosthenes had been born in 384. He lost his father, the proprietor of a sword and cutlery factory, when he was seven years old, and later accused his three guardians, left to look after the estate, of misappropriation that left him almost destitute. In the course of the prolonged legal battles that ensued, he studied rhetoric and juridical procedure under an inheritance expert, the orator Isaeus, and eventually won his case against his guardians, although by this time the estate had evaporated. To earn a living, therefore – in an age of countless, fiercely fought lawsuits – he became a professional speech-writer for private litigants, on some occasions himself appearing in court; nearly half of the sixty-one orations attributed to his authorship (of which some forty-one seem to be unmistakably genuine) are private in character.

From 355 onwards, however, while his composition of private speeches did not cease, he devoted himself more and more to orations of national or political importance. In 352 *On Symmories* (Naval Boards) urged that the Athenian navy should be brought up to date, revealing, incidentally, the financial difficulty of keeping it in operation. In *Against Aristocrates* (352), written for a certain Eurycles to deliver, he blamed an Athenian politician Charidemus for allowing the Thracian Chersonese, so important for Athens' grain route, to fall into the hands of his brother-in-law the Thracian (Odrysian) King Cersobleptes (who had to give in to Philip very soon afterwards). *On the Liberty of the Rhodians* urged the Athenians to support the democratic party of Rhodes against its ruling oligarchs who were dependants of Queen Artemisia II of Caria (Chapter 28).

That speech was delivered in 352 or 351, and so perhaps was the *First Philippic*, although it contains an allusion more appropriate to 349.

Knowledge of its exact date would have been useful because this was the first time that Demosthenes openly identified Philip II as the principal enemy, and attempted to rouse the Athenians to a consciousness of the peril directed against them by this bandit, as he declared him to be, on their doorstep. In this attempt he failed, because Eubulus and his friends, notably a respected colleague Phocion, still believed in the practicability of a balance of power, and in consequence still wanted Athens' limited resources to be concentrated on vital areas (such as the Thracian Chersonese), rather than dissipated on more sweeping and wide-ranging hostilities: and most Athenians still agreed with them.

But Demosthenes, who had lost all faith in any balance of power that involved Philip, regarded it as necessary to protect not only the Chersonese but the entire grain route along all its length, and in his three *Olynthiacs* urged the Athenians to prevent Philip from capturing the harbour city of Olynthus, headquarters of the Chalcidian League on the Macedonian coast. Once again, his persuasions failed – though whether his success, committing Athens' main forces near Philip's home ground, would have benefited the city remains questionable. The attacks on Eubulus which he took this opportunity to launch, prompted by the strained personal relations which now existed between the two men, were unfair.

After Athens had made the Peace of Philocrates with Philip in 346, Demosthenes (amid a lot of mutual abuse among Athenian politicians, and particularly between himself and his rival Aeschines) alleged, without regard for the truth, that he himself had condemned the agreement all along – and insisted on this with even greater urgency when Philip invaded Phocis immediately afterwards. Nevertheless the orator, in his speech *On the Peace*, was not in favour of actually repudiating the treaty of 346. In the *Second Philippic* (344), however, he asserted that Philip's apparent friendship with certain Greek states (notably Thebes, Messene and Argos) was just a fraudulent device designed to line them up against Athens – and he declared that negotiations with the King were not worth while.

Demosthenes' speech *On the Fraudulent Delegation* (343) returned to the attack against Eubulus and Aeschines, criticizing the former for still seeking to maintain peace with Macedonia, and denouncing the latter for having been bribed, so Demosthenes said, not to hamper Philip's attack on Phocis. With the help of Eubulus and Phocion, Aeschines was exonerated, by a narrow margin. *On the Chersonese* (341) is a plea from Demosthenes not to repudiate a fellow Athenian, Diopeithes, who had led colonists to that strategic Thracian peninsula in defiance of Philip, because in fact, declared the orator, there was now no longer any point in attempting literally to keep the Peace, seeing that Philip's actions already amounted to war. The *Third Philippic* of the same year – the most forceful speech Demosthenes ever delivered – reiterated the same arguments, and appealed for unity among the Greek states to confront the common threat.

He also sponsored a naval reform, distributing the cost of furnishing ships among the entire body of citizens in proportion to the value of each individual's wealth. In 340 he was placed in full charge of the war that he had been wanting for so long, and in his (probably genuine) *Fourth Philippic* declared it ridiculous, whatever public opinion might think, to distribute Theoric funds to the people in such an emergency. And he even proposed that Persia should be appealed to for help in stopping Philip.

Then came the battle of Chaeronea (338), for which Demosthenes had finally succeeded in rallying the Athenian people, and even mobilizing Thebes – along with a league of other allies – although this was the wrong kind of military situation for the Athenians: a pitched engagement by land. After the disastrous defeat, Demosthenes hastened back to Athens, not, as Aeschines declared, running away, but to organize the city's defences. Yet when it turned out that the Athenians' treatment at Philip's hands was to be more lenient than expected, he underwent numerous attacks in the courts for the hawkish policies that had led to Chaeronea.

Once Philip was dead Demosthenes almost immediately tried to foment troubles for his successor Alexander – at the risk of his own life – and revived the idea that Persia should be called upon to liberate Greece, although this laid him open to charges of receiving Persian bribes. In 330 came his last and greatest speech *On the Crown*, vindicating his whole political career and piling renewed and unprecedentedly savage abuse upon Aeschines. The jury supported Demosthenes' claim. Six years later, however, he was convicted for annexing funds that had belonged to a Macedonian named Harpalus (now arrested) and were held in trust for Alexander. After Alexander's death Demosthenes tried, once again, to lead a movement against the Macedonians (323–322), whose leader Antipater, in consequence, made the Athenians condemn him to death, whereupon he took a fatal dose of poison.

Although Demosthenes was often seen to be jockeying for personal power against his rivals, the dominant, pre-eminent feature of his political advocacy, maintained with determination (despite charges of inconsistency)[8] from the late 350s or, at latest, 349 onwards, was hatred and suspicion of Macedonia, in the person of Philip until his death, and thereafter of Alexander and Antipater.

This attitude was one which, for a long time, he found difficulty in persuading the majority of his fellow Athenians to share. Subsequently, too, it has earned him divergent reputations among people trying to see his career in terms of their own more recent times, varying from acclamation as a courageous and lonely champion of freedom (notably by Cicero, Cardinal Bessarion and Friedrich Jacob, and modern Anglo-Saxon writers – opposing Antony, the Turks, Napoleon and Hitler respectively) to contemptuous vituperation as a misguidedly nostalgic crank standing in the way of inevitable progress.

The principal question is this: was he right to regard Philip as a mortal threat to Athens and Hellenic civilization? Certainly, as he had warned, Philip did eventually destroy the power of Athens and other city-states (even if he never dominated them as completely as later Hellenistic kings). It could be argued, on the other side, that Philip became a menace only because Demosthenes made him one; that the king seriously turned against the city-states only because the sustained hostility of Demosthenes compelled him to do so. Yet the fact was that, despite Philip's reverence for the culture of Athens, and despite his persistent conviction that he might make use of the city (as a subordinate or at least co-operative partner), he had already, from the very first years of his reign, begun to work against its interests, by encroaching on its vital northern grain route. And the list of his later, equally damaging, activities is long.

It is not merely with hindsight, then, that Demosthenes looks justified in seeing Philip's intentions towards the Athenians as more or less continuously lethal – however unwilling his compatriots were to recognize any such thing. But this matter of hindsight raises other questions as well. We, possessing it, can see that his struggle against Philip was doomed to failure, because even if he could rally the other Greek city-states around him (as he managed, partially, to achieve at Chaeronea) the two sides, in strength, organization and direction alike, were too unevenly matched.

It was, no doubt, an intellectual failure on the part of Demosthenes if he did not recognize this – and he probably did not, since he all too often misinterpreted facts. But what was the alternative? The alternative was to give in, and submit to the eclipse and downfall of the Greek city-state, which in the eyes of Demosthenes (as of Plato and Aristotle) was the only thinkable, tolerable kind of political institution, and which had sponsored such marvels, in a huge variety of fields, during the previous two centuries.

But was its day now past? Should Demosthenes, instead of resisting its fall, have accepted or even welcomed this demise, as Isocrates did by implication when he called on Philip to lead the Greeks in a crusade against Persia? Certainly, disunity between the Greek states, as well as within them, had led to their present catastrophic weakness and vulnerability, which it was easy to see, could become terminal. Yet here, as was suggested in the previous chapter, a distinction must be made. Theoretically at least, there were two kinds of union between federated or allied Greek states: a union of equality, in which no one state or person was pre-eminent, and unequal union, under a single strong leader. The former solution, however, was impossible for the Greeks to achieve, as the whole course of Greek history had shown. That left the second, unequal solution – and second it was, in the sense of being very decisively second-best. The bulk of the Greek population might have fared better, in the long run, if it had been attained (as it was not, or soon ceased to be, owing to Hellenistic divisions), because its attainment would have enabled Hellenism to stand up against external aggressors, and in particular, during the centuries to come, to resist the Romans. However, this would have meant, it must be repeated, negating the whole city-state principle, which seemed to Demosthenes and many others an intolerably high price to pay.

However, Demosthenes' principal claim to distinction lay elsewhere. It did not consist of an agreeable personality. The obstacles he was compelled to face and overcome in early life had embittered his heart. He was an ungenial prig, whose obsessive, narrowly intense determination was accompanied by harsh and stubborn self-righteousness. Moreover, this dogged persistence contained an element of ferocity, expressed in personal attacks upon his political opponents which, even amid the considerable licence of contemporary Athenian standards, seemed scurrilous and extravagant.

About his financial integrity it is difficult to form a conclusion, because of all the contradictory outcries that the subject provoked. His appeals to Persia in the 330s were said to have been prompted by Persian bribery, and in the 320s he was accused of misappropriating Harpalus' money.[9] The political intrigues of the time leave such incidents murky and obscure, but on the whole it seems likely that Demosthenes was guilty on both counts – with the proviso, however, that he intended to use the funds for political and not wholly personal purposes.

Demosthenes' unique greatness, then, did not lie either in his political accomplishments or in his personal character. Instead, though this is not an easy thing for Greekless moderns, suspicious of rhetoric, to appreciate, his greatness lay in his oratory. For whatever may have been the merits or demerits of the causes he espoused, he was a speaker whose eloquence was unequalled in the whole of classical antiquity – and indeed, perhaps, in the entire history of the world. There are many anecdotes about the measures he had to take to overcome physical infirmities that stood in the way of this achievement, and he also had numerous oratorical rivals. Yet later critics were agreed about his pre-eminence. It is also confirmed by the quality of his extant speeches, even though their texts, in the form that has come down to us, contain passages that must have been incorporated, at leisure, after the actual debates had taken place – or sometimes different addresses, for subsequent literary purposes, were merged into one.

His passionate sincerity (for attempts to disparage this are unconvincing) contributed to the success of his orations, but so did the care – surprising to some of his contemporaries – with which he prepared them. The results were expositions of crystalline lucidity, infinitely variable and flexible, ranging from elaborate polish to a stark, sombre simplicity that created some of his most solemn and magnificent effects. Demosthenes had a delicate ear for sound and rhythm (as technical examinations of his style confirm), and made a deliberate and meticulous study of language as a device for assaulting his hearers' emotions: he knew their biases and deficiencies, and took unrelenting advantage of them all.

Among his methods were impetuous and dramatic outbursts, spectacular crescendos, recitations (sometimes in dialogue form) of anticipated objections, unfair and distorted characterizations of his adversaries, rare but masterly excursions into metaphor, repetitions of points that might not have been grasped or absorbed earlier, the avoidance of argumentative reasoning that would have proved too difficult to absorb, and carefully planned, though often scathing and nasty, touches of what was intended to be humour.

The quantity of papyrus fragments of Demosthenes' speeches that have come to light – second only to those containing passages from the Homeric poems – indicates that, despite attacks from his contemporaries, it was not long before writers began to acclaim the superlative character of his oratory. His nearest competitor in this field, Cicero, acknowledging this pre-eminence, wrote of his variety, dignity and subtlety. Cicero's borrowing, however, of the name *Philippics* for his own speeches against Antony meant that an age-long confusion between Demosthenes the orator and Demosthenes the politician had already begun.

Of course, the two roles were inextricably linked. Yet it is necessary to make a distinction between his political role, over which question marks may be thought to hang, and his oratory, which was unmistakably supreme – and received that accolade from a civilization by which speech-making was held in the highest esteem, and judged with the most critical intensity.

CHAPTER 37

ARISTOTLE: THE FRONTIERS OF CLASSICAL KNOWLEDGE

Aristotle (384–322) was born at the Ionian colony of Stagirus in Chalcidice (Macedonia). He was the son of Nicomachus, a member of the medical Asclepiad guild who was the physician of the Macedonian King Amyntas III (393/392–370/369), and probably first inspired Aristotle's interest in physical science and biology. But Nicomachus died when his son was still a boy, and he was sent, at the age of seventeen, to study at Plato's Academy at Athens, where he remained for twenty years, first as a student and then as a teacher and researcher.

After Plato's death, however, he and another prominent figure at the Academy, Xenocrates, moved away from Athens. This may have been partly because the city was at war with Macedonia, with which he enjoyed such close ties. But Aristotle was also said to have disapproved of the policy of Speusippus, who had succeeded Plato as the Academy director and was 'converting philosophy into mathematics'.[10] True, the suggestion that this was one of the motives for Aristotle's departure is not entirely reliable; although, as we shall see, it corresponds well enough with his views.

He and Xenocrates made their way to Atarneus in north-western Asia Minor, ruled over by Hermeias (*c*.355–341), who was a former member of the Academy, as well as a friend of Philip, and had encouraged a group of Platonists to found a philosophical community and school at Assus. Aristotle joined this group, marrying Hermeias' niece and adopted daughter Pythias. Then he spent two years at Mytilene on the island of Lesbos (345–343), and subsequently moved to Mieza, near the Macedonian capital Pella, where he reputedly (though the evidence is not very substantial) took charge of the education of Philip II's thirteen-year-old son Alexander (III the Great).

In 340, however, this appointment, if it ever took place, was terminated, and Aristotle may have gone home to Stagirus. But in 335 he returned to Athens, as a resident alien (metic, Appendix III) and founded his school the Lyceum, in a grove sacred to Apollo Lyceius and the Muses, where his group, at first somewhat informal, was known as the Peripatetics owing to the covered court (*peripatos*) round the building, in which instruction and discussion took place. Alexander's viceroy Antipater was Aristotle's friend, but after Alexander's death (323), when an anti-Macedonian policy prevailed at Athens, Aristotle was accused by the Athenians of impiety (as Socrates had been) and moved out of the city, leaving Theophrastus to direct the Lyceum. He settled at Chalcis in Euboea, but suffered from digestive troubles, and died in the following year.

His writings were of unparalleled scope and dimensions; and out of a vast number of treatises no less than forty-seven have survived.

Their basis was logical reasoning; for although Aristotle, unlike other ancient thinkers, did not regard logic as a science, he located it in the forecourt of the sciences, as a necessary preliminary to them all.

His *Organon* (Instrument, Tool) on the subject consists of six studies. *Categories* describes and classifies terms and phrases, offering ten basic forms of statements on Being. In spite of recurrent doubts, going right back to ancient times, most of the treatise is probably by Aristotle; and the same applies to *On Interpretation*, which discusses the parts and formulations of a sentence. The eight books of *Topics* are concerned with a survey of propositions, indicating the ways in which probable statements can be made – without involvement in contradictions – by the methods of dialectic, as established by the sophists and by Plato (Chapters 12, 31). A sequel, however, the *Sophistical Refutations*, warns against the deceptive inferences into which the arguments employed by the sophists can lead.

Aristotle's word for the study of reasoning is 'analytics', the art of discourse, rather less general than 'logic'; and the most significant parts of the *Organon* are the *Prior* and *Posterior Analytics*, containing two books each. The former work reviews the general principles of inductive inference, while the *Posterior Analytics* applies these methods of proof and definition to the nature and validity of knowledge (epistemology), indicating that there is a proper method of constructing generalizations, applicable to all the sciences, and explaining how language can and should be employed for this purpose.

Aristotle stresses the novelty of his logical writings, and even if, contrary to what has sometimes been claimed, he did not *invent* the discipline of logic (since Parmenides and the sophists and Plato had prepared the ground), he was perhaps the first to comprehend the importance, not only of the content of statements, but of their form, and their formal relation to each other. This was a major breakthrough, for no one had ever before offered a general account of what is valid in argument and what is not. Written with lucid precision and clarity, and displaying sensitiveness to the structures and connections that lie beneath the surface of languages, his *Organon*, even if it seems outdated to logicians today, is by far the most important collection of writings on this theme that has come down to us from the ancient world.

Such was the instrument with which Aristotle tackled the entire field of knowledge. Plato had believed that nature is governed by general laws; and Aristotle added the conviction that this whole panorama can be reasoned out and comprehended. For such a massive investigation he recognized, for the first time, that each of the various sciences is a separate, departmental field of enquiry, and he divided these sciences into three groups: theoretical (*theoria*), seeking knowledge of the truth; practical (*praxis*), dedicated to good behaviour; and productive (*poietike*), devoted to the creation of something beyond the activity involved. The groups sometimes merged into one another, but Aristotle wrote treatises of outstanding significance under each of these three headings.

He is the earliest Greek scientist whose writings can be adequately studied in their original form; though the chronology of their composition, and the processes by which this or that treatise moved from inception to completion, present many complex problems that receive constant attention from scholars.

In the theoretical field, a group of fourteen of Aristotle's treatises is known as the *Metaphysics*, a name that does not go back to himself (who uses the term 'first' or 'primary' philosophy)[11] but is owed to later authors who placed the collection after the *Physics* (*meta ta physika*). In these works Aristotle examines the nature of reality, that is to say its causes, the principles of existence, and the essential substance of the universe. He discerns a hierarchy of existences, each imparting form and change to the one next below it.

At the apex of the scale is the 'Unmoved First Mover', identified with God, an eternal activity of thought, free from any material admixture, imparting causal motion to the universe through a process of attraction related to love. This is a concept which Plato had already suggested, but it forms a basic feature in Aristotle's thought. It reveals his fundamentally religious attitude, and has appealed to devout people through subsequent ages, though they have been somewhat put off by the complexities he introduced, notably a suggested multiplication of Movers, created by adding fifty-five more to account for the movement of the heavenly bodies and constitute an ordered gradation in which the First Mover stands at the summit. Many will think that this multiplicity is not only a mere surrender to Plato but perilously close to nonsense.

Besides, Aristotle's interpretation of the First Mover that stood at the head of this hierarchy raises awkward questions, which his lifelong struggle with these problems was not able to solve, and which may have prompted him, in later life, to push the whole idea into the background. For example, this Mover did not create the universe, and does not (like the god later envisaged by the Stoics) pervade or direct or rule it, remaining, on the contrary, indifferent to its existence – so that Aristotle proves not to be such a 'religious' thinker after all, since his universe is not god-centred. Yet how, then, are events to be explained, if the First Mover does not control them?

The eight-book *Physics* would be better known as 'Lectures on Nature' – since its subject matter extends into metaphysics and the philosophy of science. The work examines the components of the things that exist by nature – which is described as an 'innate impulse to movement', and is discussed along with other fundamental concepts such as time and space and change and matter.

Plato's Forms (Chapter 31) were redefined by Aristotle. This concept (*eidos*) figures largely in a theme that has provoked, and continues to provoke, widespread discussion and disagreement, namely the extent of Aristotle's deviation from the teaching of Plato, whose pupil he had been and the degree to which, during the course of his life, this alienation increased or fluctuated. There was, in fact, a constant tension between his twenty years' association with Plato, inspiring deep affection and reverence, and his own in some ways un-Platonic temperament. To take one example, already noted, Aristotle failed to share the enthusiasm for mathematics which Plato had inherited from the Pythagoreans (Appendix 1) and which Speusippus emphasized in the post-Platonic Academy. It seemed to him an inappropriate foundation of the concrete physical world, being too remote for such a practical role.

To return to the Forms: Aristotle basically rejected, or came to reject, Plato's doctrine.[12] What he saw and disliked in this view (paying little attention to Plato's successive shifts and adjustments) was what he regarded as its transcendentalism: the distinction, inherited from Parmenides, between what is 'real' in an absolute sense (eternal, unchangeable) and what is mere matter (*hyle*), comprising the products of our sense-perceptions, and therefore only 'real' in a secondary and inferior sense of the word. Aristotle did not reject the Forms altogether, but preferred to regard them as immanent in concrete, perceived material objects – enabling the true, underlying nature of those objects to be comprehended; that is to say he refused to allow the Forms any independent, transcendental existence on their own account. His separate study *On Forms*, however, has survived only in fragments, and the same is true of his treatise *On Philosophy*, in which he seems to have combined his objections to mathematics and Forms into a single, interlocking argument – by attacking the doctrine of Ideal Numbers that had brought these two realms of thought together.

There remained, then, the unsolved problem of identifying and defining the principle which enables Forms to realize themselves in matter – the principle, that is to say, which makes the world go round. Aristotle identified this process as *kinesis*, movement, including both quantitative growth and qualitative change, which, together, represent the transition of a thing's potentiality (*dynamis*) – enabling it to become something else – to its actuality (*energeia*).

Aristotle's *Physics* identifies four categories, known somewhat misleadingly as the 'Four Causes'. Three of the 'Causes' have just been mentioned, material, Form, and movement. But he also identified a fourth 'cause', namely *telos*, the end or aim or purpose for which something comes into being, and the reason for its existence. Plato (and apparently Socrates before him) had gone a long way towards this 'teleological' view, maintaining that everything exists for an end, and a good end at that. But to Aristotle this concept is of central importance, and colours the whole of his thinking.

For not only, he maintained, do all things exist for an end, but an inborn impulse impels them to try to achieve that end as completely as possible: in other words, it impels them to attain self-fulfilment, to realize the full potentialities of their Form. This natural sequence of events (like the Unmoved Mover, whose relation to the process remains somewhat undefined) is another sign of what might be called the religious character of Aristotle's thinking, which dominated western thinking up to the sixteenth century and beyond, but will disappoint those who seek wholly scientific explanations of the universe. However, it also disappointed nineteenth-century religious thinkers as not being teleological *enough*, because, granted that Aristotle saw the universe as moving towards natural *ends*, it did not seem to him that nature exhibits any discoverable, providential *purpose*, although the distinction may sometimes appear evanescent.

On the Heavens, in four books, expounds the movement of heavenly and sublunary bodies, defining and distinguishing and organizing Plato's conceptions. The spherical shape of the earth was known to Aristotle, but he still believed it to be the centre of the universe. *On Generation and Corruption* (or *On Coming into Being and Passing Away*) interprets evolution in terms of a cyclical series of transformations. The four books *On Meteorology* deal mostly with phenomena relating to the weather, although comets, meteors and the nature of the sea are also discussed.

However, living things absorbed Aristotle's interest to the greatest extent, and it is here that his characteristic concepts are most at home. In the field of biology, it was his intention to cover the entire realm of nature. But he assigned the vegetable kingdom to his pupil Theophrastus, while himself undertaking the zoological part of this huge project (though perhaps with Theophrastus' help).

His *History of* (or rather, *Enquiry into*) *Animals* is an introductory collection of facts about animal life, in four books, dealing with the anatomy, physiology and habits of all sorts of animals, fishes and birds, with emphasis on the adaptation and evolution of their organs. *On the Parts (Members) of Animals* is again in four books. There are also studies *On the Generation* (Reproduction) and *Gait of Animals* – of which the former, comprising five books, earned praises from Darwin – and a further treatise *On the Movement of Animals* (of which the Aristotelian authorship is sometimes unnecessarily doubted).

Biology was Aristotle's key science, as mathematics had been Plato's, and in this field he was at his triumphal best. 'The only great philosopher', it has been said, 'who philosophized out of a passion for living nature', and at the same time virtually the earliest of all biologists and zoologists, he displayed marked originality and acumen and patience. His imposing analyses of more than five hundred species, sketching out the entire canvas, and filling most of it in, as well, were built up from a tremendous wealth of carefully sifted data, his own and others', for the organization of which he founded a library (equipped with a large museum collection) which was the model of all subsequent libraries in the ancient world.

Some of the information and interpretation that he provides has been shown in later epochs (and especially from the nineteenth century onwards) to be erroneous, but an enormous amount remains valid; and parts of his discussions seem uncannily ahead of their time. Aristotle himself sums up his biological and zoological research methods. 'If ever the facts about bees', he remarks, 'are fully grasped, then credit must be given rather to observations than to theories, and to theories only if what they affirm agrees with the observed facts.'[13]

However, despite this stirring attack on the Greek predilection for theory, he nevertheless found room for his own *idées fixes*, which scarcely harmonized with this point of view. Thus the Unmoved Mover appears once again. Moreover his studies of the adaptation and evolution of animals gave him an ample opportunity to illustrate and apply his teleological beliefs, insisting that everything is directed towards an end. Indeed it may well have been these researches into nature which convinced him that Plato had been right to maintain this teleological standpoint.

On the Soul, in three books, is not concerned with the human soul alone, but with all stages of animate life, the soul being interpreted as the internal principle – not immaterial, as Plato had suggested – which is united with the body and holds it together and endows it with life. But the human soul is above those of animals and plants, because it alone has the power of thought (*dianoetikon*). Equipped with this gift, a soul is the ordered microcosm that mirrors the macrocosm of the universe, though the extent to which Aristotle sees souls as outliving bodies is not made clear, because the Platonic picture of the hereafter does not appeal to him. Nevertheless, this elaborate and subtle analysis of the soul's functions represents the final stage of Aristotle's psychological ponderings, and no part of his philosophy has exercised a greater effect on later thought.

The ten books of the *Nicomachean Ethics*, the most famous of all studies of morality, is named after Aristotle's son, Nicomachus, and may be his edition of his father's lectures. Much of the work is written in a semi-popular fashion, endeavouring to reconcile philosophy with the outlook of the educated public – in a boringly middle-aged manner, some say today, while others find the tone bracingly commonsensical.

Better described as 'On Matters of Character' (which is what *ethos* means), the *Nicomachean Ethics* deals with a 'practical' science, being a study of the Good, that is to say of *being* good, the end (*telos*) towards which conduct should be directed. In Book I this is identified with happiness or well-being (*eudaimonia*), 'an activity of the soul in accordance with reason',[14] and the next five books define the character of such activity. Pleasure, honour and wealth are rejected as the foundation of *eudaimonia*, and the absoluteness of Plato's moral values (which he had summarized by four, named, abstract virtues) is abandoned in favour of a more realistic and pragmatic diversity. For Aristotle insists that we should start with what we find at hand, and try to perfect tendencies that are already in existence; and since, therefore, our lives are not entirely lived on a spiritual and intellectual basis, there is room not only for the virtues relating to that exalted pitch but also for qualities of character, such as courage and high-mindedness and patience and gentleness and endurance of fortune.

As to the lofty spiritual and intellectual virtues, they can be divided into two categories, at different levels of elevation. The higher of these two categories is represented by Wisdom (*sophia*). Attainable only by a few people, it finds its highest expression in *theoria* – which is translated as 'contemplation', but is, rather, the burning, indefatigable vision of philosophical truth – which enables a human being, so to speak, to 'put on immortality'[15] (and brings, incidentally, the purest and most exquisite pleasure).

The second, and lower, of these top-class categories of virtue embodies *phronesis*, which Plato had interpreted as transcendent vision but, to Aristotle, signifies a mere day-to-day capacity, the acquired habit of acting with foresight and intelligence, the best that human beings can normally and reasonably aim at. The remaining books of the *Nicomachean Ethics* deal disconnectedly with a variety of subjects, including friendship and the problem of desire, and the last book contains a eulogy of scientific research.

The seven-book *Eudemian Ethics* covers much of the same ground, though with differing emphases and slants, and may perhaps form an earlier edition of the same lecture-course copied down by Aristotle's pupil Eudemus. This treatise objects strongly to Socrates' paradoxical view that 'no man is willingly bad' – for virtue and vice, Aristotle prefers to say, are matters within our power; it is up to us to choose one or the other.

His ethical approach is once again, as one might expect, teleological: he wants to find out what human beings *are for* – to identify the functions for which nature intends them. His assumption that, despite the diversity of virtues, there must be one single, ultimate end or good was traditional, but is undemonstrated, and liable to criticism. He defines 'contemplation' as the supreme way of life, because it is the loftiest possible activity of the rational mind. But unlike Plato, as we saw, he also finds room for other more humdrum qualities relating to the lives people actually lead. However, when he attempts to delineate the personage most perfectly incorporating such useful, day-by-day qualities, the Superior or Great-Souled ('magnanimous') Man, he makes himself somewhat ridiculous; for this paragon sounds rather like a complacent, pompous ass.

Excellence, as Aristotle saw it, comes as a result of deliberately selecting the Mean, a middle course. The Greeks – prone to extremes – admired this idea, of which a great deal is heard in their folklore, and in their tragedies, and in Plato: and the Mean became one of Aristotle's best-known doctrines. Human beings must choose an intermediate course between two opposite sets of extreme behaviour – for instance, between total asceticism and extravagant self-indulgence. Although difficult to justify in logical terms, this is not, as some have assumed, a mere exaltation of mediocrity, but a proposal – probably derived from medical analogies (Chapter 20) – that it is up to each individual to seek to achieve the precise blend and proportion of qualities that is appropriate to his or her self.[16]

Aristotle exalted contemplation, but saw community life as the practical ideal: for him, as for Plato, ethics and politics are one. Neither of these two arts or sciences is the exact study, providing for no exceptions, that Plato supposed, but taken together they amount to a single, total human philosophy – politics being the central concern of humankind, since Plato had been right to maintain that people are only parts of the society to which they belong: indeed the state, Aristotle maintained, is logically prior to the individual.

Even if this belief in the centrality of politics and priority of the state, despite acceptance in some quarters even today, is questionable, Aristotle thought more deeply about the political structure of Greek society than anyone ever before, and wrote about the subject at great length. His *Politics*, although it has reached the world in a somewhat incoherent and disorganized form, remains our most ample and searching investigation into the political conditions of ancient Greece.

The treatise approaches the topic from the viewpoint of the city-state, which provided, Aristotle assumed, the fullest life for its individual citizens. Thus they are biologically defined, as he indicates in Book I, as *zoa politika*,[17] city-state beings, social animals whose natural, highest goal (*telos*) is to live in a *polis*. A discussion of slavery which follows adopts the view that the servitude of slaves to the free, and of barbarians to Greeks, is a condition of nature (cf. Appendix V). Book II offers a historical survey of politics, examining a number of 'model' constitutions, especially those of Sparta, Crete and Carthage, and discussing various legislators. There are references to Plato, and they recur in Book III, which discusses healthy constitutions (monarchy, aristocracy and moderate democracy) in contrast with degenerate and undesirable types (tyranny, oligarchy – that is to say, government by a few, not selected for merit – and radical democracy or crowd rule).

Books IV–VI analyse various defects that damage political life, and the ways of eliminating them. It is taken for granted that every state includes, within itself, two parties, divided on economic lines, and perpetually at daggers drawn with one another. Books VII and VIII go on to depict the *best* sort of state. Like Plato, Aristotle regards education, under state control, as the first essential – but an education, this time, which although still predominantly ethical, nevertheless trains a person's emotions and body as well as his intellectual and moral capacities.

Further studies of 158 Greek city-state constitutions are now lost, except for the greater part of the *Athenian Constitution* which has been unearthed on a papyrus. Though derived, somewhat hastily, from sources of varying quality, this treatise contains a useful and succinct account of the political system of Athens and its earlier historical development. The work may or may not have been written by Aristotle himself – these 'constitutions' were perhaps parcelled out for composition to his students – but it reflects the aristocratic, anti-democratic bias which he shared with Plato. It is ironical that Athens, the leading democratic city-state, should owe so much of its fame to two convinced anti-democratic writers who flourished in its midst.

Despite the revolutionary political changes introduced by Philip II and Alexander the Great (supposedly his pupil!), Aristotle, even though himself a metic and not an Athenian citizen, joined Plato and Demosthenes in still regarding the city-state as the natural, optimum kind of self-sufficient society. It was necessarily small in size, but contained – though Athenian imports seemed to contest the point – all that was necessary to enable its citizens to lead the good life.

His governing class, an exemplification of the Mean, would consist, for the sake of stability, of an aristocracy of intellect and virtue, comprising basically the middle class: those citizens who enjoyed moderate prosperity, and did not feel discontented enough to want political convulsions or imprudent adventures. Citizenship would be restricted to a smaller minority than actually possessed this privilege at Athens; agricultural labourers and artisans and shopkeepers would not be allowed to become citizens at all, because manual labour makes a person coarse (*banausos*) and leaves no time for a citizen's duties, which require leisure.[18] The 'natural slave' is another reactionary feature – in an age when opposite viewpoints were being discussed, and when Alexander took a more liberal view of barbarians – although Aristotle did qualify the severity of his definition by claiming that no Greek should enslave Greek (Appendix v).

His *Rhetoric*, in three books, comes under the heading of 'productive' writings, aimed at creating something that is worth while. It considers the methods of persuasion open to the orator, and how they can be reduced to rule. The first of its three books investigates the logical proofs and arguments derived from dialectical techniques. The second turns to psychological and ethical factors, discussing how the speaker can induce his audience to look upon him favourably and how he can whip up their emotions. The third book reviews matters relating to stylistic clarity, appropriate tone, correct arrangement, and forms and figures of speech.

This last section has the appearance of a technical manual, but the *Rhetoric* as a whole is not a handbook on the subject but an analysis of the methods by which arguments that lack intellectual validity (and here we are back with the treatises of logical procedures) can nevertheless be made to sound persuasive; and a speaker, Aristotle adds with hard-boiled common sense, cannot be blamed for making the attempt. Despite inconsistencies, this treatment of tricks and devices is the clearest and most comprehensive of its kind, and was highly relevant to the word-dominated way of life of contemporary Athenians, although it seems outdated today.

The *Poetics* is a study of poetry. Although an 'imitation' like other arts (but in its own distinctive fashion), poetry, Aristotle indicates, is more 'philosophical' than history, because it tells general truths, whereas history is limited to particular facts; and he does not therefore, like Plato, regard the poetic art as an always too dangerous stimulant, but sees that it can be instructive and beneficial as well.

Originally, the complete work dealt with epic, tragedy and comedy, but as it has come down to us tragedy is the principal theme. An analysis of tragic drama indicates the component elements of a play, the unity of action that it requires (that is to say, it should centre round a single action or experience, of a certain magnitude), and its purpose, which is defined as 'effecting the proper purgation (or purification) of the emotions through terror and pity'[19] (or 'horror and misery'): a process which will offer a cathartic outlet to the emotions of the audience and thereby cause them pleasure. Notes on certain characteristic features of tragedies are also included, such as the 'reversal' (of fortune) and 'recognition' (or discovery) and the mysterious fatal 'flaw' (*hamartia*), which brings great men like Sophocles' Oedipus down (Chapter 17). A brief discussion of epic poetry, and the rules which should apply to it has also survived and epic and tragic poetry are compared.

In spite of its fragmentary character, and the suspicion that Aristotle was temperamentally unsuited to appreciate either tragedy or epic to the full, his *Poetics* remains the earliest and also the most important of all Greek contributions to literary criticism – which he provided with a vocabulary of its own, and many permanently valuable definitions. In subsequent centuries the work became influential and famous, inspiring numerous editions and commentaries (especially after its initial separate printing in 1526) and exercising a dominant influence, in particular, upon the French classical drama of the seventeenth century. For the French theatre was founded upon a doctrine of dramatic unities which was thought to be found in Aristotle's treatise, though in fact the only unity which is lays down is unity of action.

The man who performed all these mammoth tasks was bald and spindly-legged, with diminutive eyes and a sardonic expression. His taste for elegant clothes, and jewellery, and smart dinners, was noted. It would be agreeable if some of the ancient busts labelled 'Aristotle' were accurate portraits; and despite the Greek preference for representing their philosophers generically and impersonally (since in many cases the artists had no accurate idea of what they had looked like), in one or two of these sculptures we may be able to discern the real physiognomy of Aristotle. And furthermore, if only by an effort of the imagination, the expression on the faces of these heads can be seen to reflect a certain indefinable irony and sadness that emerges from his known opinions and discussions.

It is disconcerting, however, that Cicero tells us of the sparkling style and 'golden flow',[20] because such praises are scarcely merited by the treatises that are still extant. Their language displays a concise and knotty pungency, providing an efficient vehicle for philosophical argument and scientific description, but dry and formal, and indeed at times pedantic, so that to read Aristotle is arduous. The brilliant, golden essays admired by Cicero have vanished: whereas those of his studies that have come down to us, despite a few elaborately worked-up passages, for the most part seem to have been 'esoteric', unpolished and unrevised, pieces intended not for general circulation but for employment within the student body of the Lyceum.

However, what survives does seem to include the most important works Aristotle wrote. Their gigantic range might be thought to show him as the creator of an entire, coherent, comprehensive, encyclopaedic system, and it is as a systematizer that he has often been regarded. Nevertheless, although he did, indeed, systematize a huge range of existing knowledge, he still remained, at heart, a tentative, probing, dialectically minded explorer and researcher, making acute (though sometimes distorted) use of what others had provided, and yet continually moved by his own personal, unceasing sense of wonder. For Aristotle was a man whose master passion for the acquisition of knowledge kept him always ready, with intellectual humility, to look at a point of theory again and again, and try to handle it better all the time – on the basis of newly acquired data.

The teleology he had inherited and developed may seem crankish, and the Four Causes and the Unmoved Mover represented two not entirely happy attempts to get at the problem of the ultimate nature and motivation of the universe; although the problem which Aristotle was trying to tackle has remained insoluble, giving subsequent rise to speculative fanaticisms far more harmful than his own laborious, subtle endeavours.

And when he came down to earth, his Ionian passion for investigation of natural phenomena – despite inevitable shortcomings by modern standards – illuminated innumerable subjects with his robust yet inspired passion for orderliness, displayed by inexhaustible classifications, but also, at the same time, accompanied by an unremitting responsiveness to the complexity and variety of nature and human beings. One of his eulogies of meticulous personal observation (of bees) has already been quoted. And Aristotle also remarked, in more general terms, that 'those whom indulgence in long discussions has rendered unobservant of facts are too ready to dogmatize from a few observations'.[21]

This devotion to individual facts – interpreted as the essential foundations for conceptual generalities – began, at long last, to free the sciences from the domination of philosophy. Nevertheless, philosophers of the ensuing epoch relied on Aristotle extensively, and the debts owed to his work by Stoics and Epicureans have now been shown to be more substantial than was previously believed. An Aristotelian element also found its way into subsequent versions of Platonism, and this influenced early Christian thought. Then Latin translations of Aristotle's works, taken from Arabic versions, dominated the writings of the schoolmen, and all the *Summa* of St Thomas Aquinas (*c.*1225–74). Later, too, Francis Bacon (1561–1626), adopting Aristotle's division and distinction between the Four Causes, paid him the compliment of entitling his own work the *Novum Organum.*

Indeed, Aristotle was the man who established the major and still accepted divisions of philosophy; and whereas Plato gave leading categories their names, Aristotle added numerous, more detailed, definitions. And it is from him that philosophers and scientists, of one generation after another, have derived their philosophical terminology which has entered into the inherited vocabulary of educated men and women, so that we employ these terms continually without any longer recalling their source.

He has been seen throughout the ages as the supreme scholar pursuing the life of the intellect for its own sake; and his posthumous prestige has been more enduring than any other thinker's. Although there is little point in trying to draw up a list, in order of merit, of the astonishingly numerous personages of genius who lived during the fifth and fourth centuries BC, it is impossible to think of any whose contribution to the world was greater than Aristotle's.

EPILOGUE

The foregoing pages have sought to suggest that the major achievements of classical Greece were mainly the work of less than forty outstanding men. Leading persons in the city-states were by no means just labels and cogs, since decisive events and developments were put in motion by a minute proportion of the population, the tip of an invisible iceberg. True, whatever influences of environment and inheritance and borrowing their communities underwent affected them as much as their fellow citizens, so that in that sense they are reflections of the society to which they belonged. But it was the few individuals themselves who delivered the creative responses which this society prompted, and it was they, individually, who understood and shaped and transformed the world around them according to their personal wills.

One of the most important factors that dictated the doings of the Greeks was their Mediterranean environment. Its fifth-century inhabitants were aware of this. Both Herodotus and the author of *Airs, Waters and Places* – wrongly identified with the physician Hippocrates (Chapter 20) – believed that modes of life are created and differentiated by physical surroundings and applied this to their own civilization.[1]

It is tempting to accept this doctrine, without further qualification. For the Mediterranean region is so superb, in a hundred different ways, that it seems to provide a natural framework for one of the world's greatest civilizations. Modern geographers, however, have added a more sophisticated 'possibilist' approach. Characteristics, we are told, are not *inherent* in a particular region, but the region may *whisper hints* to their inhabitants about how its problems can best be solved. Any given area, that is to say, offers certain possibilities, potentialities from which the occupants select according to their requirements, talents and whims. Climate is, of course, a vital factor, and the writer of *Airs, Waters and Places* suggested that seasonal changes encourage activity[2] – which is true provided that they are not too massive or abrupt; and the comparatively mild Mediterranean climatic cycle played its part in stimulating the civilization of the region.

The Mediterranean area provides a paradoxical blend of natural wealth and frugal austerity, which presents both obstacles, needing to be overcome, and encouragements to overcome them, at one and the same time. Life is splendid, but also precarious; determined efforts are needed to direct and correct nature and make it into an ally. Such endeavours were strenuously made in the ancient world; and the sea made it possible to extend them over the entire Mediterranean basin, and beyond it into the Propontis and the Black Sea.

But another essential feature of the region is its accessibility to the eastern, Asian and Egyptian hinterland territories where earlier communities and cultures had flourished for millennia, and the makers of classical Greek civilization owed an enormous debt to what those peoples had achieved. By the early fifth century, however – at the beginning of the period with which this book is concerned – these heritages had been fully absorbed, and although relations with Persia remained all-important, Greek political, social and cultural arrangements had become fully established, and were going their own way.

This was not, however, due to any ethnic primacy of the Greeks. Some of the ancients adopted a racialist approach, believing, simply, that they were superior to 'barbarians', notably Persians. But Isocrates (Chapter 32) was aware that the only way to define a Greek was by culture, not race,[3] and a racialist interpretation of the ancient world is now recognized to be useless, since its races were inextricably mixed from the beginning. We cannot, therefore, conclude that the makers of the classical Greek civilization achieved what they achieved because of their race.

What, then, was the reason why they achieved so much? Or, to put it another way, it becomes important to know *just why* the Greek world (not unlike the Italian Renaissance, but perhaps with even greater diversity) produced such an unprecedented, unparalleled abundance of outstanding practitioners in so very many different fields, many of them in not more than a few lifetimes. The answer is hard to find. We can indicate the range of opportunities from which the towering Greeks were able to choose, in order to give expression to their talents. But the difficulty arises when we try to give the reasons why so many of them made the fateful, earth-shaking choices that they did – and made them more or less simultaneously.

Evidently the communities to which they belonged – by some concatenation of circumstances – had just reached the stage at which these choices could be made, these deeds could be performed, these thoughts could be thought and written down, by a few people living at almost the same time. The explanation for this outburst must be the Greek city-state. The Greeks liked talking, and the Mediterranean climate (in which most of the living could be done out of doors) provided suitable room to talk – and think together, and design buildings, and devise other artistic masterpieces. They had leisure to do these things – which they prized – because they owned slaves, and could hire other men as well to do the manual and other humdrum work; and because their lifestyle was so simple and unencumbered that it did not take up too much of the day. Here, then, is the necessary corollary to the argument, developed in this book, that classical Greece was the work of outstanding individuals: they achieved what they did only because the city-states which produced them and gave them their background were what they were.

Even so, however, the city-state can hardly be said to account for *all* the prominent personages of the age: most notably in the political field. Philip II of Macedonia, for example, did not belong to such a state – although his admiration for Athens played a part in his policy. How far the Bosphoran King Leucon I was influenced by his city Panticapaeum we can scarcely say: but the city-states of Syracuse and Acragas and Halicarnassus provided the frameworks, at least, within which their autocrats operated. As for the other notable figures of the age, it was one city-state or another that nurtured and shaped them all, even if some of them treated their parent state with less than patriotic respect.

In discussing this subject, the city-state is too often implicitly identified with democracy. Yet by no means all the leading Greek states, during much or most of this period, were democratically governed: a number of the greatest personages of the age belonged to city-states that were ruled by oligarchies or dictatorships instead. True, free speech, on which so much achievement depended, flourished best under a democratic system, but it was not always totally lacking when governments were of other complexions, and even when they were democratic, restrictions existed. One could cite the prosecutions of Anaxagoras and Protagoras, for example, and the attacks on Aristophanes (who resisted them successfully), and the attacks on Socrates (who did not).

All these instances come from Athens, for two reasons: Athens was the most thoroughgoing of all Greek democracies, and it is also the democracy about which, because of the survival of so much of its literature, we have the greatest knowledge. This, in a sense, is appropriate, because a very high proportion of the makers of classical civilization belonged to this peculiarly productive state: nearly half the names of the foregoing chapter-headings are Athenians, and some will think that more should have been added. Themistocles, as he told a sneering man from a small island, was well aware of what he owed to the place of his origin.[4]

But what, in any case, did 'democracy' mean? It means very different things in different countries today, but none of these various modern interpretations correspond to what the term signified in ancient times. Ancient democracy was both broader and narrower. It was broader because, except in a few federal experiments that had so far scarcely taken root (Chapters 29, 35), it was not representative but *direct*. That is to say the citizens did not, as today, send their elected members to a parliament or house of representatives to conduct state business on their behalf, but instead they themselves, or as many of them as wanted to or could manage to, participated directly in that business in their own persons – as Pericles, according to Thucydides,[5] insisted that they should, although this would not be practicable in the larger states of today, and would not, indeed, to most people, seem an attractive prospect for themselves.

And yet, in another sense, Greek democracy was also narrower than anything to which we are accustomed, since it not only excluded women, who held no public offices and did not take part at all in government affairs, but also excluded substantial categories of non-slave inhabitants – metics and various kinds of person who could roughly be described as serfs, such as Spartan helots – as well as the slaves themselves (Appendices II–V). Democracy, then, was not a complete expression of a city-state community, but a democracy of that part of it which formed its citizen body.

Here, however, it is time to make a distinction between this political field, in which democracy was one of the rival systems, and the cultural sphere – literature, philosophy and science, and the arts. In this cultural field it is hard indeed to deny the outstanding achievements of fifth- and fourth-century Greeks. Their political achievement, however, is more questionable. Not only were the internal affairs of cities frequently convulsed (even though they involved fewer assassinations than occur in the world today), but a number of such cities, including not only autocratically ruled states such as Syracuse, but also democracies, notably Athens, derived their political power and the leisure that helped to create art and literature from the profits of empire, coercively imposed and maintained. In the ancient world that satisfying antithesis between democracies, our friends, and annexationist imperial states, our enemies, will not work, since the outstanding Greek state Athens, at its strongest (and, we are told to believe, its best) was not only a democracy but an imperialistic democracy at that.

However, if that is a query against the Athenian democratic system, it raises a moral rather than a practical question – and does not mean that the Athenian system worked any less well because of its imperialist character. Indeed it is arguable, on the contrary, that without the empire the system would not have worked at all – as the Athenian statesman Eubulus, reviewing the past, must sometimes have despairingly felt when he tried, in the mid-fourth century, to shore up his city's finances after imperial revenue had vanished. It was not, that is to say, its imperialism that prevented the direct democracy of Athens from functioning effectively; imperialism, on the contrary, had been its basis, and what prevented it from functioning effectively was something quite different, namely the frequency of the bad, foolish decisions the Athenian government made.

It has been eloquently argued, on the other side, that anti-democratic Plato and Aristotle were unduly critical of the system, which cannot have been all that bad since it endured for two hundred years, with comparatively few major convulsions. Yet it would have fared much better still if such awful decisions had not been made. Take the Peloponnesian War alone. The Athenian Assembly was ludicrously over-ambitious in voting to invade Sicily. To support the Persian dissident Amorges at the same time, or thereabouts, when Sparta still had to be reckoned with, and Persia itself was so wealthy and potentially decisive, must also be regarded as rash in the extreme. Moreover, to execute the surviving generals after the battle of Arginusae was suicidal, since, once they had gone, there was hardly anybody left to lead what resistance remained (Chapters 16, 24).

These are all questions that arose in connection with foreign policy; that is to say, they affected Athens' relations with other Greek city-states. But the charge must be geographically widened. It was not only Athens that erred in that way: mistakes in inter-state relations were committed by every other Greek city as well. In particular, there was to be seen, at all epochs, a failure of all attempts at collaboration between one state and another, so that Plato's chilling remark that the natural inter-state relation is one of war[6] was, in practice, correct. Almost every state quarrelled far too often with its own neighbours, so that any suggestion that the Panhellenism, which characterized athletic and musical festivals, should be enlarged into the political field still remained merely theoretical and hypothetical. Isocrates hoped he might channel such ideas into an anti-Persian crusade, but this scheme too, whatever its merits or demerits, remained in the clouds – relevant only because it recalled how the disunity among the Greek city-states had brought them, more than once, under that pervasive Persian influence which Isocrates was so eager to shake off.

These inter-state bickerings cannot be said to have impeded or stifled the makers of classical Greek culture. On the contrary, indeed, the rivalry which they engendered may actually, in many cases, have stimulated these men's endeavours. In the political field, on the other hand, such squabblings led to Philip II: that is to say, to the virtual destruction of the city-state as an independent political entity.

Among the makers of classical civilization there had already been formidable autocrats, for example, Gelon and Hiero I and Dionysius I of Syracuse; but the only city-states whose independence they had stifled were those of the west. Now, however, Philip subjected the nucleus of the Greek world to a similar process. There would still in future, it is true, be independently operating Greek political personages. But hitherto such figures had not only been autocrats like Dionysius but also, and far more frequently, the leaders of oligarchic and democratic city-states. From this time onwards, on the other hand, they would be almost exclusively autocrats, ruling over states in which neither oligarchy nor democracy existed.

That did not, of course, mean that Greek civilization had ended; history goes on, and the Hellenistic world was still to come. Moreover, the makers of that world would not only be politicians but, as before, writers and philosophers and artists, many of them of the utmost distinction. What had finished, however, was the era of the truly independent Greek city-state; and it is with the efflorescence of that state, and its outstanding and diverse products, that this book has been concerned.

1 Central and Northern Greece with inset of Attica

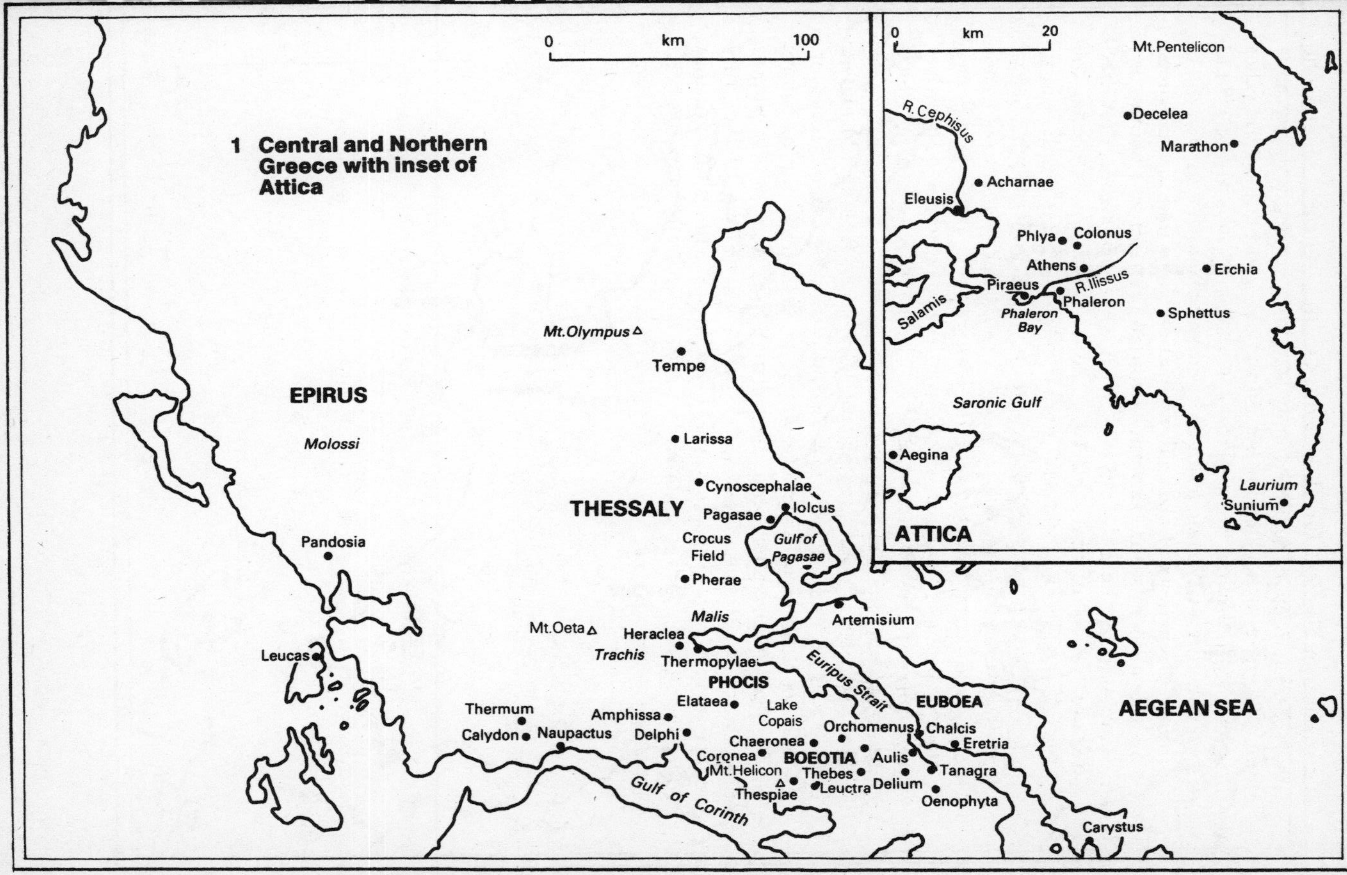

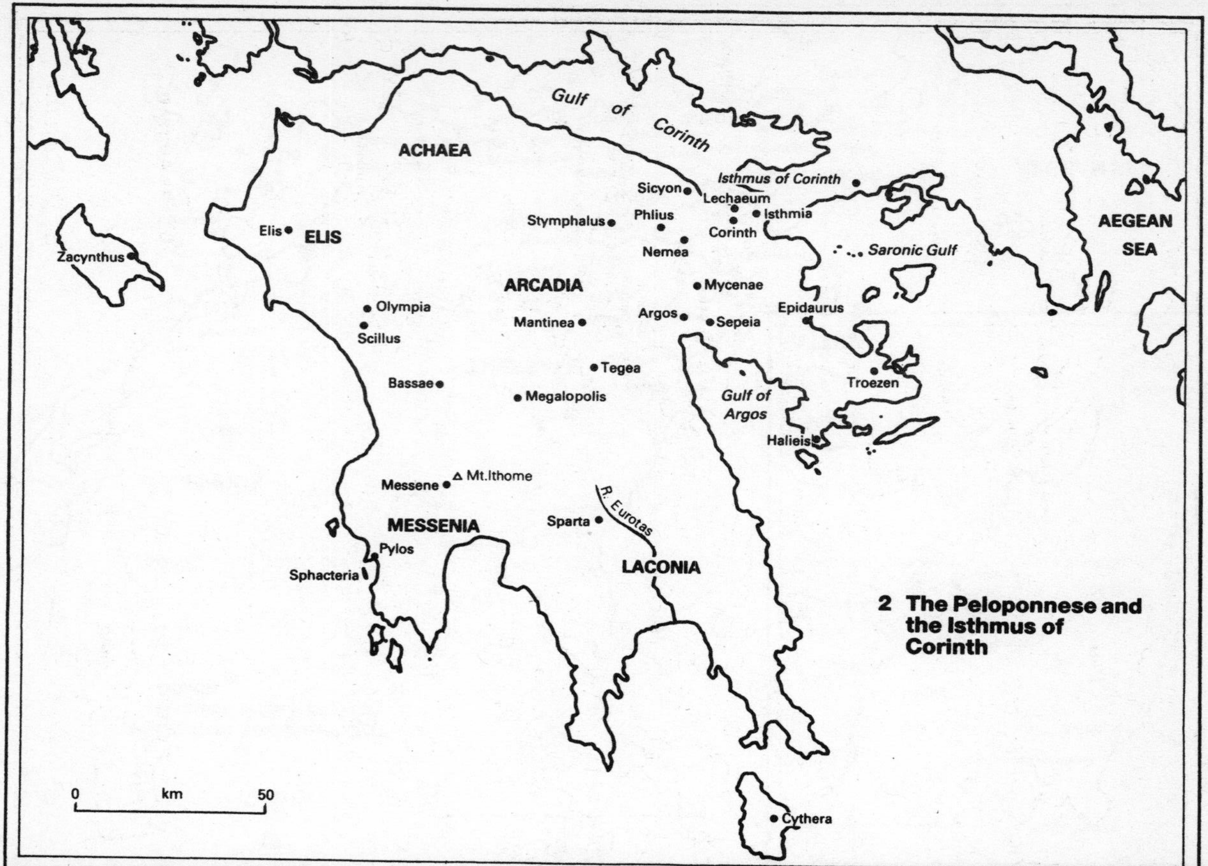

2 The Peloponnese and the Isthmus of Corinth

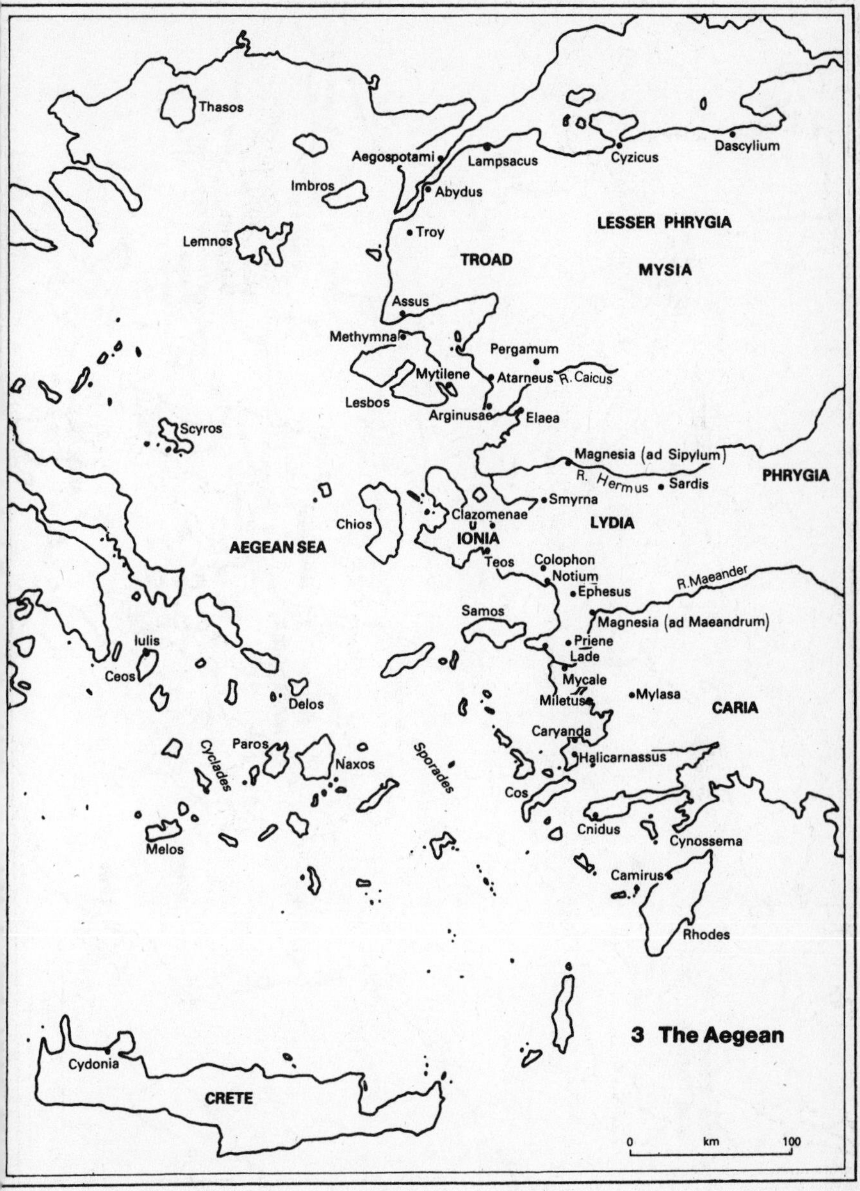
Thasos
Aegospotami
Lampsacus
Cyzicus
Dascylium
Imbros
Abydus
LESSER PHRYGIA
Lemnos
Troy
TROAD
MYSIA
Assus
Methymna
Pergamum
Mytilene
Atarneus
R. Caicus
Lesbos
Arginusae
Elaea
Scyros
Magnesia (ad Sipylum)
R. Hermus
Sardis
PHRYGIA
Smyrna
Clazomenae
Chios
IONIA
LYDIA
AEGEAN SEA
Teos
Colophon
Notium
R.Maeander
Ephesus
Samos
Magnesia (ad Maeandrum)
Iulis
Priene
Lade
Ceos
Mycale
Delos
Miletus
Mylasa
CARIA
Caryanda
Paros
Cyclades
Naxos
Sporades
Halicarnassus
Cos
Cnidus
Cynossema
Melos
Camirus
Rhodes
Cydonia
CRETE
0
km
100

3 The Aegean

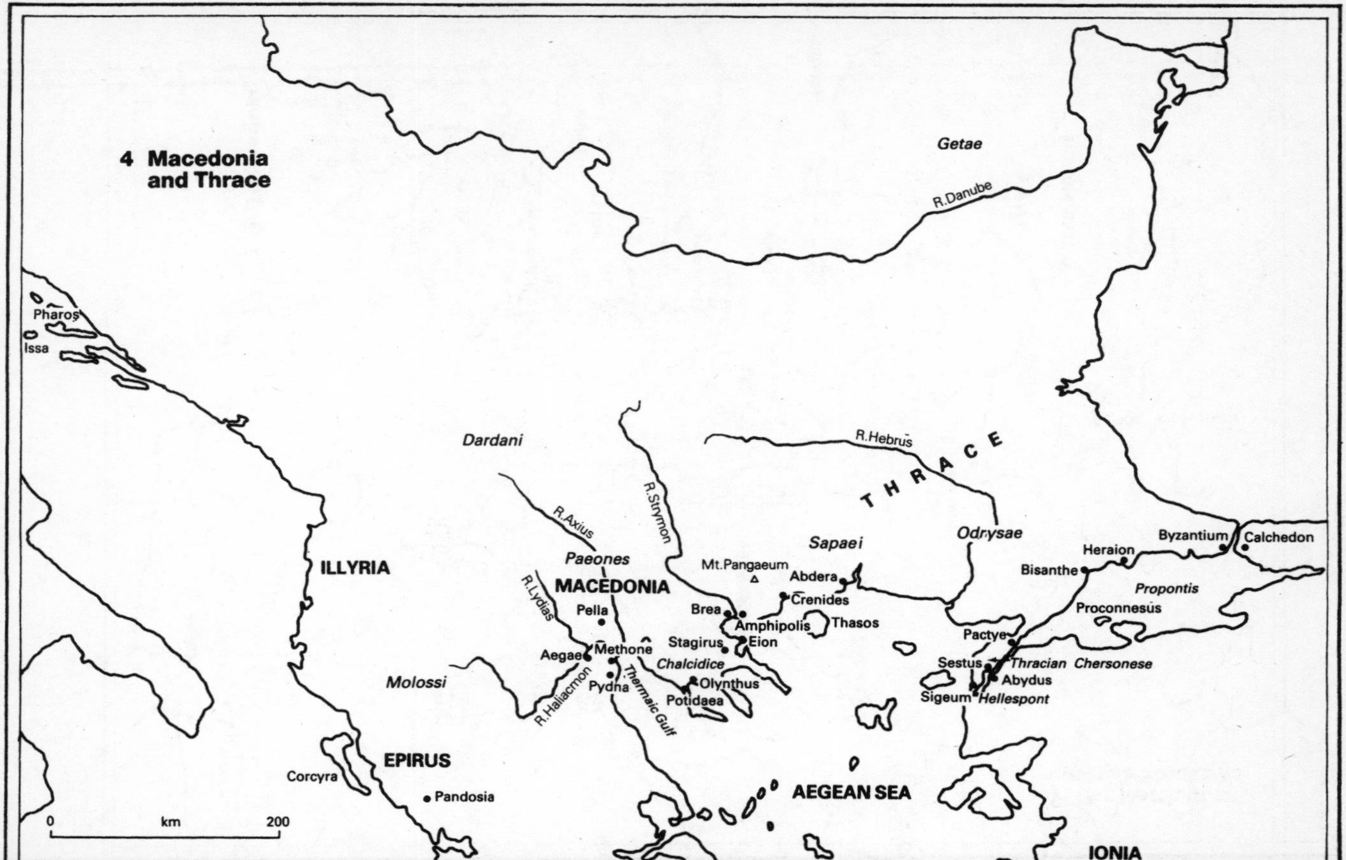
4 Macedonia and Thrace
Getae
R.Danube
Pharos
Issa
Dardani
R.Hebrus
THRACE
R.Axius
R.Strymon
Odrysae
Byzantium
Calchedon
Heraion
Sapaei
Paeones
Mt.Pangaeum
Abdera
Bisanthe
Propontis
ILLYRIA
MACEDONIA
R.Lydias
Crenides
Proconnesus
Pella
Brea
Amphipolis
Thasos
Pactye
Stagirus
Eion
Aegae
Methone
Chalcidice
Sestus
Thracian Chersonese
Molossi
Pydna
Olynthus
Abydus
R.Haliacmon
Thermaic Gulf
Potidaea
Sigeum
Hellespont
EPIRUS
Corcyra
Pandosia
AEGEAN SEA
0
km
200
IONIA

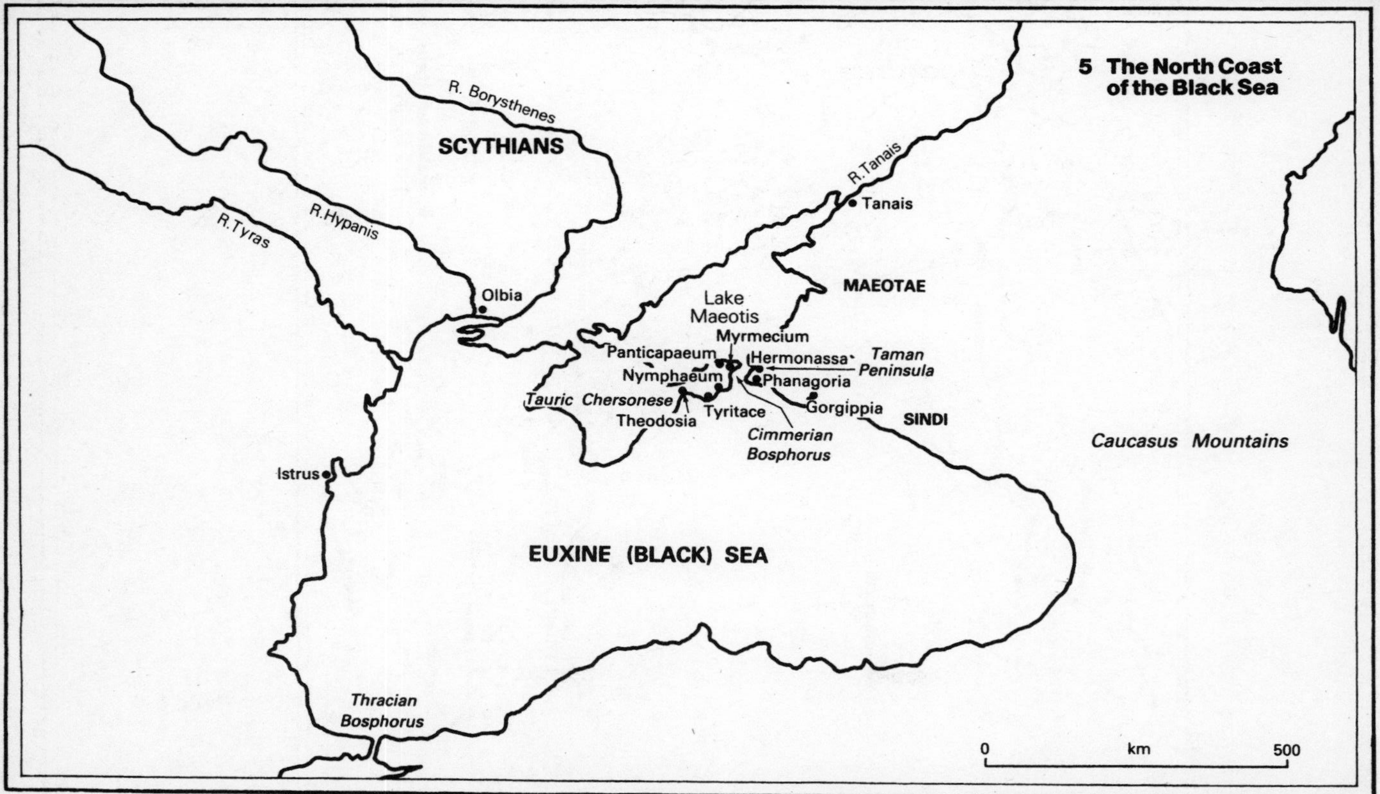
5 The North Coast of the Black Sea
R. Borysthenes
SCYTHIANS
R. Hypanis
R. Tyras
Olbia
R. Tanais
Tanais
MAEOTAE
Lake Maeotis
Myrmecium
Panticapaeum
Hermonassa
Taman Peninsula
Nymphaeum
Phanagoria
Tauric Chersonese
Tyritace
Gorgippia
SINDI
Theodosia
Cimmerian Bosphorus
Caucasus Mountains
Istrus
EUXINE (BLACK) SEA
Thracian Bosphorus
0
km
500

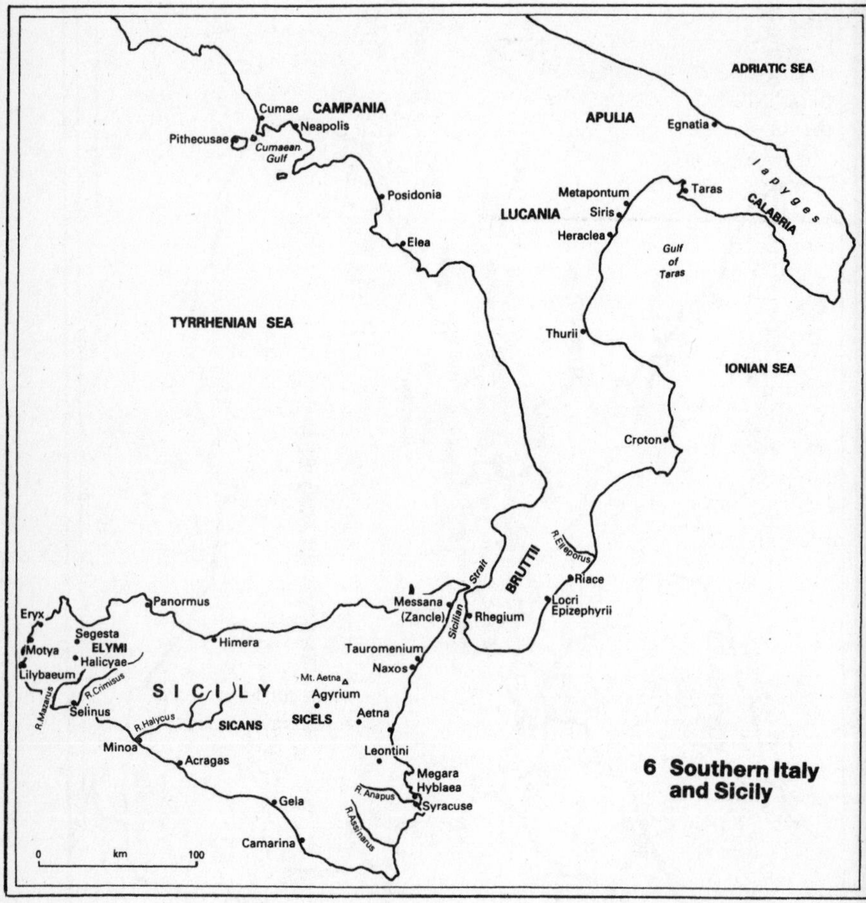

6 Southern Italy and Sicily

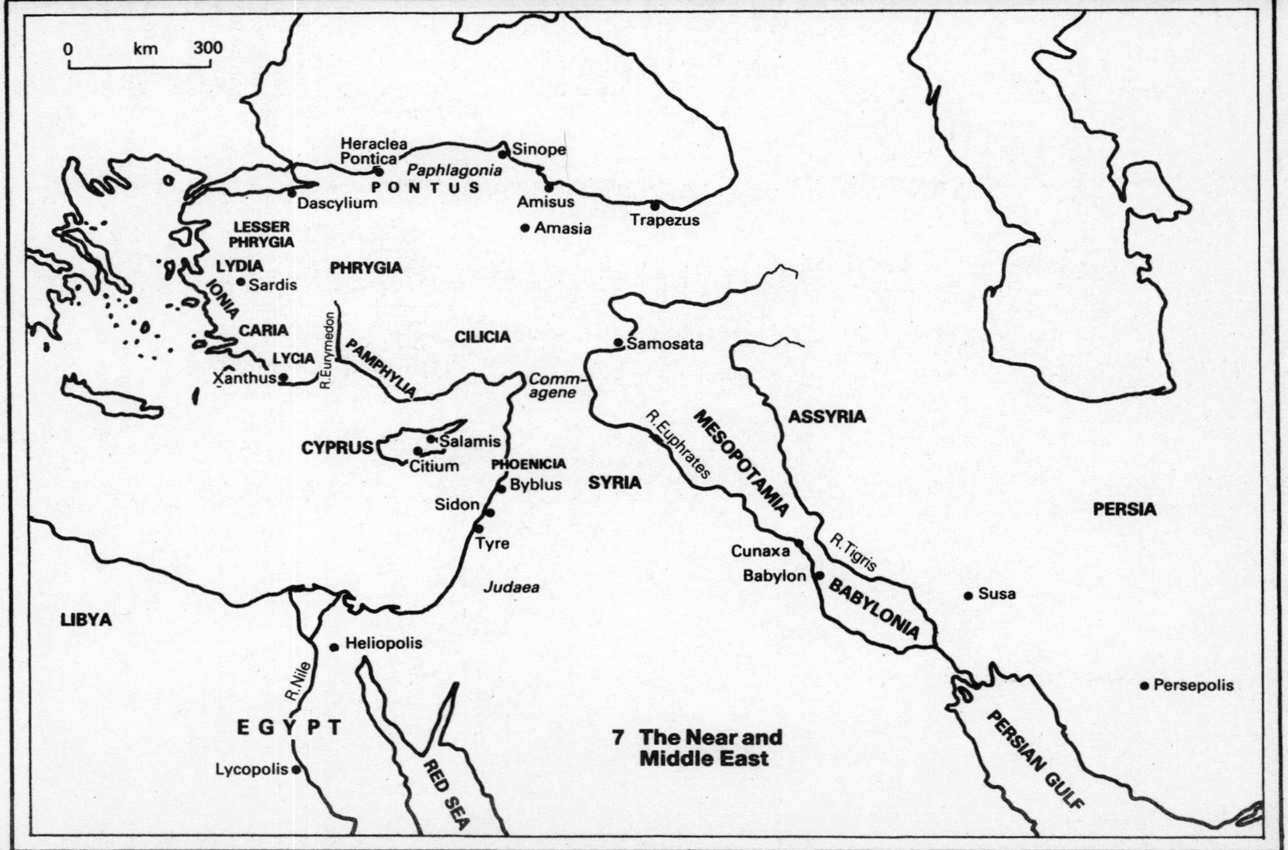

7 The Near and Middle East

APPENDIX I

PYTHAGORAS AND HIS FOLLOWERS

Born at Samos, Pythagoras emigrated in *c.*521 to Croton in south-eastern Italy. As has been shown in this book, his teachings exercised an enormous influence – especially on Plato (Chapter 31) – although, since Pythagoras never wrote his doctrines down, it is hard to disentangle them from the assertions later ascribed to him by members of his school and biographers. It seems, however, that what he professed was a disconcerting mixture of natural science (*historie*), mathematical and musical theorizing, *guru* guidance (in exhibitionist costumes) and religion or superstition.

Nature appeared to Pythagoras to be interpretable in terms of numbers, of which he inaugurated or developed or inspired the systematic investigation. Prompted by his discovery of the numerical ratios determining the principal intervals of the musical scale – and possibly also by earlier Babylonian speculations – this provocative insight elevated mathematics to a universal status, envisaging the whole of nature as a matter of countable and measurable quantity.

Pythagoras was also one of the earliest Greek thinkers, following up hints from Anaximenes and Heraclitus, to attach (ethical) significance to the human soul, thus heralding the shift, accelerated by Socrates (Chapter 21), of the centre of philosophical studies from the universe to human beings: in whom Pythagoras saw the soul as a harmonizing principle.[1] But he also – and here Indian influences, transmitted through Persia, can be detected – saw it as a fallen, polluted divinity incarcerated within the body, as in a tomb, and destined to a cycle of reincarnations (*metempsychosis*) from which it can obtain release through ritual purgation, accompanied by ascetic abstinence associated with the worship of Apollo 'the purifier'. (Indeed, Pythagoras was also said to have adopted the idea, current in Scythia and Thrace under the title of Orphism, of a process of bilocation, according to which the soul could be temporarily detached from the body.) This redemptive purification would enable the soul to achieve harmony with the order and proportion of the universe. And human beings, he maintained, could reach this goal by pure thought.

Plato represented Pythagoras as teaching a whole 'way of life'.[2] It was practised at Croton by a secret society – which took over the city's government; and similar brotherhoods temporarily seized control at Rhegium and Taras and elsewhere. At Croton, however, in the middle of the fifth century, a hostile movement burned down the local brotherhood's centre, and compelled Pythagoras to withdraw to Metapontum, where he died.

But the decline of Pythagoreanism spread and the Order in Italy was almost totally extinguished. It was revived, however, by fugitive survivors who settled at Thebes and Phlius; those at the former city included the famous Philolaus from Croton or Taras in southern Italy, who clothed Pythagorean doctrine in philosophical argument and invented or developed the school's astronomy.[3] Philolaus then led the life of a wandering philosopher, spreading Pythagorean doctrines in Sicily. It was Taras, however, which became the principal headquarters of the resuscitated order, especially under the rule of Archytas, who was visited by, and greatly affected, Plato (Chapter 26).

The membership, which was open to women as well as to men, entailed a strict ascetic discipline. But within its ranks were divergent groups, dedicated to religion and science respectively: it was the latter group which came under the leadership of Archytas (and Aristoxenus). The Hippocratic Oath may have been drawn up for a Pythagorean brotherhood (Chapter 20). Before 300, however, the Pythagorean school had vanished from view once again, only to revive as the Neo-Pythagoreanism which appeared at Rome and Alexandria in the first century BC.

APPENDIX II

WOMEN

Obviously women made the Makers of Classical Civilization who are the subject of this book – although Apollo, in the *Eumenides* of Aeschylus, saw their function as strangely passive – yet, apart from that physical role, their contribution to the civilization in question was chiefly through the imaginations of their menfolk. True, it is not easy to generalize, since far too much of our evidence comes from Athens, and since, also, their position varied considerably from one Greek state to another: at Athens, for example, women were a good deal less free than in Sparta or Crete.

In public life they played virtually no role. There are, certainly, exceptions, when they even appeared as heads of states, at least on the Greek fringes: notably Pheretime at Cyrene in the sixth century BC, and Thargelia, the widow of Antiochus in Thessaly, a little later, and the two Artemisias at Halicarnassus – not to speak of the wives or mothers of male rulers who played leading parts, such as Demarete at Syracuse and Olympias at Pella.

Yet in the city-states in general women never possessed citizenship, never held office, and took no overt part in political activities, just as in all other civilizations since the beginning of time. Deprived of control, even, over their own personal affairs, Greek women were, in terms of law, under the guardianship of a male, and enjoyed no legal right to own or dispose of property (this was where Sparta was among the exceptions). A woman's guardian was her father or, if he was dead, her male next of kin, and then, after her marriage, her husband; and in any question relating to that marriage she possessed, in law, no standing. If she had no brothers, she was married off to her nearest relative on her father's side, so as to perpetuate the family (*oikos*) into the next generation: for that was the principal task assigned to her, and for that purpose she was protected, often by stringent regulations.

Although some of the evidence is disputed today, she led a pretty secluded life, spent mostly within her home and its women's quarters; when her husband gave, or went to, a dinner party she did not accompany him, female company being provided for his entertainment by non-citizen 'companions' (*hetairai*) imported for the purpose, often cultured but, reputedly, of easy virtue, of whom the most famous was Pericles' mistress Aspasia.

Literature provides a vivid commentary on this situation. Although, in archaic times, Homer's women, if not decision-makers, played a significant background part in what was going on, and Sappho revealed the temporary existence on Lesbos of a female society that enjoyed intense emotional and practical autonomy, the extreme, obsessive, poisonous, anti-feminist malevolence of Hesiod and Semonides of Amorgos speaks for a more widespread state of affairs. For the Greek masculine world felt a nervous fear of women and of what they might be capable of doing. Indispensable for procreation though (or because) they were, they seemed a mysterious, perilous, defiling element, and their men were anxious lest they got out of line and out of step, breaking out from their ordained and domesticated niche.

And this is, very often, the implication behind their role in Greek mythology and literature. It was men who wrote nearly all of the literature, and Xenophon, for example, in his *Household Management*, offers an idealized view of the conventional picture, in which women are firmly confined to the home, and subordinate to their husbands. Plato is prepared to let them be guardians, if they are good enough, which will be rare; Aristotle sees them as irremediably inferior.

On occasion, however, more liberal attitudes had been displayed. Thus Herodotus saw the influence of women in a vast number of historical events and situations. He also dealt in a new way with the Amazons. These mythical females, who figured so prominently in classical art, represented a reversal of the correct and decorous established order, being women and yet warriors. But Herodotus married them off to the Sauromatae (Sarmatae), north of the River Tanais, in a fictitious society which laid down the appropriate functions of the two sexes, allowing neither to be entirely dominant.[4]

But the most remarkable appearance of women in the classical Greek world was their representation in tragic drama. Play after play of Aeschylus, Sophocles and Euripides presents women of widely varied characters and views, who fulfil roles which could never have been encountered in the actual contemporary life of Athens or Greece. Some of these women are noble and heroic, others are terrifying, doom-laden villains. Once again, many of them have got out of line, and are endangering man-made orderliness and regularity. This point is made clear by their equally conspicuous prominence in the Old Comedy of Aristophanes. For no less than three of his surviving plays are designed to present just such a reversal, in which the women take command, with disruptive results.

With this vast, polluting feminine entity all around them, and ready, it looked, to envelop their world, the male Greek communities provided a safety-valve. For there was one exception to the exclusion of women from public activities – and that was religion. Many of the principal deities were female: at Athens, Athena was the patron of the city. And so women were not only permitted to hold more than forty Athenian priesthoods, but were granted their own festivals and rituals, such as the Thesmophoria in honour of Demeter, in which they played a leading part, with outspoken emphasis on their role in fertility (and it was they who embroidered the robe of Athena with which she was clothed at the Panathenaea). All these officially sanctioned female participations in religion recognized that the deities had their wild, savage, untamable side – so sharply opposed to 'normal' masculine rules – and that women (by analogy with the Maenads of Dionysus) were the people who should serve this disruptive aspect of the divine world, channelling it, through officially approved festivals, into respectability.

Yet in the years before 400, and during the century that followed, attitudes were beginning to change. The change is illustrated by visual art. Female figures, *korai*, had long been a favourite sculptural form. But with very few exceptions (the flute-playing *hetaira* on the Ludovisi throne (note to Chapter 9) is one of the earliest) they had been draped. Naked girls, however, were often to be seen on fifth-century vases; and this interest in what a woman really looked like gradually widened. Zeuxis of Heraclea, planning a painting of Helen of Troy for Croton, was said to have held a parade of the local girls and chosen the best features of five of them, working from life. It was the same with the sculptors. Praxiteles' Aphrodite of Cnidus was believed to be unprecedentedly realistic (so much so that the statue prompted obscene stories). And this increased desire for physical realism, in depicting the female body, was a symptom of something else as well – a much keener interest in womanhood itself, which was to find varied expression in the Hellenistic epoch that followed.

One of the reasons why such an interest had not come earlier was because the societies of the Greek city-states, despite variations, promoted homosexual tendencies to an extent which, even in our own permissive times, remains unfamiliar. In a community whose men, engaging in politics, war, athletics or drinking parties, spent their days with members of their own sex, homosexual attitudes tended to go deeper than relations with women – as artistic emphasis on the nude male body, the *kouros*, confirms.

Indeed, at cities with old-fashioned 'heroic' social structures such as Thebes, Sparta, Elis and Thera, male partnerships – not between contemporaries but between a lover and his younger beloved – received explicit recognition. Plato made Phaedrus pronounce that the most formidable army in the world would consist of pairs of male lovers,[5] and in the fourth century just such a force was constituted, the Theban Sacred Band, which won the battle of Leuctra. Although official attitudes to the homosexual sex-act itself varied, a whole educational philosophy was built up round such relationships. In such an atmosphere the practical situation and status of women was not likely to prosper, however intensely they engaged the fantasy of the dramatists.

APPENDIX III

METICS

Metics (*metoikoi*, 'people who live with others') were resident aliens (including freed slaves) in Greek city-states. They are found in most states except Sparta, but were particularly numerous and important at Athens, from which nearly all our evidence comes – though it may be supposed that they played a considerable part in other maritime cities too, such as Corinth, Miletus and Syracuse.

They were not citizens, but they held a recognized position in the community, distinguishable from those of visiting foreigners. At Athens Solon, in the early sixth century BC, had already encouraged this class of metics, and by the time of the Persian wars their position had become fully defined. Pericles' citizen-law, by restricting citizenship to those whose father and mother were both of citizen stock, increased their number (thus reducing the proportion of the citizen-body to the total population).

Metics at Athens were obliged to have a citizen as sponsor (*prostates*), had to be registered in the deme in which they resided, and were charged an annual poll tax (*metoikion*) as well as contributions to the capital levy (*eisphora*) and other state taxes. They could also be called on to assume certain liturgies (payments for public purposes), and were liable to service in the army and navy. Metics could not contract marriages with citizens and could not own houses or land without specific legal permission. Yet they were entitled to the protection of the courts, and became eligible for a variety of privileges.

A considerable number of the artists and writers whose names have headed the chapters of this book were non-Athenians who resided at Athens as metics, although some of them subsequently obtained citizen status. Yet the metics' principal occupation arose from their debarment from owning land, for this turned them to industrial and commercial concerns instead, and meant that they became not only labourers (working side by side with citizens and slaves, for example, at the Erechtheum) but also skilled artisans, shopkeepers, traders and ship-merchants.

Thus Cephalus, the father of the orator Lysias, was induced by Pericles to move from Syracuse with his family to settle at Athens, where his weapon factory, inherited by his relatives, was the largest industrial establishment of which we know. Xenophon, in his *Ways and Means*, insisted that the Athenian metics should be increased in number and fostered, as a prime source of

Athenian economic activity and revenue.

But the greatest contribution of the metics to classical civilization was through the institution of banking. This, in a rudimentary form, had in earlier times been in the hands of temple priests; but already before 500 BC much of this business had been taken over by money-changers who set up their 'tables' (*trapezai*, hence their name of *trapezitai*) in the market-places and at festivals. In the fourth century they became bankers, dealing with loans, mortgages and deposits, although they combined this occupation (to cover its high risks) with manufacturing and commerce; so that Athens, because of its banks, became the principal money-market of Greece.

The wealthiest of the city's metic-bankers and manufacturers was Pasion (d. 370), a former slave, whose activities – typical of an age when store was set by professional expertise – are known from speeches of Demosthenes and the *Trapeziticus* of Isocrates. Pasion presented the city with various gifts, including a thousand bronze shields from his factory, and lent money to the general Timotheus (373, 372), free of interest, to gain his favour. He also alleged that his bank made extensive loans to a young man from the Tauric Chersonese (Cimmerian Bosphorus), though the youth denied receiving them. Finally Pasion was made an Athenian citizen.

APPENDIX IV

BETWEEN FREE MEN AND SLAVES

'Between free men and slaves' was the name given by Pollux (Part I, note 9) to the large categories of certain Greek city-state populations which fell short of citizenship, but were above the status of slavery, and can loosely, though somewhat anachronistically, be described as serfs. The designation of 'helots' is also applied to them, since that is what they were called at Sparta, while somewhat similar categories of inhabitants – although with differing degrees of unfreedom and under their own peculiar names – also existed at Argos, the cities of Crete and Thessaly, Sicyon, Corinth, Megara, Heraclea Pontica, Byzantium, Syracuse and the Cimmerian Bosphorus.

The helot system in Laconia seems to have developed when Dorian Sparta emerged after the breakdown of the Mycenaean civilization, and it was extended westwards, throughout Messenia, by conquest. The subjugated peoples in these territories, presumably for the most part of non-Dorian origin, belonged to the Spartan state,[6] which tied them to the soil and assigned them to individual citizens (Spartiates), to cultivate their estates. The masters of these helots could neither free them nor sell them, but were entitled to receive from them a tribute equal to one-half of the produce of the holding. This paid, the helots were permitted to keep the surplus for themselves, and to possess property of their own, within a family and even community framework. They attended their masters on campaigns and served as light-armed troops, and as oarsmen.

The problem was, however, that they outnumbered the Spartiates, if not by the seven to one ratio indicated by Herodotus, at least to a very considerable extent – most conspicuously in Messenia; but in Laconia, too, they may well have been more numerous than the rest of the non-slave population, including not only the Spartans but also the less privileged 'dwellers round about' (*perioeci*).

This meant that the task of keeping the helots down, and forestalling any attempts at rebellion, dominated the whole of Sparta's history (from the First and Second Messenian Wars of the eighth and seventh centuries onwards), and was the prime cause of the Spartiates' austere, military way of life, which was concentrated on the unending need for repression. This repression was implemented by a secret police (*krypteia*) and the ephors every year, on entering office, dramatically declared war on the helots, so that they could be killed at any time without violating religious scruple.

Throughout the period this anxious Spartiate preoccupation made itself felt on a number of critical occasions. The principal reason why Pausanias, the victor of Plataea, was put to death (469/466) was because he was suspected, rightly or wrongly, of inciting the helots to revolt (having promised those who were soldiers citizenship before Plataea – or so some alleged). Then a serious helot rebellion, the Third Messenian War, broke out (*c.*465/464–461/460 or mid-450s), and the Spartans sent their Athenian allies home, suspecting that they might co-operate with the rebels. Thus Sparta's friendship with Athens was destroyed.

During the Peloponnesian War the defeat of the Spartans at Sphacteria (Pylos) in Messenia caused them to fear a renewal of such uprisings – whereupon they 'freed' two thousand helots, who had served them particularly well in the war, and then assassinated them secretly, in order to remove potential dissident leaders. In the Peace of Nicias with Athens in 421, the Spartans stipulated that their allies should come to their help in the event of a helot revolt.

At this juncture, or a little earlier, we begin to hear of another Spartan category known as *neodamodeis*, who were new citizens, but, being ex-helots, still lacked political rights; many of them enrolled as volunteers in the army, in which they were employed for overseas or other faraway expeditions. Other subordinate classes that came into existence at Sparta were the Inferiors (*hypomeiones*), who had failed to pay their mess bills, thus losing their Spartan citizenship, and the *mothakes* or *mothones*, who were either the sons of Spartan fathers and helot mothers, or the sons of Inferiors.

An alarming event occurred at Sparta in 397, when Cinadon, probably an Inferior, was arrested for plotting with other Inferiors, helots, *neodamodeis* and *perioikoi*, and was executed along with his associates.[7] The incident showed up the fears felt by the small and diminishing number of the Spartiates, but did not, in the end, present a grave practical danger, since the majority of the unprivileged populations still remained loyal; and Agesilaus II, who had recently become king, felt secure enough to set out for Asia Minor. But he took with him (under a military council of thirty Spartans) two thousand *neodamodeis*; perhaps he was deliberately getting them out of the way.

Sparta lost its helots in Messenia when Epaminondas of Thebes liberated that country in *c.*370. But the system continued in Laconia.

APPENDIX V

SLAVES

The Greeks, as we have seen, were able to achieve what they did only because they enjoyed the leisure that made this possible. Unemployed leisure, therefore, was explicitly appreciated,[8] and although Plato's and Aristotle's distaste for physical labour was never typical, a Greek wanted to have enough to live on without working. For the concept of labour as a saleable market commodity, the idea of 'work for work's sake', was absent. And if you did have to work, observed Aristotle, 'a free man should not live for the benefit of another'.[9]

Nevertheless, it was not until the fifth century that poor, free, unskilled workers ceased to predominate numerically over slaves. All earlier states had been slave-owning, to various extents, and so were the Greeks, who from this time onwards displayed this institution to an unprecedented degree. Slaves, it is true, although essential, never became more than a subsidiary element in Greek economics; at the Erechtheum, for example, as in small specialist house-factories, they worked alongside citizens and metics (Appendix III). Yet the Greeks, despite the simplicity of their way of life, would have been badly off without them.

Numbers are very uncertain, but there may have been between 60,000 and 100,000 slaves in fifth-century Athens, representing rather more than a quarter of the population. Most slaves were foreigners, inexpensive to buy. The politician and general Nicias exceptionally owned a thousand. Sixteen slaves belonging to a contemporary metic, Cephisodorus of the Piraeus, included five from Thrace, two each from Caria and Illyria and Syria, and one each from Lydia, Cappadocia and Colchis.[10]

Slaves often owned slaves of their own, and received some education. A play of Pherecrates, we are told by Athenaeus, was called the *Slaves' School-Teacher* (*Doulodidaskalos*); and domestic schools for slaves existed at Syracuse.[11] Nevertheless, they were the property of their masters, dependent upon them in every sphere of life, and if liberation ever came their way, it came only as their master's free gift. In point of rights, slaves were no better than his tools (except that they could make him frightened). It would have been foolish to damage one's tools, so they were sometimes, or often, treated decently; in the comic drama, they appear as human but slightly ridiculous figures. But although the Scythian state slaves who served as Athenian police were no doubt adequately looked after, the treatment of those who worked in the silver mines of Laurium was deplorable.

Plato thought that slaves are born to slavery, and are better off as slaves, and Aristotle, too, propounded a doctrine portraying slavery as natural.

Others such as the fourth-century rhetorician and sophist Alcidamas of Elaea in Aeolis, in more progressive tones, denied this (especially when it was a question of Greeks enslaving Greeks). But the practice continued; and the classical achievement had owed much to it.

REFERENCES

PART I: WARS AGAINST EXTERNAL ENEMIES

1 Herodotus, VI, 137f.
2 Ibid., VI, 112.
3 Plutarch, *Themistocles*, 4, 1.
4 Ibid., 3, 4.
5 Ibid., 10, 4.
6 Thucydides, I, 74.
7 Plutarch, *Themistocles*, 15, 2.
8 Thucydides, I, 138.
9 Pollux, *Onomasticon*, III, 83; Strabo, VIII, 5, 4.
10 Diogenes Laertius, I, 168.
11 Herodotus, IX, 64.
12 Thucydides, I, 138.
13 *Supplementum Epigraphicum Graecum*, XXIII, 252–3; Pindar, *Pythians*, I, 72.
14 Herodotus, VII, 156.

PART II: BETWEEN THE WARS: FIRST PHASE

1 Plutarch, *Cimon*, 12, 1.
2 Pindar, *Olympians*, VIII, 67–9.
3 Athenaeus, VIII, 347e.
4 Plato, *Cratylus*, 402a.
5 Parmenides, fragment 1, line 22.
6 Plato, *Phaedo*, 98b; Aristotle, *Metaphysics*, I, 985a.
7 Aristotle, *On Generation and Corruption*, I, 325a2.
8 Pausanias, V, 8.
9 Ibid., X, 25–31.
10 Aristotle, *Poetics*, 2, 1448a.

PART III: THE PERICLEAN AGE

1 Thucydides, II, 65.
2 Aristotle, *Rhetoric*, III, 1411a; Plutarch, *Pericles*, 8.
3 Thucydides, I, 70.
4 Ibid., I, 76.
5 B. D. Merritt, H. T. Wade-Gery, M. F. McGregor, *The Athenian Tribute Lists* (1939–53).
6 Thucydides, I, 23ff.
7 Ibid., II, 47ff.
8 Ibid., II, 41.
9 Ibid., II, 37.
10 Plato, *Gorgias*, 515c.
11 Tacitus, *Annals*, XI, 24.
12 Plato, *Protagoras*, 317b.
13 Diogenes Laertius, IX, 54.
14 Plato, *Theaetetus*, 152a; cf. 166d.
15 Diogenes Laertius, XI, 51.
16 Plato, *Protagoras*, 322a–d.
17 Ibid., 337c.
18 Gorgias, *Olympicus*; cf. *Epitaphios*, fragment B5b.
19 Plato, *Gorgias*, 483, 491f.
20 Ibid., *Republic*, I, 343b.
21 Hecataeus, *Histories*, fragment 1.
22 Herodotus, I, preface.
23 Plutarch, *On the Malice of Herodotus* (*De Malignitate Herodoti*), 857a.
24 Herodotus, VII, 152.
25 Petronius, *Satyricon*, 88; Pliny the elder, *Natural History*, XXXIV, 58.
26 Pliny the elder, *Natural History*, XXXIV, 59; Diogenes Laertius, VIII, 46.
27 Pliny the elder, *Natural History*, XXXIV, 55.
28 Pausanias, II, 17, 4; Strabo, VIII, 372.
29 Plutarch, *Pericles*, 12.
30 Diodorus Siculus, XI, 29, 2; Lycurgus, *Leocrates*, 81.
31 Theopompus, F. Jacoby, *Fragmente der Griechischen Historiker*, p. 569, no. 115 (fragment 153).
32 Pausanias, I, 24, 7.
33 Ibid., V, 11, 1ff.
34 Quintilian, *Training of an Orator*, XII, 10, 9.

PART IV: THE PELOPONNESIAN WAR

1 Thucydides, III, 86.
2 Ibid., IV, 58–64.
3 Ibid., VI–VII.
4 Ibid., VI, 77.

5 Ibid., VII, 87.
6 Sophocles, *Antigone*, 332.
7 Ibid., *Oedipus at Colonus*, 913f.
8 Euripides, *Hippolytus*, 612; Aristophanes, *Thesmophoriazusae*, 275f.
9 Ibid., *Trojan Women*, 885–6.
10 Aristotle, *Poetics*, 15, 1454a.
11 Euripides, *Hecuba*, 1187–91.
12 Aristotle, *Poetics*, 13, 1453a.
13 Plato, *Phaedrus*, 270c–d.
14 Aristotle, *Metaphysics*, XIII, 4, 1078b, 3; *Sophistical Refutations*, 34, 183b; Plato, *Theaetetus*, 149a.
15 Aristophanes, *Frogs*, 1491–9: *cf.* Plato, *Gorgias*, 485d.
16 Plato, *Apology*, 31d (sign), 38a (unexamined life).
17 Ibid., 23c.
18 Ibid., *Euthyphro*, 2b.
19 Xenophon, *Memoirs*, I, 1, Favorinus in Diogenes Laertius, II, 40.
20 Xenophon, *Apology*, 30–1.
21 Pliny the elder, *Natural History*, XXXV, 60 (tr. H. Rackham).
22 Plato, *Republic*, II, 365c; *Critias*, 407c; *Phaedo*, 69b.
23 Pliny the elder, *op. cit.*, XXXV, 61.
24 Ibid., XXXV, 62.
25 Ibid., XXXV, 63 (tr. H. Rackham).
26 Ibid., XXXV, 68.
27 Thucydides, I, 1.
28 Ibid., I, 22.
29 Ibid., II, 61, 64.
30 Ibid., I, 22.
31 Ibid.
32 Diodorus Siculus, XIV, 13, 2.

PART V: FIRST HALF OF THE FOURTH CENTURY: WEST AND EAST

1 Diodorus Siculus, XIV, 41, 46.
2 Isocrates, *Letters*, 2, 3.
3 M.N. Tod, *Greek Historical Inscriptions*, 108 (393 BC), 133 (368 BC), 136 (367 BC).
4 Herodotus, III, 136.
5 Diogenes Laertius, VIII, 82.
6 Aeschines, *Against Ctesiphon*, 171; Craterus in F. Jacoby, *Fragmente der Griechischen Historiker*, 342f, 8.
7 *Inscriptiones Graecae*, I, 2nd edn, 91; W. Dittenberger, *Sylloge Inscriptionum Graecarum*, 3rd edn, 91.
8 Demosthenes, *Against Leptines*, 32–5.
9 Ibid., 36.

10 E. L. Hicks and G. F. Hill, *Manual of Greek Historical Inscriptions*, 111.
11 Strabo, VII, 10.
12 Herodotus, VIII, 87–8.
13 Vitruvius, II, 8, 11 (tr. B. Ashmole).
14 Lucian, *Dialogues of the Dead*, 24.
15 Pliny the elder, *Natural History*, XXXVI, 31.
16 H. Diels, *Abhandlungen der Preussischen Akademie der Wissenschaften zu Berlin*, 1904, pp. 7f.
17 Pliny the elder, *op. cit.*
18 Pausanias, VIII, 45.
19 *Inscriptiones Graecae*, V, 2, 89.
20 Vitruvius, VII, preface 13.

PART VI: FIRST HALF OF THE FOURTH CENTURY: THE GREEK MAINLAND

1 Pausanias, XI, 13, 3ff.
2 Xenophon, *Hellenica*, VII, 23.
3 Pausanias, XI, 15, 4 etc.
4 Xenophon, *Hiero*, 5, 4.
5 Arrian, *Cynegeticus*, 5, 6.
6 Aristoxenus, fragment 55.
7 Aristophanes, *Thesmophoriazusae*, 101ff.
8 Plato, *Republic*, IV, 440d.
9 Plato, *Laws*, X, 909a.
10 Ibid., I, 626a.
11 Isocrates, *Antidosis*, preface.
12 Pliny the elder, *Natural History*, XXXV, 133.
13 Pseudo-Lucian, *Loves*, 13; Lucian, *Images*, 4.
14 Pausanias, V, 17.

PART VII: THE END OF CLASSICAL GREECE

1 Diodorus Siculus, XVI, 70 (cf. 19); Plutarch, *Timoleon*, 22 and 37.
2 Plutarch, *Timoleon*, 37.
3 Ibid., *Advice on Public Life*, 2, 816e; *Self-Praise Without Offence*, 2, 542e (*automatia*).
4 Diodorus Siculus, XVII, 2, 3.
5 Cf. Aristotle, *Politics*, VI, 1311b.
6 Theopompus, F. Jacoby, *Fragmente der Griechischen Historiker*, p. 541, no. 115 (fragment 27).
7 Demosthenes, *On the Crown*, 60, 72 etc.
8 Plutarch, *Demosthenes*, 13.

9 Ibid., 14, 20 and 25; Athenaeus, VIII, 341f, 483e; Hyperides, *Against Demosthenes*, end.
10 Aristotle, *Metaphysics*, VII, 2, 1028b; cf. Speusippus, fragment 33a.
11 Aristotle, *Metaphysics*, VII, 1, 1026a.
12 Idem, *Posterior Analytics*, 83a 33.
13 Idem, *On the Generation of Animals*, III, 10, 760b.
14 Idem, *Nicomachean Ethics*, III, 1002a.
15 Ibid., x, 1177b 33.
16 Ibid., II, 1106a–b.
17 Idem, *Politics*, I, 2, 1253a.
18 Ibid., VII, 1328b 37, 1329a.
19 Idem, *Poetics*, 9, 1452a.
20 Cicero, *Academica*, II, 119.
21 Aristotle, *On Generation and Corruption*, 3160, 9.

EPILOGUE

1 Herodotus, IX, 122; Pseudo-Hippocrates, *Airs, Waters and Places* (*De Aeribus*), 3ff.
2 Pseudo-Hippocrates, *op. cit.*, 24.
3 Isocrates, *Panegyricus*, 50.
4 Herodotus, VIII, 125; Plato, *Republic*, I, 4, 329e.
5 Thucydides, II, 40.
6 Plato, *Laws*, I, 626a.

APPENDICES

1 Porphyrius, *Life of Pythagoras*, 19 ('immortal'), etc.
2 Plato, *Republic*, x, 600a–b.
3 Aristotle, *On the Sky*, B13, 293a 18; Aetius, II, 7, 7.
4 Herodotus, IV, 113–16.
5 Plato, *Symposium*, 178c–179a.
6 Strabo, VIII, 5, 4, 365.
7 Xenophon, *Hellenica*, III, 4–11.
8 Aristotle, *Politics*, VIII, 2, 4, 1337b.
9 Ibid., *Rhetoric*, 1367a, 22.
10 Athenaeus, VI, 262b; Aristotle, *Politics*, I, 1255b, 22.
11 D. M. Lewis and R. Meiggs (eds), *A Selection of Greek Historical Inscriptions to the End of the Fifth Century* BC, 1988 (no. 79 in 1969 edition).

NOTES

PART I: WARS AGAINST EXTERNAL ENEMIES

CHAPTER 1: MILTIADES: VICTOR AT MARATHON

Persia: the Persians were the first regional planners and systematic road-builders.

Marathon invasion: the Persians treated Athens' intervention in the Ionian revolt as a rebellion, since the city had allegedly acknowledged Persian suzerainty in 507.

Sparta: possibly there was a Messenian revolt in 490.

Marathon: according to a rival version it was the Persians, not the Greeks, who started the battle.

Miltiades in 489 had not told the Assembly he was going to attack Paros.

CHAPTER 2: THEMISTOCLES: VICTOR AT SALAMIS

Aegina: the war started shortly before 500 and lasted intermittently until 481.

Ostracism meant that the checking of ambition was transferred from the Areopagus Council to the people. Themistocles may have been behind some of the ostracisms from 487 onwards.

Murder of Persian envoys (481): probably Themistocles wanted to cause a fatal breach.

'Panhellenic' Congress (481): military alliance without time limit, based on oath, not treaty.

Shipbuilding was one of the first Athenian industries to expand significantly; another was mining. For the trireme see *The Rise of the Greeks*, pp. 86f.

Artemisium: two storms damaged the Persian fleet, which could not thereafter risk any diversion, e.g. against the Peloponnese.

Troezen:an Athenian 'decree' of Themistocles, found there, contradicts the picture of hasty evacuation, but is probably a later and partly fictitious composition, conflating various separate measures misleadingly.

Themistocles' threat to flee west (to Siris) before Salamis; his daughters' names (Sybaris, Italia) indicate Italian connections. Stories of an enigmatic Delphic oracle ('rely on wooden walls') are dubious, but Delphi evidently did not support the Greek side in the conflict.

Themistocles' death: reports of remorseful suicide are suspect.

His individualism: see Chapter 14 for a portrait.

CHAPTER 3: PAUSANIAS: VICTOR AT PLATAEA

Spartan system: division into messes (*syssitia*).

Plataea: the half-hearted incompetence of the Athenian contingent imposed a heavy strain on Pausanias.

His 'Medism' (*c.*477): he was said to have hoped for marriage with the daughter of Darius I's nephew Megabates, and for the Persian command against the Greeks.

CHAPTER 4: GELON AND HIERO I: VICTORS AT HIMERA AND CUMAE

Phoenicians: inhabitants of an area approximating to the modern Lebanon, speaking a Semitic language. Following the ancient example of Byblus, Tyre and Sidon replaced the Mycenaeans as the principal seafaring and trading powers of the eastern Mediterranean from the tenth century BC onwards. After the establishment of the Persian empire in the sixth century the fleets of these Phoenician city-states, serving under their own monarchs, formed the backbone of the Great King's navy. Their relations with their Sicilian and Sardinian colonies were probably loose. Since their island settlements took no land, but concentrated on trading, they remained on good terms with the natives of the hinterland.

Hippocrates succeeded Cleander at Gela (*c*.498) and in 494 conquered Leontini (where the first Sicilian dictator had established himself in 615/609).

Carthage ('Kart-Hadasht', the New City), located upon a peninsula in the Gulf of Tunis and possessing a spacious port (later supplemented by two artificial harbours), had been established in 814 BC – though some prefer an eighth-century date – by settlers from Tyre. Asserting its independence in the seventh century, Carthage began to bring other Phoenician centres in the western and eastern Mediterranean under its control or influence. For a long time its settlements in Sicily seem to have maintained a defensive rather than aggressive attitude towards the Greek city-states of the island, until Carthage decided upon invasion in 480.

Syracusan under-privileged: notably the helot-like Kyllyrioi.

Metal-supplies essential to Carthage: mercenaries demanded to be paid in gold and silver.

Himera: the battle was celebrated by the poet Simonides of Ceos. War-prisoners built the temples at Acragas.

Etruscan city-states: Tarquinii, Caere, Veii, Vulci, Vetulonia (with Populonia), Rusellae, Volaterrae, Clusium (and its offshoots Volsinii and Arretium).

Cumae (Cyme), beyond the northern extremity of the gulf named after it (the Bay of Naples), had been converted from a Euboean (Chalcidian) trading-post into a colony, and independent city-state in *c*.730/725. Before clashing with the Etruscans Cumae had taught them the alphabet and perhaps the cultivation of the olive and vine.

Aricia in Latium, on a spur at the foot of Mount Albanus, was a town with powerful legendary associations which assumed the leadership of the Latin communities in the seventh century, and, shortly after organizing resistance to the last king of Rome (Tarquinius Superbus), helped Aristodemus to repel the second Etruscan attack (506/504).

Sicilian dictators: no names or portraits of Gelon, Hiero I or Theron appear on the coins of their cities, i.e. they did not claim to be monarchs.

PART II: BETWEEN THE WARS: FIRST PHASE

CHAPTER 5: CIMON: CREATOR OF EMPIRE

Delian League: probably Athens and each individual member (there may have been about 150 in 458/457) were equal in voting power. After his first assessment of the allies' tribute Aristides virtually disappears from history. The Delian League created whole new industrial classes at Athens.

Suppressions of recalcitrant 'allies' by Athens were often followed by the installation of democracies.

Eurymedon (?469/468): Cimon had built stronger, broader, fully-decked triremes to carry more hoplites.

Ennea Hodoi (forerunner of Amphipolis): failed Athenian settlement in *c*.465.

Building at Athens: it is disputed whether the principal buildings in the Agora are attributable to Cimon, Ephialtes or Pericles.

Ephialtes' reforms: the nine archons lost their first-instance jurisdiction to the lawcourts (*dikasteria*).

The Spartans had already disapproved of Athens' suppression of Thasos, which they were prevented from helping by earthquake and revolts.

War of 460–445: 'First Peloponnesian War', cf. note on Chapter 11.

CHAPTER 6: PINDAR: THE OLD VALUES

Simonides, said to have been close to Themistocles, probably created the choral lyric as an art-form, composing for Athenian competitions like his nephew Bacchylides.

Athletic victors addressed in Pindar's forty-five surviving poems include eleven Aeginetans. Horses and breeders are praised, but never a jockey or charioteer.

Pindar's religion: he is impressed by the Pythagorean beliefs in the afterlife, purgation and transmigration (see Appendix 1).

Pindar out of fashion by the time of the comic dramatist Eupolis (first play 429).

CHAPTER 7: AESCHYLUS: GODS AND HUMAN BEINGS

Origins of tragedy: Corinth, Sicyon, Megara: at Athens, embryonic tragic plays were first produced with the façade of the old Temple of Dionysus as background. In the early fifth century the stands collapsed, and the auditorium was transferred to the Theatre of Dionysus. Shortly after 500 a second actor was added (a third in *c.*460).

Satyr plays, with wild satyrs as chorus: amoral, humorous, pathetic: usually set in the remote countryside.

Tragedies lost: out of about 150 known dramatists, plays by only three have survived (and only 32 out of about 300 that they wrote). Analyses of the many lost plays, though sometimes rewarding, remain too conjectural to be attempted here.

Fall of Miletus: by Phrynichus (= his *Phoenician Women*?) – forerunner of Aeschylus' *Persians*; probably *c.*476 rather than *c.*490.

The Oresteia. The tragedians do not distinguish carefully between Mycenae and Argos, and interchange them.

CHAPTER 8: PARMENIDES: AND THREE REACTIONS

Parmenides and others: he owed the idea of a philosophical poem to Xenophanes and was probably critical of Heraclitus (*The Rise of the Greeks*, pp. 242ff., 171ff.)

The One was perhaps identified by Parmenides with Light.

Empedocles: 'inventor of rhetoric' – i.e. taught Gorgias. As statesman at Acragas, he was said to have helped to break up the oligarchic Thousand after the expulsion of the tyrant Thrasydaeus (son of Theron), drawing up a democratic constitution. He was also considered the founder of the Sicilian school of medicine (incorporating Love and Strife as physiological opposites; later they were interpreted as Good and Evil).

Prosecution of Anaxagoras under Decree of Diopeithes (433/432 or 432/431; probably not *c.*450), proposing the impeachment of those who taught dangerous doctrines about the heavenly bodies; Anaxagoras had pronounced that the sun was a fiery ball larger than the Peloponnese. He was said to have escaped to Lampsacus and founded a school there.

Mind of Anaxagoras: human mind should rule the state as Mind rules the world, but Plato and Aristotle saw his universal mind as a mere cranking device to keep the machine running, undirected towards any specific end or purpose (*telos*).

Democritus' versatility: his Fragments (not all genuine) include many of an ethical or political nature, including an advocacy of aid by the rich to the poor. His ideal of *euthumie* (good spirits, from temperate enjoyment) foreshadowed Hellenistic *ataraxia* (imperturbable peace of mind, *From Alexander to Cleopatra*, s.v.); and his analyses of Chance (Fortune) likewise influenced later thinkers.

Democritus' fame: his disciple Nausiphanes had a school at Teos, of which Abdera was a colony. But 'I came to Athens', said Democritus, 'and no one knew me.' Plato disliked his materialism; and his atomic theory (from which the nature and motives of modern atomism

Democritus' fame—cont
are distinct) never led, in antiquity, to more advanced scientific investigation. But Galileo and Descartes revived his geometrical concept of the universe, and the first publication of Karl Marx was on Democritus.

Zeno defended Parmenides against (1) common sense, (2) the rival, mathematically based system of the Pythagoreans (Appendix 1).

Melissus was the purveyor of Parmenidean doctrine to whom the atomists paid most attention; and he shaped its presentation by Plato and Aristotle.

CHAPTER 9: THE OLYMPIA MASTER: EARLY CLASSICAL TEMPLE SCULPTURE

Aphaea, Aeginetan goddess, was identified with Dictynna and Britomartis, and similar to Artemis.

Early Classical (Severe) sculpture rejects archaic surface elaboration in favour of a greater sense of three-dimensional volume.

The Ludovisi and Boston thrones (*c*.475/450) (not strictly temple sculpture, but perhaps balustrades surrounding the sacred pit of Persephone at Locri Epizephyrii (in south-east Italy), show friezes by artists who were perhaps local but may, instead, have come from the Greek mainland or from eastern Greece. Despite questionings, both thrones seem authentic; the Boston throne is not so well executed, but has more sense of the third dimension.

CHAPTER 10: POLYGNOTUS: THE PAINTING REVOLUTION

The shrine of Theseus at Athens (*c*.475, to house his alleged bones from Scyros) contained wall-paintings which may have influenced the west pediment at Olympia.

'Better than they are': Pliny's comment on Polygnotus' human beings – or did he mean 'better than ourselves'?

'Makers' of pottery, who sign more often than painters: manufacturers or operatives?

Lekythoi (oil-flasks): fully polychrome, perhaps closer than red-figure to wall-paintings; their subject matter recalls carved grave-reliefs. Fine white-ground cups (*c*.460) are signed by the potter Sotades, who may also have been their painter.

PART III: THE PERICLEAN AGE

CHAPTER 11: PERICLES: IMPERIAL DEMOCRACY

Generalship: Pericles was outshone as general by Myronides and Tolmides.

Cimon: Pericles had earlier been quite close to him.

Piraeus: designed by the famous town-planner and political theorist Hippodamus of Miletus, who later designed Thurii.

War of 460–445: sometimes known as the 'First Peloponnesian War'.

Athenian over-commitment: an inscription of 459 names 'those who fell in the same year in Cyprus, Egypt, Phoenicia, Halieis, Aegina and Megara'.

Oenophyta (457) broke the Boeotian League, and all its cities except Thebes came temporarily under Athenian control.

Five Years' Truce between Athens and Sparta (451). Athens momentarily retained its gains in central Greece, but sacrificed its alliance with Argos, which made a Thirty Years' Peace with Sparta.

Peace of Callias (449/448). No Persian king would officially sponsor such a bilateral treaty, but satraps might establish peace in their own areas. Callias was Cimon's brother-in-law.

Crisis in Athenian empire: probably tribute was not collected in 448, but was resumed in 447 (the 446 lists were numbered as though there had been no interruption).

Samian revolt (440/439): by supporting the oligarchs (and accepting Athenian prisoners), Pissuthnes, who was probably a grandson or nephew of Xerxes I, had seemingly infringed the Peace of Callias – perhaps without specific approval of his king.

Amphipolis (437/436, replacing the failed settlement of *c*.465 at Ennea Hodoi (Nine Roads)), guarded the only practical crossing of the River Strymon. A colony was also founded at Brea, a little to the south-west, in the 440s or 430s.

Black Sea: Pericles colonized Amisus and placed settlers at Sinope. See also Chapter 27.

Incidents leading to Peloponnesian War: Athens' punitive Megarian decrees (*c.*439/438?); Corcyra; Potidaea.

Plague (430–427): identification uncertain: typhus, bubonic plague, measles, smallpox, typhoid, scarlet fever, ergotism or influenza allowing the growth of staphylococcus bacteria?

Restrictions on Athens' subjects: 'Papyrus Decree' of 450/449 tranferred 5,000 talents from the League treasury to the Treasury of Athena; the Callias Decrees (434?) and the Methone Decrees (430/429–424/423) tried to make the Aegean a closed sea: the Clearchus Decree (*c.*450/446 or in 420s?) required allies to use Athenian weights, measures and silver coins. Pericles' abortive summoning of a Panhellenic congress in 449/448 rests on dubious evidence.

Pay: by the end of the fifth century attendance at the Athenian Assembly was paid.

Pericles' Citizen Law (451/450) would have deprived Cimon of citizenship if he had not died almost immediately.

CHAPTER 12: PROTAGORAS: UNSETTLING SOPHISTS

Higher education developed by the sophists: but some pupils were in their early teens.

Physis–nomos: either *nomos* is an unjustified shackle on *physis*, or (according to the contradictory view) *physis* is violent and uncontrolled, and *nomos* the means to civilization.

Political doctrines of Protagoras: Aristoxenus believed that Plato's *Republic* was almost entirely owed to Protagoras, and he has been credited (exaggeratedly?) with the first theoretical formulation of democratic theory.

The gods of Protagoras: following an old tradition of constantly reinterpreting religion, he saw it as an anthropological fact significant in human civilization.

'Man is the Measure' protested against Parmenides' denial of the perceived world's reality; it could also be interpreted as undermining the transcendental status of the aristocracy.

Antilogiae: Protagoras also wrote on *Orthoepeia*, Correctness of Diction.

Hippias was the first systematic collector of earlier opinions (*Synagoge*), and founded the study of chronology.

Gorgias was brought up on the first handbooks of rhetorical technique, produced by Corax and Tisias in the 460s. He was also taught by the 'founder of rhetoric' Empedocles, i.e. he was instructed how to control the rhythms of prose, by analogy with verse.

Prodicus: a recently discovered papyrus ascribes to him the paradox that it is impossible to contradict – a view that probably goes back to Protagoras.

Thrasymachus: the gods neglect justice because they do not see what is going on.

CHAPTER 13: HERODOTUS: THE NEW ART OF HISTORY

Forerunners of history: historical monographs, some dealing with contemporary affairs, had already been written in the early fifth century; Persia was a favourite theme, and Lydia, too, was a subject. Scylax of Caryanda composed some sort of a biographical work in *c.*480 and then Ion of Chios developed the *genre*, as well as writing local history.

Herodotus and Athens. He knew, and was influenced by, Protagoras (they were both sent by Athens to Thurii (444/443). Herodotus' emphasis on the *physis – nomos* contrast reflects his contact with sophists at Athens.

CHAPTER 14: TO THE RIACE MASTER AND POLYCLITUS: THE MALE NUDE

Invasion of Xerxes I (480): destruction of monuments on the Acropolis, after which the Greeks levelled its surface with the remains of the sculpture, etc., left by the sack.

Delphic Charioteer: a base signed by Sotadas the Boeotian, found nearby, seems not to belong to the figure.

Portraits: a head wrongly believed to

Portraits—cont
represent Leonidas probably formed part of a pedimental group of the 480s. There are fifth-century coin-portraits of the Lycian monarchs Khäräi (stylized) and Päriklä (facing). Coin of Abdera (Thrace): head of moneyer Pythagoras. Gem (scaraboid jasper, at Boston Museum), by outstanding master Dexamenus: quasi-portrait of bearded man (*c.*440/430).

Myron: pupil of bronze-caster Ageladas of Argos.

Polyclitus: his *symmetria* was influenced by the Pythagorean doctrine of the ultimate reality of numbers (Appendix 1). His Diadumenus has richer and more plastic hair than his Doryphorus. The Hera was probably by the same Polyclitus, though this supposition gives him a long career.

CHAPTER 15: ICTINUS AND PHIDIAS: THE PARTHENON

Athena Polias (guardian of the land) and Parthenos (agrarian mother goddess, warrior maiden) were originally separate but fused by the fifth century.

Parthenon was not built to relieve unemployment (as Plutarch). In its final phase there were eighty-six workmen (twenty-four citizens, forty-two metics and twenty slaves).

Pentelic marble: finely grained, thickly crystallized, glossy, could be chiselled into sharp, undercut edges.

Ictinus at Bassae used all three Orders: his Corinthian capital on a free-standing column is one of the earliest known.

Entasis: three theories: compensation, exaggeration and tension (i.e. in the mind of the viewer, between what one expects to see and sees). Its absence makes the Hephaesteum ('Theseum') in the smiths' quarter (*c.*449/448–430s) less vibrant and alive.

Athenian festivals: numerous, and emotionally inspiring: especially the six major festivals.

Athena Parthenos: her statue stood in the east room of the Parthenon: the west room contained the Treasury.

Propylaea: ceilings of marble beams and deeply coffered slabs, painted in blue and gold.

Erechtheum: housed an ancient olive-wood statue of Athena Polias, removed to safety during Xerxes I's invasion (480).

PART IV
THE PELOPONNESIAN WAR

CHAPTER 16: HERMOCRATES: SAVIOUR OF THE WESTERN GREEKS

Syracusan Republic: large silver coins (decadrachms, 'Demareteia') not of *c.*480 as supposed but perhaps 460s (or late 470s?). Sophron, much admired by Plato, gave literary form to the mime.

Petalismos: exile for five years, not ten (as ostracism).

Leontini and Rhegium: Athens' treaties renewed 433/432.

After the Conference of Gela (424): Athenian generals Pythodorus and Sophocles (not the dramatist) exiled, Eurymedon fined.

Cleon: called 'Tanner' because he owned shops in which tanning was undertaken. He was a clever, coarse rabble-rousing statesman in an Assembly enlarged by the evacuations of Attica.

Mytilene: the Athenian debate on its fate is one of Thucydides' major dramas: leniency, he said, prevailed against Cleon's desire for savage methods (but it did not, altogether).

Sphacteria (Pylos): the Spartans sued for peace, now and later (cf. Athens in 430), but Cleon secured the rejection of their offer.

Brasidas' northern expedition preceded by the colonization of Heraclea in Trachis (426).

Athenian coalition (421–418): Argos, Elis, Mantinea. Its organizer Hyperbolus was ostracized (417; more probably than 415), the last man to suffer under this law, which was replaced, as a weapon to check ambition, by the *graphe paranomon* (prosecution for proposing an illegal law or decree). His ostracism was engineered by a temporary alliance between Nicias and Alcibiades.

Alcibiades (*c.*450–404), ward of Pericles, friend of Socrates, and architect of the coalition which collapsed at

Mantinea (418), was recalled from Sicily in 415 under suspicion (encouraged by his dissipated way of life), first of complicity in the mutilation of the Hermae (statues of Hermes around Athens) and, secondly, of staging profane parodies of the Eleusinian Mysteries, though the perpetrators had perhaps been oligarchs (including the orator Andocides) desiring to sabotage the Sicilian expedition.

Three Syracusan generals: Hermocrates and Sicanus (both later superseded) and Heraclides.

Navy (and democracy) of the Syracusans: they and the Athenians were 'too alike' (spokesman in Thucydides).

Athenian retreat from Syracuse: many lives were lost because Nicias superstitiously delayed the move, owing to an eclipse.

Athens' tax reform (413): export tax in all harbours in place of allied tribute and of *eisphora* (extraordinary property tax).

Diocles introduced a new Syracusan law-code and removed the presidency of the Assembly from the generals.

CHAPTER 17: SOPHOCLES: HARROWED HEROES AND HEROINES

Fame of Sophocles: greatly admired by Racine in seventeenth-century France and Lessing in eighteenth-century Germany.

CHAPTER 18: EURIPIDES: DRAMATIC CHALLENGER

Surviving Tragedies: the *Rhesus* is bad and of uncertain authorship, and the *Alcestis*, though genuine, not wholly or indubitably tragic.

Children of Heracles: is our text an actor's script?

Iphigenia in Aulis much abridged: was there originally a happy ending?

Bacchae: had there been an earlier Aeschylean masterpiece on the subject?

Sophists: Euripides had noted Protagoras' relativism.

Atheism is expressed by some of Euripides' characters, e.g. Bellerophon and Sisyphus (in fragments from plays named after them).

CHAPTER 19: ARISTOPHANES: COMEDY OF PROTEST

Origins of Old Comedy may go back to seventh- and sixth-century Corinth and Sicyon (cf. Tragedy, Chapter 18).

Babylonians (426): Aristophanes was brought before the Council by Cleon for slandering Athenian officials before foreigners. In the same play he called Athens' subjects the slaves of the *demos*.

Assemblywomen: Hippodamus of Miletus had been one of the first to construct an ideal state and society.

Middle Comedy: almost all lost: there are 580 extant titles, out of more than 900 plays. Mythological burlesque and the drama of everyday life were developed (foreshadowing the New Comedy of Menander), and certain current social types were satirized.

Ancient fame of Aristophanes: he was prized by subsequent generations as the purest source of old Attic.

CHAPTER 20: HIPPOCRATES: SCIENTIFIC PHYSICIAN

Alcmaeon argued for the immortality, or perpetuity, of the soul (according to Aetius) – as a substance self-moved in eternal motion, thus probably inspiring passages in Plato's *Phaedrus*.

Early fifth-century medicine still contained elements of magic.

Asclepiads: Hippocrates' father Heraclides traced his descent from Heracles. In the 420s, after the plague, a group including the dramatist Sophocles introduced the worship of Asclepius to Athens; the cult expanded rapidly in the fourth century.

Hippocrates was also credited with laying the bases of experimental physiology and empirical psychology. The best of his biographies is by Soranus of Ephesus (*c.*AD 100).

Influence of sophists in *On the Art* and *On Breath* (treatises in the Hippocratean Corpus), though early writers distance themselves from both sophists and natural philosophers (despite debts to Heraclitus).

Schools of Cos and Cnidus: the Coans felt that the Cnidians paid too much attention to the actual sensations of the patient and physical signs of the

Schools of Cos and Cnidus—cont
disease, whereas the Cnidians thought Coan books were too speculative.

On Diet prefers diet and exercise to the use of drugs.

On Ancient Medicine: by a physician devoted to traditional lore and technique, though familiar with contemporary theory (including inductive methods) and possessing some dialectical skill.

Prognosticum professes to explain how a physician can anticipate the course of an illness.

Influence: the 'Four Humours' unfortunately held sway in western medicine for nearly two millenia. Hippocratic treatment of hip injuries (including joint dislocations) was still warmly praised in the nineteenth century.

CHAPTER 21: SOCRATES: IRONICAL QUESTIONER

Soul: Socrates has been described as perhaps the first man in Europe to understand the soul (*psyche*) not merely as 'life-breath' but as the intellectual and moral personality. Whether he was influenced by the Pythagoreans (Appendix 1) is arguable.

'No one does wrong willingly' is based on the indefensible prior assumption that all voluntary action is the expression of choice (not impulse).

Definition: Socrates engaged in (invented?) inductive argument and definition by generalizations.

Teaching: he taught at street corners or in some sort of a school.

The revived democracy organized a comprehensive review and reinscription of the laws.

Anytus: general 403/402–397/396; he appears, and warns Socrates, in Plato's *Meno*. Stories of his banishment and murder are probably later inventions.

Meletus, son of a tragic poet, was probably not the Meletus who in 400/399 accused the orator Andocides of impiety (see note on Chapter 16 above). The report that Meletus was subsequently put to death by the Athenians is doubtful.

The Socratic legend: 'Socratic conversations' were attributed to no less than twelve authors; the first was reputedly Simon (a cobbler), and the best perhaps by Aeschines of Sphettus. His asceticism particularly appealed to Antisthenes, who, with Diogenes, created the Cynic philosophy.

CHAPTER 22: ZEUXIS AND PARRHASIUS: A NEW LOOK AT ART

Perspective was used only for settings, not for figures, which were kept in the foreground.

Midias Painter: thick lines, dark garment patterns, much white and yellow.

Nikes (Victories): a statue of Nike in the Agora of Athens (*c*.420/400) showed expressionistic, nervous, decorative abstraction. Marble grave reliefs, revived in the third quarter of the century, are much calmer, as their subject-matter requires.

Erechtheum: its friezes (now fragmentary) are exceptional, with a background of dark Eleusinian stone, to which white marble figures, carved separately, were fastened. The friezes of the 'Nereid monument' from Xanthus in Lycia (in the British Museum) show the further development of this art in the early fourth century.

CHAPTER 23: THUCYDIDES: HISTORIAN OF THE WAR

Clever men: Thucydides praised the extremist oligarch Antiphon for his exceptionally clever speech in his own defence.

Debts to Hippocrates: Thucydides owed to him or his school the notions of contagion and acquired immunity. In general too, after the manner of the physicians, he saw history as a casebook of human pathology.

Sources: Thucydides notoriously fails to mention documents among his sources.

Pentekontaetea: despite his own deficiencies in his respect, Thucydides blames Hellanicus of Lesbos for inadequate chronology.

Character-sketches: Thucydides' unfair treatment of Cleon detracts from his objectivity about his own career; since it was Cleon who had brought about his exile.

Speeches: their absence from the final book (VIII) is a reason for supposing that it remained incomplete. Speeches 'as near as possible': as near as he or his informant could recall, or as near as his literary sensibility would permit?

Pericles is seen by Thucydides as a moderate, but his last speech, as put together by the historian, suggested chauvinistic imperialism.

CHAPTER 24: LYSANDER: CONQUEROR OF ATHENS

Decelea commanded the road to Euboea, so that supplies had to be sent round Cape Sunium.

The Peace of Epilycus between Athens and Persia (424/423; Chapter 23) is now confirmed by a newly identified fragment of an inscription.

Pissuthnes (who had backed the Samian rebels against Athens in 441/439) revolted against Darius II Ochus, perhaps in *c*.416 – attempting to mobilize Greeks in his favour – but was overcome by Tissaphernes who succeeded him as satrap.

Amorges: date of Athens' support disputed: 414? (or after Persia's approach to Sparta in 412).

The Four Hundred, led by Antiphon and Pisander, gave way to the Five Thousand (really 9,000: artisans, more prosperous traders, and farmers) guided by Theramenes. The débâcle at Syracuse had greatly weakened the poorest class (oarsmen: *thetes*) – many of whom, moreover, were outside Athens, e.g. at Samos – so that the 5,000, or 9,000, excluded them.

Cleophon, called by his enemies a 'fatherless lyremaker' but the son of a general, managed Athens' finances (410–406), and died poor.

Cyrus the younger: Lysander had facilitated his appointment by securing the relegation of Tissaphernes to Caria. Unlike Pharnabazus, satrap of Dascylium, Cyrus refused to think of negotiating with Athens. But whether Persia's treaty with Sparta was formally renewed in 408/407 is disputed.

Notium (406): Alcibiades fled first to his own fortress-residences in Thrace (Pactye and Bisanthe) and then after the oligarchic revolution at Athens to Pharnabazus, who at Lysander's request had him killed.

Arginusae (406): the six Athenian generals executed after the battle were Erasinides, Diomedon, Lysias (not the orator of that name), Pericles (son of the statesman), Aristocrates and Thrasyllus (democratic soldier at Samos in 411). Sparta may have offered peace again after the battle.

Democracy restored at Athens (403): Sparta arranged a compromise between the democratic leader Thrasybulus and the moderate oligarchs.

PART V: FIRST HALF OF THE FOURTH CENTURY: WEST AND EAST

CHAPTER 25: DIONYSIUS I: EMPIRE BUILDER

Carthage had been provoked by Hermocrates' private warfare in Sicily. Their General Mago (I) belonged to the powerful Magonid family. Dionysius' Carthaginian Wars are sometimes numbered differently (Third = Second, Fourth = Third).

Mercenaries: in the Greek world, during the first quarter of the fourth century there were never fewer than 25,000 mercenaries in service, impelled by mass impoverishment, exile, the lack of colonizing outlets, and the increasing need for professional soldiers in an age of military specialization.

Quadrireme: heavy enough to serve as a ship of the line, yet light enough to preserve manoeuvrability.

Quinquereme: became the standard warship of the Hellenistic states and Roman Republic.

Sparta in 403 gained the loyal alliance of Dionysius I, who also helped to compel Athens to accept the Peace of Antalcidas (387). But Athens' first inscription honouring Dionysius dates back to 394/393.

The Ransoming of Hector (tragic play of Dionysius I) stressed the

The Ransoming of Hector—cont
establishment of justice and harmony; Dionysius' plays denounced tyranny as the 'mother of injustice'!

Dionysius I satirized in the *Cyclops* of Philoxenus of Cythera (d.380–379).

Timaeus: used and criticized by Diodorus Siculus (before whom ten historians wrote about Dionysius I).

Writers in favour of Dionysius I at his court: Xenarchus (composer of mimes), Aristippus the elder of Cyrene (Socratic and rhetorician), Hermeias of Methymna (court historian?).

Philistus and Theopompus created the genre of history orientated round men of force and authority.

Euaenetus and Cimon: their superb and much imitated silver decadrachms (of which the sequence is disputed) display trophies of arms taken from the defeated Athenian expedition, and may have accompanied the Assinarian Games celebrating that event, but were apparently not issued until the reign of Dionysius I.

CHAPTER 26: ARCHYTAS: PHILOSOPHICAL RULER

Iapygians were the various tribes of the heel of Italy (known to the Romans as Calabria, but the term was extended to include Apulians). The Messapians (probably of Illyrian origin) were a leading Iapygian people.

Tarantine pottery: the Apulian school started work at Taras in *c.*430–420, making large vases with elaborate compositions, sometimes on several superimposed registers. The Sisyphus Painter's statuesque style echoes the Parthenon and Bassae. Vases of *c.*360–350 (wrongly named 'Gnathia', [Egnatia] after the town of that name) reflect the perspective architecture of Agatharchus of Samos.

Popular theatre (hilarotragoedia): farces known as *phlyakes*, shown on fourth-century vases, probably before the genre assumed a literary form – as it did later in south Italy and Alexandria.

Archytas may have been the first (before Plato) to apply the notion of arithmetical and geometrical proportion to politics: anti-democrats preferred geometric to arithmetical proportion.

Taras in later fourth century: 40,000 terracotta statuettes (forerunners of 'Tanagra' figurines, which were Athenian); limestone architectural sculpture; Lysippus' colossal bronze Zeus and Heracles.

Enrolment of helpers from abroad after Archytas' death: Archidamus III of Sparta (the subject of Isocrates' *Archidamus*) was called in by Taras in *c.*342 to repel Lucanians and Bruttians (aided by Messapians and other Iapygians) but was killed at Manduria (338). Taras then invited Alexander I of Molossia (*c.*333) who fell at Pandosia (330).

CHAPTER 27: LEUCON I: THE GRAIN ROUTE

Fish preservation: salting tanks have been found at Tyritace, and pickling vats at Myrmecium.

Greek Black Sea colonies: five groups: (1) south coast (Asia Minor), (2) Milesian on north coast (Graeco-Scythian), (3) Taman peninsula (Graeco-Sindian), (4) Tauric Chersonese (Graeco-Taurian), (5) Bosphoran group (from Panticapaeum).

Scythian goldwork found in stone tomb-chambers or tumuli (with Greek cases); fourth-century Greek metalworkers depicted subjects relating to Scythian, Sindian and Maeotian life and religion in Ionian or Attic style.

Panticapaeum: protected by a ditch across the whole eastern projection of the Tauric Chersonese.

Archaeanactids, if of Milesian origin, may have come from Hermonassa on the Taman peninsula; their regime could have been founded with Scythian backing.

Athenian settlements in fifth century: Athenaeum (near Theodosia), Nymphaeum (beside the Milesian colony), Stratocleia (near Phanagoria, a colony of Teos).

Sindians: a north Caucasian or Indo-Iranian people, with their capital at Sindian Harbour, renamed Gorgippia after a member of the Spartocid house, Gorgippus, whose daughter Paerisades I married. The River Anticeites (Kuban) was also known as the Hypanis, which is better known as the name of the Bug.

Theodosia: permanently ice-free harbour (unlike Panticapaeum); first colonized by Miletus in the sixth century.

Heraclea Pontica: an important sixth-century Megarian colony, which replaced its original 'democratic' government by oligarchy, and reduced the surrounding Mariandyni to 'serf' status somewhat resembling that of the Spartan helots.

Athenian grain needs. In the fourth century imported grain was a fixed item on the agenda of one meeting of the Athenian Assembly every month. The only discoverable Athenian 'commercial policy' was to import foodstuffs (and other raw materials needed for strategic purposes); there was no corresponding export policy.

Bosphoran grainlands of Sopaeus recorded by Isocrates' *Trapeziticus* (390s).

Stratonicus, when asked to remain by Paerisades I, replied 'What, you don't intend to stay here yourself, do you?' (Athenaeus).

Coins of Panticapaeum: three-quarter profile head of Silenus or satyr; a masterpiece, approaching portraiture. The reverse shows a winged, goat-headed panther, a variety of the griffin which was the fabled guardian of the gold-producing regions of the north.

CHAPTER 28: MAUSOLUS AND PYTHIUS: THE MAUSOLEUM

Artemisia II: brother-sister marriage, perhaps borrowed from Egypt.

Mausoleum: according to an alternative reconstruction, the podia had six, and not three steps.

Pythius was also the architect of the Temple of Athena at Priene.

Bryaxis of Athens, named as one of the sculptors of the Mausoleum, may not be the man of the same name who later made a colossal statue of the god Sarapis (Serapis) for Alexandria.

Timotheus also worked on the Temple of Asclepius at Epidaurus.

Leochares, probably Athenian, portrayed Isocrates (the statue was dedicated by another Timotheus, a general) and Philip II and his family (after Chaeronea, 338).

Amazonomachy frieze of Mausoleum located as on Nereid Monument (see note on Chapter 22).

PART VI: FIRST HALF OF THE FOURTH CENTURY: THE GREEK MAINLAND

CHAPTER 29: EPAMINONDAS: THE END OF THE POLITICAL ROAD

Spartan help to Cyrus the younger: a Spartan admiral off Cilicia (south-east Asia Minor) enabled Cyrus to turn the coastal passes and enter Syria, though Cyrus' relations with two Spartan harmosts (governors) of Byzantium were insecure.

Corinthian War encouraged because Sparta was seriously shaken by the abortive conspiracy of Cinadon (Appendix III).

Argos, which provided the largest contingent for the Corinthian War, virtually absorbed Corinth (392–386), after the Corinthian democrats had killed 120 oligarchs at altars and in temples.

Iphicrates won fame by commanding light-armed troops who destroyed a Spartan hoplite division at Lechaeum (390); these mobile 'peltasts' (from *pelte*, a small light leather shield) were the major innovation of mercenary warfare, managed by a new type of professional general who subjected the rules of war to radical rethinking.

King's Peace named after Artaxerxes II Mnemon, who although lackadaisical ruled for forty-six years (404–358) over an empire which showed remarkable recuperative powers.

Spartan interference at Thebes, Mantinea and Olynthus (382–379): the Chalcidian League was suppressed.

Jason of Pherae (*c*.385–370), which had benefited from the recent growth of grain exports from the Gulf of Pagasae, was probably the son of a local ruler Lycophron; elected ruler (*tagos*) of Thessaly, he modernized its organization and extended his influence over all northern Greece.

Sacred Band at Leuctra (371): an elite Theban corps of pairs of male lovers founded by Gorgidas.

Factional strife after Leuctra: in 370, Argive democrats clubbed 1,200 opponents to death.

Before Mantinea (362): Epaminondas failed to take Sparta by surprise.

Mantinea: the second battle of that name, the first having been in 418.

After Mantinea: Persia could not intervene because it was immobilized by a satraps' revolt: in 364 King Agesilaus II of Sparta (d.360) had helped the rebellious Ariobarzanes, former satrap of Dascylium.

CHAPTER 30: XENOPHON: LITERARY LAND-OWNER

Anabasis showed (as Alexander the Great later noted) that a small, disciplined Greek army could traverse the Persian empire. But Xenophon was inclined to be pro-Persian, and saw himself as a Persian expert although he was naïve to regard Cyrus' enterprise as a 'local punitive expedition'. His principal critic was perhaps his fellow officer Sophaenetus of Stymphalus, who likewise wrote an *Anabasis of Cyrus*.

Agesilaus II played a prominent part in Greek history for a quarter of a century, but was over estimated, notably by Xenophon; he had no coherent plan.

On Ways and Means is an economic diagnosis of Athens' difficulties (or rather a study of fiscal means for political ends), stressing the lack of properly equipped ships – and of goodwill among the rich.

Xenophon's Socrates: he is at pains to show that Critias and Alcibiades, though at first restrained by Socrates, became un-Socratic. But he himself did not conform with Socrates' obedience to the state!

CHAPTER 31: PLATO: ETERNAL REALITY

Verse epigrams attributed to Plato: it seems that he was the author of none of them.

Plato an adherent of Socrates: or did he, mostly, learn about him from his own brothers and uncles?

Euclides of Megara, present at the death of Socrates, held the Good to be one single thing, though variously described (as God, Wisdom, Mind). The Megarian school which he founded was especially concerned with logical paradoxes.

The Academy was probably modelled on Pythagorean communities in south Italy.

Recollection (*anamnesis*), introduced in the *Meno* in a mythical vein, is based on the belief in the immortality of the soul which *Plato* 'had heard expounded by priests and poets' (cf. the Pythagoreans (Appendix I); also Orphics, who figure in the *Euthyphro*, and the physician Alcmaeon (note on Chapter 20)).

The Republic, according to Aristoxenus, was largely based on Protagoras (cf. note on Chapter 12).

The philospher–king: either kings should become philosophers, or philosophers kings.

Poetry and art. The poets mislead by portraying the gods as undignified and immoral: art expresses and gratifies the lowest part of the soul and its basest emotions, aping the spiritual and subtly trivializing it. Plato high-handedly conflated poetry and visual art.

The Laws: sodomy like adultery was to be illegal for citizens.

Immortality of the Soul: the belief that Plato owed this doctrine to Socrates is hard to substantiate (but cf. Alcmaeon, note on Chapter 20).

Mathematics: arithmetic and geometry: 'let no one enter who does not know geometry' was said to be inscribed outside Plato's house; for it should be possible, he maintained, by analogy with mathematics, to determine our ethical and political knowledge with some degree of exactness, order restraint and unity of purpose (cf. Archytas, note on Chapter 26).

Rationality: Plato increasingly believed in the rule of (divine) reason in the state and the universe.

Forms already in the *Euthyphro*, but not yet as transcendent. Socrates had not 'separated them' (Aristotle). Platonic idealism was revived by Neoplatonism

(Plotinus AD 205–269/70) which became the principal philosophy of the later pagan world, deeply influenced St Augustine (AD 354–430) and dominated the early Middle Ages, until displaced by Aristotle in the thirteenth century. In the sixteenth century Marsilio Ficino's Latin translation marked a revival of Platonism, exemplified by Lorenzo de'Medici's strange Platonic Academy at Florence. The Cambridge Platonists (seventeenth century), and neo-Kantians, and existentialists and analytical philosophers, all produced their own versions of Plato.

Logical limitations: unfair 'Socratic' arguments and leading questions; and Plato fails to distinguish between different ideas.

Plato's Unwritten Doctrines, championed by some as the (lost) essence of his philosophy, are less emphasized by others. Certainly, there was open, unofficial debating and lecturing, not all of which found its way into the dialogues (or necessarily met with the agreement of Plato himself, whose Greek oral culture favoured the discussion of such differences of opinion).

Plato's authoritarianism, associated with an admiration for Spartan discipline and the (legendary) Spartan state of Lycurgus, seems alien to his own, and Socrates', free-wheeling speculation.

CHAPTER 32: ISOCRATES: PANHELLENIC EDUCATIONALIST

Gorgias was encountered by Isocrates in Sicily.

Liturgies were public functions compulsorily conferred upon richer Athenian citizens and metics: trierarchy (occasional payment for ships), *choregia* (production of a chorus at music and dramatic festivals), etc.

Style of Isocrates: he was criticized for ostentatious efforts to heighten the grandeur of his themes.

Nicocles (king *c.*374, of the Teucrid royal house of Salamis) had been a pupil of Isocrates, whose speech *To Nicocles* gives him a lecture on kingship, while in the *Nicocles* the monarch addresses his subjects.

Euagoras (*c.*435–374), Nicocles' father, controlled Cyprus with Athenian help and fought Persia (390–381). Isocrates' posthumous praise becomes a rhetorical exercise on kingship.

Praise of Philip II: Isocrates hoped for his patronage of his school.

Anti-Persian Panhellenism: Lysias' *Olympic Oration* (*Olympiacus*, 388) had taken this line. Isocrates hoped for new Greek colonization of the satrapies of western Asia Minor.

Panathenaicus: attack on Sparta, contrasted with the earlier appeal to its king Archidamus III (356), of which a fragment survives. Isocrates admits a measure of opportunism, which prompted such reversals of attitude in his works.

CHAPTER 33: PRAXITELES: THE HUMANIZING OF SCULPTURE

Aphrodite of Cnidus. According to Pliny the elder Praxiteles also made a draped statue of Aphrodite, which Cos chose in preference to the naked figure, as more dignified and modest; so that the naked Aphrodite was bought by the Cnidians. More thoroughgoing three-dimensionalism was later achieved by Lysippus (*From Alexander to Cleopatra*, s.v.). Copies fail to reproduce the sensuous effects of Praxiteles' surface detail. The 'Leconfield Aphrodite' (a head at Petworth) looks like a Praxitelean original.

PART VII
THE END OF CLASSICAL GREECE

CHAPTER 34: TIMOLEON: SICILY AT ITS BEST

Dion, well-educated, haughty and cold; his aims remain disputable, though in any case he was never able to achieve them.

Dion and Platonists: his friend Timonides was in close touch with Plato's nephew and successor Speusippus, and he

Dion and Platonists—cont himself was accompanied to Sicily in 357 by Plato's pupil Callippus (who had gained his high esteem, but later murdered him).

Dion's capture of Syracuse (357) was facilitated by Dionysius II's governor of Heraclea Minoa (and the implied backing of Carthage). The historian Philistus, who had failed to intercept his arrival, committed suicide after a defeat at sea (356).

Timaeus likes Timoleon because, when overthrowing dictatorships, he had nevertheless left Timaeus' father Andromachus in control of Tauromenium.

Mago (II) committed suicide after his return to Carthage from Sicily (*c.*343).

Timoleon and Greece: he did not help the Greek alliance against Philip II at Chaeronea (338).

Coinage: Sicily was flooded by Corinthian coins, reflecting an influx of settlers from Corinthian areas; and Timoleon himself issued an extensive Corinthian-type coinage, of silver obtained from tribute and the booty from the victory at the River Crimisus (*c.*341).

Timoleon's propaganda: like Dionysius I he capitalized on Syracusan fears of Carthage.

CHAPTER 35: PHILIP II; THE CITY-STATE SUPPLANTED

Alexander I of Macedonia (498–454) shared the unreliability of the Aleuads of Larissa (Thessaly) which contributed to the withdrawal of the Greeks from Tempe in the face of Xerxes I's invasion (480); he offered to mediate. But his invitations of Greek poets to his court helped to earn him the title Philhellen, lover of the Greeks (though this implied that he himself was not Greek).

Perdiccas II (*c.*450–413) coined copiously to facilitate trading with Athens.

Army of Philip II: his phalanx (which may go back to Perdiccas III, 365/364–359) consisted of Foot Companions (*pezetairoi*, who may go back to Alexander II (369–368) or earlier), of which the *corps d'élite* were the *hypaspistai*, including the Royal Guard (*agema*).

Special units included light cavalry, peltasts, javelin-throwers, slingers and men firing torsion catapults (first perfected in Thessaly, improving on the catapults of Dionysius I).

Philip II's injuries: listed by Demosthenes.

Ivory head may be a copy of a gold and ivory portrait of Philip II made by the Athenian sculptor Leochares (see note to Chapter 28); this miniature copy, together with other heads representing royal personages, formed part of the decoration of a wooden couch.

Amphipolis: although Philip captured it in 357, in the previous year he had admitted Athens' claim to the city.

Palace at Pella: perhaps the largest in the Mediterranean area, covering at least fifteen acres. It comprised two groups of buildings, sharing a uniform façade with monumental central gateway and raised Doric colonnade.
According to an alternative view, the palace dates from Cassander (316–297). There was another large residence on the acropolis.

Wall-paintings (probably of *c.*340) in barrel-vaulted 'royal tomb': lion- and boar-hunt by men on horseback and foot. In 'small chamber tomb': Rape of Persephone by Pluto.

Appeal of Aleuadae of Larissa to Philip II was prompted by a chaotic situation in Thessaly caused by the collapse of the autocratic regime at Pherae in 352 (its ruler Alexander, Jason's nephew, had been murdered six years earlier).

Philip II in 352: it was about now that he started installing oligarchs in Greek cities.

Olynthus is the earliest site where extensive pebble mosaics have been found.

Athenian appeals to Philip II: not only by Isocrates (346) but by Plato's nephew and successor Speusippus (342), who supported the king's claim to Amphipolis and Chalcidice.

Boeotian League after Chaeronea was reconstituted on a new, equal basis, foreshadowing Hellenistic (Achaean, Aetolian) confederacies.

Persian crusade: some Greeks, after reading Ctesias' *History of Persia* and Xenophon's *Anabasis*, were over-optimistic about Persia's weaknesses.

Polygamy of Philip II: according to Satyrus (quoted by Athenaeus), his wives, in addition to Olympias and Cleopatra, included Audata (Illyrian), Phila (sister of Derdas and Machetas) and Meda (daughter of the Thracian (north Getic) King Cothelas); moreover Nicesipolis (of Pherae) and Philinna (of Larissa) had children by him, and they, too, were probably his wives.

Alexander I of the Molossi: could not be left disaffected when Philip II left for the east.

Alexander III the Great: had been clearly designated for the royal succession by a series of appointments and commands.

CHAPTER 36: DEMOSTHENES: ORATOR RESISTING THE FUTURE

Loss of Athenian generals in 'Social War'; Chabrias killed, Timotheus impeached and fined, Iphicrates impeached (but acquitted).

Eubulus: the most prominent Athenian statesman 355–342. Such financial experts arose because the generals were now wholly occupied by new military technicalities.

Legal battles: the law courts rather than the Assembly were the sovereign power in the fourth-century Athens (Aristophon of Azenia, an Attic deme, boasted he had been acquitted in seventy-five cases under the *graphe paranomon*, i.e. for putting forward illegal proposals; see note on Chapter 16).

Isaeus (*c.*420–350), said to have been a pupil of Isocrates, was famous for his skill in presenting complicated cases.

Navy: conscription since 362. But Athens' most glaring failure in this century was its inability to find money for its fleets (which were needed to protect grain supplies).

Peace of Philocrates (346): both Demosthenes and Aeschines had, in fact, supported the Peace. It contained the first clear statement that the seas should be free (from piracy) for international traffic.

Aeschines (*c.*397–*c.*322), despite Demosthenes' abuse, was an Athenian patriot rather than pro-Macedonian, though he was a member of the delegation sent to negotiate with Philip II after Chaeronea (338).

Naval financing: taxes were very low, although Antiphanes (Middle Comedy) denounced them as burdensome (wealth had to be called upon, since direct taxation was regarded as degrading).

Chaeronea: the Greek force came from Athens, Boeotia, Euboea, Achaea, Corinth, Megara, Leucas, Corcyra.

Athenian defence: the Ephebic College was founded in 336/335, on the initiative of Epicrates, for the compulsory military training of youths eighteen years old.

On the Crown was ostensibly an answer to Aeschines' *Against Ctesiphon*, whom he had accused (under the *graphe paranomon*, see note in Chapter 16) of proposing an illegal motion, i.e. the honouring of Demosthenes with a crown (337).

Attacks on Demosthenes: the orator Hyperides, who had supported him in the 340s, was one of his prosecutors in 324.

Defence of Demosthenes: by the orator Demochares, his nephew, who in 280/279 had a decree passed in his honour. Polyeuctus' statue of Demosthenes – the 'Last Patriot' rather than a portrait – dates from this period.

CHAPTER 37: ARISTOTLE: THE FRONTIERS OF CLASSICAL KNOWLEDGE

Xenocrates of Calchedon (later head of the Academy, 339–314) and Aristotle's nephew (?) Callisthenes of Olynthus (a historian who praised but was then executed by Alexander the Great) accompanied Aristotle to Assus; and Callisthenes went with him to the Macedonian court.

Aristotle's writings: he was also the part-author of many works later credited to his sole authorship.

Topics: from *topoi*, types of argument; dialectic is seen as the art of discussion by question and answer.

Aristotle's logical method: based on the syllogism, which states a general

Aristotle's logical method—cont
rule (major premise), indicates a particular case within its sphere (minor premise), and draws the conclusion ('all animals are mortal: human beings are animals: therefore human beings are mortal').

Forms: Eudoxus of Cnidus (*c.*390–340), outstanding mathematician (said to have been Archytas' pupil in geometry) and astronomer, was prepared to envisage the Forms only in concrete, material instances.

Purpose in nature: although Aristotle asserts, generally, that 'nature does nothing in vain' (so that the aetiology in *On Parts of Animals*, for example, contains extensive teleology), he recognizes that some aspects of nature are nevertheless functionless, i.e. without any discoverable final cause.

Contemplation: Aristotle's eulogy of the philosophical, spiritual way of life alarmed the followers of Isocrates, with their rhetorical teaching programme.

Moderate democracy: good living requires having some say in one's political environment – as well as possessing leisure. 'The many', whom Aristotle despised, worked for their livelihood, mostly as farmers, craftsmen and shopkeepers.

Tyranny (though not elective tyranny, *aesymneteia*) is a perversion of monarchy.

Self-sufficiency: Aristotle wants trade but not subversive contacts.

Prosperity: he contrasts legitimate, necessary acquisition with unnatural appetite for wealth.

Rhetoric, a 'productive' activity, is an aspect of dialectic (persuasion, discussion), though its premises are not universals but probabilities and signs (cf. discussion in Plato's *Phaedrus*).

Tragedy: purification, purgation (in a medical sense?) of the emotions. Are they ennobled? Or is the spectator improved by being freed from their excess or residue? – or relieved, by viewing the tragedy, from the emotions it has aroused? Or is 'clarification' the main meaning, i.e. the play makes the emotions intelligible?

Unfinished works: but the *History of Animals* is an unusually polished product.

Arabic versions: especially the translations of Avicenna of Bokhara (980–1037) (who also wrote in his native Persian) and Averroes of Cordoba (1126–1198).

St Thomas Aquinas (1225–1274): his Aristotelianism was at first highly suspect, as being 'non-Christian', and was attacked by William of Ockham (1280–1349). But Aristotelianism triumphed until the fifteenth century, when the Florentine Platonic Academy seemed to have more to offer the Humanists.

APPENDICES

APPENDIX I: PYTHAGORAS AND HIS FOLLOWERS

Orphism: *The Rise of the Greeks*, pp. 303ff.

APPENDIX II: WOMEN

Artemisia I (queen regent): her role at Salamis was perhaps exaggerated by her grandson Herodotus.

Thargelia of Miletus, married fourteen times, ruled the Thessalian state of Antiochus (her last husband) as his widow for thirty years, resisted Darius I in 490 and was killed by an Argive. But there may have been two queens of this name.

Women in politics: at Thurii a woman exceptionally spoke in the Assembly.

Spartan women: in the middle of the fourth century two-fifths of all Spartan land was said to be owned by women.

Aspasia: the comic dramatist Hermippus accused her of impiety and procuring; see also note on Appendix III.

Plato on women: he rejected the family because it created strife. He makes Socrates dismiss his wife Xanthippe brutally before his death.

Herodotus: 375 women have been counted in his *History*.

Art: on fifth-century gems the favourite subjects were no longer mythological heroes but the daily lives of women.

Homosexuality was given great encouragement by the murder of the autocrat Hipparchus by the pair of lovers, Harmodius and Aristogeiton (514 BC). The only substantial surviving work on the theme is Aeschines, *Against Timarchus*.

APPENDIX III: METICS

Metics in Athenian forces: in the fifth century they provided 3,000 hoplites to the field army and a substantial proportion of triremes' crews. Their contribution was later praised by Isocrates, but Xenophon wanted citizens to serve as soldiers instead.

Erechtheum: in the final stage forty-two out of the eighty-six workmen were metics.

Lysias gained citizenship, but it was annulled.

Aspasia came of a Milesian family.

Bankers' loans: but in the fourth century, although Athens had now swung markedly away from agriculturalism to a city-based import-export economy, its bankers took little part in maritime commercial loans, and their moneylending was not primarily directed towards business aims.

Pasion succeeded his slave-masters Antisthenes and Archestratus.

APPENDIX IV: BETWEEN FREE MEN AND SLAVES

Intermediate ('helot') classes: *klerotai*, *mnoitai* and *oikeis* in Crete, *penestai* in Thessaly, *korynephoroi* (club-carriers) or *katonakophoroi* (weavers of sheepskin cloaks) at Sicyon, wearers of dogskin caps (*kuneai*) at Corinth, Mariandyni at Heraclea Pontica, *prounikoi* (bearers of burdens) at Byzantium, *kyllyrioi* at Syracuse.

Helots in army: especially mobilized by adventurous generals (Cleomenes I, Pausanias, Brasidas, Lysander; employed as hoplites from *c*.418).

Helot revolts: did a rebellion, or the threat of one, help to make the Spartans late for the battle of Marathon (490)?

Neodamodeis were replaced in the Spartan army by mercenaries from *c*.370.

Helots vanished when many were enfranchised by Cleomenes III (235–219) and Nabis (207–192).

APPENDIX V: SLAVES

Proportion of slaves at Athens increased when Cimon, after the battle of Eurymedon, flooded the markets with 20,000 prisoners.

Slaves essential because leisure from subsistence agriculture would otherwise not have been available, since the margin over bare subsistence was so small; they were not so safe an investment as land, but safer (though less remunerative) than lending for a merchant voyage. Pseudo-Aristotle, *Estate Management*, described them as the best and most manageable form of property.

Slaves subsidiary: between two-thirds and three-quarters of the citizen population did not own them.

Thracian slaves often sold by their masters for export.

Liberation of slaves gained them the status of metic (obligations to their former master's family remained).

Fear of slaves: Spartans in camp kept them away from access to weapons (Xenophon).

Scythian slaves: Tanais was a major slave-market.

Laurium slaves, the most skilled of whom were Thracians or Paphlagonians, belonged to citizen or metic contractors who had bid for them. When the Spartans fortified Decelea (413) more than 20,000 slaves deserted from the Athenians, including many from Laurium.

BIBLIOGRAPHY

I ANCIENT SOURCES

Those whose work has not survived, or has survived only in fragments, are marked with an asterisk.*

(a) Greek

AESCHINES, of Athens, c.397–322 BC. Orator and politician.
AESCHYLUS, of Eleusis, 525/524–456 BC. Tragic dramatist. See Chapter 7.
AGATHON, of Athens, later fifth century BC. Tragic dramatist.*
ALCMAEON, of Croton, later fifth century BC. Natural scientist and physician.*
ANAXAGORAS, of Clazomenae, c.500–c.428 BC. Pre-Socratic philosopher.* See Chapter 8.
ANAXIMENES, of Miletus, soon after 600–528/525 BC. Pre-Socratic philosopher.*
ANDOCIDES, of Athens, c.440–c.390 BC. Orator, merchant and politician.
ANTIOCHUS, of Syracuse, fifth century BC. Historian of Sicily and Italy.*
ANTIPHANES, of Athens, early fourth century BC. Dramatist of Middle Comedy.*
ANTIPHON, of Athens, later fifth century BC. Orator and oligarchic politician.
ANTISTHENES, of Athens, c.445–360 BC. Founder of Cynic school of philosophy (before Diogenes).*
ARCHELAUS, of Athens, fifth century BC. Pre-Socratic philosopher.*
ARCHYTAS, of Taras, early fourth century BC. Statesman, mathematician and Pythagorean philosopher.* See Chapter 26.
ARISTOPHANES, of Athens, 457/445 – shortly before 385 BC. Dramatist of Old Comedy. See Chapter 19.
ARISTOTLE, of Stagirus, 384–322 BC. Philosopher and scientist. See Chapter 37.
ARRIAN, of Bithynia (north Asia Minor), second century AD. Historian.
ATHENAEUS, of Naucratis (Egypt), c.AD 200. Writer of encyclopaedic symposium (the *Deipnosophistae*).
AUGUSTINE, St, of Thagaste (north Africa), AD 354–430. Theologian.
BACCHYLIDES, of Iulis (Ceos), c.524/521 (?)–after 452 BC. Lyric poet.
CALLISTHENES, of Olynthus (Aristotle's nephew), died 327 BC. Historian.*
CORAX, of Syracuse, fifth century BC. First known rhetorician.*

CRATINUS, of Athens, later fifth century BC. Dramatist of Old Comedy.*
CRITIAS, of Athens, c.460–403 BC. Oligarchic politician, poet and tragic dramatist.*
CTESIAS, of Cnidus, later fifth century BC. Physician at the Persian court, historian and geographer.*
CYNICS, see Antisthenes, Diogenes.
DEMOCRITUS, of Abdera, fifth century BC. Philosopher and scientist (atomist).* See Chapter 8.
DEMOSTHENES, of Athens, 384–322 BC. Orator and statesman. See Chapter 36.
DIODORUS SICULUS, of Agyrium (Sicily), first century BC. Universal historian.
DIOGENES, of Sinope, c.400–c.325 BC. Founder of Cynic school of philosophy (after Antisthenes), probable author of dialogues and tragedies.*
DIOGENES LAERTIUS, third century AD (?). Historian and biographer of the philosophers.
DIONYSIUS I, of Syracuse, c.430–367 BC. Autocrat and tragic dramatist.* See Chapter 25.
EMPEDOCLES, of Acragas, c.493–c.433 BC. Pre-Socratic philosopher-poet, statesman, orator, physician, miracle-worker. See Chapter 8.*
EPHORUS, of Cyme, c.405–330 BC. Historian and writer on various topics.*
EPICURUS, of Samos, 341–270 BC. Founder of Epicurean school of philosophy.
EUCLIDES, of Megara, c.450–380 BC. Founder of Megarian school of philosophy.*
EUDOXUS, of Cnidus, c.390–c.340 BC. Mathematician, astronomer and geographer.*
EUPOLIS, of Athens, later fifth century BC. Dramatist of Old Comedy.*
EURIPIDES, of Phlya (Attica), c.485/480–c.406 BC. Tragic dramatist. See Chapter 18.
EUSEBIUS, of Caesarea Maritima (Syria Palaestina), c.AD 260–340. Ecclesiastical historian, biographer.
FAVORINUS, of Arelate (south Gaul), earlier second century AD. Rhetorician and popular philosopher.*
GALEN, of Pergamum (Mysia), AD 129–199 (?). Physician and medical writer.
GORGIAS, of Leontini, c.483–376 BC. Sophist.* See Chapter 12.
HECATAEUS, of Miletus, c.500 BC. Geographer, historian, mythologist.*
HELLANICUS, of Lesbos, fifth century BC. Historian, mythologist.*
HERACLITUS, of Ephesus, c.500 BC. Pre-Socratic philosopher.*
HERMEIAS, of Methymna. Historian.*
HERODOTUS, of Halicarnassus, c.480–c.425 BC. Historian. See Chapter 13.
HESIOD, of Cyme (Aeolis) and Ascra (Boeotia), eighth century BC. Epic poet.
HIPPIAS, of Elis, fifth century BC. Sophist.* See Chapter 12.
HIPPOCRATES, of Cos, fifth century BC. Physician.* See Chapter 20.
HOMER, probably born on Chios and worked in Smyrna, eighth century BC. Epic poet.
HYPERIDES, of Athens, 389–322 BC. Orator and politician.
ION, of Chios and Athens, fifth century BC. Writer of poems, tragedies, local history and memoirs.*

ISAEUS, of Athens or Chalcis, c.420–350 BC. Orator.
ISOCRATES, of Athens, 436–338 BC. Rhetorician and educationalist. See Chapter 32.
LEUCIPPUS, of Miletus (?), later fifth century BC. Philosopher and scientist (atomist).*
LUCIAN, of Samosata (Commagene), c.AD 120/125–180. Satirical popular philosopher.
LYCURGUS, of Athens, c.390–c.325/324 BC. Statesman and orator.
MANETHO, of Heliopolis (Egypt), early third century BC. Historian.*
MELISSUS, of Samos, fifth century BC. Fleet commander and Pre-Socratic (Eleatic) philosopher.*
MENANDER, of Athens, c.342–292 BC. Dramatist of New Comedy.
PARMENIDES, of Elea, sixth to fifth centuries BC. Pre-Socratic philosopher–poet. See Chapter 8.
PAUSANIAS, of Magnesia beside Sipylus (Lydia), second century AD. Travel-writer.
PHERECRATES, of Athens, second half of fifth century BC. Dramatist of Old Comedy.*
PHILISTUS, of Syracuse, c.430–356 BC. Politician, admiral and historian of Sicily.*
PHILOLAUS, of Croton or Taras, fifth century BC. Pythagorean philosopher.*
PHILOXENUS, of Cythera (off south Peloponnese), 436/435–380/379 BC. Poet at court of Dionysius I of Syracuse.*
PHRYNICHUS, of Athens, sixth to fifth centuries BC. Tragic dramatist.*
PINDAR, of Cynoscephalae (Boeotia), c.518–c.438 BC. Lyric poet. See Chapter 6.
PLATO, of Athens, c.429–347 BC. Philosopher. See Chapter 31.
PLOTINUS, of Lycopolis (Egypt), AD 205–269/70. Neo-Platonist philosopher.
PLUTARCH, of Chaeronea, before AD 50–after 120. Philosopher and biographer.
POLLUX, of Naucratis (Egypt), second century AD. Scholar and rhetorician.
POLYCLITUS of Argos, later fifth century BC. Sculptor and writer on sculpture.* See Chapter 14.
PRODICUS, of Ceos, later fifth century BC. Sophist.*
PROTAGORAS, of Abdera, fifth century BC. Sophist.* See Chapter 12.
SCYLAX, of Caryanda (Caria), late sixth century BC. Explorer (employed by Darius I) and geographer.* (Surviving geographical work of Pseudo-Scylax, fourth century BC.)
SIMONIDES, of Iulis (Ceos), c.556–468 BC. Lyric and elegiac poet and epigrammatist.
SOPHAENETUS, of Stymphalus (Arcadia), c.400 BC. General and military historian.*
SOPHOCLES, of Colonus (Attica), c.496–406 BC. Tragic dramatist. See Chapter 17.
SOPHRON, of Syracuse, fifth century BC. Writer of mimes.*
SORANUS, of Ephesus, early second century AD. Physician and medical writer.
SPEUSIPPUS, of Athens, c.407–339 BC. Philosopher and Plato's successor as head of the Academy.*

STRABO, of Amasia (Pontus), *c*.63 BC.–at least AD 21. Historian* and geographer.
THEOPHRASTUS, of Eresus (Lesbos), *c*.370–288/285 BC. Philosopher, zoologist, psychologist and Aristotle's successor as head of the Lyceum.
THEOPOMPUS, of Chios, fourth century BC. Historian.*
THESPIS, of Athens, sixth century BC. First known tragic dramatist.*
THRASYMACHUS, of Calchedon, later fifth century BC. Sophist and rhetorician.*
THUCYDIDES, of Athens, *c*.460/455–*c*.400 BC. Historian. See Chapter 23.
TISIAS, of Syracuse, fifth century BC. Rhetorician.*
XENARCHUS, of Syracuse, later fifth century BC. Writer of mimes.*
XENOCRATES, of Calchedon, later fourth century BC. Philosopher and Speusippus' successor as head of the Academy.*
XENOPHANES, of Colophon (Ionia), sixth to fifth centuries BC. Historical poet* and Pre-Socratic philosopher.
XENOPHON, of Erchia (Attica), *c*.428–*c*.354 BC. Soldier, man of letters, historian. See Chapter 30.
ZENO, of Citium (Cyprus), 335–263 BC. Founder of Stoic school of philosophy.*
ZENO, of Elea, fifth century BC. Pre-Socratic (Eleatic) philosopher.*

(b) Latin

CICERO, born at Arpinum (Latium), 106–43 BC. Statesman, orator, rhetorician, philosopher, poet, letter-writer.
CLAUDIUS, born at Lugdunum (Gaul), 10 BC–AD 54. Emperor and historian.*
NEPOS, born in north Italy, *c*.99–*c*.24 BC. Historian* and biographer.
PETRONIUS, first century AD, novelist and poet; probably the man who was Nero's courtier (died AD 66).
PLAUTUS, born at Sarsina (Umbria), third to second centuries BC. Comic dramatist.
PLINY THE ELDER, born at Comum (north Italy), AD 23/4–79. Writer on military science, language and history,* and of encyclopaedic *Natural History*.
POMPEIUS TROGUS, born at Vasio (south Gaul), later first century BC. Universal historian.*
QUINTILIAN, born at Calagurris (north Spain), *c*.AD 35–*c*.100. Educationalist and critic.
TACITUS, born in north Italy or south Gaul, *c*.AD 56–before or after 117. Historian.
TERENCE, born in north Africa, earlier second century BC. Comic dramatist.
VARRO, born at Reate (Latium), 116–27 BC. Encyclopaedic writer, official, and librarian.

II MODERN SOURCES

J. L. ACKRILL (ed.), *A New Aristotle Reader*, 1987.
F. E. ADCOCK, *Thucydides and his History*, 1963.
A. W. H. ADKINS AND P. WHITE (eds), *Readings in Western Civilization*, I. *The Greek Polis*, 1986.

D. J. ALLAN, *The Philosophy of Aristotle*, 2nd edn, 1970.
J. K. ANDERSON, *Xenophon*, 1974.
A. ANDREWES, *Greek Society*, 1975.
A. ANDREWES, *The Greek Tyrants*, 1963 (1956).
A. ANDREWES, *The Greeks*, 1967.
M. ANDRONIKOS, *The Royal Graves at Vergina*, 1980.
A. H. ARMSTRONG, *An Introduction to Ancient Philosophy*, 3rd edn, 1957.
M. ARTAMONOV, *Treasures from the Scythian Tombs*, 1970.
B. ASHMOLE, *Architect and Sculptor in Classical Greece*, 1972.
B. ASHMOLE AND N. YALOURIS, *Olympia: The Sculptures of the Temple of Zeus*, 1967.
M. M. AUSTIN AND P. VIDAL-NAQUET, *Economic and Social History of Ancient Greece*, 2nd edn, 1973.
N. AUSTIN, *The Greek Historians*, 1969.
L. AYLEN, *The Greek Theatre*, 1985.
J. BARNES, *Aristotle*, 1982.
J. BARRON, *An Introduction to Greek Sculpture*, 1981.
H. BENGTSSON *et al.*, *The Greeks and the Persians*, 1968.
C. R. BEYE, *Ancient Greek Literature and Society*, 2nd edn, 1987.
W. B. BIERS, *The Archaeology of Greece*, rev. edn, 1988.
J. BOARDMAN, *Greek Art*, rev. edn, 1985.
J. BOARDMAN, *Greek Gems and Finger Rings: Early Bronze Age to Late Classical*, 1970.
J. BOARDMAN, *Greek Sculpture: The Classical Period*, 1985.
J. BOARDMAN, *The Greeks Overseas*, rev. edn, 1980.
J. BOARDMAN *et al.* (eds), *Cambridge Ancient History*, vol. IV, 2nd edn, 1988.
H. BOLKESTEIN, *Economic Life in Greece's Golden Age*, rev. edn, 1958.
C. G. BOULTER (ed.), *Greek Art: Archaic into Classical*, 1985.
J. BOWEN, *A History of Western Education: I The Ancient World*, 1972.
C. M. BOWRA, *The Greek Experience*, 1985 (1957).
C. M. BOWRA, *Pindar*, 1964.
O. J. BRENDEL, *The Visible Idea: Interpretations of Classical Art*, 1980.
A. BROWN, *A New Companion to Greek Tragedy*, 1983.
R. BROWNING (ed.), *The Greek World*, 1985.
J. BUCKLER, *The Theban Hegemony 371–362* BC, 1980.
W. BURKERT, *Greek Religion: Archaic and Classical*, 1985.
A. R. BURN, *The Pelican History of Greece*, rev. edn, 1982.
A. R. BURN, *Persia and the Greeks*, 2nd edn (postscript by D. M. Lewis), 1984.
A. R. BURN, *The Warring States of Greece*, 1968.
A. R. BURN AND M. BURN, *The Living Past of Greece*, 1982 (1980).
J. B. BURY, *The Ancient Greek Historians*, 1958 (1908).
J. B. BURY AND R. MEIGGS, *A History of Greece*, 4th edn, 1983.
A. BUSIGNANI, *The Bronzes of Riace*, 1981.
A. CAMERON AND A. KURT (eds), *Images of Women in Antiquity*, 1983.
J. CARGILL, *The Second Athenian League*, 1981.
D. CARNE-ROSS, *Pindar*, 1985.
R. A. G. CARSON, *Coins of Greece and Rome*, 2nd edn, 1970.

L. B. CARTER, *The Quiet Athenian*, 1986.
P. A. CARTLEDGE, *Agesilaus and the Crisis of Sparta*, 1987.
M. CARY, *The Geographical Background of Greek and Roman History*, 1949.
L. CASSON, *Ships and Seamanship in the Ancient World*, 1986 (1971).
E. B. CASTLE, *Ancient Education and Today*, 1961.
J. N. CLASTER (ed.), *Athenian Democracy: Triumph or Travesty?*, 1978.
W. R. CONNOR, *The New Politicians of Fifth Century Athens*, 1971.
W. R. CONNOR, *Thucydides*, 1987.
B. F. COOK, *The Elgin Marbles*, 1984.
B. F. COOK, *Greek Inscriptions*, 1987.
J. M COOK, *The Greeks in Ionia and the East*, 1962.
J. M. COOK, *The Persian Empire*, 1983.
R. M. COOK, *Greek Art*, 1976 (1972).
R. M. COOK, *Greek Painted Pottery*, 2nd edn, 1972.
R. M. COOK, *The Greeks: Till Alexander*, 1961.
F. M. CORNFORD, *Thucydides Mythistoricus*, 1965 (1907).
J. J. COULTON, *Ancient Greek Architects at Work*, 2nd edn, (1988) 1982.
M. CRAWFORD (ed.), *Sources for Ancient History*, 1983.
M. CRAWFORD AND D. WHITEHEAD, *Archaic and Classical Greece: A Selection of Ancient Sources in Translation*, 1983.
M. CROPP, E. FANTHAM AND S. E. SCULLY (eds), *Greek Tragedy and its Legacy*, 1988.
K. CROTTY, *Song and Action: The Victory Odes of Pindar*, 1982.
J. K. DAVIS, *Democracy and Classical Greece*, 1978.
N. H. DEMAND, *Thebes in the Fifth Century*, 1982.
W. B. DINSMOOR, *The Architecture of Ancient Greece*, 1950.
E. R. DODDS, *The Greeks and the Irrational*, 1951.
K. J. DOVER (ed.), *Ancient Greek Literature*, 1980.
K. J. DOVER, *Greek and the Greeks*, vol. I (Language, Poetry, Drama), 1988.
K. J. DOVER, *Greek Homosexuality*, 1978.
K. J. DOVER, *The Greeks*, 1982.
P. DUCREY, *Warfare in Ancient Greece*, 1987.
T. J. DUNBABIN, *The Western Greeks*, 1948.
P. E. EASTERLING AND B. M. W. KNOX (eds), *The Cambridge History of Classical Literature, I: Greek Literature*, 1985.
P. E. EASTERLING AND J. V. MUIR, *Greek Religion and Society*, 1985.
A. EDEL, *Aristotle and his Philosophy*, 1982.
L. EDELSTEIN, *Ancient Medicine* (ed. O. and C.L. Temkin), rev. edn, 1988.
V. EHRENBERG, *From Solon to Socrates*, 2nd edn, 1973.
V. EHRENBERG, *The Greek State*, 2nd edn, 1974.
V. EHRENBERG, *The People of Aristophanes*, 3rd edn, 1962.
V. EHRENBERG, *Sophocles and Pericles*, 1954.
J. R. ELLIS, *Philip II and Macedonian Imperialism*, 1976.
J. A. S. EVANS, *Herodotus*, 1982.
C. FARRAR, *The Origins of Democratic Thinking*, 1988.
J. FERGUSON, *Greek and Roman Religion: A Source-Book*, 1980.

J. FERGUSON AND K. CHISHOLM (eds), *Political and Social Life in the Great Age of Athens*, 1978.

J. FERGUSON *et al.*, *Greece 478–336* BC (Units 1–16 and illustrative booklet), 1979.

A. FERRILL, *The Origins of War: From the Stone Age to Alexander the Great*, 1985.

J. N. FINDLAY, *Plato and Platonism*, 1978.

J. V. A. FINE, *The Ancient Greeks*, 1983.

M. I. FINLEY, *A History of Sicily*, I: *Ancient Sicily to the Arab Conquest* (ed. C. Duggan), rev. edn., 1987.

M. I. FINLEY, *The Ancient Economy*, rev. edn, 1985.

M. I. FINLEY, *The Ancient Greeks*, 1963.

M. I. FINLEY, *Ancient Slavery and Modern Ideology*, 1985 (1980).

M. I. FINLEY (ed.), *Classical Slavery*, 1987.

M. I. FINLEY, *Democracy Ancient and Modern*, 1973.

M. I. FINLEY, *Economy and Society in Ancient Greece* (ed. B. D. Shaw and R. P. Saller), 1982 (1981).

M. I. FINLEY (ed.), *The Legacy of Greece: A New Appraisal*, 1981.

M. I. FINLEY, *Politics in the Ancient World*, 1983.

M. I. FINLEY AND H. W. PLEKET, *The Olympic Games: The First Thousand Years*, 1976.

N. R. E. FISHER, *Social Values in Classical Athens*, 1976.

L. F. FITZHARDINGE, *The Spartans*, 1980.

H. P. FOLEY (ed.), *Women in Antiquity*, 1981.

C. W. FORNARA, *The Nature of History in Ancient Greece and Rome*, 1983.

F. J. FROST, *Greek Society*, 1971.

A. FUKS, *Social Conflict in Ancient Greece*, 1984.

D. FURLEY, *The Greek Cosmologists*, vol. I, 1987.

M. GAGARIN, *Aeschylean Drama*, 1976.

Y. GARLAN, *Slavery in Ancient Greece*, 1988.

Y. GARLAN, *War in the Ancient World: A Social History*, 1975.

R. GARNER, *Law and Society in Classical Athens*, 1987.

P. D. A. GARNSEY, *Famine and Food Supply in the Graeco-Roman World*, 1988.

P. D. A. GARNSEY (ed.), *Non-Slave Labour in the Graeco-Roman World*, 1988.

P. D. A. GARNSEY AND C. R. WHITTAKER (eds), *Imperialism in the Ancient World*, 1978.

S. GOLDHILL, *Reading Greek Tragedy*, 1986.

A. W. GOMME, *The Greek Attitude to Poetry and History*, 1954.

M. GRANT, *A Guide to the Ancient World: A Dictionary of Classical Place Names*, 1986.

M. GRANT, *Greek and Latin Authors 800* BC–AD *1000*, 1980.

M. GRANT, *The Ancient Mediterranean*, rev. edn, 1988.

M. GRANT, *The Ancient Historians*, 1970.

M. GRANT, *The Rise of the Greeks*, 1987.

M. GRANT (ed.), *Greece and Rome: The Birth of Western Civilization*, 1986 (1964).

M. GRANT AND R. KITZINGER (eds), *Civilization of the Ancient Mediterranean: Greece and Rome*, 1988.

THE GREEK HISTORIANS: *Literature and History: Papers presented to A. E. Raubitschek*, 1985.
P. GREEN, *A Concise History of Ancient Greece*, 1973.
W. C. GREENE, *The Achievement of Greece*, 1966 (1923).
T. E. GREGORY AND A. J. PODLECKI, *Panathenaia: Studies in Athenian Life and Thought in the Classical Age*, 1979.
M. GUIDO, *Syracuse*, 1958.
W. K. C. GUTHRIE, *The Greeks and their Gods*, 1950.
W. K. C. GUTHRIE, *History of Greek Philosophy*, I–VI, 1962–81.
A. E. HAIGH, *The Tragic Drama of the Greeks*, 1968 (1896).
B. W. HALL, *Plato*, 1981.
N. G. L. HAMMOND, *The Classical Age of Greece*, 1975.
N. G. L. HAMMOND, *A History of Greece to 322* BC, 3rd edn, 1986.
G. M. A. HANFMANN, *From Croesus to Constantine*, 1975.
V. D. HANSON, *Warfare and Agriculture in Ancient Greece*, 1983.
P. HARDING, *From the End of the Peloponnesian War to the Battle of Ipsus*, 1985.
R. M. HARE, *Plato*, 1982.
R. M. HARRIOTT, *Aristophanes: Poet and Dramatist*, 1985.
J. A. HARRISON, *The Athenian Law Courts in the Fourth Century* BC, 1977.
J. HART, *Herodotus and Greek History*, 1982.
F. HARTOG, *The Mirror of Herodotus*, 1988.
J. HATZFELD, *History of Ancient Greece* (ed. A. Aymard), 1966.
M. B. HATZOPOULOS AND L. D. LOUKOPOULOS (eds), *Philip of Macedon*, 1981.
E. A. HAVELOCK, *Preface to Plato*, 1963.
D. E. L. HAYNES, *Greek Art and the Idea of Freedom*, 1981.
J. F. HEALY, *Mining and Metallurgy in the Greek and Roman World*, 1978.
F. M. HEICHELHEIM, *An Ancient Economic History*, I–III, 1958–70.
J. HENDERSON (ed.), *Aristophanes: Essays in Interpretation*, 1981.
J. HERINGTON, *Aeschylus*, 1987.
J. HERINGTON, *Poetry into Drama: Early Tragedy and the Greek Poetic Tradition*, 1985.
R. A. HIGGINS, *Greek and Roman Jewellery*, 1961.
S. W. HIRSCH, *The Friendship of the Barbarians: Xenophon and the Persian Empire*, 1985.
K. HOPKINS, *Conquerors and Slaves*, 1978.
R. J. HOPPER, *Trade and Industry in Classical Greece*, 1979.
S. HORNBLOWER, *The Greek World 479–323* BC, 1983.
S. HORNBLOWER, *Mausolus*, 1982.
S. HORNBLOWER, *Thucydides*, 1987.
S. HORNBLOWER AND M. C. GREENSTOCK (eds), *The Athenian Empire*, 3rd edn, 1983.
V. HUNTER, *Thucydides: The Artful Reporter*, 1973.
E. HUSSEY, *The Presocratics*, 1972.
D. S. HUTCHINSON, *The Virtues of Aristotle*, 1987.
T. IRWIN, *Aristotle's First Principles*, 1988.
W. JAEGER, *Paideia: The Ideals of Greek Culture*, 1939–44.
G. K. JENKINS, *Ancient Greek Coins*, 1972.

G. K. JENKINS, *The Coins of Greek Sicily*, 2nd edn, 1976.
A. H. M. JONES, *Athenian Democracy*, 1987 (1957).
A. H. M. JONES, *Sparta*, 1967.
B. JORDAN, *The Athenian Navy in the Classical Period*, 1975.
R. JUST, *Women in Athenian Law and Life*, 1987.
D. KAGAN, *The Fall of the Athenian Empire*, 1988 (the last of his four-volume history of the Peloponnesian War).
G. KENNEDY, *The Art of Persuasion in Greece*, 1963.
G. B. KERFERD, *The Sophistic Movement*, 1981.
G. B. KERFERD (ed.), *The Sophists and their Legacy*, 1981.
G. S. KIRK, J. E. RAVEN AND M. SCHOFIELD, *The Presocratic Philosophers*, 2nd edn, 1983.
H. D. F. KITTO, *Greek Tragedy*, 3rd edn, 1961.
H. D. F. KITTO, *The Greeks*, rev. edn, 1957.
E. KJELLBERG AND G. SÄFLUND, *Greek and Roman Art*, 1968.
G. KLOSKO, *The Development of Plato's Political Theory*, 1986.
B. KNOX, *Word and Action: Essays on the Ancient Theater*, 1980.
C. M. KRAAY, *Archaic and Classical Greek Coins*, 1977.
C. M. KRAAY, *Greek Coins and History*, 1969.
R. KRAUT, *Socrates and the State*, 1987.
D. C. KURTZ AND B. A. SPARKES, *The Eye of Greece*, 1982.
A. LANE, *Greek Pottery*, 2nd edn, 1963.
J. A. O. LARSEN, *Greek Federal States*, 1968.
A. W. LAWRENCE, *Greek Architecture*, 4th edn (ed. R. A. Tomlinson), 1983.
A. W. LAWRENCE, *Greek and Roman Sculpture*, 1972. (rev. edn of *Classical Sculpture*, 1929).
J. LEAR, *Aristotle: The Desire to Understand*, 1988.
M. R. LEFKOWITZ AND M. B. FANT, *Women's Life in Greece and Rome*, 1982.
R. J. LENARDON, *The Saga of Themistocles*, 1978.
A. LESKY, *Greek Tragedy*, 3rd edn, 1978.
A. LESKY, *A History of Greek Literature*, 1966.
P. LEVI, *Atlas of the Greek World*, 1980.
P. LEVI, *The Pelican History of Greek Literature*, 1985.
D. M. LEWIS, *Sparta and Persia*, 1977.
D. M. LEWIS AND R. MEIGGS (eds.), *A Selection of Greek Historical Inscriptions to the End of the Fifth Century* BC, 1988.
M. LING, *The Greek World*, 1976.
A. LINTOTT, *Violence, Civil Strife and Revolution in the Classical City*, 1982.
R. J. LITTMANN, *The Greek Experiment: Imperialism and Social Conflict 800–400* BC, 1974.
G. E. R. LLOYD, *Aristotle: The Growth and Structure of his Thought*, 1968.
G. E. R. LLOYD, *Magic, Reason and Experience*, 1979.
H. LLOYD-JONES, *The Justice of Zeus*, 2nd edn, 1984.
H. LLOYD-JONES (ed.), *The Greeks*, 1975 (1962).
T. J. LUCE (ed.), *Ancient Writers: Greece and Rome*, 1982.
D. M. MACDOWELL, *The Law in Classical Athens*, 1978.
M. F. MCGREGOR, *The Athenians and their Empire*, 1987.

P. MCKECHNIE, *Outsiders in the Greek Cities of the Fourth Century*, 1988.
K. MCLEISH, *The Theatre of Aristophanes*, 1982 (1980).
H. I. MARROU, *A History of Education in Antiquity*, new edn, 1977.
T. R. MARTIN, *Sovereignty and Coinage in Classical Greece*, 1985.
M. E. MAYO (ed.), *The Art of South Italy: Vases from Magna Graecia*, 1982.
R. MEIGGS, *The Athenian Empire*, rev. edn, 1979.
F. J. MEIJER, *A History of Seafaring in the Classical World*, 1986.
D. J. MELLING, *Understanding Plato*, 1987.
A. M. MICHELINI, *Euripides and the Tragic Tradition*, 1987.
E. H. MINNS, *Scythians and Greeks*, 1913.
A. D. MOMIGLIANO, *Studies in Historiography*, 1966.
M. MONTUORI, *Socrates: An Approach*, 1987.
M. MONTUORI, *Socrates: Physiology of a Myth*, 1981.
R. O. MOON, *Hippocrates and his Successors in Relation to the Philosophy of their Time*, 1979.
W. G. MOON (ed.), *Ancient Greek Art and Iconography*, 1984.
J. M. MOORE, *Aristotle and Xenophon on Democracy and Oligarchy*, new edn, 1983.
J. S. MORRISON AND J. F. COATES, *The Athenian Trireme*, 1986.
R. G. MULGAN, *Aristotle's Political Theory*, 1986 (1977).
W. MULLEN, *Choreia: Pindar and Dance*, 1982.
J. L. MYRES, *Herodotus: Father of History*, 1953.
New Surveys in the Classics (Greece and Rome), 1967–.
J. K. AND F. S. NEWMAN, *Pindar's Art: Its Tradition and Aims*, 1985.
M. C. NUSSBAUM, *The Fragility of Goodness*, 1986.
M. OSTWALD, *From Popular Sovereignty to the Sovereignty of Law*, 1987.
H. W. PARKE, *Greek Mercenary Soldiers from the Earliest Times to the Battle of Ipsus*, 1933.
M. PARKER, *Socrates and Athens*, 1986 (1973).
Parthenos and the Parthenon (Greece and Rome, Suppl. to vol. x), 1963.
L. PEARSON, *The Art of Demosthenes*, 1976.
J. PERRADOTTO AND J. P. SULLIVAN, *Woman in the Ancient World*, 1984.
E. D. PHILLIPS, *Aspects of Greek Medicine*, 1987.
E. D. PHILLIPS, *Greek Medicine*, 1973.
A. J. PODLECKI, *The Lie of Themistocles*, 1975.
J. J. POLLITT, *The Ancient View of Greek Art*, 1974.
J. J. POLLITT, *Art and Experience in Classical Greece*, 1972.
C. A. POWELL, *Athens and Sparta: Constructing Greek Political and Social History 478–371* BC, 1988.
J. E. POWELL, *The History of Herodotus*, 1939.
W. K. PRITCHETT, *The Greek State at War*, I–IV, 1971–85.
G. PROIETTI, *Xenophon's Sparta: An Introduction* (Mnemosyne, Suppl. No. 98), 1988.
W. H. RACE, *Pindar*, 1986.
J. H. RANDALL, *Aristotle*, 1960.
H. D. RANKIN, *Sophists, Socrates and Cynics*, 1983.
P. J. RHODES, *The Athenian Empire*, 1985.
P. J. RHODES, *The Greek City-States: A Source Book*, 1986.

G. M. A. RICHTER, *Engraved Gems of the Greeks, Etruscans and Romans*, I 1968.
G. M. A. RICHTER, *A Handbook of Greek Art*, 7th edn, 1974.
G. M. A. RICHTER, *The Sculpture and Sculptors of the Greeks*, 4th edn, 1970.
B. S. RIDGWAY, *Fifth Century Styles in Greek Sculpture*, 1982.
B. S. RIDGWAY, *The Severe Style in Greek Sculpture*, 1977.
J. W. ROBERTS, *City of Socrates*, 1987 (1984).
C. M. ROBERTSON, *A History of Greek Art*, 1975.
C. M. ROBERTSON, *A Shorter History of Greek Art*, 1981.
D. S. ROBERTSON, *Greek and Roman Architecture*, 2nd edn, 1969.
C. RODENWALDT, *Democracy: Ideas and Realities*, 1975.
J. DE ROMILLY, *A Short History of Greek Literature*, 1985.
H. J. ROSE, *Ancient Greek Religion*, 1946.
T. G. ROSENMEYER, *The Art of Aeschylus*, rev. edn, 1982.
M. ROSTOVTZEFF, *Greece*, 2nd edn, 1930.
M. ROSTOVTZEFF, *Iranians and Greeks in South Russia*, 1922.
C. J. ROWE, *Plato*, 1984.
N. K. RUTTER, *Greek Coinage*, 1983.
G. E. M. DE SAINTE CROIX, *The Class Struggle in the Ancient Greek World*, rev. edn, 1983.
G. E. M. DE SAINTE CROIX, *The Origins of the Peloponnesian War*, 1972.
S. SAMBURSKY, *The Physical World of the Greeks*, 1963 (1956).
F. H. SANDBACH, *The Comic Theatre of Greece and Rome*, 1977.
L. J. SANDERS, *Dionysius* I *of Syracuse and Greek Tyranny*, 1987.
D. SANSONE, *Greek Athletics and the Genesis of Sport*, 1988.
D. M. SCHAPS, *Economic Rights of Women in Ancient Greece*, 1979.
R. SCODEL, *Sophocles*, 1984.
R. SEALEY, *The Athenian Republic: Democracy or the Rule of Law?*, 1987.
R. SEALEY, *A History of the Greek City States 700–338* BC, 1976.
C. T. SELTMAN, *Greek Coins*, 2nd edn, 1977 (1955).
H. E. SIGERIST, *A History of Medicine*, II*: Early Greek, Hindu and Persian Medicine*, 1961.
R. K. SINCLAIR, *Democracy and Participation in Athens*, 1988.
T. A. SINCLAIR, *A History of Greek Political Thought*, 2nd edn, 1967.
A. M. SNODGRASS, *An Archaeology of Greece*, 1988.
G. SOKOLOV, *Antique Art on the North Black Sea Coast*, 1974.
C. G. STARR, *History of the Ancient World*, 3rd edn, 1983.
I. F. STONE, *The Trial of Socrates*, 1988.
D. E. STRONG, *The Classical World*, 1965.
J. SWADDLING, *The Ancient Olympic Games*, 1980.
R. J. A. TALBERT (ed.), *Atlas of Classical History*, 1985.
R. J. A. TALBERT (ed.), *Timoleon and the Revival of Greek Sicily 344–317* BC, 1974.
T. TALBOT-RICE, *The Scythians*, 3rd edn, 1961.
C. A. TRYPANIS, *Greek Poetry: From Homer to Seferis*, 1981.
S. USHER, *The Historians of Greece and Rome*, rev. edn, 1985.
M. VICKERS, *Greek Symposia*, 1978.
G. VLASTOS, *Platonic Studies*, 2nd edn, 1981.
C. J. DE VOGEL, *Rethinking Plato and Platonism*, 1986.

J. VOGT, *Ancient Slavery and the Ideal of Man*, 1974.
A. J. A. WALDOCK, *Sophocles the Dramatist*, 1966.
J. M. WALTON, *The Greek Sense of Theatre: Tragedy Reviewed*, 1984.
K. H. WATERS, *Herodotus the Historian*, 1984.
T. B. L. WEBSTER, *An Introduction to Sophocles*, 2nd edn, 1969.
T. B. L. WEBSTER, *The Tragedies of Euripides*, 1967.
W. L. WESTERMANN, *The Slave Systems of Greek and Roman Antiquity*, 1955.
L. WHIBLEY, *Greek Oligarchies*, 1975 (1896).
D. WHITEHEAD, *The Ideology of the Athenian Metics*, 1977.
T. WIEDEMANN (ed.), *Greek and Roman Slavery: A Source Book*, 1981.
G. D. WILCOXON, *Athens Ascendant*, 1979.
D. WILLIAMS, *Greek Vases*, 1985.
S. WOODFORD, *An Introduction to Greek Art*, 1987.
A. G. WOODHEAD, *The Greeks in the West*, 1962.
A. J. WOODMAN, *Rhetoric in Classical Historiography*, 1988
The World of Athens (JACT), 1984.
M. R. WRIGHT, *The Presocratics*, 1985.

INDEX